PETRONIUS

SENECA
APOCOLOCYNTOSIS

15

PETRONIUS

WITH AN ENGLISH TRANSLATION BY
MICHAEL HESELTINE

REVISED BY
E. H. WARMINGTON

SENECA
APOCOLOCYNTOSIS

WITH AN ENGLISH TRANSLATION BY
W. H. D. ROUSE, M.A., Litt.D.

CAMBRIDGE, MASSACHUSETTS
HARVARD UNIVERSITY PRESS
LONDON
WILLIAM HEINEMANN LTD
MCMLXXV

American ISBN 0–674–99016–1
British ISBN 0 434 99015 9

First printed 1913
Reprinted 1916, 1922, 1925, 1930, 1936,
1939, 1951, 1956, 1961
Revised and Reprinted 1969
Reprinted 1975

Printed in Great Britain

CONTENTS

PREFACE

More than a hundred years have passed since Buecheler put the study of the text of Petronius on a good basis; and more than fifty since M. Heseltine made for the Loeb Classical Library his translation which was inevitably based on that text. In the meantime, since 1913, and especially in recent years, Petronian scholarship has much increased, in particular as regards the *Cena Trimalchionis* ("Trimalchio's Dinner") to the comparative neglect of the rest. Yet no very great advance was made on the textual side except on a modest scale by A. Ernout in his editions of *Petronius* (1922, 1931, 1950) in which the most admired achievement is the lively French translation which accompanies the text. However, in 1961 came a really vital step forward in Petronian textual history with the 1st edition of K. Müller; and the most recent half-decade has seen more good work done.

Therefore a new edition of *Petronius* in the Loeb Classical Library such as takes into account the main results of this scholarship was imperative. This made it necessary to revise the Latin text and critical notes of Heseltine's book drastically, to add a new and fuller commentary, and to substitute an introduction which also is new except where it incorporates what Heseltine wrote in 1912–13. Heseltine's translation also has been radically revised, though it remains as a whole his. We give, as Heseltine's book also gave, the complete Latin text, the printed dots indicating omissions not by the Loeb Classical Library, as has often been believed, but by the Petronian manuscript tradition, and sometimes omissions postulated by scholars but not indicated in the manuscripts. All hitherto untranslated or " bowdlerized " passages have now been translated. I give Heseltine's Introduction to our original edition of 1913, but shortened and emended a little where it no longer applies.[1] I have also added a summary of the story so far as it survives.

With regard to Dr. W. H. D. Rouse's text and translation of Seneca's *Apocolocyntosis*, the need for a fuller commentary was just as pressing as it was in the case of Heseltine's *Petronius*, and such a commentary has now been provided. Revision of the text and critical notes was a matter less vital, but more critical notes have been added, and an up-to-date introduction and bibliography prefixed.

---

[1] It must be remembered that Heseltine's attitude towards sexual matters is not to-day's.

INTRODUCTION TO PETRONIUS

[This is Heseltine's original introduction, with some editorial changes and footnotes.]

The author of the *Satyricon* is identified by the large majority of scholars with [Gaius] Petronius, the courtier of Nero. There is a long tradition in support of the identification, and the probability that it is correct appears especially strong in the light of Tacitus's account of the character and death of [Gaius] Petronius in the eighteenth and nineteenth chapters of the sixteenth book of the Annals. Mr. John Jackson has translated the passage as follows: [1]

" Petronius deserves a word in retrospect. He was a man who passed his days in sleep, his nights in the ordinary duties and recreations of life: others had achieved greatness by the sweat of their brows—Petronius idled into fame. Unlike most who walk the road to ruin, he was never regarded as either debauchee or wastrel, but rather as the finished artist in extravagance. In both word and action, he displayed a freedom and a sort of self-abandonment which were welcomed as the indiscretions of an unsophisticated nature. Yet, in his proconsulship of Bithynia, and later as consul elect, he showed himself an energetic and capable administrator. Then came the revulsion: his genuine or affected vices won him

[1] Tacitus, *Annals*, XVI, 18. The year was A.D. 66: Tacitus, *Annals*, XVI, 17. For more on Petronius as author see pp. xxxv-vi.

admittance into the narrow circle of Nero's intimates, and he became the Arbiter of Elegance, whose sanction alone divested pleasure of vulgarity and luxury of grossness.

" His success aroused the jealousy of Tigellinus against a possible rival—a professor of voluptuousness better equipped than himself. Playing on the emperor's lust for cruelty, to which all other lusts were secondary, he suborned a slave to turn informer, charged Petronius with his friendship for Scaevinus,[1] deprived him of the opportunity of defence, and threw most of his household into prison.

" At that time, it happened, the court had migrated to Campania; and Petronius had reached Cumae, when his detention was ordered. He disdained to await the lingering issue of hopes and fears: still, he would not take a brusque farewell of life. An incision was made in his veins: they were bound up under his directions, and opened again, while he conversed with his friends—not on the gravest of themes, nor in the key of the dying hero. He listened to no disquisitions on the immortality of the soul or the dogmas of philosophy, but to frivolous song and playful verses. Some of his slaves tasted of his bounty, others of the whip. He sat down to dinner, and then drowsed a little; so that death, if compulsory, should at least be natural. Even in his will, he broke through the routine of suicide, and flattered neither Negro nor Tigellinus nor any other of the mighty: instead, he described [2] the emperor's enormities; added a list of

---

[1] Flavius Scaevinus, one of the accomplices of Calpurnius Piso's unsuccessful conspiracy of A.D. 65.

[2] Not in any part of the *Satyricon*, so far as we know.

his catamites, his women, and his innovations in las-
civiousness; then sealed the document, sent it to
Nero, and broke his signet-ring to prevent it from
being used to endanger others."

The reflection arises at once that, given the *Satyricon*, this kind of book postulates this kind of author.
The loose tongue, the levity, and the love of style are
common to both. If books betray their writers'
characteristics, [Gaius] Petronius, as seen by Tacitus,
had the imagination and experience needed to depict
the adventures of Encolpius.

There is a little evidence, still based on the primary
assumption, more exact in its bearing. The *Satyricon*
contains a detailed criticism of and a poem directed
against the style of a writer who must [1] be Lucan.
[Gaius] Petronius was not the man to pass over the
poet, epigrammatist, and courtier, in whose epoch and
circle he himself shone. He may have deplored
Lucan's poetic influence, but he could not neglect it,
for Lucan was essentially the singer of his own day.
No age was so favourable as that of Nero for the introduction into a supremely scandalous tale of a reasoned
and appreciative review of the *Pharsalia*, the out-
standing poem of the time.

The criticism of the schools of rhetoric in their effect
upon education and language, and the general style
of the book in reflective and descriptive passages,
point more vaguely to a similar date of composition.

[Gaius] Petronius found in his work a form which
allowed a complete expression to the many sides
of his active and uncontrolled intellect. Its loose

---

[1] On this problem see page 380.

construction is matched by its indifference to any but stylistic reforms; it draws no moral; it is solely and properly occupied in presenting an aspect of things seen by a loiterer at one particular corner of the world. What we possess of it is a fragment, or rather a series of excerpts . . . we know not how representative of the original whole.

Of this the best-known portion, the description of Trimalchio's dinner, was hidden from the modern world until the middle of the seventeenth century, and was first printed in 1664.[1]

It is as difficult to grasp any structural outline in the *Satyricon* as it is in *Tristram Shandy*. Both alternate with flashing rapidity between exhibitions of pedantry, attacks on pedants, and indecency, in which Sterne is the more successful because he is the less obvious.

But Petronius, so far as his plan was not entirely original, was following as model Varro's Menippean satires, and had before him the libel of Seneca on Claudius, the *Apocolocyntosis*. The traditional title [2] of his work, *Satyricon*, is derived from the word *Satura*, *a medley*, and means that he was free to pass at will from subject to subject, and from prose to verse and back: it is his achievement that the threads of his story, broken as we hold them, yet show something of the colour and variety of life itself. We call his book a novel, and so pay him a compliment which he alone of Roman writers has earned.

Petronius's novel shares with life the quality of moving ceaselessly without knowing why. It differs from most existences in being very seldom dull.

---

[1] See page xxvi.   [2] But see page xxxvi.

INTRODUCTION TO PETRONIUS

An anonymous writer of the eighteenth century, making Observations on the Greek and Roman Classics in a Series of Letters to a Young Nobleman,[1] is of the opinion that: " You will in no Writer, my dear Lord, meet with so much true delicacy of thought, in none with purer language." This judgment is meant for the age of Smollett and Fielding; but there is no question of the justice of the later remark: " You will be charmed with the ease, and you will be surprised with the variety of his characters."

These characters are one and all the product of a period in history when the primary aim of the ripest civilization in the world was money-making. It was this aim which drew Trimalchio from his unknown birthplace in Asia Minor to the glitter and luxury and unnatural passion of a South Italian town. He differs from the minor personages who crowd his dining-room only in the enormous success with which he has plied the arts of prostitution, seduction, flattery, and fraud. The persons in whom the action of the novel centres, Encolpius,[2] the mouthpiece of the author, Ascyltos, and Giton, are there by the kindness of Agamemnon, a parasite teacher of the rhetoric which ate swiftly into the heart of Latin language and thought. Giton lives by his charms, Ascyltos is hardly more than a foil to Encolpius, a quarrelsome and lecherous butt.

That part of the novel which deals with Trimalchio's dinner introduces a crowd of characters, and

---

[1] Published in London, 1753.
[2] Encolpius: " Embracer " or " Lapman "; Ascyltos: " Unscathed " or " Scot-Free "; Giton: (literally neighbour) " Bymyside." All are as if Greek names.

gives the most vivid picture extant in classical literature of the life of the small town. The pulsating energy of greed is felt in it everywhere. Men become millionaires with American rapidity, and enjoy that condition as hazardously in Cumae as in Wall Street. The shoulders of one who wallows in Trimalchio's cushions are still sore with carrying firewood for sale; another, perhaps the first undertaker who made a fortune out of extravagant funerals, a gourmet and spendthrift, sits there composing lies to baffle his hungry creditors. Trimalchio towers above them by reason of his more stable fortunes and his colossal impudence. He can afford to delegate the conduct of his business, to grow a little negligent, even—for his accounts are six months in arrear—to care for the life of the spirit.

He believes, of course, in astrology; he sings excerpts out of tune from the last musical play, and takes phrases from the lips of the comic star whom Nero delights to honour. He has two [1] libraries, one of Greek, one of Latin books, and mythology courses through his brain in incorrigible confusion.

His fellow townsmen and guests, whom he insults, do not aspire to these heights. Dama, Seleucus, and Phileros are rich merely in the common coin of everyday talk, in the proverbial wisdom which seems to gather strength and brightness from being constantly exchanged. " A hot drink is as good as an overcoat "—" Flies have their virtues, we are nothing but bubbles "—" An old love pinches like a crab "—" It is easy when everything goes fair and square." In

---

[1] The MS. says three, and may be right; he may be drunk when he boasts of them.

these phrases and their like Latin literature speaks to us for once in the tones we know in England through Justice Shallow or Joseph Poorgrass. Nearly all warm themselves with this fatuous talk of riches and drink and deaths, but one man, Ganymede, a shrewd Asiatic immigrant like Trimalchio himself, blows cold on their sentimentality with his searching talk of bread-prices in Cumae, rising pitilessly through drought and the operation of a ring of bakers in league with officials. He tells us in brilliant phrases of the starving poor, of the decay of religion, of lost pride in using good flour. Then Echion, an old-clothes dealer, overwhelms him with a flood of suburban chatter about games, and children, and chickens, and the material blessings of education. But Ganymede is the sole character of Petronius's novel who brings to light the reverse side of Trimalchio's splendour. A system of local government which showers honours upon vulgarity, and allows Trimalchio his bath, his improved sanitation, his host of servants, his house with so many doors that no guest may go in and out by the same one, is invariably true to type in leaving poor men to die in the street. The very existence of poverty becomes dim for Trimalchio, half unreal, so that he can jest at Agamemnon for taking as the theme of a set speech the eternal quarrel of rich and poor.

Between rich and poor in Cumae the one link is commerce in vice.[?] Trimalchio finds Fortunata the chorus-girl standing for sale in the open market, and calls her up to be the partner of his sterile and un-meaning prodigality.[1] She has learnt all the painful

---

[1] She was a slave, not necessarily for " vice ".

lessons of the slums; she will not [1] grace Trimalchio's table until dinner is over, and she has seen the plate safely collected from his guests, and the broken meats apportioned to his slaves; she knows the sting of jealousy, and the solace of intoxication or tears; normally she rules him, as Petruchio ruled Katharina, with loud assertion and tempest of words. The only other woman present at the dinner, Scintilla, the wife of Trimalchio's friend Habinnas, a monumental mason, is more drunken and unseemly, and leaves behind her a less sharp taste of character.

Trimalchio's dinner breaks up with a false alarm of fire, and the infamous heroes of the story give Agamemnon the slip. Trimalchio vanishes, and with his loss the story becomes fragmentary once more, and declines in interest almost as much as in decency. Its attraction lies in the verse and criticism put into the mouth of Eumolpus,[2] a debased poet whom Encolpius meets in a picture gallery. With him the adventures of the trio continue. There is a lodging-house brawl, a voyage where they find themselves in the hands of old enemies, the ship's captain Lichas, whose wife Hedyle they appear to have led astray, and Tryphaena, a peripatetic courtesan who takes the Mediterranean coast for her province, and has some unexplained claim on Giton's affections. They settle these disputes only to be involved in a shipwreck and cast ashore at Croton, where they grow fat on their

---

[1] More precisely, in ch. 37 she bustles about the dining-room; in 47 her husband speaks to her; in 52 she whispers to him; in 54 she rushes in with doctors when he is hurt; in 67 she joins the party when called; and in 74 she quarrels with him.

[2] " Goodbard," or " Singwell."

pretension to be men of fortune, and disappear from sight, Encolpius after a . . . series of vain encounters with a woman named Circe, and Eumolpus after a scene where he bequeaths his body to be eaten by his heirs.

Coherence (*in the tradition*) almost fails long before the end; the episode in which Encolpius kills a goose, the sacred bird of Priapus, gives a hint, but no more, that the wrath of Priapus was [1] the thread on which the whole *Satyricon* was strung. But the life of the later portions of the novel lies in the critical and poetical fragments scattered through it. These show Petronius at his best as a lord of language, a great critic, an intelligent enthusiast for the traditions of classical poetry and oratory. The love of style which was stronger in him even than his interest in manners doubly enriches his work. It brings ready to his pen the proverbs with their misleading hints of modernity,[2] the debased syntax and abuse of gender, which fell from common lips daily, but is reproduced (*in Petronius*) alone in its fullness [3]; and side by side with these mirrored vulgarisms the gravity of the attack on professional rhetoric with which the novel begins, and the weight of the teacher's defence, that the parent will have education set to a tune of his own

[1] So E. Klebs, in *Philol.*, XLVII, 1889, 629 ff.; not so O. Schissil v. Fleschenberg, in *Wiener Studien*, XXXIII, 1911, 264 ff.

[2] See especially c. 41 to 46, 57 to 59.

[3] See e.g. *apoculamus* (c. 62), *duxissem?* (c. 57), *plovebat* (c. 44), *percolopabant* (c. 44), the nouns *agaga* (c. 69), *babaecalis* (c. 37), *bacalusias* (c. 41), *barcalae* (c. 67), *burdubasta* (c. 45), *gingilipho* (c. 73), and such expressions as *caelus hic* (c. 39), *malus Fatus* (c. 42), *olim oliorum*(?) (c. 43) *nummorum nummos* (c. 37), and the Graecisms *saplutus* and *topanta* (c. 37).

calling; Eumolpus's brilliant exposition of the supremacy of the poet's task over that of the rhetorician or historian; the curious, violent, epic fragment by which he upholds his doctrine.

Petronius employed a pause in literary invention and production in assimilating and expressing a view upon the makers[1] of poems, prose, pictures, philosophies, and statues, who preceded him, and thereby deepened his interpretation of contemporary life. His cynicism, his continual backward look at the splendours and severities of earlier art and other morals are the inevitable outcome of this self-education.

By far the most genuine and pathetic expressions of his weariness are the poems which one is glad to be able to attribute to him. The best of them speak of quiet country and seaside, of love deeper than desire and founded on the durable grace of mind as well as the loveliness of the flesh, of simplicity and escape from Court.[2]

He knew the antidote to the fevered life which burnt him up. His book is befouled with obscenity, and, like obscenity itself, is ceasing by degrees to be part of a gentleman's education. But he will always be read as a critic; he tells admirable stories of were-wolves and faithless widows[3]; he is one of

---

[1] e.g. c. 1 to 5, 55, 83, 88, 118.

[2] See e.g. Poems 2, 8, 11, 13–15, 22, and 25; of the love-poems, 25 and 26, but above all 16 and 27, which show (if they can be by him) a side of Petronius entirely hidden in the *Satyricon*.

[3] In c. 61–62 through Niceros, in c. 63 through Trimalchio, and in c. 111–113 through Eumolpus (the famous and cosmopolitan tale of the Widow of Ephesus).

the very few novelists who can distil common talk to
their purpose without destroying its flavour. The
translator dulls his brilliance . . .; he is fortunate
if he adds a few to those who know something of
Petronius beyond his name and the worst of his
reputation. . . .

H. E. Butler, [late] Professor of Latin in the University of London, is responsible for the Introduction to and text of the poems: the translator is
indebted to him for invaluable assistance in attempt-
ing to meet the difficulties which a rendering of
Petronius continues to present.

Michael Heseltine.

The Text of Petronius

From the extant evidence some reasonable
deductions about the tradition can be made. The
existing manuscripts, which give portions and scraps
only of Petronius's largely lost work, are all derived
from a lost archtype (written perhaps at Fleury) which
we may call ω. This codex had once been part of a
complete edition of all Petronius's satyric (and satirical) novel, but was so badly damaged (and decayed ?)
that the beginning and much that followed, and the
end and much that preceded, were absent and much
else was illegible or missing, though the central part
was largely intact.

During the Carolingian age, perhaps in the first
half of the ninth century,[1] some learned person made,
possibly at Fleury, excerpts or extracts of or from

---

[1] K. Müller, ed. 1, XXXVII–XXXIX; ed. 2, 414–417.

what he could read [1] and made some sense, adding some notes, mainly from the first and last portions of ω (usually putting one or more asterisks where he purposely omitted something or where ω was illegible or defective) in another lost codex which with Müller we call λ. The same person made, separately as was natural, in another lost manuscript ψ, a copy of the central part of ω consisting of the famous *Cena Trimalchionis* which formed a unit. Not long after the writer of λ and ψ had finished his work, another monastic person, using that writer's manuscript of extracts, and writing perhaps at Auxerre, shortened these extracts, especially but not always when they were very offensive. This writer, whose lost manuscript might be called o, did not mark gaps by any sign.

Thus there are three kinds of extant material—the fuller excerpts, the abridged excerpts, and the *Cena*,[2] the whole being derived from ω through two lost [3] intermediaries, λ and ψ; and we now pass on from deduced lost sources to sources which survive.

From λ then are derived two groups or classes of extant material: the class known collectively as O which comes from λ through the lost codex o, and

---

[1] This is indicated by the scrappy nature of some of the material and by apparent duplications such as *similia sicilia* and *scruta scita* which may well be alternatives of doubtfully legible words.

[2] John of Salisbury (c. 1115–1180) knew of Petronius what we know and no more, and he knew the fuller excerpts, the abridged excerpts, and the *Cena* as three separate units.

[3] Both these lost manuscripts had suffered interpolations, in part perhaps by the writer himself (of both manuscripts) or others of the Carolingian age, in part probably later.

which has the abridged form of excerpts; and the more inclusive class best known collectively as L, our authority for the older[1] and fuller collection of excerpts, derived from a copy of λ.

In the class O, codex[2] Bernensis 357, known as B, of the latter half of the ninth century, and written at Auxerre, is the best and the oldest of all the extant manuscripts of any class—indeed it is not much later than lost o itself, the chief others, both inferior to B, being codex Parisinus lat. 6842 D, known as R, and the bad codex Parisinus lat. 8049 known as P, both written in France in the twelfth century These three codices B, R, and P have no extant descendants, but Scaliger in his codex l and Tornaesius in his edition and Pithoeus in both his editions (see below) used a lost codex "Bituricus"[3] derived from P. We must take some notice of a codex (now lost again) which Müller calls δ. Written doubtless in France, it was found or acquired about the year 1420 by Poggio, probably in England (where he was from 1418 to 1423), and was the twin[4] of codex P; and from it was

---

[1] Remember however that the oldest *extant* manuscript belongs not to class L but to class O—see next paragraph.

[2] This codex B is the codex "Autissiodurensis" used undamaged by P. Pithoeus in his editions of Petronius of A.D. 1577 and 1587, whereas from Codex B are now missing chapters 81 *nec diu* to 109 *crinibus nitebas*; so are chapters 3 *meditantur* to the end of 80 *perit*, but the two folia of B containing these latter chapters are attached to codex Leidensis Vossianus Q 30 of the ninth century.

[3] It belonged to Jean Duc de Berry.

[4] That is, δ was copied from the same (lost) MS. as P was. For Calpurnius's *Bucolica* was included in both δ and P but in no other MSS. of Petronius; and δ shared with P the same faults as P has; cf. Müller pp. VIII ff. and XXIX.

derived the Petronian material of eleven codices
C, D, E, F, G, J, K, M, Q, V, and W of the fifteenth
century (nine of them still extant); that part (now
called A) of codex Parisinus lat. 7969 (see below)
which has besides the *Cena* abridged excerpts from
Petronius other than the *Cena*; and also a codex of
the sixteenth century.[1]   The *editio princeps* (not good)
of the abridged excerpts only (based on a bad
manuscript now lost, descended from δ) was prepared
by Franciscus Puteolanus (Francisco dal Pozzo) and
with other Latin works was printed at Milan about
1482.   The *editio Veneta* of Bernardino de Vitalibus of
1499 and the *editio Parisina* of R. Chalder of 1520 are
worse.   In 1565 at Antwerp J. Sambucus [2] did better;
in an edition he corrected the *ed. Par.* from a still
extant codex Vindobonensis 3198 (known as W) descended from δ.   A *stemma* for class O is on page XIII
of Müller's first edition of Petronius, and on page 389
of his second.

In the class L is the extant codex Leidensis
Scaligeranus 61 (Q61 Scaligeri) written by J. Scaliger
about 1571.   Denoted best as l, as Müller has it (not
L, as Buecheler, because L is best reserved for the

[1] Between δ and four of these MSS. with A was a lost inter-
mediary; and between δ and the other seven another lost
intermediary containing other works besides Petronius.   Cf.
Helen Milar in *Univ. of Pittsburgh Bulletin*, IX, 1933, 189 ff.;
Nancy Miller in the same, 203 ff.; Wilma Goff in *Bulletin*,
XI, 1935, 253–254.   All three are abstracts of theses.

[2] An abstract of a thesis by Mildred Daschbach, " Sambucus
and the text of Petronius " is in the *Univ. of Pittsburgh Bulletin*, VII, 1931, pp. 42–44.   There is also Lois Beatty's " The
Bellum Civile of Petronius in the editions of Sambucus,
Scaliger and Stephanus "—a thesis of which an abstract is in
the same university's *Bulletin*, XII, 1936, p. 282.

whole L-tradition), it is primarily a copy of a manuscript lent to Scaliger, Tornaesius, and Pithoeus (see
below) by J. Cujas [1] (but now lost), and supplemented
by Scaliger from sources of the O-tradition including
the now lost codex " Brituricus " (see above); extant
codex Leidensis Vossianus 111; and Sambucus's
edition. In 1575 appeared at Lyon the first edition
of the fuller collection of excerpts from Petronius;
it [2] was issued by the printer Jean de Tournes
(Ioannes Tornaesius) and the scholar Denis Lebey de
Batilly (Dionysius Lebus-Batillius) and was based on
a manuscript of Dalecamp (derived, through an intermediary, from the codex—the " Benedictinum
exemplar " (see below)—used by Pithoeus in both of
his editions), and some other sources, and the editio
Parisina and that of Sambucus (see above), until, in
the course of preparation, the editors received, from
Cujas apparently, the codex used by Scaliger. In
1577 came the first edition (of two) [3] by P. Pithoeus
(Pierre Pithou) wherein he used only one " old "
codex (derived from a copy of λ) from Fleury which
he called " Benedictinum exemplar," for the fuller
excerpts; and for the abridged excerpts he used the
then undamaged codex " Autissiodurensis " (the

---

[1] Cf. Dorothy Fulmer, " Cuiacius and the Text of Petronius," in *T.A.P.A.*, LXIV, 1933, p. lx. It seems this MS. was
derived from a copy of λ.

[2] Cf. the abstract of the thesis " The Tornaesius Edition
of Petronius," by Dorothy Fulmer, in *Univ. of Pittsburgh
Bulletin*, XII, 1936, pp. 97–104.

[3] Intervening between the two there appeared at Leyden in
1583 the Petronian commentary the *Praecidanea* of J. Dousa
and his edition of Petronius in 1585. He used Pithoeus' first
edition and the codex Lambethanus—see pp. xxiv–xxv.

extant damaged codex B—see above) and the lost codex "Bituricus" and a Florilegium.[1] In his second edition of 1587 he used also a codex which he calls "Tholosanum exemplar" (perhaps the MS. of Cujas, of class L). In effect, therefore, it is on two lost manuscripts that class L is based—the "Codex Cuiacianus" as indicated, used by Scaliger, Tornaesius, and probably Pithoeus (in his second edition); and what Pithoeus calls "Benedictinum exemplar," used by him in both of his editions and forming ultimately the source of Dalecamp's document used by Tornaesius. Hitherto the scope of class L has rested as it still largely rests on the codex l, the edition of Tornaesius, and Pithoeus's second edition. But K. Müller has added to our knowledge from several more sources. Three of these were copied from a lost codex once owned by Henri de Mesmes and hence called codex Memmianus (source of some Petronian material recorded by Turnebus and Lambinus) which itself was derived ultimately from Pithoeus's "Benedictinum exemplar": codex Vaticanus lat. 11428 written after 1565 (codex m); the sometimes useful codex Lambethanus 693 (codex r) in Lambeth Palace, London, written before 1572 by D. Rogers; and passages copied c. 1565 into a book bought by P. Daniel in Paris and now in the Stadt-

---

[1] Some Florilegia have remnants from Petronius in four extant MSS. of the twelfth to the fourteenth century, coming through a lost MS. from λ independently of the rest of the L-tradition and independently of the O-tradition. The value of their readings is small; and B. Ullman (*Classical Philology*, XXV, 1930, 11 ff.) spurns them altogether. Cf. Müller's second edition, pp. 382, 412–414. The one used by Pithoeus was in codex Par. lat. 17903.

bibliothek of Bern (N, 251.11; codex d). Müller draws also on Pithoeus's first edition; and, for *carmina* only, both in the body of Petronius's novel and separate from it, Scaliger's *Catalecta* (Lyon, 1573).[1] The editions of Petronius by Wouweren (Leyden, 1595; Paris, 1601) were not important. Of much value, however, is the last edition of Petronius issued before the discovery of the *Cena Trimalchionis*: that of M. Goldast (G. Erhard) published at Frankfurt in 1610 and Lyon, 1615, and Frankfurt again, 1621. A *stemma* for class L is on p. XXVII of Müller's first edition [2] and facing page 402 (cf. 415) of his second.

Partly from λ and partly from ψ comes a manuscript which includes the most famous portion of Petronius's novel—the *Cena Trimalchionis*. About 1420, as stated above, Poggio had found or acquired the now again lost codex δ of class O containing the abridged excerpts [3] from Petronius. Early in 1423, or late in 1422, he acquired from Cologne a manuscript which consisted of Book XV of Petronius (see p. xxxviii) and which early in 1423 he caused to be copied. This codex " Coloniensis," now lost, probably contained [4] the central part only of our Petronius—the *Cena*—

---

[1] Cf. Adalaide Wegner, " The Sources of the Petronius Poems in the *Catalecta* of Scaliger," in *T.A.P.A.*, LXIV, 1933, p. lxvii.

[2] It needs, as Müller himself discovered and indicated on his page 210 (first edition), some correction in view of the independent descent of the Florilegia from λ.

[3] So Müller, ed. 1, VIII–IX (cf. XXIX) against A. C. Clark (*Class. Rev.*, XII, 1908, 178–179) who believed that it contained the *Cena* and that H (see below) was copied from it.

[4] So Müller again against Clark who thought that it contained the abridged excerpts.

and was derived from ψ. About the end of 1423[1] was completed the famous extant Codex Parisinus lat. 7989 which contains (i) the works of Tibullus, Propertius, Catullus, and some Ovid; (ii) then the part now called A, containing abridged excerpts of class O of Petronius, copied, as they stood, from a lost copy of the lost codex δ,[2] whereas a number of these excerpts should have come in and after the *Cena*; (iii) then the part now known as H copied, independently therefore of λ and therefore of classes O and L, apparently from the copy made by Poggio of the codex " Coloniensis " and consisting of the *Cena Trimalchionis* for which H is our only source except some excerpts found in L also and Chapter 55 which occurs also in sources in classes O and L. The Petronian part of codex par. lat. 7989 ends at the end of the *Cena*, the abridged excerpts known to follow the *Cena* in Petronius's original work being placed in this codex before the *Cena*. (iv) The last part of the codex as a whole contains, not the part of Petronius which succeeds the *Cena*, but the *Moretum* and Claudian's *de Phoenice*. A *stemma* for the whole tradition of Petronius is on page XXXV of Müller.[3] Some time after 1423 the whole codex was, without surviving " Petronian " descendants, lost until its discovery about 1650 by Marino Statileo (whose real name was P. Petit) at Traù (Trogir), near Spalato (Split), Dalmatia (Yugoslavia)—hence its

[1] At the end of the part containing Catullus there seems to be a record of a date—20 November 1423.

[2] Only the two short statements in A about book-numbers derive from a source other than δ. See below, p. xxxviii.

[3] It needs slight correction—see above, note on Müller's stemma for the L-tradition.

other name, codex Traguriensis, whereas it is now at Paris.

The *editio princeps* of the *Cena—Petronii Fragmentum Traguriense—*, prepared from Statileo's own copy of the original, appeared at Padua in 1664. It was soon followed by three more editions: ANEKΔOTON *ex Petronii Satirico*, J. C. Tilebomenus (J. J. Mentel), with introduction and notes, Paris, 1664; *Petronii Fragmentum*, J. Scheffer, with notes, Upsala, 1665; and *Petronii Fragmentum*, T. Reinesius, Leipzig, 1666. For the history of the codex see R. Sabbadini, " Per la storia del codice Traurino di Petronio," in *Rivista di Filologia*, XLVIII, 1920, 27 ff.: Müller ed. I, XXVIII ff. Cf. also J.Foster, in *University of Pittsbrugh Bulletin*, XIV, 1938, pp. 86–91. There is an excellent photograph of the part which contains the *Cena*: S. Gaselee, *A Collotype Reproduction . . .* Cambridge, 1915.

EARLY MODERN AND MODERN EDITIONS [1]

(i) COMPLETE EDITIONS

The first complete edition (with others' notes), though not good, was that of M. Hadrianides, *Petronii Satyricon*, published at Amsterdam in 1669. The edition by F. Nodot, Paris, 1693, contained forged fragments. Of some value was that of P. Burman (*T. Petronii Arbitri Satyricon quae supersunt*) in two volumes with notes by N. Heinsius, Goes, Scheffer, and others, ed. 1, 1709, Utrecht; ed. 2 (a better one), 1743, Amsterdam. In 1782 at Leipzig was published, with added critical notes, C. A. Antonius's (Anton) *Petronii Satyricon ex rec.*

[1] Including some translations which give a text also.

P. Burmanni. After a long interval,[1] epoch-making in Petronian textual scholarship were *Petronii Satirarum Reliquiae*, F. Buecheler, Berlin, 1862 (editio maior); and his *Petronii Saturae et liber Priapeorum* (editio minor), Berlin, 1862; ed. 2, 1871 (with material from other Latin writers); ed. 3, 1882; ed. 4, 1904; ed. 5, revision by W. Heraeus,[2] 1912, and ed. 6, revision and augmentation by W. Heraeus, 1922. It was Buecheler who in 1862 first put the text of Petronius as a whole on a proper basis. After that year, though more progress was made in Petronian studies, much that could be revealed by further study of existing material remained unknown.

The English translation (with accompanying largely plain text) by M. Heseltine in the Loeb Classical Library (with Seneca's *Apocolocyntosis* translated by W. H. D. Rouse) was published in 1913. In 1922 came A. Ernout, *Pétrone, Le Satiricon*, Paris, with a good French translation, and text, ed. 1, 1922; ed. 2, 1931; ed. 3, 1950 (Budé); in 1929 E. T. Sage [3] *The Satiricon*, New York, text and translation. G. A. Cesareo, in *Il romanzo satirico di Petronio Arbitro*, Florence, 1930 gives text and Italian translation [while E. Paratore, *Il satyricon di Petronio* provides I, Introd.; II, Commento, Florence, 1933.]; and M. Rat, in *Le Satiricon suivi des poésies attribuées a Pétrone et des fragments épars*, Paris, 1934, gives text and French translation. In the decade before the War of 1939–1945, beginning with E. T. Sage and inspired by him, American scholars, as indicated on

---

[1] During which, as Buecheler dryly puts it, *ludebant . . . de corio Petronii sagati togati.*   [2] Heräus.

[3] For his plans and pupils, see pp. xxii, xxiii, xxv, xxix, 407.

xxviii

pp. xxi–iiii, xxv, 407, did preliminary work for a new critical edition of Petronius: Mildred Daschbach, Dorothy Fulmer, Adalaide Wegner, Lois Beatty, Helen Milar, Nancy Miller, Lillian White, Wilma Goff, and J. A. Foster. See R. Browning in *Classical Review*, N. S. XII, 1962, p. 219, note 2.

In 1961 came the greatest step forward on the textual side since Buecheler, in the important first edition by K. Müller, *Petronii Arbitri Satyricon*, Munich, in which he had the help of E. Fraenkel.[1] The Introduction, pp. VII–LX, is in Latin; but Müller followed up this edition with a second (*Petronius Satyrica*), Munich, 1965, which has his revised and recast history of the text in German on pp. 381–430, and incorporates a German translation by W. Ehlers, and (also by Ehlers) some explanatory notes and an essay on Petronius. The critical apparatus has been shortened. This second edition, primarily for German readers, takes into consideration criticisms by J. Delz in *Gnomon*, XXXIV, 1962, 676 ff., R. G. M. Nisbet in *Journal of Roman Studies*, 1962, 227 ff., and R. Browning in *Classical Review*, N.S. XII, 1962, 218–221. I have not seen A. Marzullo and M. Bonaria, *Il satiricon di Petronio*, Bologna, 1962.

Still relevant moreover are other modern editions, whole or part, and, for the text, C. Beck, *The Manuscripts of the Satyricon of Petronius Arbiter*, Cambridge, Mass., 1863 (unsound in parts, cf. F. Buecheler in *Philol.*, XX, 1863, 726 ff.); A. C. Clark, in *Classical Review*, XXII, 1908, 178–179; B. L. Ullman in

---

[1] In the present Loeb edition, wherever a contribution by Fraenkel is mentioned, it is as recorded by Müller in his first edition unless it is otherwise stated.

Classical Philology, XXV, 1930, 11 ff. and 128 ff.;
E. T. Sage in *American Journal of Philology*, 1929, 21 ff.;
and in *Transactions and Proceedings of the American
Philological Association*, LXIV, 1933, pp. xlvii ff., and
G. Pasquali, *Storia della Tradizione e critica del testo*,
Florence, 1934, 66 ff.

(ii) EDITIONS OF THE
"CENA TRIMALCHIONIS" ONLY

L. Friedlaender, *Petronii Cena Trimalchionis*, Leipzig,
ed. 1, 1891; ed. 2, 1906. With German translation and commentary.

W. D. Lowe, *Cena Trimalchionis*, Cambridge, 1905,
with English translation and commentary.

M. J. Ryan, *Cena Trimalchionis*, London, 1905, with
English translation and commentary.

W. Heraeus, *Petronii Cena Trimalchionis*, Heidelberg,
ed. 1, 1909; ed. 2, 1922; ed. 3, 1939.

W. E. Waters, *Cena Trimalchionis*, Boston, 1902;
latest ed. 1922, with English commentary.

W. B. Sedgwick, *The Cena Trimalchionis of Petronius
together with Seneca's Apocolocyntosis*, Oxford, ed. 1,
1925; ed. 2 (a revision), 1950, corrected, 1959.

[P. Perrochat, *Le festin de Trimalcion*, Commentary,
Paris, 1939, 1952, 1962.]

A. Maiuri, *La cena di Trimalchione di Petronio Arbitro*,
Naples, 1945.

E. V. Marmorale, *Cena Trimalchionis*, Folrence, 1947;
ed. 2, 1948. Text and commentary. He gives
much information in convenient form.

H. Schmeck, *Petronii cena Trimalchionis*, Heidelberg,
1952; ed. 5, 1964. Has copious critical notes on
the text, and bibliography.

INTRODUCTION TO PETRONIUS

Plain Translations without Text

Naturally these are to be found in various modern languages. Recent English plain translations are by J. W. Mackail, London, 1923; G. J. Acheson, *Dinner at Trimalchio's*, Johannesburg, 1950; J. Lindsay, *The Complete Works of Gaius Petronius*, London, 1927 and (revised) 1960; and P. Dinnage, *The Satyricon of Petronius*, London, 1953. The present revision of Heseltine's work follows not long after *The Satyricon. Petronius*, by W. Arrowsmith (University of Michigan Press; then, as a Mentor Book, The New American Library of World Literature, New York, 1960–1964), which is a translation for English readers in the United States of America; and *Petronius. The Satyricon and the Fragments*, by J. Sullivan (Penguin Books. Harmondsworth, 1965), which is a translation primarily for all other readers of English. Both translators are pungent (to my British ears Sullivan sounds smoother and plainer than Arrowsmith). Neither claims to be a consistently close renderer of the Latin throughout (though both are, especially Sullivan, in large part), the brilliant translations in the metric portions being specially free. Both write essentially for people who know little or no Latin. Neither Arrowsmith nor Sullivan gives a Latin text (so their work does not make unnecessary this revised text and closer translation in the Loeb Classical Library); both however give an introduction and explanatory notes.

Arrowsmith's rendering is, as he says, " intended to be both a contemporary version and an American one," avoiding a " neutral lifeless Anglo-American idiom ". Sullivan says of his own work that its language is " based on English vulgar language which will give the impression of slang, but not the slang of any particular period or place in England." To this self-valuation I would add that rarely does Arrowsmith or Sullivan sound or read " slangy "; that, though their translations (especially those in metre) are not meant to serve continuously throughout as a means of discovering merely the precise meaning of the Latin, their results are lively and strong; that I too, in revising Heseltine's translation of Chapter 56, for example, have been free in wordplay, and in Seneca's verse have changed but little of W. H. D. Rouse's pleasing but free rendering; and finally that, although I have left Heseltine's style mostly unchanged, and although his original and my revision differ sometimes in the interpretation of Petronius' Latin, from Arrowsmith or Sullivan or both, I have gained profit and pleasure from the classical learning and linguistic skill of both.

There is a third recent rendering into English, with notes. It is one by W. C. Firebaugh (*The Satyricon of Petronius*), New York, 1966. But I have not been able to study it, and so give no judgement or comparison of it.

Further Works on Petronius since 1914

H. C. Schnur, *The Age of Petronius Arbiter*, New York, 1957 (Cf. also C. Beck, *The Age of Petronius Arbiter*, Cambridge, Mass., 1856).

E. V. Marmorale, *Petronio*, Naples, 1936, and *Petronio nel suo tempo*, Naples, 1937, and *La questione petroniana*, Bari, 1948.

INTRODUCTION TO PETRONIUS

G. Bagnani, *Arbiter of Elegance*, Toronto, 1954.

R. Cahen, *Le Satiricon et ses origines*, Lyon and Paris, 1925.

V. Ciaffi, *Struttura del Satyricon*, Turin, 1955.

A. C. Clark, *The Cursus in Medieval and Vulgar Latin*, Oxford, 1910 and " An early use of the accentual clausula," in *American Journal of Philology*, L. 1929 374.

P. Kempe, *De Clausulis Petronianis*, Greifswald, 1922.

F. di Capua, " Il ritmo prosaico in Petronio," in *G.I.F.*, I, 1948. 37.

D. M. Paschall, *The Vocabulary of Mental Aberration in Roman Comedy and Petronius*, Baltimore, 1939.

H. L. W. Nelson, *Petronius en zijn " vulgair " Latijn*, Utrecht, 1947, and " Les rapports entre le latin littéraire, la langue de conversation et la langue vulgaire au temps de Pétrone," in *Actes du prem. congr. de la Fédération Intern. des Ass. d'Études Classiques*, Paris, 1951, 220 ff.

A. Stefenelli, *Die Volkssprache im Werk des Petron*, 1962.

A. Marbach, *Wortbildung, Wortwahl und Wortbedeutung als Mittel der Charakterzeichnung bei Petronius*, Giessen, 1931.

W. Heraeus, Die Sprache des Petronius (reprint from 1899). *Kleine Schriften*, Heidelberg, 1937.

H. Stubbe, *Die Verseinlagen im Petron*, Leipzig, 1933 (*Philol.*, Suppl. 25, 2).

D. C. Swanson, *A formal analysis of Petronius's Vocabulary*, Minneapolis, 1963.

J. P. Sullivan, *The Satyricon of Petronius. A literary study*, London, 1968.

INTRODUCTION TO PETRONIUS

ON THE CENA

L. R. Shero, " The cena in Roman Satire," in *Classical Philology*, XVIII, 1923, 126.

W. Süss, *De eo quem dicunt inesse Trimalchionis Cenae vulgari sermone*, Dorpat, 1926; and *Petronii imitatio sermonis plebei . .* , Dorpat, 1927.

A. Salonius, *Die Griechen und das Griechische in Petrons Cena Trimalchionis*. Helsingfors and Leipzig, 1927.

L. Sgobbo, " La città campana delle Saturae di Petronio," in *Rendiconti, Acad. d. Lincei*, 1923, 354, 395.

J. G. W. M. de Vreese, *Petron 39 und die Astrologie*, Amsterdam, 1927.

BIBLIOGRAPHICAL SURVEYS OF PETRONIAN SCHOLARSHIP TO 1966

(i) From the *editio princeps* (of abridged excerpts) of 1482 to 1909: S. Gaselee, " The Bibliography of Petronius," in *Transactions and Proceedings of the Bibliographical Society*, X, London, 1910, 141–233.

(ii) From 1908 to 1940: *Bursians Jahresbericht über d. Fortschritte d. Klass. Altertumswissenschaft*, vols. 175 (98 ff.); 204 (215 ff.); 235 (142 ff.); 260 (94 ff.) (E. Lommatzsch); 282 (5 ff.) (R. Helm).

Up to 1934 cf. also Schanz-Hozius, *Geschichte der römischen Literatur*, II⁴, 1935, Munich, 509–520.

(iii) 1940–1956: R. Muth, in *Anzeiger für die Altertumswissenschaft*, IX, 1956, 1 ff.; H. C. Schnur, " Recent Petronian Scholarship," in *Classical Weekly*, L, 1957, 133–136, 141–143. Cf. R. Helm in *Lustrum*, I, 1956, 229 ff.

(iv) With reference to the *Cena Trimalchionis* in particular, see especially the bibliography in H. Schmeck's *Petronii Cena Trimalchionis*, 5th edition, Heidelberg, 1964, pp. VII–X.

(v) Contributions to studies in Petronius now number about twenty a year; and record of them can be found in Marouzeau, *L'Année Philologique*.

THE AUTHOR; HIS DATE; THE TITLE OF HIS WORK
AND DIVISION INTO BOOKS

In Tacitus *Annals*, XVI, 17, the fate of Petronius is mentioned, A.D. 66, but no *praenomen* is recorded there (Nipperdey supplied ⟨T⟩). In XVI, 18, the initial of the *praenomen* is given as C (which Nipperdey deletes). There are a few brief references to Petronius in other writers. In the *N.H.* of Pliny the Elder, XXXVII, 20, and in *Quomodo adulator ab amico internoscatur* of Plutarch 19, p. 60e, Petronius is called Titus. No *praenomen* is given by later writers who mention Petronius, or by the extant Petronian MSS. except C added by Scaliger (in writing his codex 1) from Tacitus. In Tacitus, *Annals*, XVI, 18, Petronius is called *elegantiae arbiter*, and Arbiter appears as a name of his in later writers who mention Petronius (something without prefixing the name Petronius), and in some Petronian MSS. If " Arbiter " was not an inheritable *cognomen* but an *agnomen* applied to one man, then Petronius the author of the novel would be he of Tacitus and Pliny. Cf. K. F. C. Rose, in *Latomus*, XX, 1961, 821 ff.; J. Sullivan, *Petronius*, 7 ff.

A date in Nero's reign (A.D. 54–68) is firmly established for the *Satyricon* (H. C. Schnur in *Latomus*,

XVIII, 1959, 790 ff.; K. F. C. Rose in *Class. Quart.*, 1962, 166–168; E. Cizek, in *Studii Clasice*, VII, 1965, 197–207); R. Browning in *Class. Rev.*, 1949, 12. But a later date and a different person or author have been proposed without good reasons (Cf. for discussion e.g. M. Rat, *Le Satiricon*, Paris, 1934, xii ff.), even the third century A.D. (U. E. Paoli, in *S.I.F.C.*, XIV, 1937, 3; E. V. Marmorale, *La Questione Petroniana*, Bari, 1937; and others).

The title of Petronius's work is not mentioned by later writers of the Roman Empire, and even the early manuscript and editorial tradition does not reveal it for certain. Ignoring in this tradition what is at least the semblance of an adjective " satiricus " or " satyricus " qualifying Petronius himself, we have the title of the work mainly in two spellings [1] (*a*) *Satyricon* and (*b*) *Satiricon*, in both of which the *-on* is a Greek inflexion, the y also in (*a*) being Greek *u* " latinized." Is the work satyric, " satyr [2]-like " or connected with Greek satyr-dramas? Or is it satiric (sometimes misspelt satyric), that is " satirical " in the sense of Roman satire derived from *satura* (later *satira* or even *satyra*) " a medley?" Both qualities, especially perhaps the first, suit the tone of Petronius, who may indeed have intended to imply both in his title, however spelt. Again, under (*a*), if *Satyricon* is right, does it represent Satyricōn a Greek genitive plural Σατυρικῶν (i.e. Satyricon ⟨*libri*⟩, "Books of

---

[1] We have also the title *Satirarum liber* (codex P) and even *Petronii Arbitri Satyri fragmenta* (codex A). *Satirae* or *Saturae* may indeed by right as Petronius' own title. Buccheler, vi.

[2] Σάτυροι were lustful ape-like woodland " deities " with a pair of goat's feet.

Satyr (-like) Affairs)" ?[1] Or is it Satyricŏn Σατυρικὸν, neuter singular, " A Satyric Work " or " Affair " ? If alternative (b) is right, Satiricon or, as misspelt, Satyricon, though still partly Greek, would not be a genitive plural but a nominative singular neuter, " A satirical Work " or " Affair ".[2] But alternative (b) is not so likely as (a) Satyricŏn libri, with Satyrica (nominative plural) as a legitimate regular alternative as for instance Virgil's Georgicŏn libri can be called Georgica.   Leaving the actual title uncertain, and in spite of the general preference for (b) Satiricon, in this new publication as in the first we shall spell the title Satyricon. Cf. E. A. Hahn and H. C. Schnur, " The Title of Petronius's Novel," in Classical Weekly, LIII, 1959, 54 and 65; W. Heraeus, Kleine Schriften, CIX, 1.

There are vague signs of division into books:

(i) Where Fulgentius, in his Mythologiae, III, 8, alludes to " myrrhine cup " in Petronius (cf. Pliny, N.H., XXVII, 20), codex. Par. 7975 of the eleventh century interpolates into Fulgentius a reference to an incident in Chapter 20.7 of Petronius and attribution of it to book XIV of Petronius; and, although " myrrhine cup " does not occur in the extant work of Petronius at all (see Fragment VIII, pp. 390–391), this may be right.[3] For:

---

[1] This natural suggestion is supported by Ioannes Lydus, loc. cit., who alludes to Petronius and the σατυρικὸς νόμος and by a trace of division into books in the Petronian MS.-tradition (see below).   There are no other references to libri, but only references to the liber of the romance as a whole. See below.

[2] " a book . . . of satyr-things satirically treated," as Arrowsmith aptly puts it.

[3] Cf. V. Ciaffi, Fulgenzio e Petronio, 102.

(ii) **Poggio** tells us that the " codex Coloniensis " (now lost, see p. xxv) consisted of book XV, which was, it seems, the *Cena Trimalchionis*. Again:

(iii) In the extant manuscript tradition of Petronius traces of division into books, meagre though they are, can be seen in one source—Codex. Par. lat. 7989—the " Traguriensis." In it the portion which contains Petronius, beginning with the abridged excerpts in the part of this codex which we call A (see above p. xxvi) is headed by a statement that these are fragments of the XVth and XVIth books " Petronii Arbitri Satyri," and these excerpts are concluded by the statement that here end (*expliciunt*) fragments of the same books. Both statements must come from a source outside the O-tradition and the L-tradition; and that source would be Codex Coloniensis (see above, p. xxv). There follows in Codex Traguriensis the part H—the *Cena Trimalchionis*—which really does seem to have been book XV of the Satyricon. So the attribution of the shorter excerpts to book XV as well as XVI seems to be an error of the person who re-united, but in wrong order,[1] in this codex the shorter excerpts and the *Cena* into one volume. No record of any book-numbers at all was in the ultimate source of A, namely the lost codex δ (" twin " of P in the class O—see p. xxi).

It is reasonable to suppose that what precedes the *Cena* is from book XIV; that the *Cena* is book XV; and that what follows the *Cena* is from Book XVI and probably also from later books. But:

(iv) A *Glossarium S. Benedicti* (Floriacensis) of the ninth century, once belonging to P. Daniel (1530–

---

[1] See above, p. xxvi.

1603) and believed to be lost but found recently by Müller in Codex Harleianus 2735 in the British Museum, has an insertion (of the tenth century) on leaf 43 which cites the opening words of Petronius's Chapter 89 as from the fifteenth book.[1] If this is right, then book XV included also part of Petronius's work coming after the *Cena*. We might conclude, as Müller does in his 2nd edition, p. 410, that the book number should have been cited in the Glossarium as XVI. But we really cannot tell.[2]

E. H. WARMINGTON, 1968.

SUMMARY OF THE STORY

When our surviving tradition begins, Petronius has reached in his story a point where a Greek freedman Encolpius (the narrator) and Giton, Ascyltos, and Agamemnon are somewhere [3] in Italy (at Cumae argued Mommsen, Puteoli thought Friedländer); and Encolpius is inveighing against the fashion of rhetorical declamation in a reply to Agamemnon, a teacher of rhetoric, who (Chapter 3) in his further answer gives a short poem of advice (5) to any young poet. Ascyltos slips away. Encolpius pursues a vigorous hunt and finds the boy Giton (6–9) with Ascyltos whom Giton accuses of attacking him. High words and reconciliation. More violence of Ascyltos (9–11).

[1] See Müller, 2nd edition, p. 405.
[2] Cf. Müller, 2nd edition, pp. 404–411.
[3] In a Greek town (81) near Baiae and Capua (53, 62); it was a Roman colony (therefore not Naples) (44); with praetors (65). After chapter 99 they are at sea; from 124 onwards at Croton. In part of the lost portions of the novel they were at Massilia (Fragments I and IV).

Later the three (without Agamemnon) visit the local market. Quarrels with others about clothing. Return to lodgings (12–14). Quartilla, devotee or priestess of Priapus, comes with her maids and persuades them not to repeat pryings into Priapus's secrets (16–18).

[Fragmentary. At an inn, trouble with Quartilla, her maids and a eunuch.] A good dinner before a Priapean night (19–21). Wild behaviour and carousal before they go to sleep (22–26).

After unknown troubles all four are at Trimalchio's home as guests with others at a dinner-party. Luxurious preliminaries in his baths and then his living-rooms (26–29). Amusing entry into dining-room. Hors d'œuvres. Pompous entry of Trimalchio (30–32). He finishes a game with costly materials. Counterfeit peahens' eggs, etc., are served. Music and costly display (33–34). Vintage wine and *memento mori* (34). Fantastic food. T. sings. More music. Rich fare. Fortunata (wife of T.) bustles about. Another guest describes to Encolpius the luxurious ways, etc., of T. (35–38). Over wine, T. discourses on astrology (39). After an entry of Spartan dogs, a decorated and garnished boar-pig stuffed with live fieldfares is served (40). A solo performance. T. with belly-ache goes to toilet (41). Animated talk among the guests (41–46). T. returns and talks about his internal troubles. The tables are wiped to music. Three living pigs brought in. A cook slaughters one (47). T. boasts of his huge estates; and converses with Agamemnon (48). A hoax: T. says pig is not gutted; cook saved from flogging by guests' plea; guts the pig and out come

prepared sausages and black puddings (49). T. on his
" Corinthian " bronze and his silver; ignorant ideas of
his. The guests intercede for another slave (50–52).
T. is rather drunk and sings, with his slaves as a
chorus, but is restrained by Fortunata and is partly
sobered by a recital of estate-records (52–53). He is
involved in a mishap of performing acrobats. Enter
doctors and Fortunata. T. not badly hurt (53–55).
Discussion about poetry; T. recites pompous stuff.
(55–56); he remarks on the sad lot of doctors, bankers,
oxen, sheep (56). The guests receive gifts in an
amusing way (56). When Ascyltos scoffs at this,
Hermeros turns on him with a violent tirade and does
the same to Giton when he also laughs (57–58). T.
calms down the three men (59). Recital by Homeric
experts; ignorant comments by T. (59). Another
spectacular show (60). Guest Niceros tells a story
about a were-wolf (61–62). T. relates one about
witches (63). His darling and his dog; rich fare (64–
65). Arrival of the stone-mason Habinnas, half
drunk, with his wife Scintilla (65); he tells about eating elsewhere (65–66). He calls for Fortunata who
comes. The two women display to each other their
adornments (67). Performances by a slave. More
fantastic show, food and noise (68–70). T. and
his slaves (70–71). He tells of his last will and testa-
ment. He wants Habinnas to make a showy monument (71). General weeping (72). Adjournment to
the baths (72–73). Violent quarrel between T. and
Fortunata; Habinnas tries to make peace. Fury of
T. against F. (74–75). T. boasts about his successful
money-making career (75–77). He displays his
burial-clothes. Funereal music for T. (almost dead-

drunk) raises a fire-alarm. Encolpius and his friends get away from the distasteful party (77–78).

Encolpius, Giton, and Ascyltos reach their inn with difficulty (79). Ascyltos steals Giton from Encolpius. Quarrel almost comes to bloodshed (79–80). Encolpius moves alone to new lodgings and laments. He wanders in mental turmoil and is nearly arrested as an army deserter (81–82). [Fragments (82).]

In a picture-gallery Encolpius meets a fantastic old poet Eumolpus (83–84) who bursts into verse at any time. Eumolpus relates an adventure of his at Pergamum (85–87). He complains of the decadence of arts and science and philosophy (88). While they look at a picture, " Fall of Troy," Eumolpus recites a poem on its subject (89) and is stoned out of the gallery. He goes to dine with Encolpius (90) who is tearfully re-united to Giton (91) while Eumolpus, after a bath, on returning tells how he was thrown out for reciting more poetry there (92). Encolpius, Eumolpus, and Giton sup together. Recital of poetry by Eumpolpus. Neurotic and jealous conduct of Encolpius. Encolpius chides Eumolpus for his " poetising ". They are rivals over Gitan. Giton and Encolpius (pretend to ?) attempt suicide. Fracas of Eumolpus with inmates of the house, including cooks and a woman who sets a dog on him. The trouble is checked by Bargates, manager of the block (93–96). Enter a crier, Ascyltos, and others announcing the disappearance of Giton. At Encolpius's request Giton hides under a bed (97) and so deprives angry Eumolpus of the reward offered. Giton reveals himself. Eumolpus and Giton (Ascyltos has gone) are reconciled (98).

[Much apparently is missing here in the tradition. A new adventure:] Encolpius and Eumolpus are reconciled. Encolpius, Giton, and Eumolpus (apparently " on the run " after some misdeed) pack up and go on board a ship (99). Next they are in the midst of a sea voyage, the captain of the ship being Lichas of Tarentum (who turns out to be an old enemy of Encolpius). On board also is the fair Tryphaena, who has some hold on Giton. Plans for escape. Encolpius and Giton with Eumolpus's help disguise their identities (100–103). On a hint from a passenger, Lichas discovers who they are and has them flogged (104–105). Vacillating sympathy of Tryphaena (106). Mock trial? Eumolpus as counsel for the defence striving for his clients by word and deed (107–108). Violent brawling. At the height of feverish turmoil Tryphaena makes peace and renounces all her former claims on Giton (108–109); who, with Encolpius, is restored to beauty, after song, bird-catching, fishing, and recital by Eumpolus. To prove the fickleness of all women, Eumolpus tells the story of the matron of Ephesus (109–112) which gets a mixed reception (113). Tryphaena and Giton cuddle. [Fragments (113).] Great storm at sea. Lichas is blown overboard and drowned. Tryphaena is forced by her servants to leave the ship in the jolly-boat. Encolpius and Giton await death together. Fishermen to the rescue; they find Eumolpus in the master's cabin composing poetry (114–115). Shelter and food on land. Lichas's body is washed ashore and cremated. Eumolpus composed the epitaph (115–116). The castaways come near Croton and are warned that all there are either will-makers or legacy-hunters (116). Eumolpus has a plan and the rest agree to follow his leadership. Eumolpus will pretend to be a childless millionaire in bad health; the others will pretend to be his surviving servants (117). On the way to Croton, Eumolpus lectures on poetry and recites an epic on the Roman civil war of 49 to 45 B.C. (118–124). In Croton, they meet legacy-hunters. The people of Croton are pleased with Eumolpus (124). The castaways stay for some time there (125).

[Much again is missing here in the tradition. They are still in Croton:] A cheeky handmaid Chrysis talks and flirts with Encolpius (in Croton he calls himself Polyaenus) and introduces him to her mistress, Circe, whose beauty charms Encolpius. They begin to make love (126–128).

[Fragments concerning Giton (129)]. Love's slow progress (for Encolpius is hardly a woman's man): Chrysis brings to Encolpius a letter from Circe (who is jealous of Giton) and takes back a reply (129–130). Encolpius neglects Giton. Chrysis brings along an old sorceress, Proselenos, who casts spells on Encolpius and stirs him up. Encolpius meets Circe again (130–131). [Misplaced passage about Encolpius and a boy Endymion (132).] Circe has Encolpius and Chrysis flogged. Encolpius is inclined to mutilate himself in despair (132). [Fragment: Giton swears Ascyltos had never touched him (133).] Prayer of Encolpius to Priapus (133). He is bullied by Proselenos for sexual feebleness towards Circe. Oenothea, a priestess of Priapus, says she will stir him up (133–134). Mysterious cooking by Oenothea helped by Proselenos. To repair an accident she

xliv

goes off. Encolpius is mobbed by three sacred geese of Priapus and kills one of them to the distress of Oenothea on her return and that of Proselenos (135–137). When Encolpius offers gold he is forgiven. Amidst more ceremony the goose is eaten roasted (137). [Fragments. Oenothea and Proselenos apply irritants to Encolpius. Encolpius escapes pursued by both Oenothea and Proselenos drunk (138). More fragments in which Chrysis is in love with Encolpius. He is still doing an attendant's work as pretended " slave " of Eumolpus (138–139).]

A successful legacy-huntress, Philomela, now old, leaves her daughter and son in Eumolpus's care. Prowess of Eumolpus with the girl, helped by a male servant (140). Encolpius is restored to vigour. [Fragments—talk between Eumpolus and Encolpius. The legacy-hunters' patience is departing (140–141).] Eumolpus makes his will: all accepting legatees (except his freedmen) must eat pieces of Eumolpus's dead body in public.

Examples of unwilling cannibalism (141).

[The tradition here breaks off]

From Chapters 1 to 26, at the end of Section 6 *reliquam exegimus noctem*, the Latin text depends on two portions of the surviving tradition—the shorter excerpts O (including A, that is, that part of Codex. Par. lat. 7989 which has such excerpts) and the longer excerpts L. From the last part (beginning *venerat iam tertius dies*) of Chapter 26 to the end of Chapter 78 (*tam plane quam ex incendio fugimus*) the text has to rely (except Chapter 55 and much of 27–37 and a few

xlv

sayings elsewhere) on H—that part of Codex Par. lat. 7989 which has the *Cena Trimalchionis*. From Chapter 79–141 we rely again on O [1] and on L. The portions of the tradition from which the different parts of the text are thus derived are indicated by the letters *L, O, H*, as the case may be, in the left margin of the text.

Sigla [2]

l: Codex Leidensis Scaligeranus Q 61.
cod. Lambeth.: Codex Lambethanus 693.
L: The L-tradition as a whole.
B: Codex [3] Bernensis 357 and Codex Leidensis Vossianus Q30.
R: Codex Parisinus lat. 6842 D.
P: Codex Parisinus lat. 8049.
A: That part of Codex Parisinus lat. 7989 which contains the shorter excerpts.
O: The O-tradition as a whole.
δ: a codex, source of A (and other MSS.) but now lost.
H: That part of Codex Parisinus lat. 7989 which has the *Cena*.

The number of conjectures made by scholars is very large; and only a few of them have been indicated in the critical notes.

---

[1] Including A as before, though A puts all its excerpts before the *Cena*. The O-tradition ends with the words *clausum possidet arca Iovem* in Chapter 137.

[2] Of MSS. cited in the critical notes. For further details about them see Introduction.

[3] "Codex Autissiodurensis" used by Pithoeus was this codex Bernensis before it was damaged.

PETRONIUS ARBITER

PETRONI ARBITRI
SATYRICON

1 *LO* . . . " Num alio genere furiarum declamatores in-
quietantur, qui clamant: ' haec vulnera pro libertate
publica excepi; hunc oculum pro vobis impendi:
date mihi ducem,[1] qui me ducat ad liberos meos, nam
succisi poplites membra non sustinent '? Haec ipsa
tolerabilia essent, si ad eloquentiam ituris viam fac-
erent. Nunc et rerum tumore et sententiarum van-
issimo strepitu hoc tantum proficiunt, ut cum in
forum venerint, putent se in alium orbem terrarum
delatos. Et ideo ego adulescentulos existimo in
scholis stultissimos fieri, quia nihil ex his, quae in
usu habemus, aut audiunt aut vident, sed piratas
cum catenis in litore stantes, sed[2] tyrannos edicta
scribentes, quibus imperent filiis ut patrum suorum
capita praecidant, sed responsa in pestilentiam data,
ut virgines tres aut plures immolentur, sed mellitos
verborum globulos et omnia dicta factaque quasi
2 papavere et sesamo sparsa. Qui inter haec nutriun-
tur, non magis sapere possunt, quam bene olere, qui
in culina habitant. Pace vestra liceat dixisse, primi

---

[1] *Jacobs deletes* ducem.   [2] sed *Sambucus*: et.

---

[1] The narrator is Encolpius (see page xiii). Petronius
inveighs against the " declaimers," that is, teachers of rhetoric
and declamation which, vital under the free republic, tended to
degenerate into tasteless fashion under the emperors.

THE SATYRICON OF PETRONIUS ARBITER

. . . " Are our rhetoricians [1] tormented by another tribe of Furies when they cry: ' These scars I earned in the struggle for popular rights; I sacrificed this eye for you: where is a guiding hand to lead me to my children? My knees are hamstrung,[2] and cannot support my body '? Though indeed even these speeches might be endured if they smoothed the path of aspirants to oratory. But as it is, the sole result of this bombastic matter and these loud empty phrases is that a pupil who steps into a court thinks that he has been carried into another world. I believe that college makes complete fools of our young men, because they see and hear nothing of ordinary life there. Yes, it is pirates standing with chains on the beach; yes, tyrants writing edicts ordering sons to cut off their fathers' heads, yes, and oracles in time of pestilence demanding the blood of three virgins or more, honey-balls of phrases, every word and act besprinkled with poppy-seed and sesame. People who are fed on this diet can no more be sensible than people who live in the kitchen can smell good. With your permission I must tell you the truth, that you teachers more than anyone have been the ruin of

---

[2] Because he had been a prisoner-of-war, hamstrung to prevent his escape.

omnium[1] eloquentiam perdidistis. Levibus enim
atque inanibus sonis ludibria quaedam excitando
effecistis, ut corpus orationis enervaretur et caderet.
Nondum iuvenes declamationibus continebantur,
cum Sophocles aut Euripides invenerunt verba
quibus deberent loqui. Nondum umbraticus doctor
ingenia deleverat, cum Pindarus novemque lyrici
Homericis versibus canere timuerunt. Et ne poetas
[quidem][2] ad testimonium citem, certe neque Pla-
tona neque Demosthenen ad hoc genus exercitationis
accessisse video.[3] Grandis et ut ita dicam pudica
oratio non est maculosa nec turgida, sed naturali
pulchritudine exsurgit. Nuper ventosa istaec et
enormis loquacitas Athenas ex Asia commigravit
animosque iuvenum ad magna surgentes veluti
pestilenti quodam sidere afflavit, semelque corrupta
eloquentiae regula[4] stetit et obmutuit. Quis postea
ad summam[5] Thucydidis, quis Hyperidis ad famam
processit? Ac ne carmen quidem sani coloris
enituit, sed omnia quasi eodem cibo pasta non potuerunt usque ad senectutem canescere. Pictura

---

[1] omnium δ: omnem.
[2] *Deleted by Buecheler.*
[3] video *Turnebus*: et ideo.
[4] regula eloquentia *Haase. There are other conjectures.*
[5] ad summam quis postea *Scriverius.*

---

[1] To the two other famous tragic writers of Athens of the
fifth century B.C. Petronius should have added Aeschylus
before Sophocles, and perhaps did so.
[2] Besides renowned Pindar (c. 522–433 B.C.) of Thebes, the
nine lyric poets were (apart from some alternatives), Sappho,
Alcaeus, Alcman, Bacchylides, Arion, Ibycus, Stesichorus,
Anacreon, and Simonides.

true eloquence. Your tripping, empty tones stimu-
late certain absurd effects into being, with the result
that the substance of your speech languishes and dies.
In the age when Sophocles or Euripides [1] found the
inevitable word for their verse, young men were not
yet being confined to set speeches. When Pindar
and the nine lyric poets [2] were too modest to use
Homer's lines, no cloistered pedant had yet ruined
young men's brains. I need not go to the poets for
evidence. I certainly do not find that Plato or
Demosthenes took any course of training of this
kind.[3] Great style, which, if I may say so, is also
modest style, is never blotchy and bloated. It
rises supreme by virtue of its natural beauty. Your
flatulent and formless flow of words is a modern immigrant from Asia to Athens.[4] Its breath fell upon
the mind of ambitious youth like the influence of a
baleful star, and when the old tradition of eloquence
was once broken, it halted and grew dumb. Who
after this came to equal the splendid whole [5] of
Thucydides or the renown of Hyperides? Even
poetry did not glow with the colour of health, but the
whole of art, nourished on one universal diet, lacked
the vigour to reach the grey hairs of old age. The

[3] Petronius rightly implies that the philosopher Plato
(c. 429–347 B.C.) and the orator Demosthenes (384–322), both
of Athens, were the best masters of Greek prose.

[4] The florid style was called "Asiatic" in contrast to the
earlier pure plain "Attic" of Athens.

[5] The "*summa*" of the great historian Thucydides is his
severely precise muscular diction combined with superb powers
of description. Of Hyperides (389–322) the Athenian orator of
the fourth century one whole speech and parts of others were
discovered during the nineteenth century.

quoque non alium exitum fecit, postquam Aegyptiorum audacia tam magnae artis compendiariam invenit."

3   Non est passus Agamemnon me diutius declamare in porticu, quam ipse in schola sudaverat, sed "Adulescens" inquit "quoniam sermonem habes non publici saporis et, quod rarissimum est, amas bonam mentem, non fraudabo te arte secreta. Nil mirum ⟨si⟩ [1] in his exercitationibus doctores peccant, qui necesse habent cum insanientibus furere. Nam nisi dixerint quae adulescentuli probent, ut ait Cicero, 'soli in scholis relinquentur.' Sicut ficti [2] adulatores cum cenas divitum captant, nihil prius meditantur quam id quod putant gratissimum auditoribus fore: nec enim aliter impetrabunt quod petunt, nisi quasdam insidias auribus fecerint: sic eloquentiae magister, nisi tanquam piscator eam imposuerit hamis escam, quam scierit appetituros esse pisciculos, 4 sine spe praedae morabitur in scopulo. Quid ergo est? Parentes obiurgatione digni sunt, qui nolunt liberos suos severa lege proficere. Primum enim sic ut omnia, spes quoque suas ambitioni donant. Deinde cum ad vota properant, cruda adhuc studia in forum pellunt et eloquentiam, qua nihil esse maius

---

[1] nil mirum ⟨si⟩ *Leo* (non m. s. *already Jungermann*): nihil nimirum *Buecheler*: minimum in *Gulielmius*: nimirum.

[2] *Deleted by Buecheler* (*needlessly?*).

---

[1] This would allude to Greeks of Egypt from about 300 B.C. onwards. Pliny, *Nat. Hist.*, *XXXV*, 110, says that Philoxenus (of the late fourth century B.C.) of Eretria followed his master in introducing further shorthand methods of painting —*picturae compendiarias*.

[2] In this novel Agamemnon is a teacher of rhetoric. By

decadence in painting was the same, as soon as
Egyptian boldness [1] had found a short cut to this high
calling."

Agamemnon [2] would not allow me to stand de-
claiming out in the colonnade longer than he had
spent sweating inside the school. " Your talk has an
uncommon flavour, young man," he said, " and what
is most unusual, you appreciate good sense. I will
not therefore deceive you by making a mystery of my
art. No wonder the teachers are to blame for these
exhibitions. They are in a madhouse, and they must
gibber. Unless they speak to the taste of their
young masters they will be left alone in the colleges,
as Cicero says.[3] Like mock toadies (of Comedy)
cadging after the rich man's dinners, they think first
about what is calculated to please their audience.
They will never gain their object unless they lay
traps for the ear. A master of oratory is like a
fisherman; he must put the particular bait on his
hook which he knows the little fish will make for,
or he may sit waiting on his rock with no hope of a
catch. Then what is to be done ? It is the parents
who should be attacked for refusing to allow their
children to profit by stern discipline. To begin with
they consecrate even their young hopefuls, like everything else, to ambition. Then if they are in a hurry
for the fulfilment of their wishes, they drive the un-
ripe schoolboy into the law courts, and thrust eloquence, the noblest (they confess) of callings, upon

his kindness his pupils Encolpius and Ascyltos and also
Giton were invited with him to Trimalchio's dinner (Chapters
26 ff.).
   [3] In *Pro Caelio*, XVII, 41.

confitentur, pueris induunt adhuc nascentibus.
Quod si paterentur laborum gradus fieri, ut studiosi
iuvenes lectione severa irrigarentur, ut sapientiae
praeceptis animos componerent, ut verba atroci [1]
stilo effoderent, ut quod vellent imitari diu audirent,
⟨ut persuaderent⟩ [2] sibi nihil esse magnificum, quod
pueris placeret: iam illa grandis oratio haberet
maiestatis suae pondus. Nunc pueri in scholis
ludunt, iuvenes ridentur in foro, et quod utroque
turpius est, quod quisque perperam didicit, in
senectute confiteri [3] non vult. Sed ne me putes
improbasse schedium Lucilianae humilitatis, quod
sentio, et ipse carmine effingam:

5   Artis severae si quis ambit [4] effectus
      mentemque magnis applicat, prius mores
      frugalitatis lege poliat [5] exacta.
      Nec curet alto regiam trucem vultu
      cliensve cenas impotentium captet,
      nec perditis addictus obruat vino
      mentis calorem, neve plausor in scaenam [6]
      sedeat redemptus histrionis ad rictus. [7]
      Sed sive armigerae rident Tritonidis arces,

---

[1] Attico *Müller in his second edition. Fraenkel was inclined
to delete the whole clause* ut . . . effoderent.

[2] *Added by Haupt.*

[3] confutari *Rohde.*

[4] ambit *in margin of Tornaesius's ed.*: ardet *Iunius, Sambucus*: amat.

[5] poliat *N. Heinsius*: polleat *and* palleat.

[6] scenam *Heinsius*: scena.

[7] histrionis ad rictus *Ribbeck* (histrionis *already Turnebus*):
ad nutus *Anton*: ad dicta *suggests Buecheler*: histrioni *or* his-
triones addictus. *At first sight* histrioni et addictus *seems
likely, but will not do after* addictus *two lines before.*

children who are still struggling into the world. If
they would allow work to go on step by step, so that
bookish boys were steeped in serious reading, their
minds formed by wise sayings, their pens relentless
in digging out the right word, their ears giving a long
hearing to pieces they wished to imitate, and if they
would convince themselves that what took a boy's
fancy was never fine; then the grand old style of
oratory would have its full force and splendour.
As it is, the boy wastes his time at school, and the
young man is a laughing-stock in the courts. Worse
than both, they will not admit when they are old the
errors they have once imbibed at school. But pray
do not think that I quarrel with a rough-and-ready
piece [1] of Lucilian modesty. I will myself put my
own views in a poem: [2]

" If any man seeks for success in stern art and
applies his mind to great tasks, let him first perfect his
character by the rigid law of frugality. Nor must he
care for the lofty frown of the tyrant's palace, or
scheme for suppers with prodigals like a client, or
drown the fires of his wit with wine in the company
of the wicked, or sit before the stage applauding an
actor's grimaces for a price.

" But whether the fortress [3] of armoured Tritonis

---

[1] Lucilius is the early Roman satirist (c. 180–c. 102 B.C.) of
whom fragments only survive. See *Remains of Old Latin*,
Loeb Classical Library, Vol. III, pp. 366–367.

[2] The poem, like others in Petronius, is some sort of parody.
The first eight lines of it are " scazons," limping iambics, the
rest hexameters.

[3] The acropolis of Athens where still stands the Parthenon,
temple of Athena whose birth was vaguely connected with the
river and lake Triton in North Africa.

seu Lacedaemonio tellus habitata colono
Sirenumve [1] domus, det primos versibus annos
Maceoniumque bibat felici pectore fontem.
Mox et Socratico plenus grege mittat habenas
liber et ingentis quatiat Demosthenis arma.
Hinc Romana manus circumfluat et modo Graio
exonerata [2] sono mutet suffusa saporem.
Interdum subducta foro det pagina cursum
et furtiva [3] sonet celeri distincta meatu;
dein [4] epulas et bella truci memorata canore
grandiaque indomiti Ciceronis verba minetur.[5]
His animum succinge bonis: sic flumine largo
plenus Pierio defundes pectore verba."

6   Dum hunc diligentius audio, non notavi mihi
Ascylti fugam. Et dum in hoc dictorum aestu
motus [6] incedo, ingens scholasticorum turba in porticum venit, ut apparebat, ab extemporali declamatione
nescio cuius, qui Agamemnonis suasoriam exceperat.
Dum ergo iuvenes sententias rident ordinemque

---

    [1] Sirenumve *Buecheler*: sirenumque, *which may be right.*
    [2] vox ornata *Fuchs*: vox onerata *Scheidweiler*: vox operata *suggests Müller.*
    [3] furtiva *or* fortuita *Heinsius*: cortina *Palmier*: fortuna.
    [4] dein *P. Pithoeus*: dent, *perhaps rightly.*
    [5] minetur *Heinsius:* minentur: imitetur *P. du Faur.*
    [6] *Nisbet conjectures* mutus. *A false reading is* in hortis.

---

    [1] Southern Italy in general and Naples in particular, where
the coasts were, in mythology, the home of dangerous sweet-
singing maiden-faced birds, the Sirens.
    [2] Homer, son of Maeon, in one tradition. The reference
below to Demosthenes alludes to his splendid oratory (in
prose): and by Socratic he means rather the school of Plato.
Socrates founded no school.

smiles upon him, or the land where the Spartan farmer lives, or the home [1] of the Sirens, let him give the years of youth to poetry, and let his fortunate soul drink of the Maeonian fount.[2]   Later, when he is full of the learning of the Socratic school, let him loose the reins, and shake the weapons of mighty Demosthenes like a free man.   Then let the company of Roman writers pour about him, and, newly unburdened from the music of Greece, steep his soul and transform his taste.   Meanwhile, let him withdraw from the courts and suffer his pages to run free, and in secret make ringing strains in swift rhythm; then let him proudly tell tales of feasts, and wars recorded in fierce chant, and lofty words such as undaunted Cicero uttered.[3]   Gird up thy soul for these noble ends; so shalt thou be fully inspired, and shalt pour out words in swelling torrent from a heart the Muses love." [4]

I was listening to him so carefully that I did not notice Ascyltos [5] slipping away.   I was pacing along in the heat of our conversation, when a great crowd of students came out into the porch, apparently from some master whose extempory harangue had followed Agamemnon's discourse.[6]   So while the young men were laughing at his epigrams, and

[3] Probably in one of his poems (since Petronius' poem here gives advice to the would-be poet) rather than one of his speeches or other writings.

[4] " Pierian " of Mount Pierus in Thessaly, sacred to the Muses, Goddesses of poetry, dancing, history, and astronomy.

[5] On Ascyltos, see above, p. xiii.

[6] A *suasoria* was a declamation on a given deliberative theme, delivered by a teacher of rhetoric as an example to his pupils.

totius dictionis infamant, opportune subduxi me et
cursim Ascylton persequi coepi. Sed nec viam
diligenter tenebam [quia] [1] nec quod [2] stabulum esset
sciebam. Itaque quocunque ieram, eodem reverte-
bar, donec et cursu fatigatus et sudore iam madens
7 accedo aniculam quandam, quae agreste holus
vendebat, et " Rogo " inquam, " mater, numquid scis
ubi ego habitem ? " delectata est illa urbanitate tam
stulta et " Quidni sciam ? " inquit, consurrexitque et
coepit me praecedere. Divinam ego putabam et . . .

Subinde ut in locum secretiorem venimus, centonem anus urbana reiecit et " Hic " inquit " debes
habitare." Cum ego negarem me agnoscere domum, video quasdam inter titulos nudas [3] meretrices
furtim spatiantes. Tarde, immo iam sero intellexi
me in fornicem esse deductum. Execratus itaque
aniculae insidias operui caput et per medium lupanar
fugere coepi in alteram partem, cum ecce in ipso
aditu occurrit mihi aeque lassus ac moriens Ascyltos ;
putares ab eadem anicula esse deductum. Itaque
ut ridens eum consalutavi, quid in loco tam deformi
8 faceret quaesivi. Sudorem ille manibus detersit
et " Si scires " inquit " quae mihi acciderunt."
" Quid novi " inquam " ego ? " at ille deficiens
" cum errarem " inquit " per totam civitatem nec
invenirem, quo loco stabulum reliquissem, accessit
ad me pater familiae et ducem se itineris humanissime
promisit. Per anfractus deinde obscurissimos egres-

---

[1] *Deleted by Goldast.*
[2] nec quod *Buecheler*: nec quo. *Dousa suggested* quo
⟨loco⟩. *Schoppius proposed* nec qua.
[3] quasdam . . . nudas *Fraenkel*: quosdam . . . nudasque.

denouncing the tendency of his style as a whole, I took occasion to steal away and proceeded hurriedly to look for Ascyltos. But I did not remember the road accurately, and I did not know which our lodgings were. So wherever I went, I kept coming back to the same spot, till I was tired out with walking, and dripping with sweat. At last I went up to an old woman who was selling country vegetables and said, " Please, mother, do you happen to know where I live ? " She was charmed with such a polite fool. " Of course I do," she said, and got up and proceeded to lead the way. I thought her a prophetess . . . and when we had got into an obscure quarter the obliging old lady pushed back a patchwork curtain and said, " This should be your house." I was saying that I did not remember it, when I noticed some naked whores walking cautiously about among placards of price. Slowly, indeed too late, I became aware that I had been taken into a bawdy-house. I cursed the cunning old woman, and covered my head, and began to run through the brothel to another part, when just at the entrance Ascyltos met me, as tired as I was and half-dead. It looked as though the same old lady had brought him there. I hailed him with a laugh, and asked him what he was doing in such an unpleasant spot. He wiped away the sweat with his hands and said, " If you only knew what has happened to me." " What is it ? " I said. " Well," he said, on the point of fainting, " I was wandering all over the town without finding where I had left my lodgings, when a respectable person came up to me and very kindly offered to direct me. He took me round a number of dark turnings and brought me out

sus in hunc locum me perduxit prolatoque peculio

L coepit rogare stuprum. | Iam pro cella meretrix

LO assem exegerat, | iam ille mihi iniecerat manum,
et nisi valentior fuissem, dedissem poenas " . . .

L | Adeo ubique omnes mini videbantur satyrion
bibisse . . . iunctis viribus molestum contemp-

9 simus . . . Quasi per caliginem vidi Gitona in
crepidine semitae stantem et in eundem locum me
conieci. . . .[1] Cum quaererem numquid nobis in
prandium frater parasset, consedit puer super lectum
et manantes lacrimas pollice extersit.[2] Perturbatus
ego habitu fratris, quid accidisset, quaesivi. Et ille
tarde quidem et invitus, sed postquam precibus
etiam iracundiam miscui, " Tuus " inquit " iste
frater seu comes paulo ante in conductum accucurrit

LO coepitque mihi velle pudorem extorquere. | Cum ego
proclamarem, gladium strinxit et ' Si Lucretia es '
inquit ' Tarquinium invenisti.' "

L | Quibus ego auditis intentavi in oculos Ascylti
manus et " Quid dicis " inquam " muliebris patientiae
scortum, cuius ne spiritus ⟨quidem⟩ [3] purus est ? "
Inhorrescere se finxit Ascyltos, mox sublatis fortius
manibus longe maiore nisu clamavit: " Non taces "

[1] *lacuna indicated by Hadrianides.*
[2] extersit *F. Pithoeus*: expressit.
[3] *added by Buecheler.*

---

[1] Here, and in Chapters 20 and 21, the plant is not *satureia*
or *satureium*, summer savory, but *satyrion* or *satyrios* of which
Pliny, *N.H.*, XXVI, 96–98, gives four kinds, alleged to excite
sexual desire, including the man orchis, another orchid, and the
Greek fritillary. But the Greeks used the name satyrion for
any allegedly aphrodisiac plant (Pliny, XXVI, 99).

[2] On the name Giton, see above, p. xiii. In this novel he is

here, and then proceeded to offer me some of his cash and ask me for dirty intercourse. A whore had already got threepence out of me for a room, and he had already seized me. I'd have paid the penalty if I had not been stronger than he." . . .

Every one in the place seemed to be drunk [1] on aphrodisiac . . . but our united forces defied our assailant. . . .

I saw through a sort of murk Giton [2] standing on the kerb of the road in the dark, and hurried towards him. . . . I was asking my brother whether he had procured anything for us to eat, when the boy sat down at the head of the bed, and there upon proceeded to rub away the trickling tears with his thumb. My brother's looks made me uneasy, and I asked what had happened. The boy was unwilling to tell, but I added threats to entreaties, and at last he said, "That brother or friend of yours ran into our lodgings a little while ago and next wanted to rob me of my modesty. I shouted out, and he drew his sword and said, 'If you are a Lucretia, you have found your Tarquin.'" [3]

When I heard this I shook my fist in Ascyltos's face. "What have you to say?" I cried, "You! Worked on like a woman—a whore, whose very breath is unclean?" Ascyltos first pretended to be shocked, and then made a braver show of fight, and roared out much more loudly: "Hold your tongue,

called "brother," not in a true sense but as a sexually loved boy.

[3] In Roman tradition Lucretia, wife of Roman Collatinus, was raped by Sextus Tarquinius, son of L. Tarquinius the last King of Rome; and this led to the overthrow of the old monarchy at Rome and the foundation of a Republic.

inquit "gladiator obscene, quem † de ruina †[1] harena dimisit? Non taces, nocturne percussor, qui ne tum quidem, cum fortiter faceres, cum pura muliere pugnasti, cuius eadem ratione in viridario frater fui, qua nunc in deversorio puer est?" "Subdux-isti te" inquam "a praeceptoris colloquio." "Quid ego, homo stultissime, facere debui, cum fame mor-erer? An videlicet audirem sententias, id est vitrea fracta et somniorum interpretamenta? Multo me turpior es tu hercule, quid ut foris cenares, poetam laudasti." ⟨. . . .⟩[2]

Itaque ex turpissima lite in risum diffusi pacatius ad reliqua secessimus. . . .

Rursus in memoriam revocatus iniuriae "Ascylte" inquam "intellego nobis convenire non posse. Itaque communes sarcinulas partiamur ac paupertatem nostram privatis quaestibus temptemus expellere. Et tu litteras scis et ego. Ne quaestibus tuis obstem, aliud aliquid promittam; alioqui mille causae quo-tidie nos collident et per totam urbem rumoribus different." Non recusavit Ascyltos et "Hodie" inquit "quia tanquam scholastici ad cenam promisi-mus, non perdamus noctem. Cras autem, quia hoc libet, et habitationem mihi prospiciam et ali-quem fratrem." "Tardum est" inquam "differre quod placet." . . .

Hanc tam praecipitem divisionem libido facie-bat; iam dudum enim amoliri cupiebam custodem molestum, ut veterem cum Gitone meo rationem reducerem.[3] . . .

---

[1] *Fraenkel conjectures* derisum, *Housman* de ruma, *P. Walsh* meridiana. *Perhaps it was a mis-writing of* harena.

[2] *Lacuna indicated by Buecheler.*

you filthy prizefighter. You were kicked out of the ring in disgrace. Be quiet, Jack Stab-in-the-dark. You never could face a clean woman even in your best days. I was the same kind of brother to you in the garden, as this boy is now in the lodgings."

"You sneaked away from the master's talk," I said. "Well, you fool, what do you expect? I was perishing of hunger. Was I to go on listening to his views, all broken bottles and interpretation of dreams? By God, you are far worse than I am, flattering a poet to get asked out to dinner." . . . .

Then our sordid quarrelling melted into a shout of laughter, and we retired afterwards more peaceably for what remained to be done. . . .

But his insult came into my head again. "Ascyltos," I said, "I am sure we cannot agree. We will divide our luggage, and try to defeat our poverty by our own earnings. You are a scholar, and so am I. Besides, I will promise not to stand in the way of your success. Otherwise twenty things a day will bring us into opposition, and spread scandal about us all over the town." Ascyltos acquiesced, and said, "But as we are engaged to supper to-night like a couple of students, do not let us waste the evening. I shall be pleased to look out for new lodgings and a new brother to-morrow." "Waiting for one's pleasures is weary work," I replied. . . .

This headstrong quarrel is what lust produced; for I had long wanted to remove that nuisance of a watchdog, so that I might restore accounts with my Giton to their former state. . . .

---

[3] reducerem *Buecheler*: deducerem, diducerem.

11 Postquam lustravi oculis totam urbem, in cellulam redii, osculisque tandem bona fide exactis alligo artissimis complexibus puerum fruorque votis usque ad invidiam felicibus. Nec adhuc quidem omnia erant facta, cum Ascyltos furtim se foribus admovit discussisque fortissime claustris invenit me cum fratre ludentem. Risu itaque plausuque cellulam implevit, opertum me amiculo evolvit et " Quid agebas " inquit " frater sanctissime ? Quid ? Vesticontubernium [1] facis ? " Nec se solum intra verba continuit, sed lorum de pera solvit et me coepit non perfunctorie verberare, adiectis etiam petulantibus dictis : " Sic dividere cum fratre nolito " . . .

12 Veniebamus in forum deficiente iam die, in quo notavimus frequentiam rerum venalium, non quidem pretiosarum sed tamen quarum fidem male ambulantem obscuritas temporis facillime tegeret. Cum ergo et ipsi raptum latrocinio pallium detulissemus, uti occasione opportunissima coepimus atque in quodam angulo laciniam extremam concutere, si quem forte emptorem splendor vestis posset adducere. Nec diu moratus rusticus quidam familiaris oculis meis cum muliercula comite propius accessit ac diligentius considerare pallium coepit. Invicem Ascyltos iniecit contemplationem super umeros rustici emptoris [2] ac subito exanimatus conticuit. Ac ne ipse quidem sine aliquo motu [3] hominem conspexi, nam videbatur ille mihi esse, qui tunicam in solitudine invenerat.

---

[1] *So Turnebus. Another reading is* verti contubernium. *So l, with* vesticontubernium *written later in margin. In his 2nd edition, Müller conjectures* everti c.

[2] *Fraenkel would delete* emptoris.   [3] *So Tornaesius:* metu.

I went sight-seeing all over the town and then
came back to the little room.   At last I could ask
for kisses openly.   I hugged the boy close in my arms
and had my fill of a happiness that might be envied.
All was not over when Ascyltos came sneaking up to
the door, shook back the bars by force, and found
me at play with my brother.   He filled the room with
laughter and applause, pulled me out of the cloak I
had over me, and said, " What are you at, my pure-
minded brother?   Eh?   Are you for a partnership-
under-the-bedspread? "   Not content with gibing,
he pulled the strap off his bag, and proceeded to give
me a regular flogging, saying sarcastically as he did
so: " Don't make this kind of bargain with your
brother." . . .

It was already dusk when we came into the market.
We saw a quantity of things for sale, of no great
value, though the twilight very easily cast a veil over
their shaky reputations.   So for our part we stole a
cloak and carried it in, and proceeded to seize the
most lucky opportunity of displaying the extreme
edge of it in one corner of the market, hoping that
the bright colour might attract a purchaser.   In a
little while a countryman, whom I knew by sight,
came up with a girl, and went on to examine the
cloak narrowly.   Ascyltos in turn cast a glance at the
shoulders of our country customer,[1] and was suddenly struck dumb with astonishment.   I could
not look upon the man myself without a stir, for he
was the person, I thought, who had found the shirt
in the lonely spot where we lost it.   He was cer-

[1] The rustic was carrying a shirt (*tunica*) hung over his
shoulders.

Plane is ipse erat. Sed cum Ascyltos timeret fidem
oculorum, ne quid temere faceret, prius tanquam
emptor propius accessit detraxitque umeris [1] laciniam
et diligentius temptavit.[2] O lusum fortunae mira-
13 bilem. Nam adhuc nec suturae [3] quidem attulerat
rusticus curiosas manus, et [4] tanquam mendici
spolium etiam fastidiose venditabat.[5] Ascyltos postquam depositum esse inviolatum vidit et personam
vendentis contemptam, seduxit me paululum a turba
et " Scis," inquit " frater, rediisse ad nos thesaurum
de quo querebar? Illa est tunicula adhuc, ut apparet, intactis aureis plena. Quid ergo facimus, aut
quo iure rem nostram vindicamus? "

Exhilaratus ego non tantum quia praedam vide-
bam sed etiam quod fortuna me a turpissima suspicione dimiserat, negavi circuitu agendum, sed plane
iure civili dimicandum, ut si nollent [6] alienam rem
domino reddere, ad interdictum venirent.[7]

14 Contra Ascyltos leges timebat et " Quis " aiebat
" hoc loco nos novit, aut quis habebit dicentibus
fidem? Mihi plane placet emere, quamvis nostrum
sit, quod agnoscimus, et parvo aere recuperare potius
thesaurum, quam in ambiguam litem descendere:

[1] *Nisbet would delete* umeris.
[2] tentavit *Burman*: tenuit.
[3] suturae: *other readings are* futurae (*so* l, *clearly wrong*) *and*
furtivae; *cf. Müller, 1st edition, p. 12, and Buecheler. F.
Daniel suggested* nec furtive.
[4] et *Buecheler*: sed.
[5] *P. George suggests* ventilabat.

tainly the very man. But as Ascyltos was afraid to
trust his eyes for fear of doing something rash, he
first came up close as if he were a purchaser, and
pulled the shirt off the countryman's shoulders, and
then felt it carefully. By a wonderful stroke of luck
the countryman had never laid his meddling hands on
the seam even, and he was crying the thing up for
sale with a condescending air as a beggar's leavings.
When Ascyltos saw that our savings were untouched,
and what a poor creature the seller was, he took me
a little aside from the crowd, and said, "Do you
know, brother, the treasure I was grumbling at losing
has come back to us. That is the shirt, and I believe it
is still full of gold pieces: they have never been
touched. What shall we do? How shall we assert
our legal rights?"

I was delighted, not only because I saw a chance of
profit, but because fortune had relieved me of a very
disagreeable suspicion. I was against any roundabout
methods. I thought we should proceed openly by
civil process, so that they should be reduced to an
interdict in the courts if they refused to give up other
people's property to the rightful owners.

But Ascyltos was afraid of the law: "Nobody
knows us in this place," he said, "and nobody will
believe what we say. I should certainly like to buy
the thing, although it is ours, and we know it. It is
better to get back our savings cheaply than to embark
upon the perils of a lawsuit:

---

[6] nollent . . . venirent *Buecheler*: nollet . . . veniret.

[7] *After* veniret *the L-tradition places the poem* Quid faciant
leges . . . *which Buecheler, after Anton, rightly transferred to
its present position in Chapter 14.*

LO | Quid faciant leges, ubi sola pecunia regnat,
  aut ubi paupertas vincere nulla potest?
Ipsi qui Cynica traducunt tempora pera,[1]
  non nunquam nummis vendere vera [2] solent.
Ergo iudicium nihil est nisi publica merces,
  atque eques in causa qui sedet, empta probat.''

L | Sed praeter unum dipondium [sicel] ⟨quo⟩
lupinos[que quibus] [3] destinaveramus mercari, nihil
ad manum erat. Itaque ne interim praeda discede-
ret, vel minoris pallium [4] addicere placuit et [5] pretium
maioris compendii leviorem facere [6] iacturam. Cum
primum ergo explicuimus mercem, mulier operto [7]
capite, quae cum rustico steterat, inspectis diligentius signis iniecit utramque laciniae manum
magnaque vociferatione " Latrones " [tenere] [8] clamavit. Contra nos perturbati, ne videremur nihil
agere, et ipsi scissam et sordidam tenere coepimus
tunicam atque eadem invidia proclamare, nostra
esse spolia quae illi possiderent. Sed nullo genere
par erat causa, nam [9] et cociones qui [10] ad clamorem

---

[1] pera *Heinsius*: cera.
[2] vera *cd. Leid. Voss. 111*: verba *L*: verba solent emere *O,δ.*
[3] [sicel] ⟨quo⟩ lupinos[que quibus] *Fraenkel (Müller, 1st.
ed.)*: sicel *deleted by Gaselee*: ⟨quo⟩ cicer *J. F. Gronov*: [quibus]
J. F. Gronov: sicel lupinosque quibus.
[4] praemium *suggests P. George.*
[5] et *Buecheler*: ut.
[6] facere *Buecheler*: faceret: levior faceret iactura *J. F.
Gronov.*
[7] operto *Wouweren*: aperto.
[8] *Deleted by Oudendorp. Retain perhaps*: ' *to hold the
thieves.*'

22

SATYRICON

" Of what avail are laws to be where money rules alone, and the poor suitor can never succeed? The very men who mock at the times by carrying the Cynic's [1] wallet have sometimes been known to betray the truth for a price. So a lawsuit is nothing more than a public auction, and the knightly juror who sits listening to the case approves, with the record of his vote, something bought."

But we had nothing in hand except one sixpence,[2] with which we had meant to buy lupines. And so for fear our prize should escape us, we decided to sell the cloak cheaper than we had intended, and so to incur a slight loss for a greater gain. We had just unrolled our piece, when a veiled woman, who was standing by the countryman, looked carefully at the marks, and then seized the cloak with both hands, shouting at the top of her voice, " Thieves! " We were terrified, but rather than do nothing, we proceeded to tug at the dirty torn shirt, and cried out with equal bitterness that these people had taken some spoil that was ours. But the dispute was in no way even, and the dealers who were attracted by the

[1] Most Cynics led a beggar's life in the belief that money disturbs the philosopher. Their school was founded by Antisthenes, a pupil of Socrates at Athens, early in the fourth century B.C.

[2] The *dipondium* was a two-*as* coin. As to what follows, the reading *cicer* (chick-pea) for *sicel* is supported by *cicer et lupinum* in Chapter 66; but one suspects rather a Carolingian interpolation of *sicel* as a gloss to explain *dipondium* to which the *sicel* corresponded.

---

[9] nam *l*: nostra *other MSS.*: *deleted by Buecheler.*
[10] cociones qui *Saumaise*: cociones quae.

confluxerant, nostram scilicet de more [1] ridebant
insaniam,[2] quod pro illa parte vindicabant pretiosiss
imam vestem, pro hac pannuciam ne centonibus
quidem bonis dignam. Hinc Ascyltos bene [3] risum
15 discussit, qui silentio facto " Videmus " [4] inquit " su
am cuique rem esse carissimam; reddant nobis tunic
am nostram et pallium suum recipiant." Etsi rustico
mulierique placebat permutatio, advocati tamen
† iam pene † [5] nocturni, qui volebant pallium lucr
facere,[6] flagitabant uti apud se utraque deponerentur
ac postero die iudex querellam inspiceret. Neque
enim res tantum, quae viderentur in controversiam
esse, sed longe aliud quaeri ⟨quod⟩[7] in utraque parte
scilicet latrocinii suspicio haberetur. Iam sequestr
placebant, et nescio quis ex cocionibus, calvus, tuber
osissimae frontis, qui solebat aliquando etiam causas
agere, invaserat pallium exhibiturumque crastino die
affirmabat. Ceterum apparebat nihil aliud quaer
nisi ut semel deposita vestis inter praedones strangu
laretur et nos metu criminis non veniremus ad con
stitutum.

Idem plane et nos volebamus. Itaque utriusque
partis votum casus adiuvit. Indignatus enim rusti
cus, quod nos centonem exhibendum postularemus
misit in faciem Ascylti tunicam et liberatos querella

---

[1] *Fraenkel was naturally inclined to delete* scilicet de more
Ehlers suggests scilicet uno ore deridebant.

[2] insaniam *Fraenkel*: inscitiam *in margin of Tornaesius'*
ed.: invidiam.

[3] *Another reading is* pene. *Müller emends to* repente.

[4] videmus *Jungermann*: videamus.

[5] *Nisbet suggests* importune.

noise of course laughed at our madness, since one side
was laying claim to an expensive cloak, the other to a
set of rags not worthy of mending with a decent
patchwork. Ascyltos now cleverly stopped their
laughter by calling for silence and saying, " Well,
you see, every one has an affection for his own things.
If they will give us our shirt, they shall have their
cloak." The countryman and the woman were
satisfied with this exchange, but by this time some
night-policemen had been called in to [??]; they
wanted to make a profit out of the cloak, and tried
to persuade us to leave the disputed property with
them and let a judge look into our complaints the
next day. They urged that besides the counter-
claims to these garments, a far graver question arose,
since each party must lie under suspicion of thieving.
It was suggested that trustees should be appointed,
and one of the traders, a bald man with a frightfully
spotty forehead, who used sometimes to do law work,
laid hands on the cloak and declared that he would
produce it to-morrow. But clearly the object was
that the cloak should be deposited with a pack of
thieves and be seen no more, in the hope that we
should not keep our appointment, for fear of being
charged.

It was obvious that our wishes coincided with his,
and chance came to support the hopes of both sides.
The countryman lost his temper when we said his rags
must be shown in public, threw the shirt in Ascyltos's
face, and asked us, now that we had no grievance,

---

[6] qui . . . facere] *Müller deletes, rightly?*

[7] *Fraenkel would delete* quaeri.   quod *was added in the margin
of Tornaesius's edition.*

iussit pallium deponere, quod solum litem facie-
bat. . . .

Et recuperato, ut putabamus, thesauro in deversorium praecipites abimus praeclusisque foribus ridere
acumen non minus cocionum quam calumniantium
coepimus, quod nobis ingenti calliditate pecuniam
reddidissent.

> Nolo quod cupio statim tenere,
> nec victoria mi placet parata . . .

16 *LO* | Sed ut primum beneficio Gitonis praeparata nos
implevimus cena, ostium [non] [1] satis audaci strepitu
exsonuit impulsum. . . .[2]

Cum et ipsi ergo pallidi rogaremus, quis esset,
" Aperi " inquit; " iam scies." Dumque loquimur,
sera sua sponte delapsa cecidit reclusaeque subito
fores admiserunt intrantem.[3] Mulier autem erat
operto capite [illa scilicet quae paulo ante cum rustico
steterat],[4] et " Me derisisse " inquit " vos putabatis ?
ego sum ancilla Quartillae, cuius vos sacrum ante
cryptam turbastis. Ecce ipsa venit ad stabulum
petitque ut vobiscum loqui liceat. Nolite pertur-
bari. Nec accusat errorem vestrum nec punit, immo
potius miratur, quis deus iuvenes tam urbanos in suam
17 regionem detulerit." Tacentibus adhuc nobis et
ad neutram partem adsentationem [5] flectentibus

---

[1] *Deleted in cod. l and by Goldast.*
[2] *Lacuna indicated by Buecheler.*
[3] instantem *Nisbet, rightly?*
[4] illa . . . steterat] *Jacobs deleted.*

to give up the cloak which had raised the whole quarrel. . . .

As we thought, we had got back our savings. We hurried away into the inn and shut the door, and then had a laugh at the wits of our false accusers and at the dealers too, whose mighty sharpness had returned our money to us. " I never want to grasp what I desire at once, nor do easy victories delight me."

Thanks to Giton, we found supper ready, and we were making a hearty meal, when a very aggressive knock sounded at the door. . . .

We turned pale and asked who it was. " Open the door," said a voice, " and you will know." While we were speaking, the bar slipped and fell of its own accord, the door suddenly swung open, and let in our visitor. [It was the veiled woman who had stood with the countryman a little while before.] " Did you think you had deceived me ? " she said. " I am Quartilla's maid. You intruded upon her devotions [1] before her secret chapel. Now she has come to your lodgings, and begs for the favour of a word with you. Do not be uneasy; she will not be angry, or punish you for a mistake. On the contrary, she wonders how Heaven conveyed such polite young men to her quarter." We still said nothing, and showed no approval one way or the other. Then Quartilla her-

---

[1] Apparently in honour of the god of fertility Priapus—son of Aphrodite = Venus and Dionysus = Bacchus; see Chapter 17. For *sacrum* (*R,P*) *L* has *sacram*. So also had δ. *B* omits.

---

[5] *Read perhaps* assensionem *as in the margin of Tornaesius's edition; or* sententiam *as Müller suggests in his 2nd edition; or delete with Nisbet.*

intravit ipsa, una comitata virgine, sedensque super
torum meum diu flevit. Ac ne tunc quidem nos
ullum adiecimus verbum, sed attoniti expectavimus
lacrimas ad ostentationem doloris paratas. Ut ergo
tam ambitiosus detumuit [1] imber, retexit superbum
pallio [2] caput et manibus inter se usque ad articu-
lorum strepitum constrictis " Quaenam est " inquit
" haec audacia, aut ubi fabulas etiam antecessura
latrocinia didicistis ? misereor mediusfidius vestri;
neque enim impune quisquam quod non licuit, ad-
spexit. Utique nostra regio tam praesentibus plena
est numinibus, ut facilius possis deum quam hominem
invenire. Ac ne me putetis ultionis causa huc venisse
aetate magis vestra commoveor quam iniuria mea.
Imprudentes enim, ut adhuc puto, admisistis inex-
piabile scelus. Ipsa quidem illa nocte vexata tam
periculoso inhorrui frigore, ut tertianae etiam impetum timeam. Et ideo medicinam somnio petii
iussaque sum vos perquirere atque impetum morbi
monstrata subtilitate lenire. Sed de remedio non
tam valde laboro; maior enim in praecordiis dolor
saevit, qui me usque ad necessitatem mortis deducit,
ne scilicet iuvenili impulsi licentia quod in sacello
Priapi vidistis, vulgetis deorumque consilia proferatis
in populum. Protendo igitur ad genua vestra
supinas manus petoque et oro, ne nocturnas religiones
iocum risumque faciatis, neve traducere velitis tot
annorum secreta, quae vix tres [3] homines noverunt."

18 Secundum hanc deprecationem lacrimas rursus

---

[1] detumuit *Gruter*: detonuit, *which may be right.*
[2] *Fraenkel would delete* superbum, *for which Müller conjec-*
tures opertum. *Fuchs deletes* pallio.
[3] tres (*i.e.* iii *for* m) *Nisbet.* mystae *in margin of l.*

self came in with one girl by her, sat down on my bed, and cried for a long while. We did not put in a word even then, but sat waiting in amazement for the end of this carefully arranged exhibition of grief. When this very designing rain had eased off, she drew her proud head out of her cloak and wrung her hands together till the joints cracked. "You bold creatures," she said, "where did you learn to outrival the robbers of romance? Heaven knows I pity you. A man cannot look upon forbidden things and go free. Indeed the gods walk abroad so commonly in our streets that it is easier to meet a god than a man. Do not suppose that I have come here to avenge myself. I am more sorry for your tender years than for my own wrongs. For I still believe it was heedless youth that led you into deadly sin. I lay tormenting myself that night and shivering with such a dreadful chill that I even fear an attack of tertian ague. So I asked for a remedy in my dreams and was told to find you out and allay the raging of my illness by the clever plan you would show me. But I am not so greatly concerned about a cure; deep in my heart burns a greater grief, which drags me down to inevitable death. I am afraid that youthful indiscretion will lead you to publish abroad what you saw in the chapel of Priapus, and reveal our gods' counsels to the mob. So I hold out my folded hands to your knees, and beg and pray you not to make a laughing-stock of our nocturnal worship, not to deride the immemorial mystery to which less than three [1] souls hold the key."

She finished her prayer, and again cried bitterly,

---

[1] The tradition says a thousand, which, if right, is a deliberate exaggeration to give the meaning of an "open secret."

effudit gemitibusque largis concussa tota facie ac
pectore torum meum pressit. Ego eodem tempore
et misericordia turbatus et metu, bonum animum
habere eam iussi et de utroque esse securam: nam
neque sacra quemquam vulgaturum, et si quod praeterea aliud remedium ad tertianam deus illi monstras-
set, adiuvaturos nos divinam providentiam vel periculo nostro. Hilarior post hanc pollicitationem facta
mulier basiavit me spissius, et ex lacrimis in risum
mota descendentes ab aure capillos meos lenta[1]
L manu duxit | et " Facio " inquit " indutias vobiscum,
LO et a constituta lite dimitto. Quod | si non adnuissetis
de hac medicina quam peto, iam parata erat in
crastinum turba, quae et iniuriam meam vindicaret
et dignitatem:

> Contemni turpe est, legem donare superbum;
>   hoc amo, quod possum qua libet ire via.
> Nam sane et sapiens contemptus iurgia nectit,
>   et qui non iugulat, victor[2] abire solet." . . .

Complosis deinde manibus in tantum repente risum
effusa est, ut timeremus. Idem ex altera parte et
ancilla fecit, quae prior venerat, idem virguncula,
19 quae una intraverat. Omnia mimico risu exsonu-
erant, cum interim nos, quae tam repentina esset
mutatio animorum facta, ignoraremus ac modo
nosmet ipsos modo mulieres intueremur. . . .
L | " Ideo vetui hodie in hoc deversorio quemquam
mortalium admitti, ut remedium tertianae sine ulla
interpellatione a vobis acciperem." Ut haec dixit

---

[1] lenta *Bongars*: tentata *or* temptata.

and buried her face and bosom in my bed, shaken all
over with deep sobs. I was distracted with pity and
terror together. I reassured her, telling her not to
trouble herself about either point. No one would
betray her devotions, and we would risk our lives to
assist the will of Heaven, if the gods had showed her
any further cure for her tertian ague. At this promise the woman grew more cheerful, kissed me again
and again, and gently stroked the long hair that fell
below my ears, having passed from crying to laughter.
" I will make a truce with you," she said, " and withdraw the suit I have entered against you. But if you
had not promised me the cure I want, there was a
whole regiment ready for to-morrow to wipe out my
wrongs and uphold my honour:
" To be flouted is disgraceful, but to impose
terms is glorious: I rejoice that I can follow what
course I please. For surely even a wise man will take
up a quarrel when he is flouted, while the man who
sheds no blood commonly comes off victorious." . . .

Then she clapped her hands and suddenly burst
out laughing so loud that we were frightened. The
maid who had come in first did the same on one side
of us, and also the little girl who had come in with
Quartilla. The whole place rang with farcical
laughter, while we kept looking first at each other and
than at the women, not understanding how they
could have changed their tune so quickly. . . .

" I forbade any mortal man to enter this inn to-day,
just so that I might get you to cure me of my tertian
ague without interruptions." When Quartilla said

---

[2] *Nisbet suggests* iurgat, victus.

Quartilla, Ascyltos quidem paulisper obstupuit, ego
autem frigidior hieme Gallica factus nullum potui
verbum emittere. Sed ne quid tristius expectarem,
comitatus faciebat. Tres enim erant mulierculae, si
quid vellent conari, infirmissimae scilicet; contra nos,
si hihil aliud, virilis sexus. Sed et [1] praecincti
certe altius eramus. Immo ego sic iam paria compo-
sueram, ut si depugnandum foret, ipse cum Quartilla
consisterem, Ascyltos cum ancilla, Giton cum virgine. . . .

Tunc vero excidit omnis constantia attonitis, et
mors non dubia miserorum oculos coepit obducere. . . .

20 " Rogo " inquam " domina, si quid tristius paras,
celerius confice; neque enim tam magnum facinus
admisimus, ut debeamus torti perire." . . .

Ancilla quae Psyche vocabatur, lodiculam in pavimento diligenter extendit. . . .

Sollicitavit inguina mea mille iam mortibus frigida. . . .

Operuerat Ascyltos pallio caput, admonitus scilicet
periculosum esse alienis intervenire secretis. . . .

Duas institas ancilla protulit de sinu alteraque
pedes nostros alligavit, altera manus. . . .

Ascyltos iam deficiente fabularum contextu
" Quid ? ego " [2] inquit " non sum dignus qui bibam ? "
Ancilla risu meo prodita [3] complosit manus et " Ap-

---

[1] sed et *Pithoeus*: esset at *l*: esset et.
[2] ego *Goldast*: ergo.   [3] *Perhaps* procita.

this, Ascyltos was struck dumb for a moment, while I turned colder than a Swiss winter, and could not utter a syllable. But the presence of my friends saved me from my worst fears. They were three mere women, if they wanted to make any attack on us, very feeble persons, to be sure; on the other hand, we had at least our manhood in our favour, if nothing else. And certainly our dress was more fit for action. Indeed I had already matched our forces in pairs. If it came to a real fight, I was to face Quartilla, Ascyltos her maid, Giton the girl. . . .

But then all our resolution yielded to astonishment, and the darkness of certain death proceeded to fall on our unhappy eyes. . . .

" If you have anything worse in store, madam," I said, " be quick with it. We are not such desperate criminals that we deserve to die by torture." . . .

The maid, whose name was Psyche, carefully spread a blanket on the floor and proceeded to stir my groin which was by now cold, blasted with a thousand deaths. . . . Ascyltos had buried his head in his cloak. I suppose he had warning that it is dangerous to pry into other people's secrets. . . .

The maid brought two flounces out of her bosom and tied our feet with one and our hands with the other. . . .

The thread of our talk was broken. " Come," said Ascyltos, " do not I deserve a drink? " The maid was summoned by my laughter at this. She clapped her hands and said, " I put one by you, young man.

posui quidem . . . adulescens, solus tantum medica-
mentum ebibisti? " " Itane est? " inquit Quartilla
" quicquid satyrii fuit, Encolpius ebibit? " . . .

Non indecenti risu latera commovit. . . .

LO | Ac ne Giton quidem ultimo risum tenuit, utique
postquam virguncula cervicem eius invasit et non
repugnanti puero innumerabilia oscula dedit. . . .

21 L | Volebamus miseri exclamare, sed nec in auxilio
erat quisquam, et hinc Psyche acu comatoria cupienti
mihi invocare Quiritum fidem malas pungebat, illinc
puella penicillo, quod et ipsum satyrio tinxerat,
Ascylton opprimebat. . . .

Ultimo cinaedus supervenit myrtea subornatus
gausapa cinguloque succinctus. . . .

Modo extortis nos clunibus cecidit, modo basiis
olidissimis inquinavit, donec Quartilla balaenaceam [1]
tenens virgam alteque succincta iussit infelicibus
dari missionem. . . .

Uterque nostrum religiosissimis iuravit verbis inter
duos periturum esse tam horribile secretum. . . .

Intraverunt palaestritae complures [2] et nos legiti-
mo [3] perfusos oleo refecerunt. Utcunque ergo lassi-
tudine abiecta cenatoria repetimus et in proximam
cellam ducti sumus, in qua tres lecti strati erant et
reliquus lautitiarum apparatus splendidissime expositus. Iussi ergo discubuimus, et gustatione mirifica

[1] balenaciam *l.*
[2] complures *Buecheler:* quamplures.
[3] legitime *Buecheler:* selgitico (' *of Selga* ') *Triller.*

---

[1] See note on *satyrion,* Chapter 8.
[2] In the lost passage here came perhaps fragment VII, pp.

34

Did you drink the whole of the medicine yourself? "
" Did he really? " said Quartilla, " did Encolpius
drink up the whole of our loving cup? "[1] . . .[2] Her
sides shook with delightful laughter. . . . Even
Giton had to laugh at last, I mean when the little girl
took him by the neck and showered countless kisses
on his unresisting lips. . . .

We wanted to shout in our misery, but there was no
one to come to the rescue, and when I tried to cry
" Help, all honest citizens! " Psyche pricked my
cheek with a hair-pin, while the girl threatened
Ascyltos with a wet sponge which she had soaked in
the aphrodisiac. . . .

Last there arrived a sodomite in a fine brown
suit with a waistband . . . and one while almost
dislocated our buttocks with his poking, other while
slobbered us with his nasty kisses, until Quartilla,
holding her whalebone staff in her hand, with her
coats tucked up high, discharged poor us of the
service.

We both of us took a solemn oath that the dreadful
secret should die with us two. . . .

A number of wrestling-masseurs came in, rubbed us
down with proper oil, and refreshed us. Our fatigue
anyhow vanished, we put on evening dress again, and
were shown into the next room, where three couches
were laid and besides a whole rich dinner-service was
fine spread out. We were asked to sit down, and
after beginning with some wonderful hors d'oeuvres

390–1; codex Par. 7975 of Fulgentius who is our source for the
fragment says that Quartilla was sitting between Ascyltos and
Encolpius and shows that some drinking of healths was going
on.

initiati vino etiam Falerno inundamur. Excepti
pluribus ferculis cum laberemur in somnum, " Itane
est ? " inquit Quartilla " etiam dormire vobis in
mente est, cum sciatis Priapi genio pervigilium
deberi ? " . . .

22   Cum Ascyltos gravatus tot malis in somnum labe-
retur, illa quae iniuria depulsa fuerat ancilla totam
faciem eius fuligine larga [1] perfricuit et non sentientis
labra [2] umerosque sopitionibus [3] pinxit. Iam ego
etiam [tot malis] [4] fatigatus minimum veluti gustum
hauseram somni; idem et tota intra forisque familia
fecerat, atque alii circa pedes discumbentium sparsi
iacebant, alii parietibus appliciti, quidam in ipso
limine coniunctis manebant capitibus; lucernae quoque umore defectae tenue et extremum lumen
spargebant: cum duo Syri expilaturi [lagoenam] [5]
triclinium intraverunt, dumque inter argentum [6]
avidius rixantur, diductam fregerunt lagoenam.
Cecidit etiam mensa cum argento, et ancillae super
torum marcenti [7] excussum forte altius poculum caput fregit.[8] Ad quem ictum exclamavit illa pari-
terque et fures prodidit et partem ebriorum excitavit.
Syri illi qui venerant ad praedam,[9] postquam depre-
hensos se intellexerunt, pariter secundum lectum

---

[1] larga *Jungermann*: large *Fuchs*: longa.

[2] latera *Delz rightly?*

[3] sopitionibus *L: perhaps* sopionibus *as in one reading in
Catullus, xxxvii, 10.*

[4] tot malis *was perhaps repeated in error from beginning of*
22. *So Müller in his first edition, though he retains the words
in his second.*

[5] *Deleted by O. Jahn.*

we swam in wine, and that too Falernian.[1] We followed this with more courses, and were dropping off to sleep, when Quartilla said, "Well, how can you think of going to sleep, when you know that is your duty to devote the whole wakeful night to the genius of Priapus?" . . .

Ascyltos was heavy-eyed with all his troubles, and was falling asleep, when the maid who had been driven away so rudely rubbed his face over with a lot of soot, and coloured his lips and his neck with . . . ? . . . while he drowsed.   By this time I too was tired out [with adventures] and had just taken the tiniest taste of sleep.   All the servants, indoors and out, had done the same.   Some lay anyhow by the feet of the guests, some leaned against the walls, some even stayed in the doorway with their heads together. The oil in the lamps had run out, and they spread a thin dying light.   All at once two Syrians came in to rob the dining-room, and in quarrelling greedily over the silver pulled a large jug in two and broke it. The table fell over with the plate, and a cup which happened to fly rather high broke the head of the maid, who was lolling over a seat.   The knock made her scream, and this showed up the thieves and woke some of the drunken party.   The Syrians who had come to steal dropped side by side on a sofa, when they realized that they were being noticed, with the

---

[1] One of the best Italian wines, from Campania.

---

[6] inter argentum] *Nisbet would delete.*
[7] marcenti *Delz*: marcentis.
[8] tetigit *Buecheler.*
[9] *Müller deletes* illi . . . praedam.

conciderunt, ut putares hoc convenisse, et stertere tanquam olim dormientes coeperunt.

Iam et tricliniarches experrectus lucernis occidentibus oleum infuderat, et pueri detersis paulisper oculis redierant ad ministerium, cum intrans cym-
23 balistria et concrepans aera omnes excitavit. Refectum igitur est convivium et rursus Quartilla ad bibendum revocavit. Adiuvit hilaritatem comissantis cymbalistria. . . .

Intrat cinaedus, homo omnium insulsissimus et plane illa domo dignus, qui ut infractis manibus congemuit,[1] eiusmodi carmina effudit:

" Huc huc cito [2] convenite [3] nunc, spatalocinaedi,
Pede tendite, cursum addite, convolate planta
Femoreque [4] facili, clune agili et manu procaces,
Molles, veteres, Deliaci manu recisi."

Consumptis versibus suis immundissimo me basio conspuit. Mox et super lectum venit atque omni vi detexit recusantem. Super inguina mea diu multumque frustra moluit. Profluebant [5] per frontem sudantis acaciae rivi, et inter rugas malarum tantum erat cretae, ut putares detectum parietem nimbo
24 laborare. Non tenui ego diutius lacrimas, sed ad ultimam perductus tristitiam " Quaeso " inquam " domina, certe embasicoetan iusseras dari." Com-

---

[1] concrepuit *O. Jahn, rightly?*
[2] cito *added by L. Mueller.*
[3] convertite *suggests Fraenkel.*
[4] femoreque *Buecheler*: femore ⟨o⟩ *Fraenkel*: femore.
[5] profluebant *Ribbeck*: fluebant *Müller*: perfluebant.

---

[1] Or "snapped his fingers." But I suspect that *manibus* here comes from *manu* in the following verses, and that we

most convincing naturalness, and proceeded to snore as if they were asleep long ago.

By this time the butler had woken up and refilled the flickering lamps. The boys rubbed their eyes for a few minutes, and then came back to wait. Then a girl with cymbals came in, and the crash of the brass aroused everybody. Our evening began afresh, and Quartilla called us back again to our cups. The girl with the cymbals gave her fresh spirits for her revel. . . .

At last bolted in a most shameless pansy-boy, and truly worthy of the house wherein he was; who having clapt his hands violently [1] and humm'd and hawed uttered these verses:

' Now then, hurry up! Here! Gather around here, you flabby sodomites. Stretch out your legs, let 'em run too; let feet and supple thighs fly aloft, you pansy-boys, pert with wanton hands and nimble bums, soft-soddies, old rakes, hand-gelded cockerels too! [2] '

Having done with his poetry, he smeared my lips with loathsome kisses; then getting onto my bed he threw off the coverings though I stoutly resisted. For a long while he worked mightily over my groin to no purpose; streams of sweating gum oozed over his forehead, and came trickling down the wrinkles of his cheeks like pelting rain on a peeling wall. I could not forbear tears any longer, but being brought to the last extremity, says I: " Madam, I ask you— you surely had given orders that a lewd mug be

should read here *infractis vocibus* " in broken tones "—a sign of effeminacy.

[2] The castrated cockerels (capons) of Delos were famous.

plosit illa tenerius manus et " O " inquit " hominem acutum atque urbanitatis vernaculae[1] fontem. Quid? tu non intellexeras cinaedum embasicoetan vocari? " Deinde [ut] contubernali meo ⟨ne⟩[2] melius succederet, " Per fidem " inquam " vestram,[3] Ascyltos in hoc triclinio solus ferias agit? " " Ita " inquit Quartilla " et Ascylto embasicoetas detur." Ab hac voce equum cinaedus mutavit transituque ad comitem meum facto clunibus eum basiisque distri-

LO vit. | Stabat inter haec Giton et risu dissolvebat ilia sua. Itaque conspicata eum Quartilla, cuius esset puer, diligentissima sciscitatione quaesivit. Cum ago fratrem meum esse dixissem, " Quare ergo " inquit " me non basiavit? " Vocatumque ad se in osculum applicuit. Mox manum etiam demisit in sinum et pertrectato vasculo tam rudi " Haec " inquit " belle cras in promulside libidinis nostrae militabit; hodie enim post asellum diaria non sumo."

25 Cum haec diceret, ad aurem eius Psyche ridens accessit, et cum dixisset nescio quid, " Ita, ita " inquit Quartilla " bene admonuisti. Cur non, quia bellissima occasio est, devirginatur Pannychis nostra? " Continuoque producta est puella satis bella

---

[1] vernaculae *Schoppius*: vernulae.
[2] ut *deleted and* ne *added by Fraenkel's suggestion. But the text may well be sound.*
[3] vestram *Dousa*: nostram.

---

[1] *embasicoetas* was apparently (i) a drinking mug or glass of rude sexual shape and (ii) a sodomite, " pansy-boy." Hence the translation here. " A night-cap "—J. Sullivan.
[2] I take *asellus* " a little ass " to be the fish of Pliny, *N.H.*, IX, 58, 61—one or other of the hakes. The word *asellus* was

presented to me." Then she, with a gentle clapping
of her hands: " What a very smart gentleman," says
she, "—a man of excellent natural wit! What?
Hadn't *you* understood that ' lewd mug ' is a title we
give to a sodomite?"[1] Upon this, that my companion
might not escape better than myself, " By your
integrity, Madam," said I, " does Ascyltos alone
keep holiday at this table? " " Is it so? " said she,
" then let Ascyltos also be served with a lewd mug."
And therewith the sodomite changed his horse, and
turning to my pal, almost beat him to powder with
rump and kisses. Gito stood laughing all the while,
till he had well-nigh split his sides; which Quartilla
perceiving with much curiosity enquired whose boy
he was, and I telling her he was my brother, " Why
then," said she, " has he not kissed me? " And so
calling him to her, she fell to kissing him sweetly;
next she also let her hand drift into his lap, and
handled his little tool—oh! so raw—and then,
" This," said she, " will do soldierly service finely
tomorrow as a foretaste to our lusts; for today I'm
not taking a daily ration of common food after a little
donkey-fish." [2]

With that Psyche came tittering to her, and having
whispered something in her ear, " You are in the
right on't," quoth Quartilla, " 'twas well thought on;
and since we have so fine an opportunity, why should
not our Pannychis [3] be unvirgined? " Forthwith
was brought in a pretty young girl, that seemed not

used also for a lustful man. In Chapter 31 we have a bronze
donkey on a *promulsidare*, but I can see no connection with
the present passage.
  [3] " Miss All-night."

et quae non plus quam septem annos habere videbatur [et ea ipsa quae primum cum Quartilla in
cellam venerat nostram]. [1] Plaudentibus ego universis
et postulantibus nuptias [fecerunt] [2] obstupui ego et
nec Gitona, verecundissimum puerum, sufficere huic
petulantiae affirmavi, nec puellam eius aetatis esse,
ut muliebris patientiae legem posset accipere.
" Ita " inquit Quartilla " minor est ista quam ego
fui, cum primum virum passa sum? Iunonem meam
iratam habeam, si unquam me meminerim virginem
fuisse. Nam et infans cum paribus inquinata [3] sum,
et subinde procedentibus [4] annis maioribus me pueris
applicui, donec ad [hanc] [5] aetatem perveni. Hinc
etiam puto proverbium natum illud, ut dicatur posse
taurum tollere, qui vitulum sustulerit." Igitur ne
maiorem iniuriam in secreto frater acciperet, consur-
26 rexi ad officium nuptiale. Iam Psyche puellae caput
involverat flammeo, iam embasicoetas praeferebat
facem, iam ebriae mulieres longum agmen plaudentes
fecerant thalamumque incesta [6] exornaverant veste,
cum [7] Quartilla quoque [8] iocantium libidine accensa et
ipsa surrexit correptumque Gitona in cubiculum
traxit.

Sine dubio non repugnaverat puer, ac ne puella
quidem tristis [9] expaverat nuptiarum nomen. Itaque
cum inclusi iacerent, consedimus ante limen thalami,
et in primis Quartilla per rimam improbe diductam

---

[1] *Fraenkel rightly thought the whole sentence* et . . . nostram
should be deleted.

[2] *Deleted by Mommsen.*

[3] inclinata *Buecheler.*

[4] procedentibus *Brassicanus*: prodeuntibus.

[5] *Fraenkel would delete* hanc, *rightly; also* ut dicatur, *below.*

to be above seven years of age [and was the same that
came to our room at first with Quartilla]. All
approving, and desiring the nuptials, for my part I
stood amazed, and assured them that neither Gito, a
most modest lad, was able to undergo such pokery, or
the girl of years to suffer the condition of a woman to
be worked on. " Is that all ? " quoth Quartilla, " Is
she younger than I was when I first endured a man ?
May my [1] Juno curse me if I can remember that I
ever was a maid; for when I was in hanging-sleeves,
I was defiled by little boys my own size, and as I grew
in years, I applied myself to bigger, till I came of
age; and truly I think hence came the proverb, she
can bear a bull that bore a calf." Fearing then that
my brother might sustain a greater injury secretly,
I got up to celebrate the wedding. And now Psyche
put a flame-coloured veil upon the girl's head, the
lewd mug led before with a flamboe, and a long train
of drunken women fell a shouting and decked with
unchaste garb the bride-chamber; Quartilla, in-
flamed by the other jokers' lust, took hold of Gito,
and dragged him into the bedroom.

Truly the boy made no resistance, nor seemed the
girl frighted at the name of matrimony. When
therefore they lay locked up, we sat at the chamber-
door; and Quartilla having waggishly slit a chink,

[1] Just as a man had his own *genius* or guardian angel so a
woman had her *Iuno.*

---

6 intexta *Auratus*: ingesta *Scaliger*: iniecta *Heinsius.*
7 cum *Buecheler*: tum.
8 quoque] *Buecheler deletes, rightly?*
9 triste *Fraenkel.*

applicuerat oculum curiosum lusumque puerilem libidinosa speculabatur diligentia. Me quoque ad idem spectaculum lenta manu traxit, et quia considerantium cohaeserant [1] vultus, quicquid a spectaculo [2] vacabat, commovebat obiter labra et me tanquam furtivis subinde osculis verberabat. . . .

L | Abiecti in lectis sine metu reliquam exegimus noctem. . . .

H | Venerat iam tertius dies, id est expectatio liberae cenae, sed tot vulneribus confossis fuga magis placebat, quam quies. Itaque cum maesti deliberaremus, quonam genere praesentem evitaremus procellam, unus [3] servus Agamemnonis interpellavit trepidantes et " Quid? vos " inquit " nescitis, hodie apud quem fiat? Trimalchio, lautissimus homo, horologium in triclinio et bucinatorem habet subornatum, ut subinde sciat, quantum de vita perdiderit." Amicimur ergo diligenter obliti omnium malorum, et Gitona libentissime servile officium tuentem usque hoc [4]
27 iubemus in balnea [5] sequi. Nos interim vestiti errare coepimus . . . immo iocari magis et circulis
HL [ludentem] [6] accedere, cum subito | videmus senem calvum, tunica vestitum russea, inter pueros capillatos ludentem pila. Nec tam pueri nos, quamquam erat operae pretium, ad spectaculum duxerant, quam ipse

---

[1] cohaeserant *Buecheler*: haeserant.
[2] *Müller deletes* a spectaculo.
[3] Eunus *Heinsius*.
[4] usque hoc] *Heraeus deletes.*
[5] balnea *Jahn*: balneum *Heraeus*: balneo.
[6] *Deleted by Buecheler:* ludentum (*better* ludentium) *Heinsius*.

foremost and wantonly looked through it to watch their childish diversion. She pulled me also gently to the same entertainment, and since our cheeks in our contemplation were so close together, when we were not peeping she often turned her lips to me and would as it were steal a whacking kiss.

We threw ourselves into bed and spent the rest of the night without terrors. . . .

The third day had come. I mean, a free [1] dinner was promised. But we were bruised and sore from a lot of wounds. Escape was better even than rest. We were making some melancholy plans for avoiding the coming storm, when one of Agamemnon's servants came up as we stood hesitating, and said, " I say, do you not know at whose house it is to-day ? Trimalchio,[2] a very rich man—he has a clock and a uniformed trumpeter in his dining-room, to keep telling him how much of his life is lost and gone." We forgot all troubles and hurried into our clothes, and told Giton, who till now had been waiting on us very willingly, to follow us to the baths. We proceeded to take a stroll meanwhile in evening dress . . . , or rather to joke and mix with the groups of people, when all at once we saw a bald old man in a reddish shirt playing at ball with some long-haired boys. It was not the boys that attracted our notice, though they deserved it, but the old

---

[1] Such as might be available for beast-fighters at Rome during the evening before they fought beasts in the arena. The words may be an interpolation. With *Venerat* begins the part known as *Cena Trimalchionis*.

[2] Trimalchio: this name means perhaps " Thrice-lucky," perhaps " Thrice-soft; " but we do not know. *Subornatum* may mean " ready to hand."

pater familiae, qui soleatus pila prasina exercebatur.
Nec amplius eam repetebat quae terram contigerat,
sed follem plenum habebat servus sufficiebatque
ludentibus. Notavimus etiam res novas. Nam
duo spadones in diversa parte circuli stabant, quorum
alter matellam tenebat argenteam, alter numerabat
pilas, non quidem eas quae inter manus lusu expel-
lente vibrabant, sed eas quae in terram decidebant.

H Cum has ergo miraremur lautitias, | accurrit Mene-
laus et " Hic est " inquit " apud quem cubitum
ponitis,[1] et quidem [2] iam principium cenae videtis."

HL Et iam non [3] loquebatur Menelaus cum | Trimalchio
digitos concrepuit, ad quod signum matellam spado
ludenti subiecit. Exonerata ille vesica aquam poposcit ad manus, digitosque paululum adspersos in
capite pueri tersit. . . .[4]

28   Longum erat singula excipere. Itaque intravimus
balneum, et sudore calfacti momento temporis ad
frigidam eximus. Iam Trimalchio unguento perfusus
tergebatur, non linteis, sed palliis ex lana mollissima
factis. Tres interim iatraliptae in conspectu eius

H Falernum potabant, | et cum plurimum rixantes
effunderent, Trimalchio hoc suum [5] propin esse [6] dice-

HL bat. | Hinc involutus coccina gausapa lecticae im-

---

[1] ponetis *Scheffer.*   [2] quidem *Buecheler:* quid.
[3] etiamnum *Scheffer.*   [4] *Lacuna indicated by Buecheler.*
[5] solum *Waltz.*
[6] propin (προπιεῖν) esse *Heraeus:* propinasse.

---

[1] Menelaus in this novel is Agamemnon's assistant. Cf.
Chapter 81.
[2] The fact that in Martial, XII, lxxxii, 11 the older MSS
have *feret ipse propin de faece lagonae*, gives strong support for

gentleman, who was in his house-shoes, busily engaged with a green ball. He never picked it up if it touched the ground. A slave stood by with a bagful and supplied them to the players. We also observed a new feature in the game. Two eunuchs were standing at different points in the group. One held a silver jordan, one counted the balls, not as they flew from hand to hand in the rigour of the game, but when they dropped to the ground. We were amazed at such a display, and then Menelaus [1] ran up and said, " This is the man at whose table you rest your elbow: indeed what you see is the overture to his dinner." Menelaus had just finished when Trimalchio cracked his fingers. One eunuch came up at this signal and held the jordan for him as he played. He relieved his bladder and called for a basin to wash his hands and wiped them on a boy's head. . . .

I cannot linger over details. We went into the bath. We stayed till we ran with sweat, and then at once passed through into the cold water. Trimalchio was now anointed all over and rubbed down, not with towels, but with blankets of the softest wool. Three masseurs sat there drinking Falernian wine under his eyes. They quarrelled and spilt a quantity. Trimalchio said that this was his health being drunk.[2] Then he was rolled up in a scarlet woollen coat and

---

propin here in Petronius also. Otherwise we might retain the reading *propinasse* of *H*, and conclude that the full phrase would be *suum calicem propinasse* (cf. Martial, II, 15, 1), but that *calicem* was omitted by Petronius in a familiar saying. " Trimalchio said that by this method they had drunk each from his glass a health to him (Trimalchio)." The Romans, when drinking a health, used to pour some of the wine under the table deliberately, as a sort of libation to the gods.

positus est praecedentibus phaleratis cursoribus
quattuor et chiramaxio, in quo deliciae eius vehe-
bantur, puer vetulus, lippus, domino Trimalchione
deformior. Cum ergo auferretur, ad caput eius cum
minimis symphoniacus tibiis accessit et tanquam in
aurem aliquid secreto diceret, toto itinere cantavit.

Sequimur nos admiratione iam saturi et cum
H Agamemnone ad ianuam pervenimus, | in cuius poste
libellus erat cum hac inscriptione fixus: " Quisquis
servus sine dominico iussu foras exierit, accipiet pla-
HL gas centum." | In aditu autem ipso stabat ostiarius
prasinatus, cerasino succinctus cingulo, atque in
lance argentea pisum purgabat. Super limen autem
cavea pendebat aurea, in qua pica varia intrantes
29 salutabat. Ceterum ego dum omnia stupeo, paene
resupinatus crura mea fregi. Ad sinistram enim
intrantibus non longe ab ostiarii cella canis ingens,
catena vinctus, in pariete erat pictus superque
quadrata littera scriptum " Cave canem." Et col-
legae quidem mei riserunt, ego autem collecto
spiritu non destiti totum parietem persequi. Erat
autem venalicium ⟨cum⟩[1] titulis pictum, et ipse
Trimalchio capillatus caduceum tenebat Minervaque
ducente Romam intrabat. Hinc quemadmodum
ratiocinari didicisset, denique dispensator factus

---

[1] cum *added by Burman.*

---

[1] In the entrance of the remains of a house at Pompeii can
be seen a mosaic of a dog on a leash and beneath it an inscription CAVE CANEM. There are other examples.

[2] Mercury, as the god of business, was Trimalchio's patron.
It was Mercury who secured Trimalchio's selection to be a

put in a litter. Four runners decked with medals went before him, and a hand-cart on which his favourite rode. This was a wrinkled blear-eyed boy uglier than his master Trimalchio. As he was being driven off, a musician with a tiny pair of pipes came up near his head, and played the whole way as though he were whispering secrets in his ear.

We followed, lost in wonder, and came with Agamemnon to the door. A notice was fastened on the doorpost: " NO SLAVE TO GO OUT OF DOORS EXCEPT BY THE MASTER'S ORDERS. PENALTY, ONE HUNDRED STRIPES." Just at the entrance stood a porter in green clothes, with a cherry-coloured belt, shelling peas in a silver dish. A golden cage hung in the doorway, and a black and white magpie in it greeted visitors. I was gazing at all this, when I nearly fell backwards and broke my leg. For on the left hand as you went in, not far from the porter's office, a great dog on a chain was painted on the wall, and over him was written in block capitals " BEWARE OF THE DOG." [1] My friends laughed at me, but *I* plucked up courage and went on to examine the whole wall. It had a picture of a slave-market on it, with the persons' names. Trimalchio was there with long hair, holding a Mercury's staff.[2] Minerva had him by the hand and was leading him into Rome. Then the painstaking artist had given a faithful picture of his whole career with explanations: how he

Sevir or Sexvir Augustalis, an official responsible for duly carrying out the worship of the Emperor. One of the privileges of the six Sevirs was to sit on a throne. Minerva was goddess of wisdom and thought, of all arts and sciences, and of spinning and weaving.

esset, omnia diligenter curiosus pictor cum inscriptione reddiderat. In deficiente vero iam porticu
levatum mento [1] in tribunal excelsum Mercurius
rapiebat. Praesto erat Fortuna [2] cornu abundanti
copiosa [3] et tres Parcae aurea pensa torquentes.
Notavi etiam in porticu gregem cursorum cum
magistro se exercentem. Praeterea grande armar-
ium in angulo vidi, in cuius aedicula erant Lares
argentei positi Venerisque signum marmoreum et
pyxis aurea non pusilla, in quo barbam ipsius con-
ditam esse dicebant. . . .[4]

Interrogare ergo atriensem coepi, quas in medio
picturas haberent. " Iliada et Odyssian " inquit |
30 *H* " ac Laenatis gladiatorium munus." Non licebat
multiciam [5] considerare. . . .[6]

HL   Nos | iam ad triclinium perveneramus, in cuius
parte prima procurator rationes accipiebat. Et quod
praecipue miratus sum, in postibus triclinii fasces
erant cum securibus fixi, quorum unam partem quasi
embolum navis aeneum finiebat, in quo erat scriptum :
" C. Pompeio Trimalchioni, seviro Augustali, Cinnamus dispensator." Sub eodem titulo et lucerna

---

[1] mento *H, l*: merito *Tornaesius's edition and Cod. Vat. lat.
11428 and cod. Lambeth. 693*: vento *Fuchs (who also suggests
deletion)*: adiumento *Blümner. Fraenkel has suggested* ⟨de
pavi⟩mento *and also* porticu de pavimento in tribunal excelsum
⟨eum⟩.

[2] *After* Fortuna *Wehle adds* cum, *reading* Fortuna cum cornu
[abundanti] copioso.

[3] *Goes deletes* copiosa. *Wehle reads* cornu [abundanti] copioso.

[4] *Lacuna indicated by Buecheler.*

[5] *For this probably corrupt word various suggestions have been*

had learned to keep accounts, and how at last he had been made steward. At the point where the wall-space gave out, Mercury had taken him by the chin, and was whirling him up to his high official throne. Fortune stood by flowing with her horn of plenty, and the three Fates spinning their golden threads. I also observed a company of runners practising in the gallery under a trainer, and in a corner I saw a large cupboard containing a tiny shrine, wherein were silver house-gods, and a marble image of Venus, and a large golden box, where they told me Trimalchio's first beard was laid up. . . .

I proceeded to ask the house-manager what pictures they had in the hall. "The Iliad and the Odyssey," he said, "and the gladiator's show given by Laenas." I could not take the whole multi-plicacity in at once. . . .

We now went through to the dining-room. At the entrance the steward sat receiving accounts. I was particularly astonished to see rods and axes fixed on the door posts of the dining-room, and one part of them finished off with a kind of ship's brazen beak, inscribed:

" PRESENTED BY CINNAMUS THE STEWARD TO GAIUS POM-
PEIUS TRIMALCHIO, PRIEST OF THE COLLEGE OF AUGUS-
TUS." [1] Under this inscription a double lamp hung

---

[1] Rods and axes were the symbols of office of lictors, the attendants on Roman magistrates, and the six Sevirs had the right to be attended by lictors. See c. 65.

---

made: multa clam *Marbach*: multa ad aciam *Heinsius*: multa iam *Buecheler*: multa etiam *Scheffer*.
[6] *Lacuna indicated by Buecheler.*

bilychnis de camera pendebat, et duae tabulae in
utroque poste defixae, quarum altera, si bene
memini, hoc habebat inscriptum: " III. et pridie
kalendas Ianuarias C. noster foras cenat," altera
lunae cursum stellarumque septem imagines pictas;
et qui dies boni quique incommodi essent, distin-
guente bulla notabantur.

H | His repleti voluptatibus cum conaremur [in tricli-
nium] [1] intrare, exclamavit unus ex pueris, qui super
hoc officium erat positus,[2] " Dextro pede." Sine
dubio paulisper trepidavimus, ne contra praeceptum
HL aliquis nostrum limen transiret. | Ceterum ut pariter
movimus dextros [3] gressus, servus nobis despoliatus
procubuit ad pedes ac rogare coepit, ut se poenae eri-
peremus: nec magnum esse peccatum suum, propter
quod periclitaretur; subducta enim sibi vestimenta
dispensatoris in balneo, quae vix fuissent decem
sestertiorum. Rettulimus ergo dextros [4] pedes dis-
pensatoremque in atrio [5] aureos numerantem depre-
cati sumus, ut servo remitteret poenam. Superbus
ille sustulit vultum et " Non tam iactura me movet "
inquit " quam negligentia nequissimi servi. Vestimenta mea cubitoria perdidit, quae mihi natali meo
cliens quidam donaverat, Tyria sine dubio, sed iam
semel lota. Quid ergo est? Dono vobis eum."

31 Obligati tam grandi beneficio cum intrassemus tri-

---

[1] *Müller deletes.*
[2] *Fraenkel suggested deleting* qui . . . positus.
[3] *Fraenkel would delete* dextros *as below also.*
[4] *Fraenkel would delete* dextros *as above also.*
[5] in atrio *Buecheler after Heinsius* (in primore atrio): in
prooecario *Orioli*: in promptuario *Zicàri*: pro ⟨coetone den-⟩
arios *Müller in his 2nd edition*: in precario *H.L*: in praetorio
in margin of 1. in oecario *Heraeus.*

from the ceiling, and two calendars were fixed on either doorpost, one having this entry, if I remember right: " Our master C. goes out to supper on December 30th and 31st," the other being painted with the moon in her course, and the likenesses of seven stars.[1] Lucky and unlucky days were marked too with distinctive knobs.

Fed full of these delights, we tried to get in[to the dining-room], when one of the slaves, who was entrusted with this duty, cried, " Right foot first! "[2] For a moment we were naturally nervous, for fear any of us had broken the rule in crossing the threshold. But just as we were all taking a step with the right foot together, a slave stripped for flogging fell at our feet, and proceeded to implore us to save him from punishment. It was no great sin which had put him in such peril; the steward's clothes had been stolen from him in the bath, and the whole lot were scarcely worth ten sesterces. So we drew back our right feet, and begged the steward, who sat counting gold pieces in the hall, to let the slave off. He looked up haughtily, and said, " It is not the loss I mind so much as the villain's carelessness. He lost my dinner dress, which one of my clients gave me on my birthday. It was Tyrian dye,[3] of course, but it had been washed once already. Well, well, I make you a present of the fellow."

We were obliged by his august kindness, and when

---

[1] Other than the moon—that is sun, earth, and planets Mercury, Venus, Mars, Saturn, Jupiter.

[2] The left foot (*sinister*) would not be of good omen.

[3] Tyrian dark crimson dye was very costly.

clinium, occurrit nobis ille idem servus, pro quo rogaveramus, et stupentibus spississima basia impegit gratias agens humanitati nostrae. " Ad summam, statim scietis " ait " cui dederitis beneficium. Vinum dominicum ministratoris gratia est " . . .

Tandem ergo discubuimus pueris Alexandrinis aquam in manus nivatam infundentibus aliisque insequentibus ad pedes ac paronychia cum ingenti subtilitate tollentibus. Ac ne in hoc quidem tam molesto tacebant officio, sed obiter cantabant. Ego experiri volui, an tota familia cantaret, itaque potionem poposci. Paratissimus puer non minus me acido cantico excepit, et quisquis aliquid rogatus erat ut daret . . . pantomimi chorum, non patris familiae triclinium crederes. Allata est tamen gustatio valde lauta; nam iam omnes discubuerant praeter ipsum Trimalchionem, cui locus novo more primus servabatur. Ceterum in promulsidari asellus erat Corinthius cum bisaccio positus, qui habebat olivas in altera parte albas, in altera nigras. Tegebant asellum duae lances, in quarum marginibus nomen Trimalchionis inscriptum erat et argenti pondus. Ponticuli etiam ferruminati sustinebat glires melle ac papavere sparsos. Fuerunt et tomacula super craticulam argenteam ferventia posita, et infra craticulam [1] Syriaca pruna cum granis Punici mali.

32 In his eramus lautitiis, cum ipse Trimalchio ad

---

[1] *Müller deletes* craticulam.

we were in the dining-room, the slave for whom we had pleaded ran up, and to our astonishment rained kisses on us, and thanked us for our mercy. " One word, " he said; " you will know in a minute who owes you a debt of gratitude: ' The master's wine is in the butler's gift.' " . . .

At last then we sat down, and boys from Alexandria poured water cooled with snow over our hands. Others followed and knelt down at our feet, and proceeded with great skill to pare our hangnails. Even this unpleasant duty did not silence them, but they kept singing at their work. I wanted to find out whether the whole household could sing, so I asked for a drink. A ready slave repeated my order in a chant not less shrill. They all did the same if they were asked to hand anything. It was more like an actor's dance than a gentleman's dining-room. But some rich and tasty whets for the appetite were brought on; for every one had now sat down except Trimalchio, who had the first place kept for him in the new style. A donkey in Corinthian bronze stood on the side-board, with panniers holding olives, white in one side, black in the other. Two dishes hid the donkey; Trimalchio's name and their weight in silver was engraved on their edges. There were also dormice [1] rolled in honey and poppy-seed, and supported on little bridges soldered to the plate. Then there were hot sausages laid on a silver grill, and under the grill damsons and seeds of pomegranate.

While we were engaged with these delicacies,

[1] The grey edible dormouse (*Glis vulgaris*) has begun to spread in Britain, our reddish species being *Muscardinus avellanarius*.

symphoniam allatus est positusque inter cervicalia
minutissima [1] expressit imprudentibus risum.   Pallio
enim coccineo adrasum excluserat caput circaque
oneratas veste cervices laticlaviam immiserat map-
pam fimbriis hinc atque illinc pendentibus.   Habebat
etiam in minimo digito sinistrae manus anulum
grandem subauratum, extremo vero articulo digiti
sequentis minorem, ut mihi videbatur, totum aureum,
sed plane ferreis veluti stellis ferruminatum.   Et ne
has tantum ostenderet divitias, dextrum nudavit
lacertum armilla aurea cultum et eboreo circulo
33 lamina splendente conexo.[2]   Ut deinde pinna argentea dentes perfodit, " Amici " inquit " nondum mihi
suave erat in triclinium venire, sed ne diutius absens
morae vobis essem,[3] omnem voluptatem mihi
negavi.   Permittitis tamen finiri lusum."   Seque-
batur puer cum tabula terebinthina et crystallinis
tesseris, notavique rem omnium delicatissimam.
Pro calculis enim albis ac nigris aureos argenteosque
habebat denarios.   Interim dum ille omnium tex-
torum dicta inter lusum consumit, gustantibus adhuc
nobis repositorium allatum est cum corbe, in quo
gallina erat lignea patentibus in orbem alis, quales
esse solent quae incubant ova.   Accessere continuo
duo servi et symphonia strepente scrutari paleam

---

[1] tumidissima *conjectures Jacobs*: munitissima *H.*
[2] conexo *Buecheler*: connexum.
[3] *Here H has* in triclinium ·absens more (= morae) vobis
venire sed ne diutius absenti vos essem.   *L has:* in triclinium
venire sed ne diutius absentius essem.   *Heinsius first transferred* absens morae vobis *so as to follow* diutius, *but he retained*
absentivus *of Pithoeus's editions as* absentivŏs.

Trimalchio was conducted in to the sound of music, propped on the tiniest of pillows. A laugh escaped the unwary. His head was shaven and peered out of a scarlet cloak, and over the heavy clothes on his neck he had put on a napkin with a broad stripe and fringes hanging from it all round. On the little finger of his left hand he had an enormous gilt ring, and on the top joint of the next finger a smaller ring which appeared to me to be entirely gold, but was really set all round with iron cut out in little stars.[1] Not content with this display of wealth, he bared his right arm, where a golden bracelet shone, and an ivory bangle clasped with a plate of bright metal. Then he said, as he picked his teeth with a silver quill, " It was not convenient for me to come to dinner yet, my friends, but I gave up all my own pleasure; I did not like to stay away any longer and keep you waiting. But you do not mind if I finish my game? " A boy followed him with a table of terebinth wood and two crystal dice, and I noticed the prettiest thing possible. Instead of black and white counters they used gold and silver coins. Trimalchio kept passing every kind of remark as he played, and we were still busy with the hors d'oeuvres, when a tray was brought in with a basket on it, in which there was a hen made of wood, spreading out her wings as they do when they are sitting. The music grew loud: two slaves at once came up and then hunted in the

---

[1] Petronius stresses the incongruous display of wealth by Trimalchio, who wears a gold ring as if he were an *eques*—and an iron one; he " sports " the broad (purple) stripe as if he were a senator—but on his napkin, not on his cloak; and his hair is cut close like a slave or a newly made freedman.

coeperunt erutaque subinde pavonina ova divisere
convivis. Convertit ad hanc scaenam Trimalchio
vultum et " Amici " ait " pavonis ova gallinae iussi
supponi. Et mehercules timeo ne iam concepti sint;
temptemus tamen, si adhuc sorbilia sunt." Accipi-
mus nos cochlearia non minus selibras pendentia
ovaque ex farina pingui figurata pertundimus. Ego
quidem paene proieci partem meam, nam videbatur
mihi iam in pullum coisse. Deinde ut audivi veterem
convivam : " Hic nescio quid boni debet esse," persecutus putamen manu pinguissimam ficedulam inveni
piperato vitello circumdatam.

34   Iam Trimalchio eadem omnia lusu intermisso po-
poscerat feceratque potestatem clara voce, si quis
nostrum iterum vellet mulsum sumere, cum subito
signum symphonia datur et gustatoria pariter a choro
cantante rapiuntur. Ceterum inter tumultum cum
forte paropsis excidisset et puer iacentem sustulisset,
animadvertit Trimalchio colaphisque obiurgari puerum ac proicere rursus paropsidem iussit. In-
secutus est lecticarius [1] argentumque inter reliqua
H purgamenta scopis coepit everrere.[2] | Subinde intra-
verunt duo Aethiopes capillati cum pusillis utribus,

---

[1] supellecticarius *conjectures Dousa.*
[2] everrere *Goes* : verrere.

---

[1] This bird cannot be a fig-bird (*Sphecotheres* of the family of
orioles) because the several species are Australian. The name
beccafico is applied in Italy to-day to several small passerine
birds which frequent gardens in the autumn and sometimes
peck at figs for insects and are eaten. The old Roman *ficedula*

straw. Peahen's eggs were pulled out and handed to the guests. Trimalchio turned towards this fine sight, and said, " I gave orders, my friends, that peahen's eggs should be put under a common hen. And upon my oath I am afraid they are addled by now. But we will try whether they are still fresh enough to suck." We took our spoons, half-a-pound in weight at least, and hammered at the eggs, which were balls of fine meal. I was on the point of throwing away my portion. I thought a peachick had already formed. But hearing a practised diner say, " What treasure have we here? " I poked through the shell with my finger, and found a very fat fig-eater,[1] rolled up in spiced yolk of egg.

Trimalchio had now stopped his game, and asked for all the same dishes, and in a loud voice invited any of us, who wished, to take a second glass of mead. Suddenly the music gave the sign, and the light dishes were swept away by a troop of singing servants. But an entrée-dish happened to fall in the rush, and a boy picked it up from the ground. Trimalchio saw him, and directed that he should be punished by a box on the ear, and made to throw down the dish again. A chamberlain followed and proceeded to sweep out the silver with a broom among the other rubbish. Then two long-haired Ethiopians with little wineskins, just like the men who scatter

---

was probably one or more of these. Some believe it was a large warbler like the garden warbler (*Sylvia borin*). But Pliny, *N.H.*, X, 86, says that the birds are called *ficedulae* in autumn but that at all other times they are called *melancoryphi* (black-tops). This surely indicates the blackcap (*Sylvia atricapilla*), and this rather than a tit such as marsh tit or willow tit.

quales solent esse qui harenam in amphitheatro spargunt, vinumque dedere in manus; aquam enim nemo porrexit.

HL | Laudatus propter elegantias dominus " Aequum " inquit " Mars amat. Itaque iussi [1] suam cuique mensam assignari. Obiter et putidissimi [2] servi minorem nobis aestum frequentia sua facient."

Statim allatae sunt amphorae vitreae diligenter gypsatae, quarum in cervicibus pittacia erant affixa cum hoc titulo: " Falernum Opimianum annorum centum." Dum titulos perlegimus, complosit Trimalchio manus et " Eheu " inquit " ergo diutius vi-

H vit | vinum quam homuncio. Quare tangomenas fa-

HL ciamus. | Vinum vita [3] est. Verum Opimianum praesto. Heri non tam bonum posui, et multo honestiores cenabant." Potantibus ergo nobis et accuratissime lautitias mirantibus larvam argenteam attulit servus sic aptatam, ut articuli eius vertebraeque luxatae [4] in omnem partem flecterentur. Hanc cum super mensam semel iterumque abiecisset, et catenatio mobilis aliquot figuras exprimeret, Trimalchio adiecit:

[1] iussi *Burman*: iussit.
[2] putidissimi *Heinsius*: pudissimi *H*: p̄dissimi *l*.
[3] vinum vita *Goes*: vita vinum.
[4] luxatae *Heinsius*: laxatae *H*: locatae *L*.

---

[1] Since Trimalchio is apparently a character of Nero's reign (A.D. 54–68), his wine if supposed to be genuine Opimian would taste pretty bad, because Opinius was consul in 121 B.C. But the guests enjoyed it. If the labels also are supposed to be genuine, that is, put on after one hundred years' keep, and if Trimalchio is supposed to be accurate (though he is an

sand in an amphitheatre, came in and gave us wine
to wash our hands in, for no one offered us water.

We complimented our host on his arrangements.
" Mars loves a fair field," said he, " and so I gave
orders that every one should have a separate table.
In that way these filthy slaves will not make us so
hot by crowding past us."

Just then some glass jars carefully fastened with
gypsum were brought on, with labels tied to their
necks, inscribed, " Falernian of Opimius's vintage,
100 years in bottle."[1] As we were poring over the
tickets Trimalchio clapped his hands and cried, " Ah
me, so wine lives longer than miserable man. So let
us be merry.[2] Wine is life. I put on real wine of
Opimius's year. I produced some inferior stuff
yesterday, and there was a much finer set of people
to dinner." As we drank and admired each luxury in
detail, a slave brought in a silver skeleton,[3] made so
that its joints and sockets could be moved and bent in
every direction. He threw it down once or twice on
the table so that the supple sections showed several
attitudes, and Trimalchio said appropriately : " Alas

ignorant man), they were put on during the reign of Augustus
(30 B.C.–A.D. 14).

[2] The word *tangomenas* is obscure. It occurs also at the end
of Chapter 73, again with *faciamus*. *Tango menas* (Birt,
Rhein. Mus., LXXV, 118 ff.) " I touch mendoles (anchovies) "
conveys no sense; nor does *tango Manes* (Ohlert). In a
drinking mood Alcaeus (Fr. 94. Diehl; J. Edmonds, *Lyra
Graeca*, Vol. I, LCL, pp 418–419) has τέγγε πλεύμονας οἴνῳ
" wet your lungs with wine," and Buecheler suggested
tengomenas in Petronius's phrase.

[3] Some representation of a skeleton was often present where
Romans ate, apparently a reminder that though one eats now,
one will die later. *larva* usually means a ghost.

" Eheu nos miseros, quam totus homuncio nil est.
Sic erimus cuncti, postquam nos auferet Orcus.
Ergo vivamus, dum licet esse bene."

35   Laudationem [1] ferculum est insecutum plane non
pro expectatione magnum; novitas tamen omnium
convertit oculos. Rotundum enim repositorium
duodecim habebat signa in orbe disposita, super quae
proprium convenientemque materiae structor imposuerat cibum: super arietem cicer arietinum, super
taurum bubulae frustum, super geminos testiculos ac
rienes, super cancrum coronam, super leonem ficum
Africanam, super virginem steriliculam, super libram
stateram in cuius altera parte scriblita erat, in altera
H placenta, | super scorpionem pisciculum marinum, |
HL super sagittarium oculatam,[2] super capricornum
locustam marinam, super aquarium anserem, super
pisces duos mullos. In medio autem caespes cum
herbis excisus favum sustinebat. Circumferebat
Aegyptius puer clibano argenteo panem. . . .[3]

Atque ipse etiam taeterrima voce de Laserpiciario
mimo canticum extorsit. Nos ut tristiores ad tam
36 viles accessimus cibos, " Suadeo " inquit Trimalchio

---

[1] lavationem *Jacobs.*
[2] oclopetam *H*: odopetam *l.* oculatam *K. Rose and J,
Sullivan, in Class. Quart., N.S. xviii,* 180–184.
[3] *lacuna indicated by Buecheler.*

---

[1] In every case there is a connection between the Zodiacal
sign and the edible stuff placed over it " ram-like " chick-pea
was so named from its shape; the wreath of flowers over the
Crab might allude to the flowers of summer or the chaplets
that might be worn at the summer solstice because the sun is
" in the Crab " at that turn of the year; but more likely the

for us poor mortals, all that poor man is is nothing. So we shall all be, after the world below takes us away. Let us live then while it can go well with us.'

After we had praised this outburst a dish followed, not at all of the size we expected; but its novelty drew every eye to it. There was a round plate with the twelve signs of the Zodiac set in a circle,[1] and on each one the artist had laid some food fit and proper to the symbol; over the Ram ram's-head chick-pea, a piece of beef on the Bull, testicles and kidneys over the Twins, over the Crab a wreath of flowers, an African fig over the Lion, a barren sow's paunch over Virgo, over Libra a pair of scales with a muffin on one side and a cake on the other, over Scorpio a small sea-fish, over Sagittarius an oblade,[2] over Capricornus a crawfish, over Aquarius a goose, over Pisces two mullets. In the middle lay a honeycomb on a sod of turf with its weeds in it. An Egyptian boy took bread round in a silver chafingdish. . . .

Trimalchio himself too ground out a tune from the musical comedy " Assafoetida" in a most hideous voice. We came to such an evil entertainment rather depressed. " Now," said Trimalchio, " let us have

wreath is the constellation called by the Romans the " Corona " —the Northern Crown. The small fish over Scorpio would be the one called " scorpio " or " scorpaena," a sculpin (*Scorpaena scrofa* or else *S. porcus*). The connection between Capricornus, " goat-horn " and crawfish would be two goats' horns and two antennae.

[2] *oclopetam* looks like a word formed from *oculus*, eye, and *peta* from *petere*, eye-seeker, but meaning " aiming with an eye," not " aiming at an eye ", as might a crow which is edible. However I accept *oculatam*. See Note on page 430.

36 " cenemus; hoc est ius [1] cenae." Haec ut dixit, ad
symphoniam quattuor tripudiantes procurrerunt su-
perioremque partem repositorii abstulerunt. Quo
facto videmus infra [scilicet in altero ferculo] [2] altilia
et sumina leporemque in medio pinnis subornatum,
ut Pegasus videretur. Notavimus etiam circa angulos repositorii Marsyas quattuor, ex quorum utriculis
garum piperatum currebat super pisces, qui ⟨tam-
quam⟩ [3] in euripo natabant. Damus omnes plausum
a familia inceptum et res electissimas ridentes aggre-
dimur. Non minus et Trimalchio eiusmodi methodio
laetus " Carpe " inquit. Processit statim scissor et
ad symphoniam gesticulatus ita laceravit obsonium, ut
putares essedarium hydraule cantante pugnare.
Ingerebat nihilo minus Trimalchio lentissima voce:
" Carpe, Carpe." Ego suspicatus ad aliquam urbanitatem totiens iteratam vocem pertinere, non erubui
eum qui supra me accumbebat, hoc ipsum interrogare.
At ille, qui saepius eiusmodi ludos spectaverat,
" Vides illum " inquit " qui obsonium carpit: Carpus
vocatur. Itaque quotiescunque dicit ' Carpe,' eodem
verbo et vocat et imperat."

37 Non potui amplius quicquam gustare, sed conversus
ad eum, ut quam plurima exciperem, longe accersere
fabulas coepi sciscitarique, quae esset mulier illa,

---

[1] ius *l*: in *H*: initium *Reiske, who with Wehle would delete*
hoc est ius cenae.

[2] *Deleted by Pithoeus in his second edition.*

[3] *Added by Wehle*: ⟨quasi⟩ *Gaselee.* quiq3 *H*.

---

[1] Pegasus was Bellerophon's winged horse. Marsyas the
satyr was flayed alive by Apollo whom Marsyas had challenged
to a contest in pipe-playing and had lost.

dinner. This is sauce for the dinner." As he spoke,
four dancers ran up in time with the music and took
off the top part of the dish. Then we saw in the well
of it fat fowls and sow's bellies, and in the middle a
hare got up with wings to look like Pegasus.[1] Four
figures of Marsyas at the corners of the dish also
caught the eye; they let a spiced sauce run from their
wine-skins over the fishes, which swam about in a kind
of tide-race. We all took up the clapping which the
slaves started, and attacked these delicacies with
hearty laughter. Trimalchio was delighted with the
trick he had played us, and said, " Now, Carver."
The slicer came up at once, and making flourishes in
time with the music hacked the meat to pieces; you
would have said that a gladiator in a chariot was fighting to the accompaniment of a water-organ. Still
Trimalchio kept on in a slow voice, " Oh, Carver,
Carver." I thought this word over and over again
must be part of a joke, and I made bold to ask the
man who sat next me this very question. He had
seen performances of this kind quite often. " You
see the fellow who is carving his way through the
meat? Well, his name is Carver. So whenever
Trimalchio says the word, he calls his name, and also
gives orders." [2]

I was now unable to eat any more, so I turned to
my neighbour to get as much news as possible. I
proceeded to seek for far-fetched stories, and to
enquire who the woman was who kept running about

[2] As Lowe put it, " Carver, carve 'er "; as Sedgwick
suggested, " Hackett, hack it."

quae huc atque illuc discurreret. " Uxor " inquit
" Trimalchionis, Fortunata appellatur, quae nummos
modio metitur. Et modo, modo quid fuit? Ignoscet
mihi genius tuus, noluisses de mani illius panem accipere. Nunc, nec quid nec quare, in caelum abiit et
Trimalchionis topanta [1] est. Ad summam, mero
H meridie si dixerit illi tenebras esse, credet. | Ipse
nescit quid habeat, adeo saplutus [2] est; sed haec
lupatria [3] providet omnia et [4] ubi non putes. Est
sicca, sobria, bonorum consiliorum [tantum auri
vides],[5] est tamen malae linguae, pica pulvinaris.
Quem amat, amat; quem non amat, non amat. Ipse
Trimalchio [6] fundos habet, qua milvi volant, nummorum nummos. Argentum in ostiarii illius cella
plus iacet, quam quisquam in fortunis habet.
Familia vero babae babae, non mehercules puto
decumam partem esse quae dominum suum noverit.
Ad summam, quemvis ex istis babaecalis [7] in rutae
38 folium coniciet. Nec est quod putes illum quicquam emere. Omnia domi nascuntur: laina [8]
credrae,[9] piper, lacte gallinaceum si quaesieris, in-

---

[1] τὰ πάντα in margin of l.   [2] Greek ζάπλουτος.
[3] lupa trita Goes.
[4] omnia est Müller in his 2nd edition.
[5] Deleted by Nodot, probably rightly, though Müller retains
the words in his second edition. " You see so much gold ".
[6] Müller deletes Trimalchio.
[7] babaecali = Greek βαβαὶ καλοί.   [8] laina P. George: lana.
[9] credrae H which may be corrupt. cedriae Muncker:
cedrea Heraeus: cerae Heinsius: citria Jacobs. The last
conjecture, or citrea, may well be right.

---

[1] Literally " May your genius pardon me." See above,
note on chapter 25.

everywhere. " She is Trimalchio's wife Fortunata,"
he said, " and she counts her money by the bushel.
And what was she a little while ago? You[1] will pardon me if I say that you would not have taken a
piece of bread from her hand. Now without why or
wherefore she is queen of Heaven, and Trimalchio's
all in all. In fact, if she tells him that it is dark at
high noon, he will believe it. He is so enormously
rich that he does not know himself what he has; but
this wolf-bitch woman has a plan for everything, even
where you would not think it. She is temperate,
sober, and prudent, but she has a nasty tongue, and
henpecks him on his own sofa.[2] Whom she likes, she
likes; whom she dislikes, she dislikes. Trimalchio
has estates wherever a kite can fly in a day, is
millionaire of millionaires. There is more plate lying
in his hall-porter's room than other people have in
their whole fortunes. And his slaves! My word! I
really don't believe that one out of ten of them knows
his master by sight. Why, he can knock any of
these young la-de-das into a nettle-bed[3] if he
chooses. You must not suppose either that he buys
anything. Everything is home-grown: mastich,[4]
citrons, pepper; you can have hen's milk for the ask-

[2] The phrase means literally " she is a magpie belonging to
a pillow," and clearly refers to domestic tyranny.
[3] *In rutae folium coniciet.* Literally " will throw into a
rue-leaf." *Rutae folium* is said by Friedländer to be a proverbial expression for a small space. He refers to Martial, xi,
31. The phrase occurs again in c. 58.
[4] P. George's emendation *laina* seems a good one, because
the point is that what Trimalchio grows at home is exotic,
which *lana*, wool, is not.

venies. Ad summam, parum illi bona lana nasceba-
tur; arietes a Tarento emit, et eos culavit in gregem.
Mel Atticum ut domi nasceretur, apes ab Athenis
iussit afferri; obiter et vernaculae quae sunt, melius-
culae a Graeculis fient. Ecce intra hos dies scripsit,
ut illi ex India semen boletorum mitteretur. Nam
mulam quidem nullam habet, quae non ex onagro
nata sit. Vides tot culcitas: nulla non aut con-
chyliatum aut coccineum tomentum habet. Tanta
est animi [1] beatitudo. Reliquos autem collibertos eius
cave contemnas. Valde sucos[s]i sunt. Vides illum
qui in imo imus recumbit: hodie sua octingenta possidet. De nihilo crevit. Modo solebat collo [2] suo
ligna portare. Sed quomodo dicunt—ego nihil scio,
sed audivi—quom [3] Incuboni pilleum rapuisset, [et] [4]
thesaurum invenit. Ego nemini invideo, si quid [5]
deus dedit. Est tamen sub alapa et non vult sibi
male. Itaque proxime casam [6] hoc titulo proscripsit:
' C. Pompeius Diogenes ex kalendis Iuliis cenaculum
locat; ipse enim domum emit.' Quid ille qui
libertini loco iacet, quam bene se habuit. Non
impropero illi. Sestertium suum vidit decies, sed
male vacillavit. Non puto illum capillos liberos

---

[1] homini *Reinesius*.
[2] modo solebat collo *Wehle*: solebat collo modo *H*.
[3] quom *Buecheler*: cum modo *Scheffer*: quomodo.
[4] *Deleted by Scheffer*.   [5] quid *Buecheler*: quoi *Goes*; quo.
[6] casam *Buecheler* (or cenaculum): oecum *Jak. Gronov*: cum.

---

[1] *Incubo* was a goblin who guarded hidden treasure. If
one stole his cap, he was compelled to reveal the treasure.

ing. Why, his wool was not growing of fine enough
quality. He bought rams from Tarentum and
bummed them into his flock. He had bees brought
from Athens to give him Attic honey on the premises;
the Roman-born bees incidentally will be improved
by the Greeklings. Within the last few days, I
may say, he has written for a cargo of mushroom
spawn from India. And he has not got a single
mule which is not the child of a wild ass. You see all
the cushions here: every one has purple or scarlet
stuffing. So high is his felicity. But do not look
down on the other freedmen who are his friends.
They are very juicy people. That one you see lying
at the bottom of the end sofa has his eight hundred
thousand. He grew from nothing. A little time ago
he was carrying loads of wood on his back. People do
say—I know nothing, but I have heard—that he
pulled off a goblin's cap and found a fairy hoard.[1] If
God makes presents I am jealous of nobody. Still,
he shows the marks of his master's fingers,[2] and has a
fine opinion of himself. So he has just put up a
notice next to his hovel: ' This attic, the property of
Caius Pompeius Diogenes, to let from the 1st of July,
the owner having purchased a house.' That person
there too who is lying in the freedman's place [3] is well
pleased with himself. I do not blame him. He had
his million in his hands, but he has had a bad shaking.
I believe he cannot say his hair is free from mortgage.

[2] On setting a slave free the master gave him a slap (alapa)
as a symbol of his former power over him.
[3] Apparently a recognized place at table was assigned to a
freedman invited to dine with freemen. Its position is not
known.

habere, nec mehercules sua culpa; ipso enim homo
melior non est; sed liberti scelerati, qui omnia ad se
fecerunt. Scito autem: sociorum olla male fervet,
et ubi semel res inclinata est, amici de medio. Et
quam honestam negotiationem exercuit, quod illum
sic vides. Libitinarius fuit. Solebat sic cenare,
quomodo rex: apros gausapatos, opera pistoria, avis,
cocos,[1] pistores. Plus vini sub mensa effundebatur,
quam aliquis in cella habet. Phantasia, non homo.
Inclinatis quoque rebus suis, cum timeret ne credi-
tores illum conturbare existimarent, hoc titulo
auctionem [2] proscripsit: ' C. Iulius Proculus auctionem faciet rerum supervacuarum.' "

39   Interpellavit tam dulces fabulas Trimalchio; nam
iam sublatum erat ferculum, hilaresque convivae vino
sermonibusque publicatis operam coeperant dare.   Is
ergo reclinatus in cubitum " Hoc vinum " inquit
"vos oportet suave faciatis. Pisces natare oportet.
Rogo, me putatis illa cena esse contentum, quam in
theca repositorii videratis ?   ' Sic notus Vlixes ? ' quid
ergo est ? Oportet etiam inter cenandum philo-
logiam nosse. Patrono meo ossa bene quiescant, qui
me hominem inter homines voluit esse. Nam mihi
nihil novi potest afferri, sicut ille † fericulusta mel † [3]

---

[1] avis, cocos *Scheffer*: viscocos.   *There are other conjectures.*
Jacobs thought opera pistoris *should be deleted.*
[2] auctionem *Scheffer*: caucionem.   C. *or* T. *before* Iulius
was added by Buecheler.
[3] fericulus iam *Buecheler*.   *The corruption certainly contains*
ferculus (*J. F. Gronov*).   *Studer suggests* talem *for* ta mel.

No fault of his I am sure; there is no better fellow
alive; but it is the damned freedmen who have
pocketed everything. You know how it is: the company's pot goes off the boil, and the moment business
takes a bad turn your friends desert you. You see
him in this state: and what a fine trade he drove!
He was an undertaker.[1] He used to dine like a
prince: boars cooked in a cloth, pastry-cooks' con-
coctions, chefs, and confectioners! There used
to be more wine spilt under the table than many a
man has in his cellars. He was a fairy prince, not a
mortal. When his business was failing, and he was
afraid his creditors might guess that he was going
bankrupt, he advertised a sale in this fashion: ' Caius
Julius Proculus will offer for sale some articles for
which he has no further use.' ''

Trimalchio interrupted these delightful tales; the
course had now been removed, and the cheerful company proceeded to turn their attention to the wine,
and to general conversation. He lay back on his
couch and said: " Now you must make this wine go
down pleasantly. A fish must have something to
swim in. But I say, did you suppose I would put up
with the dinner you saw on the top part of that round
dish—' Is this the old Ulysses whom ye knew? '[2]—
well, well, one must not forget one's culture even at
dinner. God rest the bones of my patron; he
wanted me to be a man among men. No one can
bring me anything new, as that last dish already

---

[1] The word is derived from Libitina, goddess of funerals.
From her temple they got their hired equipment.
[2] See Virgil, *Aeneid*, ii, 44. Don't you know me better than
that?

habuit praxim. Caelus hic, in quo duodecim dii habitant, in totidem se figuras convertit, et modo fit aries. Itaque quisquis nascitur illo signo, multa pecora habet, multum lanae, caput praeterea durum, frontem expudoratam, cornum acutum. Plurimi hoc signo scholastici nascuntur et arietilli." [1] Laudamus urbanitatem methematici; itaque adiecit: " deinde totus caelus taurulus fit. Itaque tunc calcitrosi nascuntur et bubulci et qui se ipsi pascunt. In geminis autem nascuntur bigae et boves et colei et qui utrosque parietes linunt. In cancro ego natus sum. Ideo multis pedibus sto, et in mari et in terra multa possideo; nam cancer et hoc et illoc quadrat. Et ideo iam dudum nihil super illum posui, ne genesim meam premerem. In leone cataphagae nascuntur et imperiosi; in virgine mulieres [2] et fugitivi et compediti; in libra laniones et unguentarii et quicunque aliquid expendunt; [3] in scorpione venenarii et percussores; in sagittario strabones, qui holera spectant, lardum tollunt; in capricorno aerumnosi, quibus prae mala sua cornua nascuntur; in aquario copones et cucurbitae; in piscibus obsonatores et rhetores. Sic orbis vertitur tanquam mola,

---

[1] arietilli *Heinsius*: arieti illi.   [2] mulierosi *Jak. Gronov.*
[3] expendunt *Burman*: expediunt.

---

[1] Cf. J. G. W. M. de Vreese, *Petron 39 und die Astrologie*, Amsterdam, 1927. The twelve chief Roman gods were Jupiter, Juno, Mars, Venus, Apollo, Vulcan, Mercury, Minerva, Diana, Vesta, Ceres, and Neptune. On the signs Trimalchio gives his own ideas.

[2] Literally " those who daub dividing walls on both sides," or " those who whitewash two dividing walls from one pail "— kill two birds with one stone.

proved in its consummation. The firmament where the twelve gods inhabit turns into as many figures, and at one time becomes a ram.[1] So anyone who is born under that sign has plenty of flocks and wool, a hard head and a shameless forehead and sharp horns. Very many pedants and young bucks are born under this sign." We applauded the elegance of his astrology, and so he went on: " Then the whole sky changes into a young bull. So men who are free with their heels are born now, and oxherds and people who have to find their own food. Under the Twins tandems are born, and pairs of oxen, and men with balls, and those who sit on both sides of the fence.[2] *I* was born under the Crab. So I have many legs to stand on, and many possessions by sea and land; for either one or the other suits your crab. And that was why just now I put nothing on top of the Crab, for fear of weighing down the house of my birth. Under the Lion gluttons and masterful men are born; under Virgo women, and runaway slaves, and chained gangs; under Libra butchers, and perfumers, and any people who weigh something out; poisoners and assassins under Scorpio; under Sagittarius cross-eyed men, who take the bacon while they look at the vegetables; under Capricornus the poor folk whose troubles make horns sprout on them; under Aquarius innkeepers and men with water on the brain; under Pisces chefs and rhetoricians.[3] So the world turns

[3] *Libra:* Balance *or* Scales. *Sagittarius:* " Archer." *Capricornus:* " Goat-horn." *Aquarius:* " Water-carrier," " Water-bearer " (perhaps inn-keepers put water in the wine). *Pisces:* " Fishes," under which probably fish-mouthed people were born.

et semper aliquid mali facit, ut homines aut nascantur
aut pereant. Quod autem in medio caespitem videtis
et supra caespitem favum, nihil sine ratione facio.
Terra mater est in medio quasi ovum corrotundata, et
omnia bona in se habet tanquam favus."

40 " Sophos " universi clamamus et sublatis manibus
ad cameram iuramus Hipparchum Aratumque com-
parandos illi homines [1] non fuisse, donec advenerunt
ministri ac toralia praeposuerunt toris,[2] in quibus retia
erant picta subsessoresque cum venabulis et totus
venationis apparatus. Necdum sciebamus ⟨quo⟩ [3]
mitteremus suspiciones nostras, cum extra triclinium
clamor sublatus est ingens, et ecce canes Laconici
etiam circa mensam discurrere coeperunt. Secutum
est hos repositorium, in quo positus erat primae
magnitudinis aper, et quidem pilleatus, e cuius
dentibus sportellae dependebant duae palmulis
textae, altera caryotis altera thebaicis repleta. Circa
autem minores porcelli ex coptoplacentis facti,
quasi uberibus imminerent, scrofam esse positam
significabant. Et hi quidem apophoreti fuerunt.
Ceterum ad scindendum aprum non ille Carpus
accessit, qui altilia laceraverat,[4] sed barbatus ingens,
fasciis cruralibus alligatus et alicula subornatus
polymita, strictoque venatorio cultro latus apri
vehementer percussit, ex cuius plaga turdi evo-

---

[1] homini *Heinsius.*

[2] toralia praeposuerunt *Mentel*: tolaria proposeurunt *H*:
toralia proposeurunt [toris] *Fraenkel.*

[3] ⟨quo⟩ *added by Mentel.*　　　　[4] *J. Sullivan deletes* q.a.l.

like a mill, and always brings some evil to pass, causing the birth of men or their death. You saw the green turf in the middle of the dish, and the honeycomb on the turf; I do nothing without a reason. Mother Earth lies in the world's midst rounded like an egg, and in her all blessings are contained as in a honeycomb."

"Bravo!" we all cried, swearing with our hands lifted to the ceiling that Hipparchus and Aratus [1] were men not to be compared with him, until the servants came and spread over the couches coverlets painted with nets, and men lying in wait with hunting spears, and all the instruments of the chase. We were still wondering where to turn our expectations, when a great shout was raised outside the dining-room, and in came some Spartan hounds too, and proceeded to run round the table. A tray was brought in after them with a wild boar of the largest size upon it, wearing a cap of freedom, with two little baskets woven of palm-twigs hanging from the tusks, one full of dry dates and the other of fresh. Round it lay sucking-pigs made of simnel cake with their mouths to the teats, thereby showing that we had a sow before us. These sucking-pigs were for the guests to take away. Carver, who had mangled the fowls, did not come to divide the boar, but a big bearded man with bands wound round his legs, and a spangled hunting-coat of damasked silk, who drew a hunting-knife and plunged it hard into the boar's side. A number of fieldfares flew out at the blow.

[1] Aratus (c. 315–c. 245 B.C.) of Soli and Hipparchus (c. 190–124 B.C.) of Nicaea were famous astronomers, the latter deservedly.

laverunt. Parati aucupes cum harundinibus fuerunt
et eos circa triclinium volitantes momento excepe-
runt. Inde cum suum cuique iussisset referri Trimalchio, adiecit: " Etiam videte, quam porcus ille
silvaticus lotam [1] comederit glandem." Statim pueri
ad sportellas accesserunt, quae pendebant e dentibus,
thebaicasque et caryotas ad numerum divisere
cenantibus.

41   Interim ego, qui privatum habebam secessum, in
multas cogitationes diductus sum, quare aper pilleatus intrasset. Postquam itaque omnis bacalusias [2]
consumpsi, duravi interrogare illum interpretem
meum, quod [3] me torqueret. At ille: " Plane etiam
hoc servus tuus indicare potest; non enim aenigma
est, sed res aperta. Hic aper, cum heri summa cena
eum [4] vindicasset, a convivis dimissus est; itaque
hodie tanquam libertus in convivium revertitur."
Damnavi ego stuporem meum et nihil amplius inter-
rogavi, ne viderer nunquam inter honestos cenasse.

Dum haec loquimur, puer speciosus, vitibus hederis-
que redimitus, modo Bromium, interdum Lyaeum
Euhiumque confessus, calathisco uvas circumtulit et
poemata domini sui acutissima voce traduxit. Ad
quem sonum conversus [5] Trimalchio " Dionyse "
inquit " liber esto." Puer detraxit pilleum apro
capitique suo imposuit. Tum Trimalchio rursus
adiecit: " Non negabitis me " inquit " habere

---

[1] lotam *Muncker: Buecheler conjectures* cultam: *H has* totam.
[2] *So H. Various suggestions have been made to alter it.*
[3] quod *Buecheler:* quid.
[4] summa cena eum *Buecheler:* summam cenam *Scheffer:*
summa cenam.
[5] *Fraenkel suggested deleting* conversus. *Compare chapter 98.*

As they fluttered round the dining-room there were
fowlers ready with limed reeds who caught them in a
moment. Trimalchio ordered everybody to be given
his own portion, and added: " Now you see what fine
acorns the woodland boar has been eating." Then
boys came and took the baskets which hung from her
jaws and distributed the fresh and the dry dates to
the guests.

Meantime I had got a quiet corner to myself, and
had gone off on a long train of speculation,—why the
boar had come in with a cap of freedom on. After
turning the problem over every way [1] I ventured to
put the question which was troubling me to my old
informant. " Your humble servant can explain that
too ; " he said, " there is no riddle, the thing is quite
plain. Yesterday when this animal appeared as *pièce
de résistance* at dinner, the guests let him go; and
so to-day he comes back to dinner as a freedman." I
cursed my dullness and asked no more questions, for
fear of showing that I had never dined among decent
people.

As we were speaking, a beautiful boy with vine-
leaves and ivy in his hair brought round grapes in a
little basket, impersonating Bacchus now as the
Noisy one, sometimes as the Loosener and as Good-
Joy, and rendering his master's verses in a most shrill
voice. Trimalchio turned round at the noise and
said, " Dionysus, rise and be liberated." The boy
took the cap of freedom off the boar, and put it on his
head. Then Trimalchio went on: " I am sure you

---

[1] *Bacalusias* may be derived from *baceolus* (Gk. βάκηλος) a
blockhead, and *ludere*, hence meaning perhaps "every kind
of foolish explanation of the riddle."

Liberum patrem." Laudavimus dictum Trimalchionis et circumeuntem [1] puerum sane perbasiamus.[2]

Ab hoc ferculo Trimalchio ad lasanum surrexit.
Nos libertatem sine turanno nacti coepimus invitare [3]
convivarum sermones. Dama [4] itaque primus cum
† pataracina † [5] poposcisset, " Dies " inquit " nihil
est. Dum versas te, nox fit. Itaque nihil est melius, quam de cubiculo recta in triclinium ire. Et
mundum frigus habuimus. Vix me balneus calfecit.
Tamen calda potio [6] vestiarius est. Staminatas
duxi, et plane matus sum. Vinus mihi in cerebrum
abiit."

42   Excepit Seleucus fabulae partem et " Ego " inquit
" non cotidie lavor; baliscus [7] enim fullo est, aqua
dentes habet, et cor nostrum cotidie liquescit. Sed
cum mulsi pultarium obduxi, frigori laecasin dico.
Nec sane lavare potui; fui enim hodie in funus.
Homo bellus, tam bonus Chrysanthus animam ebulliit. Modo, modo me appellavit. Videor mihi cum
illo loqui. Heu, eheu. Utres inflati ambulamus.

---

[1] circumeuntem *Scheffer*: circumeuntes.
[2] *Perhaps* perbasiavimus.
[3] *Perhaps* iungere.
[4] Dama *Buecheler*: Damas *Heinsius*: clamat.
[5] patera acina *Scheffer*: amaracina *J. F. Gronov*: pateram
vini *Jacobs*: patera capaci vina *Heinsius*.
[6] lotio *Goes*.
[7] balneus *J. F. Gronov*: balaniscus *Reinesius*: balniscus
Scheffer: aliptes *suggests Müller*.

---

[1] The name of the Italian god Liber, god of planting and
fructification, has nothing to do with *liber* " free " or *liberare*,
" to set free," but was fancifully derived from the fact that
wine frees people from cares. Trimalchio, who confers

will agree that the god of Liberation is my father." [1]
We applauded Trimalchio's phrase, and kissed the
boy heartily as he went round.

After this course Trimalchio rose to go to the pot.
With the tyrant away we had our freedom, and we
proceeded to draw the conversation of our neighbours. Dama began after calling for bumpers [?]:
" Day is nothing. Night is on you before you can
turn round. Then there is no better plan than going
straight out of bed to dinner. It was precious cold.
I could scarcely get warm in a bath. But a hot drink
is as good as an overcoat. I have taken some deep
drinks [?] and I am quite soaked.[2] The wine has
gone to my head."

Seleucus took up the tale and said : " I do not wash
every day; the bath [?] pulls you to pieces like a
fuller, the water bites, and the heart of man melts
away daily. But when I have put down some mugs
of mead I let the cold go to hell.[3] Besides, I
could not wash; I was at a funeral to-day. A fine
fellow, the excellent Chrysanthus, has bubbled his
last. It was but the other day he greeted me. I
feel as if I were speaking with him now. Dear, dear,
how we bladders of wind strut about. We are of less

freedom on slaves, therefore takes Liber as his patron and his
father. His real father in fact had not been a free man.
Liber was identified with the Greek god Dionysus, or Bacchus,
god of fruitfulness and vegetation, and particularly of wine.

[2] If *staminatas* is not corrupt, as *pataracina* apparently is
six sentences before, it may well mean draughts of neat wine.
It has been variously derived from the Greek στάμνος or the
Latin *stamen*, and variously emended.

[3] *laecasin* = Greek λαικάζειν, go wenching. So Burman for
laecasim in cod. *H*. See Martial, XI, lviii, 12.

Minoris quam muscae sumus, ⟨muscae⟩ [1] tamen aliquam virtutem habent, nos non pluris sumus quam
bullae. Et quid si non abstinax fuisset? Quinque
dies aquam in os suum non coniecit, non micam panis.
Tamen abiit ad plures. Medici illum perdiderunt,
immo magis malus fatus; medicus enim nihil aliud
est quam animi consolatio. Tamen bene elatus est,
vitali lecto, stragulis bonis. Planctus est optime—
manu [2] misit aliquot—etiam si maligne illum ploravit
uxor. Quid si non illam optime accepisset! Sed
mulier quae [3] mulier milvinum genus. Neminem
nihil boni facere oportet; aeque est enim ac si in
puteum conicias. Sed antiquus amor cancer est."

43 Molestus fuit, Philerosque proclamavit: "Vivorum
meminerimus. Ille habet, quod sibi debebatur:
honeste vixit, honeste obiit. Quid habet quod que-
ratur? Ab asse crevit et paratus fuit quadrantem de
stercore mordicus tollere. Itaque crevit quicquid
tetigit [4] tanquam favus. Puto mehercules illum reliquisse solida centum, et omnia in nummis habuit.
De re [5] tamen ego verum dicam, qui linguam caninam
comedi: durae buccae fuit, linguosus, discordia, non
homo. Frater eius fortis fuit, amicus amico, manu
plena, uncta [6] mensa. Et inter initia malam parram

---

[1] muscae *added by Heinsius*: quae *by Anton*: illae *by
Ernout.*

[2] stragulis *and* planctus *and* manu *ed. Patav.*: stagulis *and*
plautus *and* manum *H.*

[3] qua *Reiske*: quaeque *Muncker*: mulier quae – mulier
Burriss.

[4] tetigit *Delz*: crevit.

[5] vere *Heinsius.*

[6] plena uncta *Reinesius, Heinsius*: uncta plena.

value than flies; flies have their virtues, we are worth no more than bubbles. And what would have happened if he had not tried the fasting cure? No water touched his lips for five days, not a morsel of bread. Yet he went over to the majority. The doctors killed him—no, it was his unhappy destiny; a doctor is nothing but a sop to conscience. Still, he was carried out in fine style on a bier covered with a good pall. The mourning was very good too—he had freed a number of slaves—even though his own wife was very grudging over her tears. I daresay he did not treat her particularly kindly. But women † one and all † are a set of kites. You should never do no good to nobody; it is all the same as if you put your kindness in a well. But an old love pinches like a crab."

He was a bore, and Phileros shouted out: " Oh, let us remember the living. He has got his deserts; he lived decently and died decently. What has he got to grumble at? He started with twopence, and he was always ready to pick a halfpenny out of the dung with his teeth. So whatever he touched grew like a honeycomb. Upon my word, I believe he left a clear hundred thousand, and all in hard cash. Still, I have eaten hound's tongue,[1] I must speak the truth on our subject. He had a rough mouth, was talkative, and was more of a discord than a man. His brother was a fine fellow, stood by his friends, openhanded and kept a good table. To begin with, he

---

[1] Probably the plant κυνόγλωσσος " dog's tongue," " hound's tongue," still so called, used in ancient times in medicine for people hard of hearing, and in wine to improve its cheering effect.

pilavit, sed recorrexit costas illius prima vindemia:
vendidit enim vinum, quanti tum [1] ipse voluit. Et
quod illius mentum sustulit, hereditatem accepit, ex
qua plus involavit, quam illi relictum est. Et ille
stips, dum fratri suo irascitur, nescio cui terrae filio
patrimonium elegavit. Longe fugit, quisquis suos
fugit. Habuit autem oricularios [2] servos, qui illum
HL pessum dederunt. | Nunquam autem recte faciet, qui
H cito credit, | utique homo negotians. Tamen verum
quod frunitus est, quam diu vixit . . .[3] cui datum
est, non cui destinatum. Plane Fortunae filius, in
manus illius plumbum aurum fiebat. Facile est autem, ubi omnia quadrata currunt. Et quot putas
illum annos secum tulisse? Septuaginta et supra.
Sed corneolus fuit, aetatem bene ferebat, niger tanquam corvus. Noveram hominem † olim oliorum † [4]
et adhuc salax erat. Non mehercules illum puto in
domo canem reliquisse. Immo etiam pullarius [5]
erat, omnis Minervae homo. Nec improbo, hoc
solum enim secum tulit."

44 Haec Phileros dixit, illa Ganymedes: " Narratis
quod nec ad caelum nec ad terram pertinet, cum

---

[1] quanti tum *Scheffer*: quanti *Buecheler*: quantum.

[2] oricularios *Reinesius*: gracularios *Jak. Gronov*: oracular-
ios.

[3] *Some words have dropped out here. Perhaps* ⟨bene vixit⟩
or, as Muncker suggests, cui ⟨datum est,⟩ datum est.

[4] olim olimorum *Wehle*: molli molliorem *Fröhner. Perhaps*
oliorum *should be deleted (if* olim *is right). There are various
efforts to recover a lost epithet. Read perhaps simply* olim oli-
dum.

[5] pullarius *Burman*: puellarius.

caught a Tartar:[1] but his first vintage put his ribs
right again: for he sold his wine for any price he then
wanted. And what made him hold up his chin was
that he came into an estate out of which he got more
than had been left to him. And that blockhead, in a
fit of passion with his brother, left the family property
away to some son of the soil. He that flies from his
own family has far to travel. But he had some
eaves-dropping slaves who did for him. A man who
is always ready to believe what is told him will never
do well, especially a business man. Still no doubt he
enjoyed himself every day of his life. † Blessed is he
who gets the gift, not he for whom it is meant. He
was a real Fortune's darling, lead turned gold in his
hands. Yes, it is easy when everything goes fair
and square. And how many years do you think he
had on his shoulders? Seventy and more. But he
was a tough old thing, carried his age well, as black
as a crow. I had known him world without end,[2]
and he was still lecherous. I really do not think he
left even his dog unmolested in his house. No, he
was still a boy-catcher, a man of every fine art.
Well, I do not blame him: it is only his past pleasures
he could take with him."

So said Phileros, but Ganymede[3] broke in: " You
go talking about things which are neither in heaven
nor earth, and none of you care all the time how the

---

[1] Literally " he plucked a bad *parra*," some bird of ill omen:
Horace, *Odes*, iii, 27.
[2] *Olim oliorum* is doubtful; *oliorum* may be a partial dupli-
cation of an adjacent word as elsewhere in MSS. of Petronius.
Cf. note on p. 84.
[3] Ganymedes is here the name of one of the guests.

interim nemo curat, quid annona mordet. Non
mehercules hodie buccam panis invenire potui. Et
quomodo siccitas perseverat. Iam annum esuritio[1]
fuit. Aediles male eveniat, qui cum pistoribus collu-
dunt ' Serva me, servabo te.' Itaque populus minu-
tus laborat; nam isti maiores maxillae semper
Saturnalia agunt. O si haberemus illos leones, quos
ego hic inveni, cum primum ex Asia veni. Illud erat
vivere. † similia sicilia interiores et †[2] laruas sic
istos percolopabant, ut illis Iupiter iratus esset.
[Sed][3] memini Safinium: tunc habitabat ad arcum
veterem, me puero, piper, non homo. Is quacunque
ibat, terram adurebat. Sed rectus, sed certus, amicus amico, cum quo audacter posses in tenebris
micare. In curia autem quomodo singulos [vel][4]
pilabat [tractabat],[5] nec schemas loquebatur sed
directum.[6] Cum ageret porro in foro, sic illius vox
crescebat tanquam tuba. Nec sudavit unquam nec
expuit, puto eum[7] nescio quid Asiadis[8] habuisse.

---

[1] esuritio *Buecheler*: esurio.
[2] *For efforts to emend this corruption see the critical notes of
Buecheler and Schmeck; G. Whittick in Classical Review LXVI,
= N.S. II, 1952, 11–12, keeps the reading of H.*
[3] *Deleted by Scheffer.*
[4] *Deleted by Scheffer and others.*
[5] *Deleted by Scheffer and others.*
[6] directum *or* derectum *Reiske*: dilectum.
[7] eum *Mentel*: enim.
[8] assi a dis *Burman, perhaps rightly*: asia dis *H. Possibly*
aridi. *There are various suggestions.*

---

[1] The text here, after various attempts to emend it, remains
a problem. *Similia* and *sicilia* seem to me to be alternatives or
by dittography duplicates (almost). The same might be true
if the writer of *H* ought to have written *si milia si cilia* (that is

price of food pinches. I swear I cannot get hold of a mouthful of bread to-day. And how the drought goes on. There has been a famine for a whole year now. Damn the magistrates, who play ' Scratch my back, and I'll scratch yours,' in league with the bakers. So the little people come off badly; for the jaws of the upper classes are always keeping carnival. I do wish we had the lion-hearts I found here when I first came out of Asia. That was life. [. . .] they beat those inner rail-huggers and bogey men to a jelly and so put the fear of God into them.[1] I remember Safinius: he used to live then by the old arch when I was a boy. He was more of a pepper-pot than a man: used to scorch the ground wherever he trod. Still he was straight: you could trust him, a true friend: you would not be afraid to play at morra[2] with him in the dark. How he used to dress them down in the senate-house, every one of them, never using roundabout phrases, making a straightforward attack. And when he was pleading in the courts, his voice used to swell like a trumpet. Never any sweating or spitting: I imagine he had a touch of the Asiatic style. And how kindly he returned one's

ιλια) as Heraeus suggests, though in this case *si milia* might be an intended gloss on *si cilia* " if a thousand." But Whit-tick may be right in suggesting the general sense " whatever the odds," as well as in interpreting *interiores* as racers who try to hold the inner position on a curving track.

[2] *micare* means to quiver, to move quickly to and fro. Here Petronius alludes to the game still played in Italy and called there " morra." Of two players, one raises suddenly one hand showing for an instant one or more fingers out-stretched; and the other player must at once guess the number. A person who could win in the dark would be a miracle.

Et quam benignus resalutare, nomina omnium reddere, tanquam unus de nobis. Itaque illo tempore annona pro luto erat. Asse panem quem emisses non potuisses cum altero devorare. Nunc oculum bublum vidi maiorem. Heu heu, quotidie peius. Haec colonia retroversus crescit tanquam coda vituli. Sed quare nos [1] habemus aedilem trium cauniarum, qui sibi mavult assem quam vitam nostram? Itaque domi gaudet, plus in die nummorum accipit, quam alter patrimonium habet. Iam scio, unde acceperit denarios mille aureos. Sed si nos coleos haberemus, non tantum sibi placeret. Nunc populus est domi leones, foras vulpes. Quod ad me attinet, iam pannos meos comedi, et si perseverat haec annona, casulas meas vendam. Quid enim futurum est, si nec di nec homines huius coloniae miserentur? Ita meos fruniscar, ut ego puto omnia illa a diibus [2] fieri.

_HL_ | Nemo enim caelum caelum putat, nemo ieiunium servat, nemo Iovem pili facit, sed omnes opertis

_H_ oculis bona sua computant. | Antea stolatae ibant nudis pedibus in clivum, passis capillis, mentibus [3] puris, et Iovem aquam exorabant. Itaque statim urceatim plovebat: aut tunc aut nunquam: et omnes redibant [4] udi [5] tanquam mures. Itaque dii pedes lanatos habent, quia nos religiosi non sumus. Agri iacent"—

45 "Oro te" inquit Echion centonarius "melius

---

[1] nos _Mentel_: non, _which Müller deletes_: quare habemus aedilem non trium _is suggested by Buecheler_.

[2] a diibus _Buecheler_: aedilibus.

[3] vestibus _Leo needlessly_.

[4] redibant _Jacobs_: rodebant _Heinsius_: ridebant.

[5] udi _Triller_: uvidi _Reiske_: avidi _Heinsius_: ut dii.

greeting, calling every one by name quite like one of ourselves. So at that time food was dirt-cheap. You could buy a larger loaf for twopence than you and your companion together could get through. One sees an ox-eye [1] bigger now. Lord, things are worse daily. This town grows backwards like a calf's tail. But why do we put up with a magistrate not worth three little figs,[2] who cares more about putting twopence in his purse than keeping us alive? He sits grinning at home, and pockets more money a day than other people have for a fortune. I happen to know where he came by a thousand in gold. If we had any balls he would not be so pleased with himself. Nowadays people are lions in their own houses, and foxes when they go out of doors. *I* have already eaten my rags, and if food-prices keep up, I shall have to sell my cottages. Whatever is to happen if neither the gods nor man will take pity on this town? As I hope to have joy of my children, I believe all these things come from Heaven. For no one now believes that the gods are gods. There is no fasting done, no one cares a button for religion: they all shut their eyes and count their own goods. In old days the mothers in their best robes used to climb the hill with bare feet and lose hair, pure in spirit, and pray Jupiter to send rain. Then it used promptly to rain by the bucket: it was now or never: and they all came home, wet as drowned rats. As it is, the gods steal upon us with woolly feet because we are sceptics. So our fields lie baking——"

"Oh, don't be so gloomy," said Echion, the old

---

[1] What sort of "ox eye" is obscure.
[2] From Caunus in Caria in Asia Minor.

PETRONIUS ARBITER

loquere. ' Modo sic, modo sic ' inquit rusticus
HL varium porcum perdiderat. | Quod hodie non est
H cras erit: sic vita truditur. | Non mehercules patri
melior dici potest, si homines haberet. Sed labora
hoc tempore, nec haec sola.[1] Non debemus delicat
esse, ubique medius caelus est. Tu si aliubi fueris
dices hic porcos coctos ambulare. Et ecce habitur
sumus munus excellente in triduo [2] die festa; famili
non lanisticia, sed plurimi liberti. Et Titus noste
magnum animum habet et est caldicerebrius; au
hoc aut illud erit, quid [3] utique. Nam illi domesticu
sum, non est miscix.[4] Ferrum optimum daturus est
sine fuga [5] carnarium in medio, ut amphitheater vi
deat. Et habet unde: relictum est illi sestertiun
tricenties, decessit illius pater † male.† [6] Ut quad
ringenta impendat, non sentiet patrimonium illius
et sempiterno nominabitur. Iam Manios [7] aliquo
habet et mulierem essedariam et dispensatoren
Glyconis, qui deprehensus est, cum dominam suan
delectaretur. Videbis populi rixam inter zelotypos
et amasiunculos. Glyco autem, sestertiarius homo
dispensatorem ad bestias dedit. Hoc est se ipsun
traducere. Quid servus peccavit, qui coactus es
facere? Magis illa matella digna fuit quam tauru
iactaret. Sed qui asinum non potest, stratum caedit
Quid autem Glyco putabat Hermogenis filicen

[1] sola *Reiske*: sua.
[2] in triduo *Heinsius*: inter duo.
[3] quid *Heinsius*: quod.
[4] miscix *Antonius*: *H has* mixcix, *rightly?*
[5] fuga *Scheffer*: fuco *Heinsius*: fuca.
[6] Maleius *Reiske*: et mater *Jacobs*.
[7] nannos *Scheffer*: mannos *Reinesius*.

88

clothes dealer. " 'There's ups and there's downs,' as the country bumpkin said when he lost his pied pig. What is not to-day, will be to-morrow: so we trudge through life. I engage you could not name a better country to call one's own, if only the men in it had sense. It has its troubles now like others. We must not be too particular when there is a sky above us all. If you are anywhere else, you would say that roast pigs walked in the streets here. Just think, we are soon to be given a superb spectacle lasting three days; not simply a troupe of professional gladiators, but a large number of them freedmen. And our good Titus has a big imagination and is hot-headed: it will be one thing or another, something real anyway. I know him very well, and he is all against half-measures. He will give you the finest blades, no running away, butchery done in the middle, where the whole audience can see it. And he has the wherewithal; he came into thirty million when his father departed this life [—bad job ?]. If he spends four hundred thousand, his estate will never feel it, and his name will live for ever. He has already collected some Jacks, and a woman to fight from a chariot, and Glyco's steward, who was caught amusing Glyco's wife. You will see the crowd quarrel, jealous husbands against gallants. A two-penny-halfpenny fellow like Glyco goes throwing his steward to the beasts. He only gives himself away. It is not the slave's fault; he had to do as he was told. That filthy pizz-pot whore of his rather deserved to be tossed by the bull. But a man who cannot beat his donkey, beats the saddle. How did Glyco suppose that a weedy fern of Hermogenes's sowing would

unquam bonum exitum facturam? Ille milvo volanti
poterat ungues resecare; colubra restem non parit.
Glyco? Glyco [1] dedit suas; [2] itaque quamdiu vixerit,
habebit stigmam, nec illam nisi Orcus delebit. Sed
sibi quisque peccat. Sed subolfacio, quod nobis
epulum daturus est Mammaea, binos denarios mihi
et meis. Quod si hoc fecerit, eripiat Norbano totum
favorem. Scias oportet plenis velis hunc vinciturum.
Et revera, quid ille nobis boni fecit? Dedit gladiatores sestertiarios iam decrepitos, quos si sufflasses,
cecidissent; iam meliores bestiarios vidi. Occidit
de lucerna equites, putares eos gallos gallinaceos;
alter burdubasta, alter loripes, tertiarius mortuus pro
mortuo, qui habebat [3] nervia praecisa. Unus alicuius
flaturae fuit Thraex, qui et ipse ad dictata pugnavit.
Ad summam, omnes postea secti sunt; adeo de
magna turba ' adhibete ' acceperant, plane fugae
merae. ' Munus tamen ' inquit ' tibi dedi ': et ego
tibi plodo. Computa, et tibi plus do quam accepi.
46 Manus manum lavat. Videris mihi, Agamemnon,
dicere: ' Quid iste argutat molestus? ' quia tu, qui
potes loquere, non loquis. [4] Non es nostrae fasciae,
et ideo pauperorum verba derides. Scimus te prae
litteras fatuum esse. Quid ergo est? aliqua die te

[1] exitio *Heinsius*. [2] suos *Scheffer*.
[3] habebat *Buecheler*: habet. [4] loquis *Burman*: loqui.

---

[1] Literally " a viper does not bring forth a rope."
[2] A prosperous lawyer. See Chapter 46.
[3] " with wind-full sails." The whole phrase means, as *we*
might say, " will beat him hands down."
[4] Presumably little images of clay.
[5] Gladiators who wore Thracian weapons were called
Thracians.

ever come to a good end? He was one for paring
the claws of a kite on the wing, and you do not father
figs from thistles.[1] Glyco? why, Glyco has given
away his own flesh and blood. He will be branded
as long as he lives, and nothing but death will wipe it
out. But a man must have his faults. My nose
prophesies what meal we shall get from Mammaea,
twopence each for me and mine. If he so behaves, he
will put Norbanus [2] quite in the shade. You should
know we will tie him up, sails full spread.[3] After all,
what has Norbanus ever done for us? He produced
some decayed twopenny-halfpenny gladiators, who
would have fallen flat if you breathed on them; I
have seen better ruffians turned in to fight the wild
beasts. He shed the blood of some mounted in-
fantry that might have come off a lamp; [4] dunghill
cocks you would have called them: one a spavined
mule, the other bandy-legged, and the holder of
the bye, just one corpse instead of another, and hamstrung. One man, a Thracian,[5] had some stuffing,
but he too fought according to the rule of the schools.
In short, they were all flogged afterwards. How the
great crowd roared at them, ' Lay it on! ' They
were mere runaways, to be sure. ' Still,' says Norbanus, ' I did give you a show.' Yes, and I clap my
hands at you. Reckon it up, and I give you more
than I got. One good turn deserves another. Now,
Agamemnon, you look as if you were saying, ' What
is this bore chattering for? ' Only because you have
the gift of tongues and do not speak. You are not
of our cloth, and so you make fun of the way we poor
men talk. We know you are mad with much learning. But I tell you what; can I persuade you to

persuadeam, ut ad villam venias et videas casulas
nostras? Inveniemus quod manducemus, pullum,
ova: belle erit, etiam si omnia hoc anno tempestas
† dispare pallavit † [1] inveniemus ergo unde saturi
fiamus. Et iam tibi discipulus crescit cicaro meus.
Iam quattuor partis dicit; si vixerit, habebis ad
latus servulum. Nam quicquid illi vacat, caput de
tabula non tollit. Ingeniosus est et bono filo,
etiam si in aves [2] morbosus est. Ego illi iam tres
cardeles occidi, et dixi quia mustella comedit.
Invenit tamen alias nenias, et libentissime pingit.
Ceterum iam Graeculis calcem impingit et Latinas
coepit non male appetere, etiam si magister eius sibi
placens fit [3] nec uno loco consistit, † sed venit dem † [4]
litteras, sed non vult laborare. Est et alter non
quidem doctus, sed curiosus, qui plus docet quam scit.
Itaque feriatis diebus solet domum venire, et quicquid
dederis, contentus est. Emi ergo nunc puero aliquot
libra rubricata, quia volo illum ad domusionem aliquid
de iure gustare. Habet haec res panem. Nam litteris satis inquinatus est. Quod si resilierit, destinavi
illum artificium [5] docere, aut tonstrinum [6] aut praeconem aut certe causidicum, quod illi auferre non
possit nisi Orcus. Ideo illi cotidie clamo: ' Primi-

---

[1] dispar pallavit *Antonius*: dispare pullavit *Reiske*: dispare
pellavit *Siewert*. *There are other guesses.*
[2] aves *Triller*: naves.   [3] fit *Buecheler*: sit.
[4] *There are various attempts to correct this. Perhaps* sed
vendit idem.
[5] artificium *Scheffer*: artificii.
[6] tonstrinum *Scheffer*: constreinum.

come down to my place some day and see my little property? We shall find something to eat, a chicken and eggs: it will be delightful, even though the weather this year has [ruined]¹ everything: we shall find something to fill ourselves up with. My little boy is growing into a follower of yours already. He can do simple division now; if he lives, you will have a little servant at your side. Whenever he has any spare time, he never lifts his nose from the slate. He is clever, and comes of a good stock, even though he is too fond of birds. I killed three of his gold-finches just lately, and said a weasel had eaten them. But he has found some other trifles, and has taken to painting with great pleasure. He has stuck a heel in his Greek now, and begins to relish Latin finely, even though his master is conceited and will not stick to one thing at a time. The boy comes † asking me to give him some writing to do,† though he does not want to work. I have another boy who is no scholar, but very enquiring, and can teach you more than he knows himself. So on holidays he generally comes home, and is quite pleased whatever you give him. I bought the child some books with red-letter headings in them a little time ago. I want him to have a smack of law in order to manage the property. Law has bread and butter in it. He has dipped quite deep enough into literature. If he is restless, I mean to make him learn a trade, as a barber or an auctioneer, or at least a barrister, something that he can carry to the grave with him. So I drum it into him every day: ' Mark my words,

---

¹ This corruption has no good remedy yet.

geni, crede mihi, quicquid discis, tibi discis. Vides
Phileronem causidicum: si non didicisset, hodie
famem a labris non abigeret. Modo, modo collo
suo circumferebat onera [1] venalia, nunc etiam adver-
sus Norbanum se extendit. Litterae thesaurum est,
et artificium nunquam moritur.' ''

47 Eiusmodi fabulae vibrabant, cum Trimalchio intravit et detersa fronte unguento manus lavit spatioque
minimo interposito " Ignoscite mihi " inquit " amici,
multis iam diebus venter mihi non respondit. Nec
medici se inveniunt. Profuit mihi tamen malicorium [2]
et taeda ex aceto. Spero tamen, iam veterem [3] pudorem sibi imponit. Alioquin circa stomachum mihi
sonat, putes taurum. Itaque si quis vestrum voluerit
sua re [causa] [4] facere, non est quod illum pudeatur.
Nemo nostrum solide natus est. Ego nullum puto
tam magnum tormentum esse quam continere. Hoc
solum vetare ne Iovis potest. Rides, Fortunata,
quae soles me nocte desomnem facere ? Nec tamen
in triclinio ullum vetuo [5] facere quod se iuvet, et
medici vetant continere. Vel si quid plus venit,
omnia foras parata sunt: aqua, lasani et cetera
minutalia. Credite mihi, anathymiasis in cerebrum
it et in toto corpore fluctum facit. Multos scio sic
periisse, dum nolunt sibi verum dicere.'' Gratias
agimus liberalitati indulgentiaeque eius, et subinde

---

[1] olera *Scheffer*.   [2] malicorium *Scheffer*: maleicorum.
[3] veterem *Heinsius*: ventrem *which Müller deleted*.
[4] *Deleted by Scheffer*.   [5] vetuo *Buecheler*: vetui.

---

[1] *Primigenius* (" first of his kind ") is here a proper name.
He was not necessarily *primogenitus* (first-born) also. He is
son of the guest Echio.

Primigenius,[1] whatever you learn, you learn for your own good. Look at Philero [2] the barrister: if he had not worked, he would not be keeping the wolf from the door to-day. It is not so long since he used to carry loads round on his back and sell them, and now he makes a brave show even against Norbanus. Yes, education is a treasure, and culture never dies.' "

Gossip of this kind was in the air, when Trimalchio came in mopping his brow, and washed his hands in scent. After a short pause, he said, " You will excuse me, gentlemen? My bowels have not been working for several days. All the doctors feel lost. Still, I found pomegranate rind useful, and pinewood boiled in vinegar. I hope now my stomach learns to observe its old decencies. Besides, I have such rumblings inside me you would think there was a bull there. So if any of you gentlemen wishes to do private business, there is no need to be shy about it. We were none of us born quite solid. I cannot imagine any torture like holding oneself in. The one thing Jupiter himself cannot forbid is that we should have relief. Why do you laugh, Fortunata? It is you who are always keeping me awake all night. Of course, as far as I am concerned, anyone may do what he likes in the dining-room. The doctors forbid retention. But if the matter is serious, everything is ready outside: water, pots, and all the other little comforts. Take my word for it, vapours go to the brain and make a disturbance throughout the body. I know many people have died this way, by refusing to admit the truth to themselves." We thanked him for his generosity and kindness, and then tried to sup-

[2] Philero: presumably Phileros of Chapters 43 and 44.

castigamus crebris potiunculis risum. Nec adhuc
sciebamus nos in medio [lautitiarum],[1] quod[2] aiunt,
clivo laborare. Nam cum mundatis ad symphoniam
mensis tres albi sues in triclinium adducti sunt
capistris et tintinnabulis culti, quorum unum bimum
nomenculator esse dicebat, alterum trimum, tertium
vero iam sexennem,[3] ego putabam petauristarios
intrasse et porcos, sicut in circulis mos est, portenta
aliqua facturos; sed Trimalchio expectatione discussa " Quem " inquit " ex eis vultis in cenam statim
fieri? gallum enim gallinaceum, penthiacum[4] et
eiusmodi nenias rustici faciunt: mei coci etiam vitu-
los aeno coctos[5] solent facere." Continuoque cocum
vocari iussit, et non expectata electione nostra maxi-
mum natu iussit occidi, et clara voce: " Ex quota
decuria es?" Cum ille se ex quadragesima respon-
disset, " Empticius an " inquit " domi natus?"
" Neutrum " inquit cocus " sed testamento Pansae
tibi relictus sum." " Vide ergo " ait " ut diligenter
ponas; si non, te iubebo in decuriam viatorum
conici." Et cocum quidem potentiae[6] admonitum in
48 culinam obsonium duxit, Trimalchio autem miti ad
nos vultu respexit et " Vinum " inquit " si non
placet, mutabo; vos illud oportet bonum faciatis.
Deorum beneficio non emo, sed nunc quicquid ad

---

[1] lautitiarum] *Fraenkel deletes.*   [2] quod *Heinsius:* quo.
[3] sexennem *Wehle:* senem (*perhaps rightly*).
[4] phasiacum *is suggested by Rheinesius.*
[5] aeno coctos *Mentel:* oenococtos *Orioli:* eno cocto.
[6] potentiae *Scheffer:* potentia. *For* cocum . . . admonitum *Mentel proposed* cocus admonitus.

---

[1] Pentheus, traditional King of Thebes, was torn to pieces
by women frenzied by Dionysus.

press our laughter by drinking hard and fast. We did not yet realize that we had only got halfway through [the delicacies], and still had an uphill task before us, as they say. The tables were cleared to the sound of music, and three white pigs, adorned with muzzles and bells, were led into the dining-room. One was two years old, the announcer said, the second three, and the other as much as six. I thought some rope-walkers had come in, and that the pigs would perform some wonderful tricks, as they do for crowds in the streets. Trimalchio ended our suspense by saying, " Now, which of them would you like turned into a dinner this minute ? Any country hand can turn out a fowl or a Pentheus mincemeat [1] or trifles of that kind. My cooks are quite used to serving whole calves done in a cauldron." Then he told them to fetch a cook at once, and, without waiting for us to choose, ordered the eldest pig to be killed, and said in a loud voice, " Which division of the household do you belong to ? " The man said he came from the fortieth. " Were you purchased or born on the estate ? " " Neither; I was left to you under Pansa's will." " Well then," said Trimalchio, " mind you serve this carefully, or I will have you degraded to the messengers' division." So the cook was reminded of his master's power, and the dish that was to be carried him off to the kitchen. Trimalchio turned to us with a mild expression and said, " I will change the wine if you do not like it. You will have to give it its virtues. Under God's providence, I do not have to buy it. Anything here which makes your mouths water is grown on a country

salivam facit, in suburbano nascitur eo,[1] quod ego
adhuc non novi. Dicitur confine esse Tarraciniensi-
bus et Tarentinis. Nunc coniungere agellis Siciliam
volo, ut cum Africam libuerit ire, per meos fines navi-
gem. Sed narra tu mihi, Agamemnon, quam controversiam hodie declamasti? Ego etiam [2] si causas non
ago, in domusione [3] tamen litteras didici. Et ne
me putes studia fastiditum, II [4] bybliothecas habeo,
unam Graecam, alteram Latinam. Dic ergo, si me
amas, peristasim declamationis tuae." Cum dixisset
Agamemnon: " Pauper et dives inimici erant," ait
Trimalchio " Quid est pauper? " " Urbane " inquit
Agamemnon et nescio quam controversiam exposuit.
Statim Trimalchio " Hoc " inquit " si factum est,
controversia non est; si factum non est, nihil est."
Haec aliaque cum effusissimis prosequeremur lauda-
tionibus, " Rogo " inquit " Agamemnon mihi carissime, numquid duodecim aerumnas Herculis tenes,
aut de Vlixe fabulam, quemadmodum illi Cyclops
† pollicem forcipe [5] extorsit? † Solebam haec ego

[1] meo *Goes.*   [2] etiam *Wehle*: autem.
[3] domusionem *Wehle*: divisione.
[4] duas *Mentel*: II *Buecheler*: tres.
[5] *H has* pollicem poricino extorsit *for which various emendations have been proposed.* forcipe *or* per iocum *Studer.* Delete
perhaps poricino (*so Fuchs*). *The word may hide* periculum
' *the quick' under finger-nails—cf. Fragment III ad* periculum.

[1] Terracina and Taranto are more than two hundred miles
apart. Trimalchio's knowledge of geography is vague.
[2] A *controversia* was a declamation on some controversial
subject.
[3] The mythological twelve labours of Hercules (Heracles)
are not given in full by Homer who, however, does mention or
allude to some of them. The Cyclopes were an imaginary

estate of mine which I know nothing about as yet.
I believe it is on the boundary of Terracina and
Tarentum.[1] Just now I want to join up all Sicily
with properties of mine, so that if I take a fancy to go
to Africa I shall travel through my own land. But do
tell me, Agamemnon, what declamation [2] did you
deliver in school to-day? Of course, I do not practise
in court myself, but I learned literature for domestic
purposes. And do not imagine that I despise learning. I have got two libraries, one Greek and one
Latin. So give me an outline of your speech, if you
love me." Then Agamemnon said: " A poor man
and a rich man were once at enmity." " But what
is a poor man? " Trimalchio replied. " Very clever,"
said Agamemnon, and went on expounding some
problem or other. Trimalchio at once retorted: "If
the thing really happened, there is no problem; if it
never happened, it is all nonsense." We followed up
this and other sallies with the most extravagant
admiration. " Tell me, dear Agamemnon," said
Trimalchio, " do you know anything of the twelve
labours of Hercules, or the story of Ulysses and how
the Cyclops † twisted his thumb with the tongs? † [3]

race of one-eyed shepherds in Sicily. The story of Ulysses and
Polyphemus the Cyclops is in Book IX of Homer's *Odyssey*.
The text of the incident mentioned here by Petronius is
apparently corrupt—*poricino* in cod. *H* looks as if it hides
another of those partial duplications as well as an instrumental
ablative case. In Chapter 56 *porrum* a leek and *flagellum* a
whip or the like seem to be connected, as if a whipping instru-
ment could be called a *porrum*. But all is vague. If *pollicem*
is right, the incident is not in Homer. Trimalchio's knowledge
of literature is as vague as his geography—see especially
Chapter 59.

puer apud Homerum legere. Nam Sibyllam quidem
Cumis ego ipse oculis meis vidi in ampulla pendere,
et cum illi pueri dicerent: Σίβυλλα, τί θέλεις;
respondebat illa: ἀποθανεῖν θέλω."

49 Nondum efflaverat omnia, cum repositorium cum
sue ingenti mensam occupavit. Mirari nos celeri-
tatem coepimus et iurare, ne gallum quidem gallinaceum tam cito percoqui potuisse, tanto quidem
magis, quod longe maior nobis porcus videbatur esse,
quam paulo ante aper fuerat.[1] Deinde magis magisque Trimalchio intuens eum " Quid? quid? " inquit
" porcus hic non est exinteratus? Non mehercules
est. Voca, voca cocum in medio." Cum constitisset
ad mensam cocus tristis et diceret se oblitum esse
exinterare, " Quid? oblitus? " Trimalchio exclamat,
" Putes illum piper et cuminum non coniecisse.
Despolia." Non fit mora, despoliatur cocus atque
inter duos tortores maestus consistit. Deprecari
tamen omnes coeperunt et dicere: " Solet fieri;
rogamus, mittas;[2] postea si fecerit, nemo nostrum pro
illo rogabit." Ego, crudelissimae severitatis, non
potui me tenere, sed inclinatus ad aurem Agamemnonis " Plane " inquam " hic debet servus esse
nequissimus; aliquis oblivisceretur porcum exinterare? Non mehercules illi ignoscerem, si piscem
praeterisset." At non Trimalchio, qui relaxato in

[1] apparuerat *Heinsius.*
[2] mittas *Heinsius*: mittes.

---

[1] In Roman mythology Sibyls were prophetesses who
might be immortal but were not free from the effects of old age.
Trimalchio claims to have seen the famous Sibyl of Cumae

I used to read these things in Homer when I was a boy. Yes, and I myself with my own eyes saw the Sibyl at Cumae hanging in a flask; and when the boys cried at her: ' Sibyl, Sibyl, what do you want? ' ' I would that I were dead,' she used to answer." [1]

He had still more talk to puff out, when the table was filled by a dish holding an enormous pig. We went on to express astonishment at such speed, and took our oath that not even a fowl could have been properly cooked in the time, especially as the pig seemed to us to be much bigger than the boar [2] had been a little while earlier. Trimalchio looked at it more and more closely and then said, " What, what, has not this pig been gutted? I swear it has not. The cook, send the cook up here to us." The poor cook came and stood by the table and said that he had forgotten to gut it. " What? Forgotten? " shouted Trimalchio. " You would think the fellow had only forgotten to season it with pepper and cummin. Off with his shirt! " In a moment the cook was stripped and stood dolefully between two executioners. But we all set to to beg him off and say: " These things will happen; do let him go; if he does it again none of us will say a word for him." I was as stiff and stern as could be; I could not restrain myself, but leaned over and said in Agamemnon's ear: " This must be a most wretched servant; how could anyone forget to gut a pig? On my oath I would not forgive him if he had let a fish go like that." But not Trimalchio; *his* face softened into

so withered as to be preserved in a flask. The sentence might imply that the dinner was not held right inside Cumae.
    [2] The boar brought in as related in Chapter 40.

hilaritatem vultu " Ergo " inquit " quia tam malae
memoriae es, palam nobis illum exintera." Recepta
cocus tunica cultrum arripuit porcique ventrem hinc
atque illinc timida manu secuit. Nec mora, ex plagis
ponderis inclinatione crescentibus tomacula cum
botulis effusa sunt.

50   Plausum post hoc automatum familia dedit et
" Gaio feliciter " conclamavit. Nec non cocus
potione [1] honoratus [2] est et argentea corona, pocu-
lumque in lance accepit Corinthia. Quam cum Agamemnon propius consideraret, ait Trimalchio
" Solus sum qui vera Corinthea habeam." Expecta-
bam, ut pro reliqua insolentia diceret sibi vasa Corin-
tho afferri. Sed ille melius: " Et forsitan " inquit
" quaeris, quare solus Corinthea vera possideam
quia scilicet aerarius, a quo emo, Corinthus vocatur
Quid est autem Corintheum, nisi quis Corinthum
habet? Et ne me putetis nesapium esse, valde bene
scio, unde primum Corinthea nata sint. Cum Ilium
captum est, Hannibal, homo vafer et magnus stelio,[3]
omnes statuas aeneas et aureas et argenteas in unum
rogum congessit et eas incendit; factae sunt in unum
aera miscellanea. Ita ex hac massa fabri sustulerunt

[1] portione *Jak. Gronov.*
[2] honoratus *Scheffer*: oneratus. *For* et (*so Buecheler*) *after*
est *H has* etiam.
[3] stelio *Heinsius*: scelero *Reinesius*: scelio.

---

[1] Trimalchio's confusion in what follows is wonderful
There was a false story (see Pliny, *N.H.*, XXXIV, 6–8) that the
alloy " Corinthian " bronze was discovered accidentally
through mixture of melted metals during the burning o:

smiles. "Well," he said, "if your memory is so bad, clean him here in front of us." The cook put on his shirt, seized a knife, and carved the pig's belly in various places with a shaking hand. At once the slits widened under the pressure from within, and sausages and black puddings tumbled out.

At this the slaves burst into spontaneous applause and shouted, "God bless Gaius!" The cook too was rewarded with a drink and a silver crown, and was handed the cup on a Corinthian dish. Agamemnon began to peer at the dish rather closely, and Trimalchio said, "I am the sole owner of genuine Corinthian plate." I thought he would declare with his usual effrontery that he had cups imported direct from Corinth. But he went one better: "You may perhaps inquire," said he, "how I come to be alone in having genuine Corinthian stuff: the obvious reason is that the name of the dealer I buy it from is Corinthus. But what is real Corinthian, unless a man has Corinthus at his back? Do not imagine that I am an ignoramus. I know perfectly well how Corinthian plate was first brought into the world.[1] At the fall of Ilium, Hannibal, a trickster and a great knave, collected all the sculptures, bronze, gold, and silver, into a single pile, and set light to them. They all melted into one amalgam of bronze. The workmen took bits out of this lump and made

Corinth by the Roman L. Mummius in 146 B.C. But Trimalchio transfers the "discovery" to the burning of Troy (Ilium) by the Greeks about a thousand years earlier, and there brings in Hannibal, Rome's famous Carthaginian opponent in Italy in the latter years of the third century B.C. We do not know the composition of Corinthian bronze as distinct from other bronze.

et fecerunt catilla et paropsides et statuncula. Si‹
Corinthea nata sunt, ex omnibus in unum, nec ho‹
nec illud. Ignoscetis mihi, quod dixero: ego mal‹
mihi vitrea, certe non olunt.[1] Quod si non frange
rentur, mallem mihi quam aurum; nunc autem vili‹
51 sunt. Fuit tamen faber qui fecit phialam vitream
quae non frangebatur. Admissus ergo Caesarem es‹
cum suo munere, deinde fecit reporrigere Caesarem
et illam in pavimentum proiecit. Caesar non pot‹
valdius quam expavit. At ille sustulit phialan
de terra; collisa erat tanquam vasum aeneum
deinde martiolum de sinu protulit et phialam oti‹
belle correxit. Hoc facto putabat se solium[3] Iovi‹
tenere, utique postquam ⟨Caesar⟩[4] illi dixit: ' Num
quid alius scit hanc condituram vitreorum? ' vide
modo. Postquam negavit, iussit illum Caesar decol
lari: quia enim, si scitum esset, aurum pro lut‹
52 haberemus. In argento plane studiosus sum. Habe‹
scyphos urnales plus minus ⟨C⟩:[5] quemadmodum
Cassandra occidit filios suos, et pueri mortui iacent
sic ut vivere[6] putes. Habeo capides M[7], qua‹

---

[1] non olunt *Buecheler*: non olent *Jahn*: nolunt. *There ar‹
other conjectures.*

[2] Caesarem *Scheffer*: Caesari *which Fraenkel suggeste‹
deleting.*

[3] solium *Heinsius*: coelum *John of Salisbury*: coleum.

[4] *Added by Buecheler.*

[5] C *added by Wehle. But probably more words are lost here,*
as Heinsius and Goes indicated.

[6] sic ut vivere *Heinsius*: sicuti vere.

[7] capides M *Buecheler*: capidem; *ed. Patav. has* c. quam.

plates and entrée dishes and statuettes. That is
how Corinthian metal was born, from all sorts lumped
together, neither one kind nor the other. You will
forgive me if I say that personally I prefer glass;
glass at least does not smell. If it were not so
breakable I should prefer it to gold; as it is, it is so
cheap. But there was once a workman who made a
glass cup that was unbreakable. So he was given
an audience of the Emperor [1] with his invention; he
made Caesar give it back to him and then threw it on
the floor. Caesar was as frightened as could be.
But the man picked up his cup from the ground: it
was dinted like a bronze bowl; then he took a little
hammer out of his pocket and made the cup quite
sound again without any trouble. After doing this
he thought he had himself seated on the throne of
Jupiter,[2] especially when Caesar said to him: ' Does
anyone else know how to blow glass like this ? ' Just
see what happened. He said not, and then Caesar
had him beheaded. Why ? Because if his invention
were generally known we should treat gold like dirt.
Myself I have a great passion for silver. I own about
a hundred four-gallon cups engraved with Cassandra [3]
killing her sons, and the boys lying there dead—but
you would think they were alive. I have a thousand

---

[1] The Emperor Tiberius (A.D. 14–37), according to Pliny,
N.H., XXXVI, 198; Dio Cassius, LVII, 57.

[2] But cod. *H* has *coleum*. So, by a glorious piece of blas-
phemy, " thought he had Jupiter by the balls."

[3] Cassandra was a prophetess in Troy. Apollo, offended
at her resistance to him, caused the Trojans to disbelieve
her. Instead of saying Cassandra, Trimalchio should have
said Medea, who killed her children by Jason in revenge on
him.

reliquit † patronorum meus † [1] ubi Daedalus Niobam in equum Troianum includit. Nam Hermerotis pugnas et Petraitis in poculis habeo, omnia ponderosa; meum enim intellegere nulla pecunia vendo."

Haec dum refert, puer calicem proiecit. Ad quem respiciens Trimalchio " Cito " inquit " te ipsum caede, quia nugax es." Statim puer demisso labro orare.[2] At ille " Quid me " inquit " rogas? Tanquam ego tibi molestus sim. Suadeo, a te impetres, ne sis nugax." Tandem ergo exoratus a nobis missionem dedit puero. Ille dimissus circa mensam percucurrit ⟨. . .⟩[3]

et " Aquam foras, vinum intro " clamavit. Excipimus urbanitatem iocantis, et ante omnes Agamemnon, qui sciebat, quibus meritis revocaretur ad cenam. Ceterum laudatus Trimalchio hilarius bibit et iam ebrio proximus " Nemo " inquit " vestrum rogat Fortunatam meam, ut saltet? Credite mihi: cordacem nemo melius ducit."

Atque ipse erectis supra frontem manibus Syrum histrionem exhibebat concinente tota familia: μάδεια

---

[1] *There are various emendations of which* patronorum unus (*Goes*) *and* patronus meus (*ed. Patav.*) *are the simplest.*

[2] labro orare *Scheffer*: labrore.

[3] *Lacuna indicated by Buecheler.*

---

[1] Not L. Mummius, as Buecheler suggested; he died too early, and Trimalchio is imagined as knowing nothing about him.

[2] Triple confusion by Trimalchio: In Greek mythology Niobe, wife of Amphion, a traditional King of Thebes, had nothing to do with the Trojan war and the wooden horse; nor had Daedalus the Athenian architect and craftsman who built or designed the labyrinth at Cnossos in Crete. He did,

jugs which a patron † [1] bequeathed, where you see
Daedalus shutting Niobe into the Trojan horse.[2]
And I have got the fights between Hermeros and Petraites [3] on my cups, and every cup is a heavy one;
for I do not sell my connoisseurship for any money."

As he was speaking, a boy dropped a cup. Trimalchio looked at him and said, " Quick, off with your
own head, since you are so stupid." The boy's lip
fell and he began to petition. " Why do you ask
me?" said Trimalchio, " as if I should be hard on
you! I advise you to prevail upon yourself not to
be stupid." In the end we induced him to let the
boy off. As soon as he was forgiven the boy ran
round the table. . . .

Then Trimalchio shouted, " Out with water! In
with wine!" We took up the jokes, especially
Agamemnon, who knew how to earn a second invitation to dinner. Trimalchio warmed to his drinking
under our flattery, and was almost drunk when he
said: " None of you ask dear Fortunata to dance. I
tell you no one can dance the cancan [4] better." He
then lifted his hands above his brow and gave us the
actor Syrus, while all the slaves sang in chorus:

> Madeia!
> Perimadeia! [5]

however, make a wooden cow for Pasiphaë (wife of King Minos
for whom that labyrinth was built) who loved a fine white bull
and hid inside the cow so as to be covered by it. She gave
birth to the monstrous Minotaur for which the labyrinth at
Cnossos was built.
[3] Gladiators. cf. H. T. Rowell, in *T.A.P.A.*, 1958, 14 ff.,
and chapter 71.
[4] The *cordax* was a rude Greek dance.
[5] These are words of unknown meaning.

περιμάδεια. Et prodisset in medium, nisi Fortunata
ad aurem accessisset; [et] [1] credo, dixerit non decere
gravitatem eius tam humiles ineptias. Nihil autem
tam inaequale erat; nam modo Fortunatam ⟨vere-
batur⟩, modo ad naturam suam revertebatur.[2]

53 Et plane interpellavit saltationis libidinem actuarius, qui tanquam urbis acta recitavit: " VII. kalendas sextiles: in praedio Cumano, quod est Trimalchionis, nati sunt pueri xxx, puellae xl; sublata in
horreum ex area tritici millia modium quingenta;
boves domiti quingenti. Eodem die: Mithridates
servus in crucem actus est, quia Gai nostri genio male
dixerat. Eodem die: in arcam relatum est, quod
collocari non potuit, sestertium centies. Eodem die:
incendium factum est in hortis Pompeianis, ortum
ex aedibus Nastae vilici." " Quid ? " inquit Trimalchio " quando mihi Pompeiani horti empti sunt ? "
" Anno priore " inquit actuarius " et ideo in rationem
nondum venerunt." Excanduit Trimalchio et " Quicunque " inquit " mihi fundi empti fuerint, nisi intra
sextum mensem sciero, in rationes meas inferri
vetuo." Iam etiam edicta aedilium recitabantur et
saltuariorum testamenta, quibus Trimalchio cum
elogio exheredabatur; iam nomina vilicorum et
repudiata a circitore [3] liberta in balneatoris contu-

[1] *Deleted by Buecheler.*
[2] modo fortunatam suam revertebatur modo ad naturam
H, variously emended, verebatur *is added by Heinsius,* suam
revertebatur *put after* naturam *by Buecheler.*
[3] *So Buecheler:* circumitore.

And Trimalchio would have come out into the middle of the room if Fortunata had not whispered in his ear. I suppose she told him that such low fooling was beneath his dignity. But never was anything so variable; at one moment he was afraid of Fortunata, and then he would return to his natural self.

But a clerk quite interrupted his passion for the dance by reading as though from the city's daily gazette: " July the 26th. Thirty boys and forty girls were born on the estate at Cumae which is Trimalchio's.[1] Five hundred thousand pecks of wheat were taken up from the threshing-floor into the barn. Five hundred oxen were broken in. On the same date: the slave Mithridates was led to crucifixion for having damned the soul of our lord Gaius. On the same date: ten million sesterces which could not be invested were returned to the strong-box. On the same day: there was a fire in our gardens at Pompeii, which broke out in the house of Nasta the bailiff." " Stop," said Trimalchio, " When did I buy any gardens at Pompeii? " " Last year," said the clerk, " so that they are not entered in your accounts yet." Trimalchio glowed with passion, and said, "I will not have any property which is bought in my name entered in my accounts unless I hear of it within six months." We now had a further recitation of police notices, and some foresters' wills, in which Trimalchio was cut out in a codicil;[2] then the names of bailiffs, and of a freed-woman who had been caught with a bathman and divorced by her husband, a night watchman; the

---

[1] *quod est Trimalchionis*: words of a legal formula rather than an explanatory interpolation.　　[2] " in flattering terms "?

bernio deprehensa et atriensis Baias relegatus; iam
reus factus dispensator et iudicium inter cubicularios
actum.

Petauristarii autem tandem venerunt.   Baro insulsissimus cum scalis constitit puerumque iussit per
gradus et in summa parte odaria saltare, circulos
deinde ardentes transilire [1] et dentibus amphoram
sustinere.   Mirabatur haec solus Trimalchio dice-
batque ingratum artificium esse.   Ceterum duo esse
in rebus humanis, quae libentissime spectaret,
petauristarios et cornicines; [2] reliqua [animalia] [3]
acroamata tricas [4] meras esse.   " Nam et comoedos " inquit " emeram, sed malui illos Atellaniam [5]
facere et choraulen meum iussi Latine cantare."

54   Cum maxime haec dicente eo [6] puer ⟨. . .⟩ [7] Trimalchionis delapsus est.   Conclamavit familia, nec
minus convivae, non propter hominem tam putidum,
cuius etiam cervices fractas libenter vidissent, sed
propter malum exitum cenae, ne necesse haberent
alienum mortuum plorare.   Ipse Trimalchio cum
graviter ingemuisset superque brachium tanquam
laesum incubuisset, concurrere medici, et inter primos
Fortunata crinibus passis cum scypho, miseramque
se atque infelicem proclamavit.   Nam puer quidem,
qui ceciderat, circumibat iam dudum pedes nostros
et missionem rogabat.   Pessime mihi erat ne his

---

[1] transilire *Heinsius*: transire.

[2] cornicines *Heinsius*: cornices.

[3] *Deleted by Buecheler*: anomala *or* anilia *Heinsius*: enim
talia *Gilbert*.

[4] acroamata trieas *Scheffer*: cromataricas.

[5] Atellaniam *Buecheler*: Atellanam *Scheffer*: atellam.

[6] eo *Müller*: Gaio.

[7] *lacuna indicated by Scheffer*.

name of a porter who had been banished to Baiae;[1] the name of a steward who was being prosecuted, and details of an action between some valets.

But at last the acrobats came in. A very dull bloke stood there with a ladder and made a boy dance from rung to rung and on the very top to the music of popular airs, and then made him hop through burning hoops, and pick up a wine jar with his teeth. No one was excited by this but Trimalchio, who kept saying that it was a thankless profession. He said there were only two things in the world that he could watch with real pleasure, acrobats and trumpeters; all other shows were silly nonsense. "Why," said he, "I once bought a Greek comedy company, but I preferred them to do Atellane plays,[2] and I told my pipe-player to have Latin songs."

Just as Trimalchio was speaking the boy slipped and fell [against his arm].[3] The slaves raised a cry, and so did the guests, not over a disgusting creature whose very neck they would have been glad to see broken, but because it would have been a gloomy finish to the dinner to have to shed tears over the death of a perfect stranger. Trimalchio groaned aloud, and nursed his arm as if it was hurt. Doctors rushed up, and among the first Fortunata, with her hair down, and a cup in her hand, calling out what a poor unhappy woman she was. The creature who had fallen down was crawling round at our feet by this time, and begging to be let off. I was very much

[1] Coastal resort, now Baia; a nice place for exile.
[2] Native Latin comedy as opposed to *comoedia palliata*, which was translated or adapted from the Greek.
[3] Perhaps Fragment XV comes somewhere here.

precibus † per ridiculum [1] aliquid catastropha †
quaereretur. Nec enim adhuc exciderat cocus ille,
qui oblitus fuerat porcum exinterare. Itaque totum
circumspicere triclinium coepi, ne per parietem
automatum aliquod exiret, utique postquam servus
verberari coepit, qui brachium domini contusum alba
potius quam conchyliata involverat lana. Nec longe
aberravit suspicio mea; in vicem enim poenae [2]
venit decretum Trimalchionis, quo puerum iussit
liberum esse, ne quis posset dicere, tantum virum
esse a servo vulneratum.[3]

55 *HLO/H* | Comprobamus nos factum | et quam in praecipiti
HLO res humanae essent, | vario sermone garrimus. |
H " Ita " inquit Trimalchio " non oportet hunc casum
sine inscriptione transire " statimque codicillos
poposcit et non diu cogitatione distorta haec
recitavit:

HL | " Quod non expectes, ex transverso fit. . . .
. . . [4] et supra nos Fortuna negotia curat.

II | quare da nobis vina Falerna, puer."

HLO Ab hoc epigrammate | coepit poetarum esse mentio
diuque summa carminis penes Mopsum Thracem
memorata est donec Trimalchio " Rogo " inquit

---

[1] per ridiculum *Keller*: periculo. *The whole passage is
variously emended.*

[2] poenae *Hadrianides*: cene.

[3] vulneratum *Scheffer*: tuberatum *Garrod*: liberatum.

[4] *To fill the gap, Heinsius suggests* ubique | nostra.

afraid that his petition † was leading up to some comic turn. † ¹ The cook who had forgotten to gut the pig had not yet faded from my recollection. So I proceeded to look all round the dining-room, in case any clockwork toy should jump out of the wall, especially after they went on to beat a servant for dressing the bruise on his master's arm with white wool instead of purple. And my suspicions were not far out. Instead of punishment there came Trimalchio's decree that he should be made a free man, for fear anyone might be able to say that so great a hero had been wounded by a slave.

We applauded his action, and made small talk in different phrases about the uncertainty of man's affairs. " Ah," said Trimalchio, " then we should not let this occasion slip without a record." And he called at once for paper, and after no long writhing reflection declaimed these verses:

" What men do not look for turns about and comes to pass. . . . . And high over us Fortune directs our affairs. Wherefore, slave, hand us Falernian wine."

A discussion about poets arose out of this epigram, and for a long time it was maintained that Mopsus ² of Thrace held the crown of song in his hand, until Trimalchio said, " Now, I ask you as a scholar, how would

¹ In this passage of uncertain reading, I feel that *catastropha* (καταστροφή) means some action such as tackling or up-tripping or throwing down as in a ball-game or in wrestling. The word usually means a sudden reversal of fortune in a tragic drama.

² We know of several soothsayers but no poet named Mopsus.

" magister, quid putas inter Ciceronem et Publilium [1]
interesse? Ego alterum puto disertiorem fuisse,
alterum honestiorem. Quid enim his melius dici
potest?

" ' Luxuriae rictu Martis marcent moenia.
Tuo palato clausus pavo pascitur [2]
plumato amictus aureo Babylonico,[3]
gallina tibi Numidica, tibi gallus spado;
ciconia etiam, grata [4] peregrina hospita
pietaticultrix gracilipes crotalistria,
avis exul hiemis,[5] titulus tepidi temporis,
nequitiae nidum in caccabo fecit modo.[6]
Quo margaritam caram [7] tibi, bacam Indicam? [8]
An ut matrona ornata phaleris pelagiis
tollat pedes indomita in strato extraneo?
Zmaragdum ad quam rem viridem, pretiosum
    vitrum?
Quo Carchedonios optas ignes lapideos,
nisi ut scintillet probitas e carbunculis? [9]
Aequum est induere nuptam ventum textilem,
palam prostare nudam in nebula linea?'

56 H | " Quod autem " inquit " putamus secundum
litteras difficillimum esse artificium? Ego puto

---

[1] Publilium *Buecheler*: Publium.
[2] pascitur *Scaliger in the margin of l*: nascitur.
[3] Babylonicus, *thinks Fraenkel.*
[4] Graia *Scaliger.*
[5] hieme *Fraenkel and Fuchs.*
[6] modo *Jacobs*: tuae *Fraenkel*: merae *or* tuo *Heinsius*: meo.
[7] margaritam caram *Ribbeck*: margarita cara.
[8] tibi bacam Indicam *Heinsius*: *There are other suggestions.*
tribaca Indica.

you compare Cicero and Publilius?[1] In my opinion
the first has more eloquence, the second more
beauty. For what could be better written than these
lines?

" 'The high walls of Mars crumble beneath the
gaping jaws of luxury. To please thy palate the
peacock in his Babylonian vesture of gilded feathers
is prisoned and fed, for thee the guinea-fowl, and for
thee the capon. Even our beloved foreign guest the
stork, type of parental love, with thin legs and sound-
ing rattle, the bird exiled by winter, the harbinger
of the warm weather, has now built a nest in thy
cooking-pot of rascality. Why get pearls of price for
yourself—blobs, fruits of India? For thy wife to be
adorned with sea-spoils when she lifts her feet unchecked on a strange man's bed? For what end dost
thou require the green emerald, the precious crystal,
or the fire that lies in the gems of Carthage, save that
honesty should shine forth from amid the carbuncles?
Should a young bride clothe herself with a garment
of the wind or stand forth publicly naked under her
mere mist of muslin?'

" And now," said he, " what do we think is the
hardest profession after writing? I think a doctor's

---

[1] Publilius Syrus (not the unknown actor of Chapter 52)
was a composer of mimes or farces and publisher of moral
sayings during the first century B.C. (see *Minor Latin Poets*,
Loeb Classical Library, 3–111). The pompous verses which
follow may be by him, but sound more like a parody. Trimalchio of course admires them. The " walls of Mars "
mean Rome.

---

⁹ probita se *B*: probitas est *H, L, and other MSS.* carbunculis *Buecheler*: carbunculus *or* -os *or* -as.

115

medicum et nummularium: medicus, qui scit quid
homunciones intra praecordia sua habeant et quando
febris veniat, etiam si illos odi pessime, quod mihi
iubent saepe anetinam[1] parari; nummularius, qui
per argentum aes videt. Nam mutae bestiae laborio-
sissimae boves et oves: boves, quorum beneficio
panem manducamus; oves, quod lana illae nos
gloriosos faciunt. Et facinus indignum, aliquis ovil-
lam est et[2] tunicam habet. Apes enim ego divinas
bestias puto, quae mel vomunt, etiam si dicuntur

HL illud a Iove afferre; | ideo autem pungunt, quia
ubicunque dulce est, ibi et acidum invenies."

H | Iam etiam philosophos de negotio deiciebat, cum
pittacia in scypho circumferri coeperunt, puerque
super hoc positus officium apophoreta recitavit.
"Argentum[3] sceleratum": allata est perna, super
quam acetabula erant posita. "Cervical": offla
collaris allata est. "Serisapia[4] et contumelia":

---

[1] anethinam *Jahn*: aloetinam *Reinesius*: anatinam.
[2] est et *Statileo, Scheffer*: esset.
[3] *Perhaps* armentum "*plough-cattle*".
[4] sevisapia *Heinsius*: seria sapae *Scheffer*.

---

[1] *H* has *anatinam*, "a dose of duck." This may be right.
Pliny, *N.H.*, XXV, 6, says that Mithridates VI, King of
Pontus, who allegedly drank poison after remedies daily, to
make himself immune from poisoning, mixed with antidotes
the blood of Pontic ducks which, says Pliny, lived on poison.
However, the context here does not give a dose of duck any
point.
[2] Of base-metal coins coated with silver.

or a money-changer's. The doctor's, because he knows what poor men have in their insides, and when a fever will come—though I detest them specially, because they so often order a prescription for a dose of dill [1] for me. The money-changer's, because he sees the copper under the silver.[2] Just so among the dumb animals, oxen and sheep are the hardest workers: the oxen, because thanks to the oxen we have bread to eat; the sheep, because their wool clothes us in splendour. It is a gross outrage when people eat lamb and wear shirts. Yes, and I hold the bees to be the most divine insects. They vomit honey, although people do say they bring it from Jupiter: and they have stings, because wherever you have a sweet thing there you will find something bitter too."

He was just throwing the philosophers out of work, when tickets were carried round in a cup, and a boy who was entrusted with this duty read aloud the names of the presents for the guests.[3] " Tainted silver ": [4] a ham was brought in with vinegar bowls on top of it. " Something soft for the neck ": a scrap of neck-end was put on. " That feeling ' wise

[3] *Apophoreta* are presents for guests to carry away. It was customary to hand tickets to them on which riddles concealing the names of the presents were written. Trimalchio's jokes depend upon allusions to likenesses (even appalling puns) between the words in the riddle and the name of the present, and are therefore impossible to render naturally in English.

[4] *argentum sceleratum* " rascally silver " suggests impure silver or Nero's depreciation of Rome's gold and silver coinage; but the connection with ham and vinegar is not clear, unless the *acetabula* were of silver and unless *perna* suggests Greek σκέλος, leg.

xerophagiae e sale [1] datae sunt et contus [2] cum malo.
" Porri et persica ": flagellum et cultrum accepit;
" passeres et muscarium ": uvam passam et mel
Atticum. " Cenatoria et forensia ": offlam et tabulas accepit. " Canale et pedale ": [3] lepus et solea
est allata. " Muraena et littera ": murem cum rana
alligata fascemque betae ⟨accepit⟩.[4] Diu risimus:
sexcenta huiusmodi fuerunt, quae iam exciderunt [5]
memoriae meae.

57 Ceterum Ascyltos, intemperantis licentiae, cum
omnia sublatis manibus eluderet et usque ad lacrimas
rideret, unus ex conlibertis Trimalchionis excanduit,
is ipse qui supra me discumbebat,[6] et " Quid rides "
inquit " vervex? An tibi non placent lautitiae
domini mei? Tu enim beatior es et convivare melius
soles. Ita tutelam huius loci habeam propitiam, ut
ego si secundum illum discumberem, iam illi bala-
tum [7] clusissem.[8] Bellum pomum, qui rideatur

---

[1] xerophagiae *Reiske*: xerophagi *Friedländer*: aecrophagie
H. e sale *Burman*: ex sapa *Friedländer*: saele *H.*

[2] contus *Burman*: centus.

[3] canale *Buecheler*: canalem. pedale *Hadrianides*: pedalem.

[4] accepit *added by Buecheler.*

[5] exciderunt *Hadrianides*: ceciderunt.

[6] *Fraenkel was inclined to delete the whole clause* is . . . discumbebat.

[7] alapam *Scheffer*: talatrum *Heraeus*: colaphum *Reiske.*
There are other suggestions combined with what follows.

[8] clusissem *Friedländer, Marbach*: duxissem *H. There are
other suggestions combined with what precedes.*

---

[1] I assume here a double meaning *malo* " evil " and *mālo*
" apple."

[2] *passer* was a name applied to several small birds. You
can see why I choose siskin in translating.

but it's all so late ' and ' appalling impoliteness ' ": *he* was given dry biscuits all so salty, and a little pole with a bad apple.[1] " Flip of leeks and peaches *piquant*: *he* got a whip and a knife *coupant*. " Siskins [2] and fly-paper ": up came dry-skin grapes and Attic honey. " Dinner-dress and public dress ": [3] *he* received a piece of meat and note-books. " Something for a dog and something for a foot ": a hare and a slipper were served up. " A murry *muraena* and a letter ": *he* received a " mury "-mouse with a *rana*-frog tied to it and a bunch of b-eet.[4] We laughed loud and long: there were any number of these jokes, which have now escaped my memory.

But Ascyltos let himself go completely, threw up his hands and made fun of everything and laughed till he cried. This annoyed one [5] of Trimalchio's fellow-freedmen, the man who was sitting next above me.

" What are you laughing at, mutton head? " he said. " Are our host's good things not good enough for you? I suppose you are richer and used to better living. As I hope to have the spirits of this place on my side, if I had been sitting next him I should have put a stopper on his bleating by now. A nice young

---

[3] These are the ordinary meanings of the Latin words as normally used. What follows substitutes something more general: *cenatoria* " connected with dinner "; *forensia* " connected with the forum."

[4] *beta* " beetroot " because *beta* ($\beta\hat{\eta}\tau\alpha$) is also the second letter of the alphabet. On this chapter in general cf. H. D. Rankin, in *Classica et Mediaevalia*, XXXIII, 1962, 86 ff. I have given few only of the many conjectures about the text.

[5] Hermeros—see Chapter 59.

alios; [1] larifuga nescio quis, nocturnus, qui non valet
lotium suum. Ad summam, si circumminxero illum,
nesciet qua fugiat. Non mehercules soleo cito fervere, sed in molle carne vermes nascuntur. Ridet.
Quid habet quod rideat? Numquid pater fetum [2]
emit lamna? Eques Romanus es: et ego regis filius.
' Quare ergo servivisti?' Quia ipse me dedi in
servitutem et malui civis Romanus esse quam
tributarius. Et nunc spero me sic vivere, ut nemini
iocus sim. Homo inter homines sum,[3] capite aperto
ambulo; assem aerarium nemini debeo; constitutum
habui nunquam; nemo mihi in foro dixit redde quod
debes.' Glebulas emi, lamellulas paravi; viginti
ventres pasco et canem; contubernalem meam
redemi, ne quis in ⟨sinu⟩ [4] illius manus tergeret;
mille denarios pro capite solvi; sevir gratis factus
sum; spero, sic moriar, ut mortuus non erubescam.
Tu autem tam laboriosus es, ut post te non respicias?
In alio peduclum vides, in te ricinum non vides.
Tibi soli ridiclei videmur; ecce magister tuus homo
maior natus: placemus illi. Tu lacticulosus,[5] nec
mu nec ma argutas, vasus fictilis, immo lorus in
aqua, lentior, non melior. Tu beatior es: bis prande,

---

[1] rideat alios *ed. Patav.*: rideat curalios *Fröhner, Schneck*:
rideat uranios *Jacobs*.

[2] foenum *Mentel.*   [3] sum *Burman*: suos.

[4] sinu *added by Heinsius. There are other suggestions.*

[5] lacticulosus *Scheffer*: lendiculosus *Heinsius*: laeticulosus.

---

[1] This indicates that Ascyltos wears a gold ring like a Roman
eques or knight.

fruit to laugh at other people! Some vagabond fly-
by-night not worth his own pizz. In fact, when I've
piddled round him he won't know where to take
refuge. Upon my word, I am not easily annoyed as
a rule, but in rotten flesh worms will breed. He
laughs. What has he got to laugh about? Did his
father pay solid gold for him when he was a baby? A
Roman knight,[1] are you? Well, I am a king's son.
' Then why have you been a slave? ' Because I
went into service to please myself, and preferred
being a Roman citizen to going on paying taxes as a
provincial. And now I hope I live such a life that no
one can jeer at me. I am a man among men; I
walk about bare-headed; I owe nobody a brass
farthing; I have never been in the Courts; no one
has ever said to me in public, ' Pay me what you owe
me.' I have bought a few small clods and collected a
little plate; I have to feed twenty bellies and a dog:
I ransomed my fellow slave lest someone should
wipe his hands in her lap;[2] I paid a thousand
silver pennies for my own freedom; I was made a
priest of Augustus and excused the fees; I hope to
die so that I need not blush in my grave. But are
you so full of business that you have no time to look
behind you? You can see a louse on others, but
not the big tick on yourself. No one finds us comic
but you: there is your schoolmaster, older and
wiser than you: he likes us. You are a child just
weaned, you cannot squeak out mu or ma, you are
a clay-pot, or rather a wash-leather in water, softer,
not superior. If you are richer, then have two break-

[2] Perhaps Petronius made the speaker omit a " four-letter "
word here. Cf. E. Burriss in *Class. Phil.*, 1947, 204 ff.

bis cena. Ego fidem meam malo quam thesauros. Ad summam, quisquam me bis poposcit? Annis quadraginta servivi; nemo tamen sciit, utrum servus essem an liber. Et puer capillatus in hanc coloniam veni; adhuc basilica non erat facta. Dedi tamen operam, ut domino satis facerem, homini maiesto [1] et dignitosso, cuius pluris erat unguis, quam tu totus es. Et habebam in domo, qui mihi pedem opponerent hac illac; tamen—genio illius gratias—enatavi. Haec sunt vera athla; nam [in] [2] ingenuum nasci tam facile est quam ' accede istoc.' Quid nunc stupes tanquam hircus in ervilia ? "

58 Post hoc dictum Giton, qui ad pedes stabat, risum iam diu compressum etiam indecenter effudit. Quod cum animadvertisset adversarius Ascylti, flexit convicium in puerum et " Tu autem " inquit " etiam tu rides, caepa cirrata? [3] Io Saturnalia, rogo, mensis december est? Quando vicesimam numerasti? ⟨Nescit⟩ [4] quid faciat crucis offla, corvorum cibaria. Curabo, iam tibi Iovis iratus sit, et isti qui tibi non imperat. Ita satur pane fiam, ut ego istud conliberto meo dono; alioquin iam tibi depraesentiarum reddidissem. Bene nos habemus, at isti nugae,[5] qui tibi non imperant.[6] Plane qualis dominus, talis et servus.

---

[1] maiesto *Muncker*: maiiesto *Buecheler*: macisto *Hilt-brunner*: mali isto.

[2] *Deleted by Buecheler.*

[3] pica cirrata *Reinesius*: caepa piperata *Scheffer*: caepa pirrata.

[4] *added by Buecheler.*

[5] nugae *Buecheler*: geuge. *There are other conjectures.*

[6] *Fraenkel would delete the clause* qui . . . imperant.

---

[1] At the *Saturnalia* in mid-December in honour of Saturn, as mythical bringer of agriculture to Italy, slaves were granted

fasts and two dinners a day. I prefer my reputation to any riches. One word more. Who ever had to ask me twice? I was a slave for forty years, and nobody knew whether I was a slave or free. I was a boy with long curls when I came to this place; they had not built the town-hall then. But I tried to please my master, a fine dignified gentleman whose finger-nail was worth more than your whole body. And there were people in the house who put out a foot to trip me up here and there. But still—God bless my master!—I struggled through. These are real victories: for being born free is as easy as saying, 'Come here.' But why do you look scared at me now like a goat in a field of vetch?"

At this remark Giton, who was standing by my feet, burst out with an unseemly laugh, which he had now been holding in for a long while. Ascyltos's enemy noticed him, and turned his abuse on to the boy. "What," he said, "are you laughing too, you curly-headed onion? Merry Saturnalia indeed: what, have we December here? When did you pay five per cent on your freedom?[1] He doesn't know what to do, the gallows-meat, the crows'-food. I will call down the wrath of Jupiter at once on you and the fellow who cannot keep you in order. As sure as I get my bellyfull of bread, I would have given you what you deserve now on the spot, but for my respect for my fellow-freedman. We are getting on splendidly, but those fellows are fools, who don't keep you in hand. Yes, like master, like man. I can scarcely

some licence. The tax mentioned was the one normally paid by a master on the assessed value of a slave set free by him.

Vix me teneo, nec [1] sum natura caldicerebrius, sed [2]
cum coepi, matrem meam dupundii non facio.   Recte,
videbo te in publicum, mus, immo terrae tuber:
nec sursum nec deorsum non cresco, nisi dominum
tuum in rutae folium non conieci,[3] nec tibi parsero,[4]
licet mehercules Iovem Olympium clames.   Curabo,
longe tibi sit comula ista besalis et dominus dupun-
duarius.   Recte, venies sub dentem: aut ego non
me novi, aut non deridebis, licet barbam auream
habeas.   Athana tibi irata sit, curabo, et qui te
primus deurode [5] fecit.

   " Non didici geometrias critica [6] et alogias [7]
menias,[8] sed lapidarias litteras scio, partes centum
dico ad aes, ad pondus, ad nummum.   Ad summam,
si quid vis, ego et tu sponsiunculam: exi, defero
lamnam.[9]   Iam scies patrem tuum mercedes perdi-
disse, quamvis et rhetoricam scis.[10]   Ecce

   ' Qui de [11] nobis longe venio, late venio?   solve me.'

[1] nec *Jahn*: et.
[2] caldicerebrius *John:* caldus cicer eius. sed *added by*
Buecheler.
[3] conieci *Scheffer*: coniecit.
[4] parsero *Reinesius*: par ero.
[5] δεῦρο δή *Buecheler*: deuro de.
[6] critica *Reiske*: creticas *Scheffer*: criticen *Mentel*:
cretica. *Perhaps* chreias *or* chrias (χρείας).
[7] alogas *Scheffer.*
[8] menias *H*: naenias *Scheffer, Heinsius. If we omit* et,
then possibly geometrias criticas (se. τέχνας) analogias menias.
[9] lamnam *Heinsius*: lāna.
[10] scis *Reiske*: scias *Goes*: scio.
[11] qui de *Buecheler*: quidem.

---

[1] See note on the beginning of Chapter 38.
[2] *Athana* is Heinsius's correction of Sathana. *Deurode* is a

hold myself in, and I am not naturally hot-tempered, but when I once begin I do not care twopence for my own mother. Depend upon it, I shall meet you somewhere in public, you rat, you puff-ball. I will not grow an inch up or down until I have put your master's head in a nettle-bed [1] and I shall have no mercy on you, I can tell you, however much you may call upon Jupiter in Olympus. I'll see to it that those pretty eight-inch curls and that twopenny master of yours will be no use to you. Depend upon it, you will come under the harrow; if I know my own name you will not laugh any more, though you may have a gold beard like a god. I will bring down the wrath of Athena on you and the man who first made you a 'come here man.' [2]

" No, I never learned your geometries, criticisms, non-logics, Wraths.[3] But I know my block capitals, and I can do any sum into pounds, shillings and pence. In fact, if you like, you and I will have a little bet. Come on, I put down the metal. Now I will show you that your father wasted the fees, even though you are a scholar in rhetoric. Look here:

' What part of us am I? I come far, I come wide.[4]
  Solve this riddle about me.'

transliteration of the Greek δεῦρο δή " come hither," used of a person trained to be obsequious.
[3] It is tempting to read *nenias* or *naenias* with Scheffer and Heinsius in this uncertain passage. But the reading *menias* of *H* can be taken to represent, like the three preceding nouns, another Greek word (as we should expect) μήνιας, accusative plural of μῆνις the first word (μῆνιν) of Homer's *Iliad*: " Wrath of Achilles son of Peleus—sing about *that*, goddess " (*Iliad*, I, 1). So the speaker says he never learnt Homer. Hermeros speaks to Ascyltos. [4] Very doubtful.

Dicam tibi, qui de nobis currit et de loco non movetur; qui de nobis crescit et minor fit.   Curris, stupes,
satagis, tanquam mus in matella.   Ergo aut tace aut
meliorem noli molestare, qui te natum non putat;
nisi si me iudicas anulos buxeos curare, quos amicae
tuae involasti.   Occuponem [1] propitium.   Eamus in
forum et pecunias mutuemur: iam scies hoc ferrum
fidem habere.   Vah, bella res est volpis uda.   Ita
lucrum faciam et ita bene moriar ut [2] populus per
exitum meum iuret, nisi te ubique toga perversa
fuero persecutus.   Bella res et iste, qui te haec
docet, mufrius, non magister.   ⟨Nos⟩ [3] didicimus,
dicebat enim magister: ' Sunt vestra salva? recta
domum; cave, circumspicias; cave, maiorem male-
dicas.   At nunc mera [4] mapalia; nemo dupundii
evadit.'   Ego, quod me sic vides, propter artificium
meum diis gratias ago."

59   Coeperat Ascyltos respondere convicio, sed Trimalchio delectatus colliberti eloquentia " Agite " inquit
" scordalias de medio.   Suaviter sit potius, et tu,
Hermeros, parce adulescentulo.   Sanguen illi fervet,
HL   tu melior esto. | Semper in hac re qui vincitur, vin-

[1] o bucconem *Heinsius*: o cleponem *Reinesius.*
[2] ut *Heinsius*: aut.
[3] ⟨nos⟩ *added by Jacobs who reads* nos magis.   *Heraeus reads*
nos aliter.
[4] at nunc mera *Heraeus, surely rightly*; *we have* mera
mapalia *in Seneca, Apocolocyntosis,* 9.   sat numero *Wehle.*
There are other suggestions.   aut numera *H.*

---

[1] The answer to these riddles according to Buecheler is
" the eye, the foot, and the hair."
[2] *Occupo* is a goblin who helps people in business, like the
Lares mentioned in c. 60.

I'll tell you something else—what part of us runs and does not move from its place; what grows out of us and grows smaller?[1]   Ah! you run about and look scared and hustled, like a mouse in a pot.   So keep your mouth shut, or do not worry your betters who are unaware of your existence; unless you think I have any respect for the boxwood rings you stole from your young woman.   May the God of grab be on my side![2]   Let us go on 'Change and borrow money: then you will see that my iron ring commands credit.   My word, a draggled fox is a fine creature!   I hope I may never get rich and make a good end, so that the people swear by my death, if I do not put on the black cap[3] and hunt you down everywhere.   It was a fine fellow who taught you to behave like this, too; a chattering ape, not a master. We had some real schooling, for the master used to say, 'Are all your belongings safe?   Go straight home, and don't stop to look round you; and mind you do not abuse your elders.   As things are, everything is plain shoddy;[4] not one person is worth two-pence in the end.'   Yes, I thank God for my education; it made me what I am, as you see."

Ascyltos was proceeding to retort to his abuse, but Trimalchio was delighted with his fellow-freedman's readiness, and said, " Come now, stop all this wrangling.   It is nicer to go on pleasantly, and *you*—please do not be hard on the young man, Hermeros.   Young blood is hot in him; you must be indulgent.   A man

[3] *Toga perversa:* a magistrate wore his toga reversed when he had to pronounce a capital sentence.
[4] *mapalia* were properly huts or cottages of Africans. Cp. Seneca, *Apocolocyntosis*, 9.

H cit. | Et tu cum esses capo, coco coco,[1] atque cor non
habebas.[2] Simus ergo, quod melius est, a primitiis
hilares et Homeristas spectemus.'' Intravit factio
statim hastisque scuta concrepuit. Ipse Trimalchio
in pulvino consedit, et cum Homeristae Graecis versibus colloquerentur, ut insolenter solent, ille canora
voce Latine legebat librum. Mox silentio facto
'' scitis '' inquit '' quam fabulam agant? Diomedes
et Ganymedes duo fratres fuerunt. Horum soror
erat Helena. Agamemnon illam rapuit et Dianae
cervam subiecit. Ita nunc Homeros dicit, quemadmodum inter se pugnent Troiani et Parentini.[3]
Vicit scilicet[4] et Iphigeniam, filiam suam, Achilli
dedit uxorem. Ob eam rem Aiax insanit et statim
argumentum explicabit.'' Haec ut dixit Trimalchio,

---

[1] *Perhaps, after the manner of many cockerels,* coco coco co.
[2] habebas *Mentel:* habeas.
[3] Tarentini *Scheffer, rightly?*
[4] *after* scilicet *Scheffer adds* ⟨Agamemnon⟩.

---

[1] Trimalchio's perversion of Greek mythology which follows
is superb. The '' true '' mythology is: Ganymedes was not a
Greek but a Trojan boy carried away to '' heaven '' by Zeus to
be his favourite and his (and the other gods') cup-bearer.
Diomedes was a great Greek captain and hero in the traditional
war against Troy in north-western Asia Minor. Ganymedes
and Diomedes were not related in any way to each other or to
Helen (wife of Menelaus, King of Sparta) whose brothers
were Castor and Pollux. Paris, the Trojan, carried Helen
off to Troy and so caused the war. Agamemnon (King of
Mycenae city, brother of Menelaus, and commander-in-chief
of the Greeks in the war) lured his daughter Iphigenia
to Aulis on the pretext of marrying her to prince Achilles;
and, to gain favourable winds, and relief from plague in

who admits defeat in this kind of quarrel is always the winner. And you, too, when you were a young cockerel cried Cock-a-doodle-doo! and hadn't any sense in your head. So let us do better, and start the fun over again, and have a look at these reciters of Homer." A troop came in at once and clashed spear on shield. Trimalchio sat up on his cushion, and when the reciters talked to each other in Greek verse, as their conceited way is, he intoned Latin from a book. Soon there was silence, and then he said,[1] " You know the story they are doing? Diomede and Ganymede were two brothers. Helen was their sister. Agamemnon carried her off and took in Diana by sacrificing a deer to her instead. So Homer is now telling the tale of the war between Troy and Parentium. Of course he won and married his daughter Iphigenia to Achilles. That drove Ajax mad, and he will show you the story in a minute." As he spoke the reciters raised a shout, and the slaves

---

his army, would have sacrificed her, but Artemis (Diana) substituted a hart and translated her elsewhere before the ten years' war began, part of which is related by Homer. During the war Achilles died. [This is not in the *Iliad*.] After Achilles' arms had been awarded to Odysseus (Ulysses), Ajax went mad because he had wanted them. Trimalchio's mythology is: Ganymedes and Diomedes were brothers of Helen. She was carried off by King Agamemnon who deceived Diana by sacrificing a deer instead. Homer tells the story of fighting between the Trojans and the Parentini (connecting these with Paris?) of a town in the Italian country of Istria at the north end of the Adriatic, unless indeed for *parentini* in cod. *H* Scheffer was right in conjecturing Tarentini the people of Taranto in south Italy. After his victory Agamemnon gave Iphigenia in marriage to Achilles so that Ajax went mad through jealousy of Achilles.

clamorem Homeristae sustulerunt, interque familiam
discurrentem vitulus in lance donaria [1] elixus allatus
est, et quidem galeatus.   Secutus est Aiax strictoque
gladio, tanquam insaniret,[2] concidit, ac modo versa
modo supina [3] gesticulatus mucrone frusta collegit
mirantibusque vitulum partitus est.

60   Nec diu mirari licuit tam elegantes strophas; nam
repente lacunaria sonare coeperunt totumque triclinium intremuit.   Consternatus ego exsurrexi et
timui, ne per tectum petauristarius aliquis descen-
deret.   Nec minus reliqui convivae mirantes [4] erex-
ere vultus, expectantes quid novi de caelo nuntiare-
tur.   Ecce autem diductis [5] lacunaribus subito circulus
ingens, de cupa videlicet grandi excussus,[6] demittitur,
cuius per totum orbem coronae aureae cum alabastris
unguenti pendebant.   Dum haec apophoreta iube-
mur sumere, respiciens ad mensam . . .
iam illic repositorium cum placentis aliquot erat positum, quod medium Priapus a pistore factus tenebat,
gremioque satis amplo omnis generis poma et uvas
sustinebat more vulgato.   Avidius ad pompam [7]
manus porreximus, et repente nova ludorum missio [8]
hilaritatem [hic] refecit.   Omnes enim placentae
omniaque poma etiam minima vexatione contacta

[1] donaria *Buecheler*: ducenaria *Burman*: dunaria.
[2] *After* insaniret *Müller puts* vitulum *instead of leaving it
after* mirantibusque *below.*
[3] supina *Scheffer*: spuma.
[4] *Fraenkel suggested deleting* mirantes.
[5] diductis *Scheffer*: deductus.
[6] *Fraenkel would delete the words* de . . . excussus.

ran about and a boiled calf on a presentation dish
was brought in. There was a helmet on its head.
Ajax followed and attacked it with his sword drawn as
if he were mad; and after making passes with the
edge and the flat he collected slices on the point,
and divided the calf among the astonished company.[1]

We were not given long to admire these elegant
tours de force; suddenly there came a noise from the
ceiling, and the whole dining-room trembled. I rose
from my place in a panic: I was afraid some acrobat
would come down through the roof. All the other
guests too looked up astonished, wondering what
new portent from heaven was announced. The
whole ceiling parted asunder, and an enormous hoop,
apparently knocked out of a giant cask, was let down.
All round it were hung golden crowns and alabaster
boxes of perfumes. We were asked to take these
presents for ourselves, when I looked back at the
table. . . .

A dish with some cakes on it had now been put there,
a Priapus [2] made by the confectioner standing in the
middle, holding up every kind of fruit and grapes in
his wide apron in the conventional style. We reached
greedily after his treasures, and a sudden fresh start
to the games renewed our merriment. All the cakes
and all the fruits, however lightly they were touched,

---

[1] This would be an allusion to the way in which Ajax in his
fits of madness attacked herds and flocks of farm animals.
[2] See note on p. 27.

---

[7] poma *Fröhner.*
[8] missio *Buecheler*: commissio *Delz, perhaps rightly*: re-
missio. *Friedlaender deletes* hic.

coeperunt effundere crocum, et usque ad os [1] molestus umor accidere. Rati ergo sacrum esse fer[i]-
culum [2] tam religioso apparatu perfusum, consur-
reximus altius et " Augusto, patri patriae, feliciter "
diximus. Quibusdam tamen etiam post hanc venera-
tionem poma rapientibus et ipsi iis [3] mappas implevimus, ego praecipue, qui nullo satis amplo munere
putabam me onerare Gitonis sinum.

Inter haec tres pueri candidas succincti tunicas intraverunt, quorum duo Lares bullatos super mensam
posuerunt, unus pateram vini circumferens " dii pro-
pitii " clamabat. ⟨. . .⟩ [4]

Aiebat autem unum Cerdonem, alterum Felicionem, tertium Lucrionem [5] vocari. Nos etiam
auream [6] imaginem ipsius Trimalchionis, cum iam
omnes basiarent, erubuimus praeterire.

61   Postquam ergo omnes bonam mentem bonamque
valitudinem sibi optarunt, Trimalchio ad Nicerotem
respexit et " solebas " inquit " suavius esse in con-
victu; nescio quid nunc [7] taces nec muttis.[8] Oro te,
sic felicem me videas, narra illud quod tibi usu venit."
Niceros delectatus affabilitate amici " omne me "
inquit " lucrum transeat, nisi iam dudum gaudi-
monio dissilio, quod te talem video. Itaque hilaria

---

[1] os *Buecheler*: nos.
[2] fericulum *Reinesius* (*perhaps rather* ferculum): peniculum
Scheffer: periculum.
[3] ipsi iis *Heinsius*: ipsas.
[4] *lacuna indicated by Buecheler.*
[5] Lucrionem *Reinesius*: lucronem.
[6] auream *Jahn*: ueram.
[7] nunc *Scheffer*: nec.
[8] muttis *Scheffer*: mutes.

proceeded to spurt out saffron, and the nasty juice flew even into our faces. We thought it must be a sacred dish [1] that was anointed with such holy appointments, and we all stood straight up and cried, "The gods bless Augustus,[2] the father of his country." But as some people even after this solemnity snatched at the fruit, we filled our napkins too with them, myself especially, for I thought that I could never fill Giton's lap with a large enough present. Meanwhile three boys came in with their white tunics well tucked up, and two of them put images of the Lares [3] with lockets round their necks on the table, while one carried round a bowl of wine and cried, "God be gracious unto us.". . . .

Trimalchio said that one of the images was called Gain, another Luck, and the third Profit. And as everybody else kissed Trimalchio's golden portrait we were ashamed to pass it by.

So after they had all wished themselves good sense and good health, Trimalchio looked at Niceros and said, "You used to be better company at a dinner; something or other makes you dumb now, and you do not utter a sound. Do please, to make me happy, tell us of your adventure." Niceros was delighted by his friend's amiability and said, "May I never turn another penny if I am not ready to burst with joy at seeing you in such a good humour. Well, it shall

---

[1] Because saffron was often used by the Romans in sacred procedure.

[2] This title, assumed by Octavian when he became the first emperor (reigned 30 B.C.–A.D. 14), was applied to his successors also.

[3] The Lares and Penates were the household gods.

mera sint, etsi timeo istos scholasticos, ne me rideant.[1]
Riserint;[2] narrabo tamen: quid enim mihi aufert,
qui ridet? Satius est rideri quam derideri." " Haec
ubi dicta dedit," talem fabulam exorsus est:

" Cum adhuc servirem, habitabamus in vico an-
gusto; nunc Gavillae domus est. Ibi, quomodo dii
volunt, amare coepi uxorem Terentii coponis:
noveratis Melissam Tarentinam, pulcherrimum bacciballum. Sed ego non mehercules corporaliter illam[3]
aut propter res venerias curavi, sed magis quod benemoria[4] fuit. Si quid ab illa petii, nunquam mihi
negatum; fecit assem, semissem habui; ⟨quicquid
habui⟩,[5] in illius sinum demandavi, nec unquam fefel-
litus sum. Huius contubernalis ad villam supremum
diem obiit. Itaque per scutum per ocream egi agi-
navi,[6] quemadmodum ad illam pervenirem: ⟨scitis⟩[7]
62 autem, in angustiis amici apparent. Forte dominus
Capuam[8] exierat ad scruta [scita][9] expedienda.
Nactus ego occasionem persuadeo hospitem nostrum,
ut mecum ad quintum miliarium veniat. Erat autem
miles, fortis tanquam Orcus. Apoculamus[10] nos circa

---

[1] rideant *Mentel*: derideant.
[2] riserint *Scheffer*: viderint *ed. Patav.*: viderit.
[3] illam *Buecheler*: autem.
[4] benemoria *Orelli*: bene morata *Hadrianides*: bene moriar
H which might be an interjection (so Jacobs and Burriss).
[5] *Added by Buecheler.*
[6] *Heinsius suggests* aegre agitavi: ecraginavi *Reiske.*
[7] scitis *added by Buecheler.*
[8] Capuam *Scheffer*: Capuae, *perhaps rightly.*
[9] *Deleted by P. George.*
[10] apoculamus *Scheffer* (*see Chapter 67*): apoculanius.

be pure fun then, though I am afraid your clever friends will laugh at me. Still, let them; I will tell my story; what harm does a man's laugh do me? Being laughed at is more satisfactory than being sneered at." So spake the hero,[1] and began the following story:

" While I was still a slave, we were living in a narrow street; the house now belongs to Gavilla. There it was God's will that I should fall in love with the wife of Terentius the inn-keeper; you remember her, Melissa of Tarentum, a pretty round thing.[2] But I swear it was no base passion; I did not care about her for physical love, but rather because she had a beautiful nature. If I asked her for anything it was never refused me; if she made twopence I had a penny; whatever I had I put into her pocket, and I was never taken in. Now one day her husband died on the estate.[3] So I buckled on my shield and greaves, and schemed how to come at her: and as you know, one's friends turn up in tight places. My master happened to have gone to Capua to look after some silly business[4] or other. I seized my opportunity, and persuaded a guest in our house to come with me as far as the fifth milestone. He was a soldier, and as brave as Hell. So we bummed our-

---

[1] A phrase of Roman epic poetry. Cf. Chapter 121, line 100.
[2] This is probably the meaning of *bacciballum*, from *baca* or *bacca*, a berry. "Around little peach."
[3] Terentius was a slave managing the tavern for his master.
[4] *scita* looks like an alternative effort for *scruta* arising partly from *scitis* just before; but if it is right, then: "elegant trash."

gallicinia, luna lucebat tanquam meridie. Venimus
inter monimenta: homo meus coepit ad stelas facere,
sedeo [1] ego cantabundus et stelas [2] numero. Deinde
ut respexi ad comitem, ille exuit se et omnia vestimenta secundum viam posuit. Mihi anima [3] in
naso esse, stabam tanquam mortuus. At ille cir-
cumminxit vestimenta sua, et subito lupus factus est.
Nolite me iocari putare; ut mentiar, nullius patrimonium tanti facio. Sed, quod coeperam dicere, postquam lupus factus est, ululare coepit et in silvas
fugit. Ego primitus nesciebam ubi essem, deinde
accessi, ut vestimenta eius tollerem: illa autem
lapidea facta sunt. Qui mori timore nisi ego? Gladium tamen strinxi et in tota via [4] umbras cecidi,
donec ad villam amicae meae pervenirem. Larva [5]
intravi, paene animam ebullivi, sudor mihi per
bifurcum volabat,[6] oculi mortui, vix unquam refectus
sum. Melissa mea mirari coepit, quod tam sero
ambularem, et ' Si ante ' inquit ' venisses, saltem
nobis adiutasses; lupus enim villam intravit et omnia
pecora ⟨momordit⟩,[7] tanquam lanius sanguinem illis
misit. Nec tamen derisit, etiam si fugit; servus

---

[1] sedeo *Scheffer*: sed.
[2] *H has* stellas *here but it doubtless stands for* stelas.
[3] anima *Muncker*: in animo.
[4] in tota via *Scheffer*: matavita tau. *There are various
conjectures, some rather fantastic. Perhaps* media via.
[5] larva *Fraenkel*: ut larva *Buecheler*: ianuam *Scheffer*: in
larvam. *There are other suggestions.*
[6] undabat *suggests Nisbet.*
[7] *Added by Müller. There are other conjectures.*

---

[1] If we have this word right, it is some slang for going away,
formed of *apo*, Greek ἀπό " from," and *culus* " arse," or

selves off [1] about cockcrow; the moon shone like high
noon. We got among the monuments; [2] my man
proceeded to do business at the gravestones, I sat
down with my heart full of song and began to count
the gravestones. Then when I looked round at my
friend, he stripped himself and put all his clothes by
the roadside. My heart was in my mouth, [3] but I
stood like a dead man. He piddled all round
his clothes and suddenly turned into a wolf. Please
do not think I am joking; I would not lie about this for
any fortune in the world. But as I was saying, after
he had turned into a wolf, he proceeded to howl, and
ran off into the woods. At first I hardly knew where
I was, then I went up to take his clothes; but they
had all turned into stone. No one could be nearer
dead with terror than I was. But I drew my sword
and went slaying shadows [4] all the way till I came
to my love's house. I went in—a mere ghost and
nearly bubbled out my life; the sweat ran down my
legs, my eyes were dull, I could hardly be revived.
My dear Melissa proceeded to express surprise at my
being out so late, and said, ' If you had come earlier
you might at least have helped us; a wolf got into the
farm and worried all our sheep, and let their blood like
a butcher. But he did not make fools of us, even

Greek ἀποκυλίω, ἀποκυλίνδω " roll away " ? Possibly, however, it is ap- (ἀπ') and oculus " take ourselves from sight,"
" vanish "; or, since in Chapter 67 H has apocalo, we
might read this in both chapters, as if from calare (καλεῖν)
" call ourselves off."
    [2] Presumably by the roadside, as often.
    [3] The Latin has naso " nose."
    [4] It seems impossible to emend the corruption here in any
convincing way. matavi may hide mactavi a gloss on cecidi.

enim noster lancea collum eius traiecit.' Haec ut
audivi, operire oculos amplius non potui, sed luce clara
Gai nostri [1] domum fugi tanquam copo compilatus, et
postquam veni in illum locum, in quo lapidea vestimenta erant facta, nihil inveni nisi sanguinem. Ut
vero domum veni, iacebat miles meus in lecto tanquam bovis, et collum illius medicus curabat. Intellexi illum versipellem esse, nec postea cum illo
panem gustare potui, non si me occidisses. Viderint
alii quid de hoc [2] exopinissent; ego si mentior, genios
vestros iratos habeam."

63   Attonitis admiratione universis "Salvo" inquit
"tuo sermone" Trimalchio "si qua fides est, ut
mihi pili inhorruerunt, quia scio Niceronem nihil
nugarum narrare: immo certus est et minime linguosus. Nam et ipse vobis rem horribilem narrabo:
asinus in tegulis. Cum adhuc capillatus essem,
nam a puero vitam Chiam gessi, ipsimi nostri [3]
delicatus decessit, mehercules margaritum, zacritus [4]
et omnium numerum. Cum ergo illum mater misella
plangeret et nos tum plures [5] in tristimonio essemus,
subito strigae ⟨stridere⟩ [6] coeperunt; putares canem

---

[1] Gai nostri *Buecheler*: raptim *suggests Müller*: maturius
Ehlers: hac n̄r̄i.
[2] alii quid de hoc *Buecheler*: quid de hoc alii *Heinsius*: qui
hoc de alibi.
[3] ipsimi nostri *Scheffer, Buecheler*: ipim mostri.
[4] zacritus *Roensch*: catamitus *Jacobs, perhaps rightly.
There are other guesses*: caccitus.
[5] plorantes *suggests Müller in his 2nd edition*.
[6] stridere *added by Jacobs*.

---

[1] Literally "a Chian life," i.e. luxurious and vicious.
Thucydides calls the Chians shameless.

though he got off; for our slave made a hole in his neck with a spear.' When I heard this, I could not keep my eyes shut any longer, but at break of day I rushed back to my master Gaius's house like a defrauded inn-keeper, and when I came to the place where the clothes were turned into stone, I found nothing but a pool of blood. But when I reached home, my soldier was lying in bed like an ox, with a doctor looking after his neck. I realized that he was a werewolf, and I never could sit down to a meal with him afterwards, not if you had killed me first. Other people may think what they like about this; but may all your guardian angels punish me if I am lying."

We were all dumb with astonishment, but Trimalchio said, " I pick no holes in your story; by the soul of truth, how my hair stood on end! For I know that Niceros never talks nonsense: he is very dependable, and not at all a chatterbox. Now I want to tell you a tale of horror myself: but I'm a donkey on the tiles compared with him. While I still had hair down my back, for I lived delicately [1] from my youth up, my master's favourite died. Oh! he was a pearl, one in a thousand, a mirror of all perfection! [2] So while his poor mother was bewailing him, and several of us were sharing her sorrow, suddenly the witches began to screech; you would have thought there was a dog

---

[2] *ipsimus*: " his very self " " the master "; zacritus, representing the Greek διάκριτος " distinguishedly excellent," is an effort to emend *caccitus*, for which *catamitus* (so Jacobs) " pansy-boy " is perhaps preferable. *omnium numerŭm = omnium numerorum* " a person of all categories " (of excellence).

leporem persequi. Habebamus tunc hominem Cappadocem, longum, valde audaculum et qui valebat: poterat[1] bovem[2] iratum tollere. Hic audacter stricto gladio extra ostium procucurrit, involuta sinistra manu curiose, et mulierem tanquam hoc loco —salvum sit, quod tango—mediam traiecit. Audimus gemitum, et—plane non mentiar—ipsas non vidimus. Baro autem noster introversus se proiecit in lectum, et corpus totum lividum habebat quasi flagellis caesus, quia scilicet illum tetigerat mala manus.[3] Nos cluso ostio redimus iterum ad officium, sed dum mater amplexaret corpus filii sui, tangit et videt manuciolum de stramentis factum. Non cor habebat, non intestina, non quicquam: scilicet iam puerum strigae involaverant et supposuerant stramenticium vavatonem.[4] Rogo vos, oportet credatis, sunt mulieres plussciae, sunt nocturnae, et quod sursum est, deorsum faciunt. Ceterum baro ille longus post hoc factum nunquam coloris sui fuit, immo post paucos dies phreneticus periit."

64   Miramur nos et pariter credimus, osculatique mensam rogamus nocturnas, ut suis se[5] teneant, dum redimus a cena.

Et sane iam lucernae mihi plures videbantur ardere totumque triclinium esse mutatum, cum Trimalchio "tibi dico" inquit "Plocame, nihil narras? Nihil

---

[1] poterat *deleted in the ed. Patav.*
[2] bovem *Reiske*: iovem.
[3] *I would delete the clause* quia . . . manus, *as Fraenkel suggested.*
[4] *There are several conjectures for* vavatonem.

pursuing a hare. We had a Cappadocian in the
house at the time, a tall fellow, quite brave and a
man of muscle; he could lift an angry bull off the
ground. He rushed boldly out of doors with a naked
sword, having carefully wrapped up his left hand, and
ran a woman through the middle, just about here—
may the spot my finger is on be safe! We heard a
groan, but to tell the honest truth we did not see the
witches themselves. But our big fellow came back
and threw himself on a bed: and his whole body was
blue as if he had been flogged, of course because the
witch's hand had touched him. We shut the door
and returned to our observances, but when the
mother put her arms round the body of her son, she
felt it and saw that it was a little bundle of straw. It
had no heart, no inside or anything: of course the
witches had carried off the boy and put a straw
squaller [1] in his place. Ah! yes, I would beg you
to believe there are wise women, and night-riders,
who can turn the whole world upside down. Well,
the tall bloke never came back to his proper colour
after this affair, but died raving mad in a few days."

We were full of wonder and faith, and we kissed
the table and prayed the Night-riders to stay at home
as we returned from dinner.

By this time, I own, the lamps were multiplying
before my eyes, and the whole dining-room was altering; then Trimalchio said, "Come you, Plocamus,

[1] The word *vavato* suggests early efforts of very young children to speak.

---

[5] *After* se *Buecheler adds* sedibus, *reasonably.* *Perhaps* se
sede.

nos delectaris? Et solebas suavius esse, canturire
belle deverbia, adicere melica.[1] Heu heu, abistis
dulces caricae."[2] "Iam" inquit ille "quadrigae
meae decucurrerunt, ex quo podagricus factus sum.
Alioquin cum essem adulescentulus, cantando paene
tisicus factus sum. Quid saltare? Quid deverbia?
Quid tonstrinum? Quando parem habui nisi unum
Apelletem?" Oppositaque[3] ad os manu nescio
quid taetrum exsibilavit, quod postea Graecum esse
affirmabat.

Nec non Trimalchio ipse cum tubicines esset imitatus, ad delicias suas respexit, quem Croesum appellabat. Puer autem lippus, sordidissimis dentibus,
catellam nigram atque indecenter pinguem prasina
involvebat fascia panemque semissem ponebat super
torum [atque] ac[4] nausea recusantem saginabat.
Quo admonitus officii[5] Trimalchio Scylacem iussit
adduci "praesidium domus familiaeque." Nec mora,
ingentis formae adductus est canis catena vinctus,
admonitusque ostiarii calce, ut cubaret, ante mensam
se posuit. Tum Trimalchio iactans candidum panem
"nemo" inquit "in domo mea me plus amat."
Indignatus puer, quod Scylacem tam effuse laudaret,
catellam in terram deposuit hortatusque est, ut ad
rixam properaret. Scylax, canino scilicet usus

---

[1] melica *Scheffer*: melicam *which may well be right*.
[2] dulces caricae *Scheffer*: dulcis carica.
[3] appositaque *Heinsius*.   [4] *So Buecheler*: atque hac.
[5] officii *Buecheler*: officio. *Fraenkel suggests* ⟨ae⟩ quo
[admonitus] officio.

---

[1] Not the famous Greek painter but an actor in tragedies
who flourished c. A.D. 40.

have you got no story? Will you not entertain us?
You used to be more pleasant company, and recite
blank verse very prettily, and put in songs too.
Dear, dear, all the sweet green figs are fallen!"
"Ah, yes," the man replied, "my galloping days are
over since I was taken with the gout. Otherwise,
in the days when I was a young fellow I nearly got
consumption with singing. How I could dance and
recite and imitate the talk in a barber's shop! Was
there ever my equal, except the one and only
Apelles?"[1] And he put his hand against his
mouth and whistled out some offensive stuff I did not
catch: he declared afterwards it was Greek.

Trimalchio himself also, after imitating a man with
a trumpet, looked round for his favourite, whom he
called Croesus. The creature had blear eyes and
very bad teeth, and was tying up an unnaturally
obese black puppy[2] in a green handkerchief, and
then putting a broken piece of bread on a chair, and
cramming it down the throat of the dog, who did not
want it and felt sick. This reminded Trimalchio of
his duties, and he ordered them to bring in Scylax,[3]
"the guardian of the house and the slaves." An
enormous dog on a chain was at once led in, and on
receiving a kick from the porter as a hint to lie down,
he curled up in front of the table. Then Trimalchio
threw him a bit of white bread and said, "No one
in my house loves me better than Scylax." The
favourite took offence at his lavish praise of the dog,
and put down the puppy, and encouraged her to
attack at once. Scylax, after the manner of dogs,

[2] Named *Margarita* "Pearl;" see below.
[3] Greek for young animal, a puppy in particular.

143

ingenio, taeterrimo latratu triclinium implevit Margaritamque Croesi paene laceravit. Nec intra rixam tumultus constitit, sed candelabrum etiam super mensam eversum et vasa omnia crystallina comminuit et oleo ferventi aliquot convivas respersit. Trimalchio ne videretur iactura motus, basiavit puerum ac iussit super dorsum ascendere suum. Non moratus ille usus est equo manuque plena[1] scapulas eius subinde verberavit, interque risum proclamavit: " Bucca, bucca,[2] quot sunt hic? " repressus ergo aliquamdiu Trimalchio camellam grandem iussit misceri . . . potiones dividi omnibus servis, qui ad pedes sedebant, adiecta exceptione: " Si quis " inquit " noluerit accipere, caput illi perfunde. Interdiu severa, nunc hilaria."

65   Hanc humanitatem insecutae sunt matteae, quarum etiam recordatio me, si qua est dicenti fides, offendit. Singulae enim gallinae altiles pro turdis circumlatae sunt et ova anserina pilleata, quae ut comessemus, ambitiosissime a nobis Trimalchio petiit dicens exossatas esse gallinas. Inter haec triclinii valvas lictor percussit, amictusque veste alba cum ingenti frequentia comissator intravit. Ego maiestate conterritus praetorem putabam venisse. Itaque temptavi assurgere et nudos pedes in terram deferre. Risit hanc trepidationem Agamemnon et

---

[1] plana *Scheffer.*
[2] bucco bucco *Mentel, Heinsius.*

---

[1] Perhaps *bucca* was a child's game (Hoodman Blind in English) where one child was blindfolded and the others touched him on the cheek, and asked him how many fingers,

of course, filled the dining-room with a most hideous barking, and nearly tore Croesus's little Pearl to pieces. And the uproar did not end with a dog-fight, for a lamp upset over the table, and broke all the crystal to pieces, and sprinkled some of the guests with hot oil. Trimalchio did not want to seem hurt at his loss, so he kissed his favourite, and told him to jump on his back. He mounted his horse at once and went on smacking Trimalchio's shoulders with his open hand, saying amid laughter, " How many are here, blind man's cheek? " [1] After some time Trimalchio calmed himself, and ordered a great bowl of wine to be mixed, and drinks to be served round to all the slaves, who were sitting at our feet, adding this provision: " If anyone refuses to take it, pour it over his head; business in the daytime and pleasure at night."

After this display of kindness, some savouries were brought in, the memory of which, as sure as I tell you this story, still makes me shudder. For instead of a fieldfare a fat chicken was brought round to each of us, and goose-eggs in caps, which Trimalchio kept asking us to eat with the utmost insistence, saying that they were chickens without the bones. Mean-while a priest's attendant [2] knocked at the dining-room door, and a reveller dressed in white came in with a large number of others. I was frightened by his official looks, and thought the mayor had arrived. So I tried to get up and plant my bare feet on the ground. Agamemnon laughed at my anxiety and

or how many children, had touched him. Or perhaps the modern *morra* is meant, as in Chapter 44.

[2] The attendant on a Sevir Augusti. See pp. 48–51.

" Contine te " inquit " homo stultissime. Habinnas
sevir est idemque lapidarius, qui videtur [1] monu-
menta optime facere."

Recreatus hoc sermone reposui cubitum, Habin-
namque intrantem cum admiratione ingenti spectabam. Ille autem iam ebrius uxoris suae umeris
imposuerat manus, oneratusque aliquot coronis
et unguento per frontem in oculos fluente praetorio
loco se posuit continuoque vinum et caldam poposcit.
Delectatus hac Trimalchio hilaritate et ipse capa-
ciorem poposcit scyphum quaesivitque, quomodo
acceptus essent. " Omnia " inquit " habuimus
praeter te; oculi enim mei hic erant. Et mehercules
bene fuit. Scissa [2] lautum novendiale [3] servo suo
misello faciebat, quem mortuum manu miserat. Et
puto, cum vicensimariis magnam mantissam habet;
quinquaginta enim millibus aestimant mortuum.
Sed tamen suaviter fuit, etiam si coacti sumus dimi-
66 dias potiones super ossucula eius effundere." " Tamen " inquit Trimalchio " quid habuistis in cena ? "
" Dicam " inquit " si potuero; nam tam bonae
memoriae sum, ut frequenter nomen meum obliviscar.
Habuimus tamen in primo porcum poculo [4] coronatum
et circa saviunculum [5] et gizeria optime facta [6] et

---

[1] videtur *Scheffer*: videretur. *Müller deletes the whole
clause* qui . . . facere.

[2] *The name is variously emended.*

[3] lautum novendiale *Buecheler*: laucum novendialem.
Heinsius reads lautam novendialem, *the word* cenam *to be
understood.* sacrum novendiale *Mentel, Scheffer.*

[4] botulo *Jak. Gronov.*

[5] saviunculum *Hildebrand*: sangunculum *Heraeus*: saucun-
culum.

[6] farcta *Jahn.*

said, " Control yourself, you silly fool! It is Habinnas of the priests' college, a monumental mason with a reputation for making first-class tombstones."

I was relieved by this news, and lay down in my place again, and watched Habinnas' entrance with great astonishment. He was already drunk, and had put his hands on his wife's shoulders; he had several wreaths on, and ointment was running down his forehead into his eyes. He sat down in the chief magistrate's place,[1] and at once called for wine and hot water. Trimalchio was delighted at his good humour, and demanded a larger cup for himself, and asked him how he had been received. " We had everything there except you," was the reply, " for my eyes were here with you. Yes, it was really splendid. Scissa [2] was having a funeral feast on the ninth day for her poor dear slave, whom she set free on his deathbed. And I believe she will have an enormous profit to record with the five per cent tax-collector, for they reckon that the dead man was worth fifty thousand.[3] But anyhow it was a pleasant affair, even if we did have to pour half our drinks over his lamented bones." " Ah," said Trimalchio, " but what did you have for dinner? " " I will tell you if I can," he said, " but my memory is in such a fine way that I often forget my own name. Well, first we had a pig crowned with a wine-cup, garnished with honey cakes, and giblets very well done, and

---

[1] The lowest seat on the middle couch, usually called the consul's seat, but here the highest official present took it.

[2] The name *Scissa* may be that of a man.

[3] She would pay a tax of five per cent, i.e. 2,500 sesterces, on his value.

certe betam [1] et panem autopyrum de suo sibi, quem
ego malo quam candidum; et vires facit, et cum mea
re [causa] [2] facio, non ploro. Sequens ferculum fuit
scriblita [3] frigida et super mel caldum infusum excellente Hispanum. Itaque de scriblita quidem non
minimum edi, de melle me usque tetigi. Circa cicer
et lupinum, calvae arbitratu et mala singula. Ego
tamen duo sustuli et ecce in mappa alligata habeo;
nam si aliquid muneris meo vernulae non tulero,
habebo convicium. Bene me admonet domina mea.
In prospectu habuimus ursinae frustum, de quo cum
imprudens Scintilla gustasset, paene intestina sua
vomuit; ego contra plus libram comedi, nam ipsum
aprum sapiebat. Et si, inquam, ursus homuncionem
comest, quanto magis homuncio debet ursum
comesse? In summo habuimus caseum mollem
ex sapa et cocleas singulas et cordae [4] frusta et
hepatia in catillis et ova pilleata et rapam et
senape et catillum concacatum, pax Palamedes.[5]
Etiam in alveo circumlata sunt oxycomina, unde
quidam etiam improbe ternos pugnos [6] sustulerunt.
67 Nam pernae missionem dedimus. Sed narra mihi,
Gai, rogo, Fortunata quare non recumbit?'' ''Quomodo nosti'' inquit ''illam'' Trimalchio ''nisi
argentum composuerit, nisi reliquias pueris diviserit,
aquam in os suum non coniciet.'' ''Atqui'' respondit

---

[1] cerebellam *Fröhner.*
[2] *deleted by Buecheler.*
[3] scriblita *here and in the next sentence ed. Patav.*: sciribilita.
[4] fordae *Heinsius*: cordis *Scheffer.*
[5] concacatum *Burman*: concagatum. *Perhaps* anguillam
conchas garum, mox pelamidas.
[6] improbe ternos pugnos *Buecheler*: improbi t.p. *Jak.
Gronov*: improbiter nos pugno.

eetroot of course, and pure wholemeal bread, which
prefer to white myself; it puts strength into you,
nd when I do my business I don't grumble. The
ext dish was a cold tart, with excellent Spanish
ine poured over warm honey. Indeed I ate a lot
f the tart, and gave myself such a soaking of honey.
'ease and lupines were handed, a choice of nuts and
n apple each. I took two myself, and I have got
hem here tied up in my napkin: for if I do not bring
ome present back for my pet slave-boy there will be
rouble. Oh! yes, my wife reminds me. There
vas a piece of bear in view.[1] Scintilla was rash
nough to taste it, and nearly brought up her own
aside. I ate over a pound myself, for it tasted like
roper wild boar. What I say is this, since bears eat
p us poor men, how much better right has a poor
han to eat up a bear? To finish up with we had
heese mellowed in new wine, and snails all round,
nd pieces of tripe, and liver in little dishes, and eggs
n caps, and turnip, and mustard, and a mucked up
lish—but hold hard, Palamedes.[2] Pickled olives
vere brought round in a dish, too, and some greedy
reatures took three fistfuls. For we had let the
am go. But tell me, Gaius, why is Fortunata not
t dinner?" "Do you not know her better?"
aid Trimalchio. "Until she has collected the silver,
nd divided the remains among the slaves, she will
ot let a drop of water pass her lips." "Oh," replied

---

[1] Or "in high regard."

[2] Meaning unknown. Perhaps the words hide (as a gloss?)
nx Palamedes—a dish "Palamedes"—i.e. of cranes. Cf.
*Martial XIII, lxxv. Earlier in the sentence I think *catillum*
t least is wrong, coming from *catillis* a little before.

Habinnas " nisi illa discumbit, ego me apoculo " [1] e
coeperat surgere, nisi signo dato Fortunata quate
amplius a tota familia esset vocata. Venit erg
galbino succincta cingillo, ita ut infra cerasina appare
ret tunica et periscelides tortae phaecasiaeque inau
ratae. Tunc sudario manus tergens, quod in coll
habebat, applicat se illi toro, in quo Scintilla [2] Habin
nae discumbebat uxor, osculataque plaudentem " es
te " inquit " videre ? "

Eo deinde perventum est, ut Fortunata armilla
suas crassissimis detraheret lacertis Scintillaequ
miranti ostenderet. Ultimo etiam periscelides re
solvit et reticulum aureum, quem ex obrussa ess
dicebat. Notavit haec Trimalchio iussitque afferr
omnia et " Videtis " inquit " mulieris [3] compedes
sic nos barcalae despoliamur. Sex pondo et selibra
debet habere. Et ipse nihilo minus habeo decen
pondo armillam ex millesimis Mercurii factam.
Ultimo etiam, ne mentiri videretur, stateram iussi
afferri et circumlatum approbari pondus. Nec melio
Scintilla, quae de cervice sua capsellam detraxi
aureolam, quam Felicionem appellabat. Inde du
crotalia protulit et Fortunatae in vicem consideranda
dedit et " Domini " inquit " mei beneficio nem
habet meliora." " Quid ? " inquit Habinnas " ex
catarissasti me, ut tibi emerem fabam vitream. Plan

---

[1] apoculo *ed. Patav.*: apocalo.
[2] *Fraenkel suggested deleting* Scintilla.
[3] mulieris *Scheffer*: muliebres *Heinsius*: mulieres.

---

[1] *barcala* is akin to *bardus* and *baro*, blockhead.

Habinnas, " but unless she is here I burn myself off," and he was just getting up, when at a given signal all the slaves called " Fortunata " four times and more. So she came in with a high yellow waist-band on, which allowed a cherry-red slip to appear under it, and twisted anklets, and white shoes embroidered with gold. She wiped her hands on a cloth which she had round her neck, took her place on the sofa, where Scintilla, Habinnas's wife, was lying, kissed her as she was clapping her hands, and said, ' Is it really you I see, dear ? "

Fortunata then went so far as to take the bracelets off her fat arms to exhibit them to Scintilla's admiring gaze. At last she even took off her anklets and her hair-net, which she said was eighteen carat. Trimal-chio saw this, and ordered the whole lot to be brought to him. " There," he said, " are a woman's fetters; that is how we poor fools [1] are plundered. She must have six pounds and a half of gold on her. I have got a bracelet myself, made out of the thou-sandth which I owe to Mercury,[2] that weighs not an ounce under ten pounds." At last, for fear we should think he was lying, he ordered the scales to be brought and had the weight carried round and tested. Scintilla was just as bad. She took off a little gold box from her neck, which she called her lucky box. Then she brought out two rattling earrings, and gave them to Fortunata to look at in her turn, and said, " Thanks to my husband's kindness, nobody has finer ones." " What ? " said Habinnas, " you cleaned me out to buy you a glass bean. I declare if I

[2] God of merchants; to him rich Romans apparently dedicated a contribution.

si filiam haberem, auriculas illi praeciderem. Mul
eres si non essent, omnia pro luto haberemus; num
hoc est caldum meiere et frigidum potare."

Interim mulieres sauciae inter se riserunt ebria
que [1] iunxerunt oscula, dum altera diligentiam matr
familiae iactat, altera delicias et indiligentiam vir
Dumque sic cohaerent, Habinnas furtim consurrex
pedesque Fortunatae correptos super lectum immisi
" Au au " illa proclamavit aberrante tunica supe
genua. Composita ergo in gremio Scinillae in
censissimam [2] rubore faciem sudario abscondit.

68   Interposito deinde spatio cum secundas mensa
Trimalchio iussisset afferri, sustulerunt servi omne
mensas et alias attulerunt, scobemque croco et mini
tinctam sparserunt et, quod nunquam ante videran
ex lapide speculari pulverem tritum. Statim Trima
chio " poteram quidem " inquit " hoc fericulo ess
contentus; secundas enim mensas habetis. Sed
quid belli habes, affer."

Interim puer Alexandrinus, qui caldam ministra
bat, luscinias coepit imitari clamante Trimalchion
subinde: " Muta." Ecce alius ludus. Servus q
ad pedes Habinnae sedebat, iussus, credo, a domin
suo proclamavit subito canora voce:

" Interea medium Aeneas iam classe tenebat."

---

[1] ebriaque *Müller*: ebrieque.
[2] incensissimam *or* indecentissimam *Reinesius*: indecer
imam.

---

[1] This means apparently we sweat for women and get col
thanks.

had a daughter I would cut off her ears. If there were no women, we should look on all gems as so much dirt; as it is, we piddle warm and drink cold."[1]

Meanwhile the tipsy wives laughed together, and gave each other drunken kisses, one prating of her merits as a housewife, the other of the favourites of her husband and his own demerits. While they were hobnobbing, Habinnas got up quietly, took Fortunata by the legs, and threw them up on the sofa. She shouted out, " Ow! Ow! " as her dress flew up over her knees. She took refuge in Scintilla's arms, and buried her burning red face in a napkin.

After an interval, Trimalchio ordered a further dessert-course of food to be brought in. The slaves took away all the tables, brought in others, and sprinkled about sawdust coloured with saffron and vermilion, and, what I had never seen before, powdered mica. Trimalchio at once said, " I might really be satisfied with this course; for you have got your fresh relays. But if there is anything nice, put it on."

Meanwhile a boy from Alexandria, who was handing hot water, proceeded to imitate a nightingale, and made Trimalchio shout " Oh! change the tune." Then there was another joke. A slave, who was sitting at the feet of Habinnas, began, by his master's orders I suppose, suddenly to declaim in a sing-song voice:

" Now with his fleet Aeneas held the main".[2]

[2] See Virgil, *Aeneid*, V, 1. Aeneas was the fictional founder of Rome, connecting Rome with Troy.

Nullus sonus unquam acidior percussit aures meas;
nam praeter errantis barbariae aut adiectum aut de-
minutum clamorem miscebat Atellanicos versus, ut
tunc primum me etiam Vergilius offenderit.   Lassus [1]
tamen, cum aliquando desisset,[2] [adiecit][3] Habinnas et " nunquam " inquit [4] " didicit, sed ego ad
circulatores eum mittendo erudibam.[5]   Itaque parem
non habet, sive muliones volet sive circulatores
imitari.   Desperatum [6] valde ingeniosus est: idem
sutor est, idem cocus idem pistor, omnis musae man-
cipium.   Duo tamen vitia habet, quae si non haberet,
esset omnium numerum: [7] recutitus est et stertit.
Nam quod strabonus est, non curo: sicut Venus
spectat.   Ideo nihil tacet, vix oculo mortuo unquam.
69 Illum emi trecentis [8] denariis."   Interpellavit loquentem Scintilla et " plane " inquit " non omnia
artificia servi nequam narras.   Agaga est; at curabo,
stigmam habeat."   Risit Trimalchio et " adcog-
nosco " inquit " Cappadocem: nihil sibi defraudat,
et mehercules laudo illum; hoc enim nemo parentat.
Tu autem, Scintilla, noli zelotypa esse.   Crede mihi,
et vos novimus.   Sic me salvum habeatis, ut ego sic
solebam ipsumam meam debattuere, ut etiam
dominus suspicaretur; et ideo me in vilicationem
relegavit.   Sed tace, lingua,[9] dabo panem."   Tanquam laudatus esset nequissimus servus, lucernam

[1] plausum *Buecheler.*   [2] desisset *Scheffer*: dedisset.
[3] *Fraenkel suggested deleting* adiecit.
[4] nunquam inquit *Buecheler*: nunquid.
[5] erudibam *Buecheler*: erudiebam *Jahn*: audibant.
[6] desperatum *Buecheler*: desperatus.
[7] numerum *Haase*: numerorum *Scheffer*: nummorum.
[8] emi trecentis *Scheffer*: emit retentis.
[9] lingua *Scheffer*: lingua iam *Heinsius*: linguam.

No sharper sound ever pierced my ears; for besides his making barbarous mistakes in raising or lowering his voice, he mixed up Atellane verses [1] with it, so that even Virgil jarred on me for the first time in my life. All the same, when he was tired and at last left off, Habinnas said, " He never went to school, but *I* educated him by sending him round the hawkers in the market. So he has no equal when he wants to imitate mule-drivers or hawkers. He is hopelessly clever; he is a cobbler too, a cook, a confectioner, a slave of all the talents. He has only two faults, and if he were rid of them he would be simply perfect. He is a Jew and he snores. For I do not mind his being cross-eyed; he has a look like Venus. So that is why he cannot keep silent, and scarcely ever shuts his eyes. I bought him for three hundred denarii." Scintilla interrupted his story by saying, " To be sure you have forgotten some of the tricks of the vile slave. He is a pimp; but I will see to it that he is branded." Trimalchio laughed and said, " Oh! I perceive he is a Cappadocian; [2] he does not deny himself anything, and, upon my word, I admire him; for no one honours a dead man's tomb with *that*. And please do not be jealous, Scintilla. Take my word for it, we know you women too. By my hope of salvation, I used to batter my own mistress, until even the master became suspicious; and so he banished me to a country stewardship. But peace, my tongue, and you shall have some bread." The worthless slave took a clay lamp out of his dress, as if

---

[1] See note at end of Chapter 53.
[2] Slaves from Cappadocia seem to have had a bad reputation.

de sinu fictilem protulit et amplius semihora tubicines
imitatus est [1] succinente Habinna et inferius labrum
manu deprimente. Ultimo etiam in medium processit et modo harundinibus quassis choraulas imitatus est, modo lacernatus cum flagello mulionum fata
egit, donec vocatum ad se Habinnas basiavit, po-
tionemque illi porrexit et " Tanto melior " inquit
" Massa, dono tibi caligas."

Nec ullus tot malorum finis fuisset, nisi epidipnis
esset allata, turdi siliginei [2] uvis passis nucibusque
farsi.[3] Insecuta sunt Cydonia etiam mala spinis con-
fixa, ut echinos efficerent. Et haec quidem tolerabilia erant, si non fericulum [4] longe monstrosius
effecisset, ut vel fame perire mallemus. Nam cum
positus esset, ut nos putabamus, anser altilis circaque
pisces et omnium genera avium, " ⟨Amici⟩ " [5] inquit
Trimalchio " quicquid videtis hic positum, de uno
corpore est factum." Ego, scilicet homo prudentissimus, statim intellexi quid esset, et respiciens
Agamemnonem " mirabor " inquam " nisi omnia ista
de ⟨cera⟩ [6] facta sunt aut certe de luto. Vidi Romae
Saturnalibus eiusmodi cenarum imaginem fieri."
70 Necdum finieram sermonem, cum Trimalchio ait :
" Ita crescam patrimonio, non corpore, ut ista cocus
meus de porco fecit. Non potest esse pretiosior

---

[1] *Fraenkel was inclined to delete* imitatus est.
[2] turdi siliginei *Heinsius*: turdis iligine.
[3] farsi *Heinsius*: farsis.
[4] fericulum *ed. Patav.*
[5] amici *added by Buecheler.*

he had been complimented, and imitated trumpeters for more than half an hour, Habinnas humming an accompaniment by pulling his lower lip down. Finally, he came right into the middle of the room, and shook a bunch of reeds in imitation of pipe-players, or gave us the mule-drivers' life, with a cloak and a whip, till Habinnas called him in and gave him a kiss, and offered him a drink, saying, " Better than ever, Massa. I will give you a pair of boots for that."

There would have been no end to our troubles if a last course had not been brought in, fieldfares made of fine meal and stuffed with raisins and nuts. There followed also quinces, stuck all over with thorns to look like sea-urchins. We could have borne this, if a far more fantastic dish had not driven us even to prefer death by starvation. What we took to be a fat goose, with fish and all kinds of birds round it, was put on, and then Trimalchio said, " My friends, whatever you see here on the table is made out of one body." With my usual intelligence, I knew at once what it was; I looked at Agamemnon and said, " I shall be surprised if the whole thing is not made out of wax, or, at any rate clay. I have seen sham dinners of this kind served in Rome at the Saturnalia." [1] I had not finished speaking when Trimalchio said, " As I hope to grow in gains and not in girth, my cook made the whole thing out of a pig. There could not be a more valuable fellow. If you

---

[1] See note on Chapter 58.

---

[6] defacta *H*: cera *added by Heinsius so as to read* de cera facta: de face facta *Brožele*: *Other suggestions have been made.*

homo. Volueris, de vulva [1] faciet piscem, de lardo palumbum, de perna turturem, de colaepio gallinam. Et ideo ingenio meo impositum est illi nomen bellissimum; nam Daedalus vocatur. Et quia bonam mentem habet, attuli illi Roma munus cultros Norico ferro.'' Quos statim iussit afferri inspectosque miratus est. Etiam nobis potestatem fecit, ut mucronem ad buccam probaremus.

Subito intraverunt duo servi, tanquam qui rixam ad lacum fecissent; certe in collo [2] adhuc amphoras habebant. Cum ergo Trimalchio ius inter litigantes diceret, neuter sententiam tulit decernentis, sed alterius amphoram fuste percussit. Consternati nos insolentia ebriorum intentavimus oculos in proeliantes notavimusque ostrea pectinesque e gastris [3] labentia, quae collecta puer lance circumtulit. Has lautitias aequavit ingeniosus cocus; in craticula enim argentea cochleas attulit et tremula taeterrimaque voce cantavit.

Pudet referre, quae secuntur: inaudito enim more pueri capillati attulerunt unguentum in argentea pelve pedesque recumbentium unxerunt, cum ante crura talosque corollis vinxissent. Hinc ex eodem unguento in vinarium atque lucernam aliquantum [4] est infusum.

Iam coeperat Fortunata velle saltare, iam Scintilla

---

[1] vulva *Hadrianides*: bulba *Scheffer*: bulla.
[2] collo *Heinsius*: iugo *Fröhner*: loro *Muncker*: loco.
[3] gastris *Muncker*: castris.
[4] aliquantum *Heinsius*: liquatum.

want it, he will make you a fish out of a sow's womb, a
woodpigeon out of bacon, a turtledove out of a ham,
and a chicken out of a knuckle of pork. That gave
me the idea of putting a very pretty name on him;
he is called Daedalus.[1] And because he is so intelligent, I brought him back from Rome some knives,
made of steel of Noricum,[2] as a present." He had
these knives brought in at once, and contemplated
them with admiration. He even allowed us to try the
edge on our cheeks.

Suddenly two slaves came in who had apparently
been fighting at a water-tank; at least they still had
waterpots on their necks. Trimalchio sat in judgment on the dispute, but neither of them accepted
his decision, and they smashed each other's waterpots
with sticks. We were amazed at their drunken folly,
and stared at them fighting, and then we saw oysters
and scallops fall out of the pots, and a boy picked
them up and brought them round on a dish. The
clever cook was a match for this exhibition; he
offered us snails on a silver gridiron, and sang in an
extremely ugly quavering voice.

I am ashamed to tell you what followed: in defiance of all convention, some long-haired boys
brought ointment in a silver basin, and anointed our
feet as we lay, after winding little garlands round our
feet and ankles. A quantity of the same ointment
was then poured into the mixing-bowl and the lamp.

Fortunata had now grown anxious to dance; Scin-

---

[1] On Daedalus, see note on Chapter 52. The name was used
for a Jack-of-all-trades.

[2] Noricum was a territory between the River Danube and
the Alps.

frequentius plaudebat quam loquebatur, cum Trimalchio " Permitto " inquit " Philargyre [et Carrio] [1] etsi prasinianus es famosus, dic et Menophilae, contubernali tuae, discumbat." Quid multa? paene de lectis deiecti sumus, adeo totum triclinium familia occupaverat. Certe ego notavi super me positum cocum, qui de porco anserem fecerat,[2] muria condimentisque fetentem. Nec contentus fuit recumbere, sed continuo Ephesum tragoedum coepit imitari et subinde dominum suum sponsione provocare " si prasinus proximis circensibus primam palmam."

71   Diffusus hac contentione Trimalchio " amici " inquit " et servi homines sunt et aeque unum lactem biberunt, etiam si illos malus fatus oppresserit.[3] Tamen me salvo cito aquam liberam gustabunt. Ad summam, omnes illos in testamento meo manu mitto. Philargyro etiam fundum lego et contubernalem suam, Carioni [4] quoque insulam et vicesimam et lectum stratum. Nam Fortunatam meam heredem facio, et commendo illam omnibus amicis meis. Et haec ideo omnia publico, ut familia mea iam nunc sic me amet tanquam mortuum." Gratias agere omnes indulgentiae coeperant domini, cum ille oblitus nugarum exemplar testamenti iussit afferri et totum a primo ad ultimum ingemescente familia recitavit. Respiciens deinde Habinnam " quid dicis " inquit

---

[1] et Carrio H: et Cario Buecheler: Kaibel deletes. Cp. Chapter 71.

[2] Fraenkel would delete the clause qui . . . fecerat.

[3] oppressit Buecheler.   [4] Carioni Buecheler: Carrioni.

---

[1] These persons were two of Trimalchio's slaves. He addresses one of them, Philargyrus, as a supporter of the green

tilla clapped her hands more often than she spoke,
when Trimalchio said, " Philargyrus, you, though
you are a damned wearer of the green,[1] may sit
down and tell your good woman, Menophila, to do
the same." I need hardly say that we were nearly
pushed off the sofas with the slaves crowding into
every seat. Anyhow, I noticed that the cook, who
had made a goose out of the pig, sat stinking of pickle
and sauces just above me. Not satisfied with having
a seat, he at once proceeded to imitate the tragedian [2]
Ephesus, and then invited his own master to make a
bet on the green winning the first prize in the next
games.

Trimalchio expanded at this dispute and said,
" Ah, my friends, a slave is a man and drank his
mother's milk like ourselves, even if cruel fate has
trodden him down. Yes, and if I live they shall soon
taste the water of freedom. In fact I am setting
them all free in my will. I am leaving a property and
his good woman to Philargyrus as well, and to Cario
a block of buildings, and his manumission fees, and a
bed and bedding. I am making Fortunata my heir,
and I recommend her to all my friends. I am making
all this known so that my slaves may love me now as
if I were dead." They all went on to thank their
master for his kindness, when he turned serious, and
had a copy of the will brought in, which he read aloud
from beginning to end, while the slaves moaned and
groaned. Then he looked at Habinnas and said,

colours in competitions in the circus. Competitors there wore
one of four colours: blue, green, white, red.
    [2] Ephesus: no tragic actor or composer with this name is
known.

" amice carissime? Aedificas monumentum meum, quemadmodum te iussi? Valde te rogo, ut secundum pedes statuae meae catellam ponas [1] et coronas et unguenta et Patraitis omnes pugnas, ut mihi contingat tuo beneficio post mortem vivere; praeterea ut sint in fronte pedes centum, in agrum pedes ducenti. Omne genus enim poma volo sint circa cineres meos, et vinearum largiter. Valde enim falsum est vivo quidem domos cultas esse, non curari eas, ubi diutius nobis habitandum est. Et ideo ante omnia adici volo: ' hoc monumentum heredem non sequitur.' [2] Ceterum erit mihi curae, ut testamento caveam, ne mortuus iniuriam accipiam. Praeponam enim unum ex libertis sepulcro meo custodiae causa, ne in monumentum meum populus cacatum currat. Te rogo, ut naves etiam . . . monumenti mei [3] facias plenis velis euntes, et me in tribunali sedentem praetextatum cum anulis aureis quinque et nummos in publico de sacculo effundentem; scis enim, quod epulum dedi binos denarios. Faciantur,[4] si tibi videtur, et triclinia. Facias [5] et totum populum sibi suaviter facientem. Ad dexteram meam ponas

---

[1] ponas *Buecheler*: fingas *Scheffer*: pingas, *which may be right.*
[2] sequitur *Buecheler*: sequatur.
[3] *Keller suggested adding* ⟨in fronte⟩ *before* monumenti. *Müller in his 2nd edition deletes* monumenti mei.
[4] faciantur *Goes*: faciatur.
[5] facias *Buecheler*: facies.

---

[1] See note on Chapter 52.
[2] The initials *h.m.h.n.s.* of the Latin words were often put upon monuments.
[3] The words indicating the part of the monument on which Trimalchio wants ships to be carved are missing.

" Now tell me, my dear friend: you will erect a monument as I have directed? I beg you earnestly to put up round the feet of my statue my little dog, and some wreaths, and bottles of perfume, and all the fights of Petraites,[1] so that your kindness may bring me a life after death; and I want the monument to have a frontage of one hundred feet and to be two hundred feet in depth. For I should like to have all kinds of fruit growing round my ashes, and plenty of vines. It is quite wrong for a man to decorate his house while he is alive, and not to trouble about the house where he must make a longer stay. So above all things I want added to the inscription, ' This monument does not descend to my heir.'[2] I shall certainly take care to provide in my will against any injury being done to me when I am dead. I am appointing one of the freedmen to be caretaker of the tomb and prevent the common people from running up and defiling it. I beg you to put ships in full sail . . .[3] of monument, and me sitting in official seat, wearing five gold rings and distributing coin publicly out of a bag;[4] you remember that I gave a free dinner worth two denarii a head. I should like you to make a representation of a dining-room set of couches, if you can arrange it. And represent also the whole people there enjoying themselves. On my right hand put a statue of dear

[4] Members of the college of Augustus were allowed on important public occasions to sit on a throne and to wear a *toga praetexta*. Trimalchio may have earned the right to wear gold rings by giving a public dinner: after his term of office as a Sevir Augusti (pp. 48–51) expired, he would not be entitled to wear them. See c. 32, where he wears a ring made to look like gold at a distance.

statuam Fortunatae meae columbam tenentem: et
catellam cingulo alligatam ducat: et cicaronem
meum, et amphoras copiosas [1] gypsatas, ne effluant
vinum. Et urnam [2] licet fractam sculpas, et super
eam puerum plorantem. Horologium in medio, ut
quisquis horas inspiciet, velit nolit, nomen meum
legat. Inscriptio quoque vide diligenter si haec satis
idonea tibi videtur: ' C. Pompeius Trimalchio Maece-
natianus hic requiescit. Huic seviratus absenti
decretus est. Cum posset in omnibus decuriis Romae
esse, tamen noluit. Pius, fortis, fidelis, ex parvo
crevit, sestertium reliquit trecenties, nec unquam
philosophum audivit. Vale: et tu.' "

72   Haec ut dixit Trimalchio, flere coepit ubertim.
Flebat et Fortunata, flebat et Habinnas, tota denique
familia, tanquam in funus rogata, lamentatione triclinium implevit. Immo iam coeperam etiam ego
plorare, cum Trimalchio " Ergo " inquit " cum
sciamus nos morituros esse, quare non vivamus? Sic
vos felices videam, coniciamus nos in balneum, meo
periculo, non paenitebit. Sic calet tanquam furnus."
" Vero, vero," inquit Habinnas " de una die duas

---

[1] copiose *P. George.*   [2] urnam *Jak. Gronov:* unam.

---

[1] I feel that the words *ne effluant* (or *effluat?*) *vinum* are an
intruded remark.
[2] Trimalchio was allowed to have this name because he had
been in the service of a patron named Maecenas before he
became a slave in the family of the Pompeii. Slaves were
allowed to retain their old master's name on transfer in order

Fortunata holding a dove, and let her be leading a
little dog with a waistband on; and my dear little
boy, and big jars sealed with gypsum, so that they
may not let the wine run out.[1] And have a broken
urn carved with a boy weeping over it. And a sun-
dial in the middle, so that anyone who looks at the
time will read my name whether he likes it or not.
And again, please think carefully whether this inscription seems to you quite appropriate: 'Here
lieth Gaius Pompeius Trimalchio, freedman of
Maecenas.[2] The degree of Priest of Augustus was
conferred upon him in his absence. He might have
been attendant on any magistrate in Rome, but
refused it.[3] God-fearing, gallant, constant, he grew
from very little and left thirty millions. He never
listened to a philosopher. Fare thee well, Trimalchio: and thou too, passer-by.'"

After saying this, Trimalchio began to weep floods
of tears. Fortunata wept, Habinnas wept, and then
all the slaves began as if they had been invited to his
funeral, and filled the dining-room with lamentation.
I had even begun to lift up my voice myself, when
Trimalchio said, "Well, well, if we know we must die,
why should we not live? As I hope for your happiness, let us jump into a bath. My life on it, you will
never regret it. It is as hot as a furnace." "Very
true, very true," said Habinnas, "making two days

to prevent confusion arising from similarities in their names
where they were very numerous.
  [3] Trimalchio boasts that if he had chosen to go to Rome as
a freedman he could have become a member of the decuries,
the orders or guilds which supplied the lower branches of the
public service, e.g. lictors, scribes, criers, and street officers.

facere, nihil malo " nudisque consurrexit pedibus et
Trimalchionem gaudentem [1] subsequi ⟨coepit.⟩ [2]

Ego respiciens ad Ascylton " Quid cogitas? "
inquam " ego enim si videro balneum, statim expira-
bo." " Assentemur " ait ille " et dum illi balneum
petunt, nos in turba exeamus." Cum haec placuis-
sent, ducente per porticum Gitone ad ianuam venimus, ubi canis catenarius tanto nos tumultu excepit,
ut Ascyltos etiam in piscinam ceciderit. Nec non
ego quoque ebrius,[3] [qui etiam pictum timueram
canem,[4]] dum natanti opem fero, in eundem gurgitem
tractus sum. Servavit nos tamen atriensis, qui
interventu suo et canem placavit et nos trementes
extraxit in siccum. Et Giton quidem iam dudum
se ratione [5] acutissima redemerat a cane; quicquid
enim a nobis acceperat de cena, latranti sparserat, at
ille avocatus cibo furorem suppresserat. Ceterum
cum algentes udique [6] petissemus ab atriense, ut nos
extra ianuam emitteret, " Erras " inquit " si putas
te exire hac posse, qua venisti. Nemo unquam
convivarum per eandem ianuam emissus est; alia
intrant, alia exeunt." Quid faciamus homines miser-
rimi et novi generis labyrintho inclusi, quibus lavari
iam coeperat votum esse? Ultro ergo rogavimus,
ut nos ad balneum duceret, proiectisque vestimentis,
quae Giton in aditu siccare coepit, balneum intravimus, angustum scilicet et cisternae frigidariae simile,

73

---

[1] gaudentem *H*: gradientem *Reinesius*: plaudentem *Jacobs*,
Wehle.
[2] coepit *added by Burman.*   [3] exterritus *Jahn.*
[4] *Müller deletes* qui . . . canem, *rightly.*
[5] se ratione *Scheffer*: servatione.
[6] udique *Buecheler*: utique.

out of one is my chief delight." And he got up with bare feet and proceeded to follow Trimalchio, who was now happy again.

I looked at Ascyltos and said, " What do you think? I shall die on the spot at the very sight of a bath." " Oh! let us say yes," he replied, " and we will slip away in the crowd while they are making for the bath." This was agreed, and Giton led us through the gallery to the door, where the dog on the chain welcomed us with such a noise that Ascyltos fell straight into the fish-pond. As I [who had been terrified even of a painted dog] [1] was drunk too, I fell into the same abyss while I was helping him in his struggles to swim. But the porter by his intervention pacified the dog and saved us, and pulled us shivering on to dry land. Giton had ransomed himself from the dog some time before by a very cunning plan; when it barked he threw it all the pieces we had given him at dinner, and food distracted the beast from his anger. But when, chilled to the bone and wet, we asked the porter at least to let us out of the door, he replied, " You are wrong if you suppose you can go out at the door you came in by. None of the guests are ever let out by the same door; they come in at one and go out by another." There was nothing to be done, we were victims enwound in a new labyrinth, and the idea of washing had begun to grow pleasant, so we asked him instead to show us the bath, and after throwing off our clothes, which Giton then dried in the front hall, we went in. It was a tiny place like a cold-water cistern,[2] and

---

[1] See Chapter 29.   [2] J. Sullivan suspects this clause.

in quo Trimalchio rectus stabat. Ac ne sic quidem
putidissimam eius iactationem [1] licuit effugere; nam
nihil melius esse dicebat quam sine turba lavari, et eo
ipso loco aliquando pistrinum fuisse. Deinde ut
lassatus consedit, invitatus balnei sono diduxit usque
ad cameram [2] os ebrium et coepit Menecratis cantica
lacerare, sicut illi dicebant, qui linguam eius intellege-
bant. Ceteri convivae circa labrum manibus nexis
currebant et gingilipho ingenti clamore exsonabant.
Alii autem [aut] [3] restrictis manibus anulos de pavimento conabantur tollere aut posito genu cervices
post terga flectere et pedum extremos pollices
tangere. Nos, dum alii sibi ludos faciunt, in solium,
quod Trimalchioni vaporabatur,[4] descendimus.

Ergo ebrietate discussa in aliud triclinium deducti
sumus, ubi Fortunata disposuerat lautitias [suas] [5]
ita ut supra ⟨. . .⟩ lucernas aeneolosque piscatores
notavimus [6] et mensas totas argenteas calicesque circa
fictiles inauratos et vinum in conspectu sacco defluens.
Tum Trimalchio " Amici " inquit " hodie servus meus
barbatoriam fecit, homo praefiscini frugi et micarius.
Itaque tangomenas faciamus et usque in lucem cene-
74 mus." Haec dicente eo gallus gallinaceus cantavit.
Qua voce confusus Trimalchio vinum sub mensa iussit

---

[1] eius iactationem *Heinsius*: ei actionem.
[2] *Nisbet would delete* usque ad cameram.
[3] *Deleted by Buecheler.*
[4] vaporabatur *Buecheler : there are other suggestions*: perva-
patur *H, but* al parabatur *in margin; which supports Heinsius'*
praeparabatur.
[5] *apparently marked for deletion in H* (su̱a̱s): *Müller deletes*
ita ut supra *also and puts a lacuna after* supra.
[6] notavimus *Müller*: notaverim.

Trimalchio was standing upright in it. We were not allowed to escape his filthy bragging even there; he declared that there was nothing nicer than washing out of a crowd, and told us that there had once been a bakery on that very spot. He then became tired and sat down, and the echoes of the bathroom encouraged him to open his tipsy jaws to the ceiling and go on to murder Menecrates's songs,[1] as I was told by those who could understand what he said. Other guests joined hands and ran round the bath, roaring with obstreperous laughter at the top of their voices. Some again had their hands tied behind their backs and tried to pick up rings from the floor, or knelt down and bent their heads backwards and tried to touch the tips of their big toes. While the others were amusing themselves, we went down into a deep bath which was being heated for Trimalchio.

Then, having got rid of the effects of our liquor, we were led into another dining-room, where Fortunata had laid out her treasures, so that over the lamps we saw . . . little bronze fishermen, and tables of solid silver, and clay-made cups with gold settings, and wine being strained through a cloth before our eyes. Then Trimalchio said, " Gentlemen, a slave of mine is celebrating his first shave to-day: an honest, cheese-paring fellow, in a good hour be it spoken. So let us drink deep [2] and keep up dinner till dawn."

Just as he was speaking, a cock crew. The noise upset Trimalchio, and he had wine poured under the

[1] Menecrates was a harp-player specially honoured by Nero (Suetonius, *Nero*, c. 30).

[2] See note on Chapter 34.

effundi lucernamque etiam mero spargi.   Immo anulum traiecit in dexteram manum et " non sine causa "
inquit " hic bucinus signum dedit; nam aut incendium oportet fiat, aut aliquis in vicinia animam abi-
ciet.   Longe a nobis.   Itaque quisquis hunc indicem
attulerit, corollarium accipiet."   Dicto citius de
vicinia [1] gallus allatus est, quem Trimalchio ⟨occidi⟩ [2]
iussit, ut aeno coctus [3] fieret.   Laceratus igitur ab
illo doctissimo coco, qui paulo ante de porco aves
piscesque fecerat, in caccabum est coniectus.   Dumque Daedalus potionem ferventissimam haurit,
Fortunata mola buxea piper trivit.

Sumptis igitur matteis respiciens ad familiam Trimalchio " Quid vos " inquit " adhuc non cenastis?
Abite, ut alii veniant ad officium."   Subiit igitur alia
classis, et illi quidem exclamavere: " Vale Gai," hi
autem: " Ave Gai."   Hinc primum hilaritas nostra
turbata est; nam cum puer non inspeciosus inter
novos intrasset ministros, invasit eum Trimalchio et
osculari diutius coepit.   Itaque Fortunata, ut ex
aequo ius firmum approbaret, male dicere Trimalchioni [4] coepit et purgamentum dedecusque praedi-
care, qui non contineret libidinem suam.   Ultimo
etiam adiecit: " canis."   Trimalchio contra offensus
convicio calicem in faciem Fortunatae immisit.   Illa,
tanquam oculum perdidisset, exclamavit manusque

----

[1] *Müller deletes* de vicinia.
[2] occidi *added by Buecheler, perhaps needlessly.*
[3] oenococtus *Orioli.*
[4] Trimalchioni *Buecheler:* Trimalchionem.

table,[1] and even the lamp sprinkled with pure wine. Further, he changed a ring onto his right hand, and said, " That trumpeter did not give his signal without a reason. Either there must be a fire, or some one close by is just going to give up the ghost. Lord, save us! So anyone who catches the informer shall have a reward." He had scarcely spoken, when the cock was brought in from somewhere near. Trimalchio ordered it to be killed and cooked in a saucepan. So he was cut up by the learned cook who had made birds and fishes out of a pig a little while before, and thrown into a cooking-pot. And while Daedalus took a long drink very hot, Fortunata ground up pepper in a box-wood mill.

After the delicacies were eaten, Trimalchio looked at the slaves and said, " Why have you not had dinner yet? Be off, and let some others come and wait." So another brigade appeared, and the old lot shouted, " Gaius, good-bye," and the new ones, " Hail! Gaius." After this, our jollity received its first shock; a rather comely boy came in among the fresh waiters, and Trimalchio took him and proceeded to kiss him warmly. So Fortunata, to assert her rights at law, proceeded to abuse Trimalchio, and called him a dirty disgrace for not holding his lust in check. At last she even added, " You hound." Her cursing annoyed Trimalchio, and he let fly a cup in her face. She shrieked as if her eye had been put

[1] Wine under the table: see note on p. 47. But here Trimalchio thinks there must be a fire somewhere and causes wine to be spilt under the table instead of the usual water which, to avert the omen, was so poured if fire has been mentioned at a banquet. Pliny, *N.H.*, XXVIII, 26.

trementes ad faciem suam admovit.   Consternata est
etiam Scintilla trepidantemque sinu suo texit.   Immo puer quoque officiosus urceolum frigidum ad malam eius admovit, super quem incumbens Fortunata
gemere ac flere coepit.   Contra Trimalchio " Quid
enim ? " inquit " ambubaia non meminit [1] se de [2]
machina ?   Inde illam [3] sustuli, hominem inter homines feci.   At inflat se tanquam rana, et in sinum
suum non spuit,[4] codex, non mulier.   Sed hic, qui in
pergula natus est, aedes non somniatur.   Ita genium
meum propitium habeam, curabo, domata sit Cassandra caligaria.   Et ego, homo dipundiarius, sestertium centies accipere potui.   Scis tu me non mentiri.
Agatho unguentarius † here proxime † [5] seduxit me
et ' Suadeo ' inquit ' non patiaris genus tuum
interire.'   At ego dum bonatus ago et nolo videri
levis, ipse mihi asciam in crus impegi.   Recte, curabo,
me unguibus quaeras.   Et ut depraesentiarum intel-
ligas, quid tibi feceris : Habinna, nolo, statuam eius
in monumento meo ponas, ne mortuus quidem lites
habeam.   Immo, ut sciat me posse malum dare, nolo,
me mortuum basiet."

75   Post hoc fulmen Habinnas rogare coepit, ut iam
HL desineret irasci et | " Nemo " inquit " nostrum non
H peccat.   Homines sumus, non dei." | Idem et Scintilla

---

[1] meminit *Heinsius*: me misit.   *The suggestion* ambubaiam
non meminisse!   *of Nisbet is reasonable.*

[2] se de *H*: sed de *Buecheler.*

[3] machina? inde illam *Fraenkel*: machina illam *Reiske*:
machillam illam *H.*   *In his 2nd edition Müller reads* meminit?
[se] de machina illam.

[4] non spuit *Reiske*: conspuit.

[5] *Of various conjectures I prefer Nisbet's.   He would simply
delete* here.

out, and lifted her trembling hands to her face. Scintilla was frightened too, and shielded her quivering friend with her arms. While an officious slave held a cool little jar to her cheek, Fortunata leaned over it and went on to groan and cry. But Trimalchio said, "What is it all about? Doesn't this chorus-girl remember that she's from the sale-platform? That's where I took her from, and made her one of ourselves. But she puffs herself up like a frog, and does not spit [1] onto her bosom; a log she is, not a woman. But if you were born in a hut you cannot dream of a palace. Damn my soul if I do not properly tame this shameless Cassandra.[2] And I might have married ten million, two-penny fool that I was! You know I am speaking the truth. Agatho, a perfumer of the rich woman next door, took me aside quite recently and said, ' I entreat you not to let your family die out.' But I, acting like a good chap, didn't wish to seem fickle, and so I have stuck the axe into my own leg. Very well, I will make you want to dig me up with your finger-nails. But you shall understand what you have done for yourself straight away. Habinnas, do not put any statue of her on my tomb, or I shall have nagging even when I am dead. And to show that I can do her a bad turn, I will not have her kiss me even when I am laid out."

After this flash of lightning Habinnas proceeded to ask him to moderate his wrath. " We all have our faults," he said, " we are men, not gods," Scintilla

---

[1] Which she ought to do, being so lucky.
[2] Cassandra, Trojan priestess who had fits of madness, was a type of passion, and a Cassandra " in a soldier's top-boots " (*caligaria*) is a brutal strong woman.

flens dixit ac per genium eius Gaium appellando
rogare coepit, ut se frangeret.[1] Non tenuit ultra
lacrimas Trimalchio et " Rogo " inquit " Habinna,
sic peculium tuum fruniscaris: si quid perperam feci,
in faciem meam inspue. Puerum basiavi frugalis-
simum, non propter formam, sed quia frugi est:
decem partes dicit,[2] librum ab oculo legit, thraecium [3]
sibi de diariis fecit, arcisellium de suo paravit et duas
trullas. Non est dignus quem in oculis feram? sed
Fortunata vetat. Ita tibi videtur, fulcipedia?
suadeo, bonum tuum concoquas, milva, et me non
facias [4] ringentem, amasiuncula: alioquin experieris
cerebrum meum. Nosti me: quod semel destinavi,
clavo tabulari [5] fixum est. Sed vivorum meminderi-
mus. Vos rogo, amici, ut vobis suaviter sit. Nam
ego quoque tam fui quam vos estis, sed virtute mea
ad hoc perveni. Corcillum est quod homines facit,
cetera quisquilia omnia. ' Bene emo, bene vendo';
alius alia vobis dicet. Felicitate dissilio. Tu autem,
sterteia,[6] etiamnum ploras? iam curabo, fatum tuum
plores. Sed, ut coeperam dicere, ad hanc me fortunam frugalitas mea perduxit. Tam magnus ex
Asia veni, quam hic candelabrus est. Ad summam,

---

[1] se frangeret *Heinsius*: effrangeret.
[2] didicit *Goes*.
[3] Thraecium *or* thoracium *Orelli*: pretium *Scheffer*:
teruncium *Heinsius*: thretium.
[4] facias *Mentel*: facies.
[5] trabali *Scheffer*.
[6] sterceia *Orioli*.

cried and said the same, called him Gaius and proceeded to ask him by his guardian angel to unbend.
Trimalchio no longer restrained his tears, and said,
" Habinnas, please, as you hope to enjoy your money,
spit in my face if I have done anything wrong. I
kissed that excellent boy not because he is beautiful,
but because he is excellent: he can do division and
read books at sight, he has bought a suit of Thracian [1]
armour out of his day's wages, purchased a round-
backed chair with his own money, and two ladles.
Does he not deserve to be treated well by me?
But Fortunata will not have it. Is that your feeling,
my high-heeled hussy? I advise you to chew what
you have bitten off, you she-kite, and not make me
show my teeth, my little dear: otherwise you shall
know what my anger is. Mark my words: when
once my mind is made up, the thing is fixed with a
drawing-pin.[2] But we will think of the living.
Please make yourselves comfortable, gentlemen.
I was once just what you are, but by my own merits
I have come to this. A bit of sound sense is what
makes men; the rest is all rubbish. ' I buy well
and sell well ': some people will tell you differently.
I am bursting with happiness. What, you snorer
in bed, are you still whining? I will take care that
you have something to whine over. Well, as I was
just saying, self-denial has brought me into this
fortune. When I came from Asia I was about as
tall as this candle-stick. In fact I used to measure

[1] As if for use by a certain kind of gladiator in the arena.
See pages 90–91.
[2] *clavus tabularis*, a nail for thin wood; but one expects
clavus trabalis, a nail for thick wood.

quotidie me solebam ad illum metiri,[1] et ut celerius
rostrum barbatum haberem, labra de lucerna unge-
bam. Tamen ad delicias [femina] [2] ipsimi [domini]
annos quattuordecim fui. Nec turpe est, quod
dominus iubet. Ego tamen et ipsimae [dominae]
satis faciebam. Scitis, quid dicam: taceo, quia non
76 sum de gloriosis. Ceterum, quemadmodum di
volunt, dominus in domo factus sum, et ecce cepi
ipsimi cerebellum. Quid multa? coheredem me
Caesari fecit, et accepi [3] patrimonium laticlavium.
Nemini tamen nihil satis est. Concupivi negotiari.
Ne multis vos morer, quinque naves aedificavi, oneravi vinum—et tunc erat contra aurum—misi Romam.
Putares me hoc iussisse: omnes naves naufragarunt,
factum, non fabula. Uno die Neptunus trecenties
sestertium devoravit. Putatis me defecisse? Non
mehercules mi haec iactura gusti fuit, tanquam nihil
facti. Alteras feci maiores et meliores et feliciores,[4]
ut nemo non me virum fortem diceret. Scitis,
magna navis magnam fortitudinem habet. Oneravi
rursus vinum, lardum, fabam, seplasium, mancipia.
Hoc loco Fortunata rem piam fecit; omne enim
aurum suum, omnia vestimenta vendidit et mi
centum aureos in manu posuit. Hoc fuit peculii
mei fermentum. Cito fit, quod di volunt. Uno
cursu centies sestertium corrotundavi. Statim re-

---

[1] metiri *Scheffer*: me uri.
[2] femina *and* domini *and* (*below*) dominae *deleted by Bue-*
cheler.
[3] accepi *Scheffer*: accepit.
[4] *P. George would delete* et feliciores.

myself by it every day, and grease my lips from the lamp to grow a beard the quicker. Still, I was my master's favourite for fourteen years. No disgrace in obeying your master's orders. Well, I used to amuse my mistress too. You know what I mean; I say no more, I am not a conceited man. Then, as the Gods willed, I became the real master of the house, and simply had his brains in my pocket. I need only add that my master made me joint residuary legatee with Caesar,[1] and came into an estate fit for a senator.[2] But no one is satisfied with nothing. I conceived a passion for business. I will not keep you a moment—I built five ships, got a cargo of wine—which was worth its weight in gold at the time—and sent them to Rome. You may think it was a put-up job; every one was wrecked, truth and no fairy-tales. Neptune gulped down thirty million in one day. Do you think I lost heart? Lord! no, I no more tasted my loss than if nothing had happened. I built some more, bigger, better and also luckier, so that no one could say I was not a brave man. You know, a huge ship has great gallantry about her. I got another cargo of wine, bacon, beans, perfumes, and slaves. Fortunata did a noble thing at that time; she sold all her jewellery and all her clothes, and put a hundred gold pieces into my hand. They were the leaven of my fortune. What God wishes soon happens. I made a clear ten million on one voyage. I at once

---

[1] It was common, and often prudent, for a rich man under the early Empire to mention the Emperor in his will.

[2] *laticlavius* means " belonging to the broad edging of purple " which senators were entitled to wear.

demi fundos omnes, qui patroni mei fuerant. Aedi-
fico domum, venalicia coemo iumenta; quicquid tan-
gebam, crescebat tanquam favus. Postquam coepi
plus habere, quam tota patria mea habet, manum
de tabula: sustuli me de negotiatione et coepi
libertos faenerare. Et sane nolentem me negotium
meum agere exhortavit mathematicus, qui venerat
forte in coloniam nostram, Graeculio, Serapa[1]
nomine, consiliator deorum. Hic mihi dixit etiam ea,
quae oblitus eram; ab acia et acu mi omnia exposui;[2] intestinas meas noverat; tantum quod
mihi non dixerat, quid pridie cenaveram. Putasses
77 illum semper mecum habitasse. Rogo, Habinna—
puto, interfuisti—: 'Tu dominam tuam de rebus
illis[3] fecisti. Tu parum felix in amicos[4] es. Nemo
unquam tibi parem gratiam refert. Tu latifundia
possides. Tu viperam sub ala nutricas' et, quod
vobis non dixerim, et nunc mi restare vitae annos
triginta et menses quattuor et dies duos. Praeterea
cito accipiam hereditatem. Hoc mihi dicit fatus
meus. Quod si contigerit fundos Apuliae iungere,
satis vivus pervenero. Interim dum Mercurius
vigilat, aedificavi hanc domum. Ut scitis, casula[5]
erat; nunc templum est. Habet quattuor cenationes,
cubicula viginti, porticus marmoratos duos, susum
cenationem,[6] cubiculum in quo ipse dormio, viperae

---

[1] Serapio *Heinsius.*
[2] exposuit *Scheffer*: exposcit.
[3] pusillis *Heinsius.*
[4] amicis *Scheffer.*
[5] casula *Heinsius*: casa *ed. Patav.*: cusuc.
[6] cenationem *Scheffer*: lavationem *Salonius*: cellationem.

bought up all the estates which had belonged to my
patron. I built a house, and bought slaves and
cattle; whatever I touched grew like a honey-comb.
When I came to have more than the whole revenues
of my own country, I threw up the game: I retired
from active work and proceeded to finance freedmen.
I was quite unwilling to go on with my work when I
was encouraged by an astrologer who happened to
come to our town, a little Greek called Serapa, who
knew the secrets of the Gods. He told me things
that I had forgotten myself; explained everything
from thread and needle upwards; knew my own
inside, and only fell short of telling me what I had
had for dinner the day before. You would have
thought he had always lived with me. You remember, Habinnas?—I believe you were there?—' You
got your wife from those profits. You are not lucky
in your friends. No one is ever as grateful to you as
you deserve. You are a man of property. You are
nourishing a viper in your bosom ' and, though I
must not tell you this, even now I have thirty years
four months and two days left to live. Moreover I
shall soon come into an estate. My oracle tells me
so. If I could only extend my boundaries to Apulia [1]
I should have gone far enough for my lifetime.
Meanwhile I built this house while Mercury watched
over me.[2] As you know, it was a tiny place; now
it is a temple. It has four dining-rooms, twenty
bedrooms, two marble colonnades, an upstairs dining-
room, a bedroom where I sleep myself, this viper's

---

[1] Apulia (Puglia)—the " heel " of Italy.
[2] Mercury was Trimalchio's patron. Also he was the god
of gain and good luck. See note, p. 440.

huius sessorium, ostiarii cellam perbonam; hospitium
hospites ⟨C⟩ [1] capit. Ad summam, Scaurus cum huc
venit, nusquam mavoluit hospitari, et habet ad
mare paternum hospitium. Et multa alia sunt,
quae statim vobis ostendam. Credite mihi: assem
habeas, assem valeas; habes, habeberis. Sic amicus
vester, qui fuit rana, nunc est rex. Interim, Stiche,
profer vitalia, in quibus volo me efferri. Profer
et unguentum et ex illa amphora gustum, ex qua
iubeo lavari ossa mea."

78   Non est moratus Stichus, sed et stragulam albam
et praetextam in triclinium attulit ⟨. . .⟩ [2] iussitque
nos temptare, an bonis lanis essent confecta. Tum
subridens " Vide tu " inquit " Stiche, ne ista mures
tangant aut tineae; alioquin te vivum comburam.
Ego gloriosus volo efferri, ut totus mihi populus
bene imprecetur." Statim ampullam nardi aperuit
omnesque nos unxit et " Spero " inquit " futurum ut
aeque me mortuum iuvet tanquam vivum." Nam
vinum quidem in vinarium iussit infundi et " Putate
vos " ait " ad parentalia mea invitatos esse."

   Ibat res ad summam nauseam, cum Trimalchio
ebrietate turpissima gravis novum acroama, cornicines, in triclinium iussit adduci, fultusque cervicali-
bus multis extendit se super torum extremum et
" Fingite me " inquit " mortuum esse. Dicite aliquid belli." Consonuere cornicines funebri strepitu.

---

  [1] ⟨C⟩ *added by Heinsius.*   [2] *lacuna indicated by Buecheler.*

---

  [1] Roman history had produced a number of famous men of
this name.

boudoir, an excellent room for the porter; there is a guest-room to take a hundred guests. In fact when Scaurus [1] came he preferred staying here to anywhere else, and he has a family place by the sea. There are plenty of other things which I will show you in a minute. Take my word for it: if you have a penny, that is what you are worth; by what a man hath shall he be reckoned. So your friend who was once a frog is now a king. Meanwhile, Stichus, bring me the grave-clothes in which I mean to be carried out. And some ointment, and a sample out of that jar which has to be poured over my bones."

In a moment Stichus had fetched a white winding-sheet and dress into the dining-room and . . . [Trimalchio] asked us to feel whether they were made of good wool. Then he gave a little laugh and said, "Mind neither mouse nor moth corrupts them, Stichus; otherwise I will burn you alive. I want to be carried out in splendour, so that the whole crowd calls down blessings on me." He immediately opened a flask of spikenard and anointed us all and said, " I hope I shall like this as well in the grave as I do on earth." Besides this he ordered wine to be poured into a bowl, and said, " Now you must imagine you have been asked to a festival in honour of my past life."

The thing was becoming perfectly sickening, when Trimalchio, now deep in the most vile drunkenness, had a new set of performers, some trumpeters, brought into the dining-room, propped himself on a heap of cushions, and stretched himself on his death-bed, saying, " Imagine that I am dead. Play something pretty." The trumpeters broke into a loud

Unus praecipue servus libitinarii [1] illius, qui inter hos
honestissimus erat, tam valde intonuit, ut totam
concitaret viciniam.   Itaque vigiles, qui custodiebant
vicinam regionem [2] rati ardere Trimalchionis domum,
effregerunt ianuam subito et cum aqua securibusque
tumultuari suo iure coeperunt.   Nos occasionem
opportunissimam nacti Agamemnoni verba dedimus
raptimque tam plane quam ex incendio fugimus. ⟨ . . . ⟩
79 L | . . . ⟩ [3] Neque fax ulla in praesidio erat, quae iter
aperiret errantibus, nec silentium noctis iam mediae
promittebat occurrentium lumen.   Accedebat huc
ebrietas et imprudentia locorum etiam interdiu
obfutura.[4]   Itaque cum hora paene tota per omnes
scrupos[5] gastrarumque eminentium fragmenta traxis-
semus cruentos pedes, tandem expliciti acumine
Gitonis sumus.   Prudens enim [pridie],[6] cum luce
etiam clara timeret errorem, omnes pilas columnas-
que notaverat creta, quae lineamenta evicerunt spis-
sissimam noctem et notabili candore ostenderunt
errantibus viam.   Quamvis non minus sudoris habuimus   etiam   postquam   ad   stabulum   pervenimus.
Anus enim ipsa inter deversitores diutus ingurgitata
ne ignem quidem admotum sensisset.   Et forsitan
pernoctasemus   in   limine,   ni   tabellarius   Trimal-

---

[1] libitinarii *Scheffer*: libertinarii.
[2] *Müller deletes the clause* qui . . . regionem.
[3] *lacuna indicated by Buecheler.*
[4] obfutura *Buecheler*: obscurorum *Burman*: obscura.
[5] scrupos *in margin of l*: scirpos.
[6] pridie *cod. Vat. lat. 11428 and in margin of cod. Lambeth.
693, apparently from a conjecture* sumus. pridie enim cum *of F.
Daniel; otherwise cod. Lambeth. as also cod. l repeats* prudens;
*but l however then underlines it.   Both readings are rightly
rejected.   Nisbet suggest* puer.

funeral march. One man especially, a slave of the
undertaker who was the most decent man in the
party, blew such a mighty blast that the whole
neighbourhood was roused. So the watch,[1] who were
patrolling the streets close by, thought Trimalchio's
house was alight, and suddenly burst in the door and
proceeded with water and axes to do their duty in
creating a disturbance. My friends and I seized this
most welcome opportunity, outwitted Agamemnon,[2]
and took to our heels as quickly as if there were a real
fire. . . .

. . . There was no guiding torch to show us the
way as we wandered; it was now midnight, and the
silence gave us no prospect of meeting anyone with a
light. Moreover we were drunk, and our ignorance
of the quarter would have puzzled us even in the daytime. So after dragging our bleeding feet nearly a
whole hour over the flints and broken pots which lay
out in the road, we were at last put straight by Giton's
cleverness. The careful child had been afraid of
losing his way even in broad daylight, and had
marked all the posts and columns with chalk; these
lines shone through the blackest night, and their brilliant whiteness directed our lost footsteps. But even
when we reached our lodgings our agitation was not
relieved. For our friend the old woman had had a
long night swilling with her lodgers, and would not
have noticed if you had set a light to her. We might
have had to sleep on the doorstep if Trimalchio's

---

[1] Either a municipal or a private brigade of firemen or
watchmen.
[2] Who had secured for them an invitation to Trimalchio's
dinner. The *Cena* ends with this sentence.

chionis intervenisset † X vehiculis † [1] dives. Non
diu ergo tumultuatus stabuli ianuam effregit et nos
† per eandem intro † [2] admisit . . .

Qualis nox fuit illa, di deaeque,
quam mollis torus. Haesimus calentes
et transfudimus hinc et hinc labellis
errantes animas. Valete, curae
mortales. Ego sic perire coepi.

Sine causa gratulor mihi. Nam cum solutus mero
remisissem [3] ebrias manus, Ascyltos, omnis iniuriae
inventor, subduxit mihi nocte puerum et in lectum
transtulit suum, volutatusque liberius cum fratre
non suo, sive non sentiente iniuriam sive dissimulante,
indormivit alienis amplexibus oblitus iuris humani.
Itaque ego ut experrectus pertrectavi gaudio de-
spoliatum torum . . . si qua est amantibus fides, ego
dubitavi, an utrumque traicerem gladio somnumque
morti iungerem. Tutius dein secutus consilium
Gitona quidem verberibus excitavi, Ascylton autem
truci intuens vultu " quoniam " inquam " fidem
scelere violasti communem amicitiam, res tuas
ocius tolle et alium locum, quem polluas, quaere."

Non repugnavit ille, sed postquam optima fide
partiti manubias sumus, " age " inquit " nunc et
80 puerum dividamus." Iocari putabam discedentem.
At ille gladium parricidali manu strinxit et " non

---

[1] *Perhaps not corrupt. Tornaesius's edition has* * *instead of*
X.
[2] intro *Bourdelot*: terram. *Gurlitt conjectures* per eam
⟨tan⟩dem [terram]: *Müller suggests* per eam ⟨tan⟩dem intro-
misit *in his 1st edition,* eam dein aper⟨turam⟩ *in his 2nd.*

courier had not come up † in state with ten carts.†
After making a noise for a little while he broke down
the house-door and let us in by it. . . .

" Ah! gods and goddesses, what a night that was,
how soft was the bed. We lay in a warm embrace
and with kisses everywhere made exchange of our
wandering spirits. Farewell, all earthly troubles.
So I proceeded to meet my ruin."

I blessed my luck too soon. I was overcome with
drink and let my shaking hands fall, and then
Ascyltos, that fountain of all wickedness, took my
boy at night away into his own bed, and taking all
manner of liberties with one who was no comrade of
his, who either felt no hurt or hid his feelings, at last
fell asleep with another man's lover, in defiance of
all human justice. When I awoke and felt all over
the bed stripped of its delight . . . if there is any
faith in lovers! I hesitated whether to run my
sword through them both and make sleep and death
one.[1] But I came to a safer resolution, and awaking
Giton with my blows, I looked angrily at Ascyltos,
and said, " As you have wickedly broken our agreement and the friendship between us, collect your
things at once, and find some other place to corrupt."

He did not resist, but after we had divided our
spoils with scrupulous honesty he said, " And now we
must divide the boy too." I thought this was a part-
ing joke. But he drew his sword murderously, and

[1] The clausula suggests the end of a line of dramatic poetry.

There are various other conjectures. fenestram *Richard.*
Perhaps per candem errantes admisit.
[3] remisissem *Jacobs:* amisissem.

frueris " inquit " hac praeda, super quam solus
incumbis. Partem meam necesse est vel hoc gladio
contemptus [1] abscidam." Idem ego ex altera parte
feci et intorto circa brachium pallio composui ad
proeliandum gradum. Inter hanc miserorum dementiam infelicissimus puer tangebat utriusque
genua cum fletu petebatque suppliciter, ne The-
banum par humilis taberna spectaret, neve sanguine
mutuo pollueremus familiaritatis clarissimae sacra.
" Quod si utique " proclamabat " facinore opus est,
nudo ecce iugulum, convertite huc manus, imprimite
mucrones. Ego mori debeo, qui amicitiae sacramentum delevi." Inhibuimus ferrum post has
preces, et prior Ascyltos " ego " inquit " finem
discordiae imponam. Puer ipse, quem vult, sequatur, ut sit illi saltem in eligendo fratre [salva] [2]
libertas." Ego ⟨qui⟩ [3] vetustissimam consuetudinem putabam in sanguinis pignus transisse, nihil
timui, immo condicionem praecipiti festinatione rapui
commisique iudici litem. Qui ne deliberavit quidem,
ut videretur cunctatus, verum statim ab extrema
parte verbi consurrexit ⟨et⟩ [4] fratrem Ascylton elegit.
Fulminatus hac pronuntiatione, sic ut eram, sine
gladio [5] in lectulum decidi, et attulissem mihi
damnatus manus, si non inimici victoriae invidissem.

[1] contemptus *Burman*: contentus. *Jacobs suggested* di-
midio contentus.
[2] salva *only in the editions of Tornaesius and Pithoeus and
cod. Lambeth. Buecheler deletes.*
[3] qui *added in Pithoeus's 2nd edition.*

said, " You shall not enjoy this treasure that you brood over all alone. I am rejected, but I must carve off my share too, even with this sword."

So I did the same on my side; wrapped my cloak round my arm and put myself in position for a fight. As we raved in folly, the poor boy touched our knees, and humbly besought us with tears not to let that quiet lodging-house be the scene of a Theban duel,[1] or stain the sanctity of a beautiful friendship with each other's blood. " But if you must commit your crime," he cried, " look here, here is my throat. Turn your hands this way and imbrue your blades. I deserve to die for breaking the oath of friendship." We put up our swords at his prayers, and Ascyltos spoke first, " I will put an end to this quarrel. Let the boy follow the one he prefers, so that he at any rate may have a free choice of brothers."

I had no fears, imagining that long-standing familiarity had passed into a tie of blood, and I accepted the arrangement in hot haste, and referred the dispute to the judge. He did not even pretend to take time to consider, but got up at once as I finished speaking, and chose Ascyltos for his brother. I was thunderstruck at his choice, and fell down on the bed just as I was, without my sword; I should have committed suicide at the sentence if I had not grudged my enemy this triumph. Ascyltos went

---

[1] Such as the struggle between Eteocles and Polyneices, two sons of Oedipus, for the throne of Thebes, in Greek traditional history.

---

[4] *Added by Buecheler.*
[5] *Müller deletes* sine gladio.

Egreditur superbus cum praemio Ascyltos et paulo
ante carissimum sibi commilitonem fortunaeque
etiam similitudine parem in loco peregrino destituit
abiectum.

LO | Nomen amicitiae sic, quatenus expedit, haeret;
 calculus in tabula mobile ducit opus.
Cum fortuna manet, vultum servatis, amici;
 cum cecidit, turpi vertitis ora fuga.

———

Grex agit in scaena mimum: pater ille vocatur,
 filius hic, nomen divitis ille tenet.
Mox ubi ridendas inclusit pagina [1] partes,
 vera redit facies, dum simulata [2] perit. . . .

81 Nec diu tamen lacrimis indulsi, sed veritus, ne
Menelaus etiam antescholanus inter cetera mala
solum me in deversorio inveniret, collegi sarcinulas
locumque secretum et proximum litori maestus
conduxi. Ibi triduo inclusus redeunte in animum
solitudine atque contemptu verberabam aegrum
L planctibus pectus | et inter tot altissimos gemitus
frequenter etiam proclamabam: "ergo me non
ruina terra potuit haurire? Non iratum etiam
innocentibus mare? Effugi iudicium, harenae imposui, hospitem occidi, ut inter ⟨tot⟩ [3] audaciae
nomina mendicus, exul, in deversorio Graecae urbis
iacerem desertus? Et quis hanc mihi solitudinem
imposuit? Adulescens omni libidine impurus et sua

———

[1] pergula *Nisbet*. *Buecheler suggested* machina.
[2] dum simulata *Buecheler*: assimulata *Dousa*: dissimulata.
[3] *Added by Jacobs. For* ut inter audaciae *Fraenkel suggests*
ut meritus tot audaciae.

stalking out with his winnings, and left his comrade, whom he had loved a little while before, and whose fortunes had been so like his own, in despair in a strange place.

"The name of friendship endures so long as there is profit in it: the counter on the board plays a changeable game. While my luck holds you give me your smiles, my friends; when it is out, you turn your faces away in shameful flight.

[1] A company acts a farce on the stage: one is called the father, one the son, and one is labelled the Rich Man. Soon the comic parts are shut in a † book †, the men's real faces come back, and the made-up disappear."

But still I did not spend much time in weeping. I was afraid that Menelaus the assistant tutor [2] might increase my troubles by finding me alone in the lodgings, so I got together my bundles and sadly took a room in a remote place right on the beach. I shut myself up there for three days; I was haunted by the thought that I was deserted and despised; I beat my breast, already worn with blows, groaned deeply, and even cried aloud many times, "Could not the earth have opened and swallowed me, or the sea that shows her anger even against the innocent? I fled from justice, I cheated the ring, I killed my host, and with all these badges of courage I am left forsaken in lodgings in a Greek town, a beggar and an exile! And who condemned me to this loneliness? A young man tainted by excess of every kind,

---

[1] The four lines following seem not to belong here. A mime was a farce in which stock characters were introduced.

[2] Menelaus: cf. Chapter 27.

quoque confessione dignus exilio, stupro liber, stupro
ingenuus, cuius anni ad tesseram venierunt, quem
tanquam puellam conduxit etiam qui virum putavit.
Quid ille alter? Qui [tamquam] [1] die togae virilis
stolam sumpsit, qui ne vir esset, a matre persuasus
est, qui opus muliebre in ergastulo fecit, qui postquam conturbavit et libidinis suae solum vertit, reliquit veteris amicitiae nomen et, pro pudor, tanquam
mulier secutuleia unius noctis tactu omnia vendidit.
Iacent nunc amatores obligati [2] noctibus totis, et
forsitan mutuis libidinibus attriti derident solitudinem meam. Sed non impune. Nam aut vir
ego liberque non sum, aut noxio sanguine parentabo
iniuriae meae."

82   Haec locutus gladio latus cingor et ne infirmitas
militiam perderet, largioribus cibis excito vires. Mox
in publicum prosilio furentisque more omnes circum-
eo porticus. Sed dum attonito vultu efferatoque
nihil aliud quam caedem et sanguinem cogito fre-
quentiusque manum ad capulum, quem devoveram,
refero, notavit me miles, sive ille planus fuit sive
nocturnus grassator, et " Quid tu " inquit " com-
milito, ex qua legione es aut cuius centuria?"
Cum constantissime et centurionem et legionem
essem ementitus, " Age ergo " inquit ille " in
exercitu vestro phaecasiati milites ambulant?"
Cum deinde vultu atque ipsa trepidatione mendacium
prodidissem, ponere iussit arma et malo cavere.
Despoliatus ergo, immo praecisa ultione retro ad

---

[1] *Deleted by Gataker.*
[2] adligati *Buecheler, rightly?*

deserving banishment even by his own admission, free in lewdness;   a gentleman in lewdness; his years were for sale at a dice-throw, and even those who supposed him to be a man hired him like a girl. And his friend?   A boy who went into skirts instead of trousers, whose mother persuaded him never to grow up, who played the part of a woman in a slaves' prison, who after going bankrupt, and changing the tune of his vices, has broken the ties of an old friendship, and shamelessly sold everything in a single night's work like a follow-me-girl.   Now the lovers lie all night long in each other's arms, and very likely laugh at my loneliness when they are tired out.   But they shall suffer for it.   I am no man, and no free citizen, if I do not avenge my wrongs with their hateful blood."

With these words I put on my sword, and recruited my strength with a square meal to prevent my losing the battle through weakness.   I rushed out of doors next and went round all the arcades like a madman.   My face was as of one dumbfoundered with fury, I thought of nothing but blood and slaughter, and kept putting my hand to the sword-hilt which I had consecrated to the work.   Then a soldier, who may have been a swindler or a footpad by night, noticed me, and said, " Hullo, comrade, what regiment and company do you belong to ? "   I lied stoutly about my captain and my regiment, and he said, " Well, do soldiers in your force walk about in white shoes ? "   My expression and my trembling showed that I had lied, and he ordered me to hand over my arms and look out for myself.   So I was not only robbed, but my revenge was nipped in the bud.

deversorium tendo paulatimque temeritate laxata [1]
coepi grassatoris audaciae gratias agere . . .

Non bibit inter aquas poma aut pendentia carpit
    Tantalus infelix, quem sua vota premunt.
Divitis haec magni facies erit, omnia cernens
    qui timet et sicco concoquit ore famem. . . .

Non multum oportet consilio credere, quia suam
habet fortuna rationem . . .

83   In pinacothecam perveni vario genere tabularum
mirabilem. Nam et Zeuxidos manus vidi nondum
vetustatis iniuria victas, et Protogenis rudimenta cum
ipsius naturae veritate certantia non sine quodam
horrore tractavi. Iam vero Apellis quam Graeci [2]
μονόκνημον appellant, etiam adoravi. Tanta enim
subtilitate extremitates imaginum erant ad similtudi-
nem praecisae, ut crederes etiam animorum esse
picturam. Hinc aquila ferebat caelo [3] sublimis [4]
Idaeum,[5] illinc candidus Hylas repellebat improbam
Naida. Damnabat Apollo noxias manus lyramque

       [1] laxata *Muncker*: lassata.
       [2] Graeci *might be deleted*.
       [3] *Fraenkel suggested deleting* caelo.
       [4] sublimen *Buecheler*.
       [5] Idaeum *Wehle*: deum.

---

    [1] See note on Seneca's *Apocolocyntosis*, 14.
    [2] Zeuxis (born c. 450 B.C.), famous Greek realistic painter,
of Heraclea (probably the one by the Black Sea).
    [3] Greek painter of Rhodes (?), fourth century B.C.
    [4] Apelles, late fourth century B.C., was perhaps the most
renowned of Greek painters.
    [5] Ganymedes (see above, pp. 128–9); Mount Ida (cf.

I went back to the inn, and by degrees my rashness cooled, and I proceeded to bless the footpad's effrontery. . . .

" Poor Tantalus [1] stands in water and never drinks, nor plucks the fruit above his head: his own desires torment him. So must a rich great man look when, with everything before his eyes, he fears starvation, and digests hunger dry-mouthed. . . ."

It is not much use depending upon calculation when Fate has methods of her own. . . .

I came into a gallery hung with a wonderful collection of various pictures. I saw the works of Zeuxis [2] not yet overcome by the defacement of time, and I studied with a certain terrified wonder the rough drawings of Protogenes,[3] which rivalled the truth of Nature herself. But when I came to the work of Apelles [4] the work which the Greeks call The One-legged, I positively worshipped it. For the outlines of his figures were defined with such subtle accuracy, that you would have declared that he had painted their souls as well. In one the eagle on high was carrying the Shepherd of Ida [5] to heaven, and in another fair Hylas [6] resisted a tormenting Naiad. Apollo [7] passed judgment on his accursed hands, and

89 and 134) is the mountain from which Zeus (Jupiter) carried him off in the shape of an eagle.

[6] In mythology, Hylas, loved by Heracles, went with the Argonauts seeking the golden fleece and, when drawing water, was dragged in by an amorous Naiad (fresh-water nymph) and disappeared.

[7] Apollo, the god, killed the Spartan boy, Hyacinthus, whom he loved, by a mis-throw of a discus. The " hyacinth " flower (corn-flag, *Gladiolus segetum*) sprang up from the boy's blood.

resolutam modo nato flore honorabat. Inter quos
etiam pictorum [1] amantium vultus tanquam in solitudine exclamavi: " Ergo amor etiam deos tangit.
Iuppiter in caelo suo non invenit quod diligeret, sed [2]
peccaturus in terris nemini tamen iniuriam fecit.
Hylan Nympha praedata imperasset amori suo,
si venturum ad interdictum Herculem credidisset.
Apollo pueri umbram revocavit in florem; [et] [3]
omnes [fabulae quoque] [4] sine aemulo habuerunt
complexus. At ego in societatem recepi hospitem
Lycurgo crudeliorem."

Ecce autem, ego dum cum ventis litigo, intravit
pinacothecam senex canus, exercitati vultus et qui
videretur nescio quid magnum promittere, sed cultu
non proinde speciosus, ut facile appareret eum ⟨et⟩ [5]
hac nota litteratum esse, quos odisse divites solent.
Is ergo ad latus constitit meum . . .

" Ego " inquit " poeta sum et ut spero, non humil-
limi spiritus, si modo coronis aliquid credendum est,
quas etiam ad immeritos [6] deferre gratia solet.
'Quare ergo' inquis 'tam male vestitus es?'
Propter hoc ipsum. Amor ingenii neminem unquam
divitem fecit.

LO | Qui pelago credit, magno se faenore tollit;
qui pugnas et castra petit, praecingitur auro;
vilis adulator picto iacet ebrius ostro,
et qui sollicitat nuptas, ad praemia peccat:

---

[1] *Fraenkel would delete* etiam pictorum.
[2] diligeret *P. Daniel and* sed *Jacobs*: eligeret et.
[3] *Deleted by Fraenkel.*
[4] *Deleted by Fraenkel.*
[5] *Added by Dousa.*
[6] immeritos *suggests Buecheler*: imperitos.

adorned his unstrung lyre with the newborn flower.
I cried out as if I were in a desert, among these
faces of mere painted lovers, " So even the gods feel
love. ' Jupiter in his heavenly home ' could find no
object for his passion, but came down on earth to sin,
yet did no one any harm. The Nymph who ravished
Hylas would have restrained her passion had she
believed that Hercules would come to dispute her
claim. Apollo recalled the ghost of a boy into a
flower. All these divinities enjoyed love's embraces
without a rival. But I have taken for my comrade
a friend more cruel than Lycurgus [1] himself."

Suddenly, as I strove thus with the empty air, a
white-haired old man [2] came into the gallery. His
face was troubled, but there seemed to be the promise
of some great thing about him; though he was
shabby in appearance, so that it was quite plain by
this sign alone that he was a man of letters, of the
kind that rich men are accustomed to hate. Well,
he came and stood by my side. . . .

" I am a poet," he said, " and one, I hope, of no
mean imagination, if one can reckon at all by crowns
of honour, which influence can set even on unworthy
heads. ' Why are you so badly dressed, then?'
you ask. For that very reason. The worship of
genius never made a man rich.

" "The man who trusts the sea carries off high
profits; the man who follows war and the camp is
girded with gold; the base flatterer lies drunk on
a couch of purple dye; the man who tempts young

---

[1] Traditional name of the early law-giver of Sparta. Early
laws were always believed to be severe.
[2] Eumolpus.

sola pruinosis horret facundia pannis
atque inopi lingua desertas invocat artes.

84 Non dubie ita est: si quis vitiorum omnium inimicus
rectum iter vitae coepit insistere,[1] primum propter
morum differentiam odium habet; quis enim potest
probare diversa?   Deinde qui solas extruere divitias
curant, mihil volunt inter homines melius credi, quam
quos ipsi tenet. Inescant[2] itaque, quacunque
ratione possunt, litterarum amatores, ut videantur
illi quoque infra pecuniam positi " . . .

L | " Nescio quo modo bonae mentis soror est
paupertas " . . .
    " Vellem, tam innocens esset frugalitatis meae
hostis, ut deliniri posset. Nunc veteranus est latro
et ipsis lenonibus doctior " . . .

85   " In Asiam cum a quaestore[3] essem stipendio
eductus, hospitium Pergami accepi. Ubi cum
libenter habitarem non solum propter cultum
aedicularum, sed etiam propter hospitis formosissi-
mum filium, excogitavi rationem, qua non essem
patri familiae suspectus [amator].[4] Quotiescunque
enim in convivio de usu formosorum mentio facta est,

---

[1] insistere *Brassicanus*: inspicere *O*: respicere coepit *the
Florilegia. Cf. Müller, ed. 1, p. 91.*
[2] *Müller's suggestion* inescant *is accepted. In his 2nd
edition he prefers Buecheler's* insectantur. *Fraenkel suggests*
inlactant = illectant. *The MSS. have* iactantur.
[3] *perhaps* a quaestura.
[4] *Fraenkel would delete* amator, *rightly, because of the clausula*
sŭspēctŭs ămātŏr.

---

[1] Ascyltos.
[2] Asia was the Roman province—only a smallish part of

wives gets money for his sin; eloquence alone shivers in rags and cold, and calls upon a neglected art with unprofitable tongue.'

" Yes, that is certainly true: if a man dislikes all vices, and proceeds to tread a straight path in life, he is hated first of all because his character is different; for who is able to like what differs from himself? Further, those who only trouble about heaping up riches do not want anything to be considered better than what is in their own hands. So they offer a bait to men with a passion for learning in every possible way, to make them also look an inferior article to money. . . .

" Somehow or other poverty is own sister to good sense. . . .

" I wish he [1] that hates me for my virtue were so guiltless that he might be mollified. As it is he is a past master of robbery, and more clever than any pimp. . . .

" When I had been brought out to Asia [2] by a quaestor on salary, I lodged in a home at Pergamum by invitation. [3] Here I stayed with pleasure not only because of the entertainment of that refined establishment, but also because of a very beautiful boy—the son of my host. My contrivance was to act [the lover] unsuspected by his father; and to effect my wishes, I used this method. Whenever at table we happened to discourse of amours with

Asia Minor. In the provinces quaestors were financial officers. Codex *l* indicates that Eumolpus is the speaker.

[3] *Pergami* is locative case of *Pergamum*, the famous Greek capital of the Roman province of Asia, not genitive of *Pergamus*, a man's name.

tam vehementer excandui, tam severa tristitia violari
aures meas obsceno sermone nolui, ut me mater
praecipue tanquam unum ex philosophis intueretur.
Iam ego coeperam ephebum in gymnasium deducere,
ego studia eius ordinare, ego docere ac praecipere, ne
quis praedator corporis admitteretur in domum . . .

" Forte cum in triclinio iaceremus, quia dies sollem-
nis ludum artaverat [1] pigritiamque recedendi imposuerat hilaritas longior, fere circa mediam noctem
intellexi puerum vigilare. Itaque timidissimo murmure votum feci et ' domina ' inquam ' Venus, si ego
hunc puerum basiavero, ita ut ille non sentiat, cras
illi par columbarum donabo.' Audito voluptatis
pretio puer stertere coepit. Itaque aggressus simu-
lantem aliquot basiolis invasi. Contentus hoc princi-
pio bene mane surrexi electumque par columbarum
86 attuli expectanti ac me voto exsolvi. Proxima nocte
cum idem liceret, mutavi optionem et ' si hunc '
inquam ' tractavero improba manu, et ille non senserit, gallos gallinaceos pugnacissimos duos donabo
[patienti].' [2] Ad hoc votum ephebus ultro se admovit
et, puto, vereri coepit, ne ego obdormissem.[3] Indulsi
ergo sollicito, totoque corpore citra summam voluptatem me ingurgitavi. Deinde ut dies venit,
attuli gaudenti quicquid promiseram. Ut tertia
nox licentiam dedit, consurrexi,[4] ad aurem male
dormientis ' dii ' inquam ' immortales, si ego huic

---

[1] *In his 2nd edition Müller conjectures* apportaverat, *but
Nisbet prefers* ampliaverat *or* prolataverat.

[2] *P. George deletes* patienti.

[3] obdormiscerem *Muncker.*

[4] *After* consurrexi, *Müller (1st edition) adds* accessique, *but
later (2nd edition) adds* inclinatusque. *Fraenkel would add* et.

young beauties, I fell into a passion, and pretended
my modesty suffered so much by obscene talk, that
the boy's mother in particular looked on me as a
philosopher above the sensual pleasures of the world.
Soon I proceeded to escort the boy to the gymnasium, to arrange his studies, to be his teacher and
to warn his parents to admit no preyer on his body
into the house. . . .

" It happened that we were resting in the dining-
room, because a public holiday had cut short our play,
and prolonged merry-making had made us too lazy to
retire. About midnight I noticed that the boy was
awake; so in a cautious whisper I made my vow—
' Queen Venus, if I could kiss this boy, without his
knowing it, I will give him to-morrow a pair of doves! '
Hearing the price of the pleasure, the boy proceeded
to snore; so I approached the little impostor and
pressed several kisses upon his lips. Satisfied with
this beginning, I stopped there, and early the next
morning performed my promise, chose a pair of doves
and gave them to the eager boy. Next night I had
another chance, altered my choice, and said ' If I
can handle him in saucy style without his knowing
it, I'll give him a pair of the best fighting-cocks.'
At this the boy readily accommodated himself,
and indeed I think he went on to fear that I fell
asleep myself; so I humoured him in his anxiety
and wallowed with my whole body, but not reaching
the supreme height of pleasure. Then as day came I
brought all that I had promised, to his delight.
When the third night gave me scope, I got up. . . .
I whispered close to the ear of the restless sleeper,
' immortal gods!' I said. If only I can get from

[dormienti] [1] abstulero coitum plenum et optabilem, pro hac felicitate cras puero asturconem Macedonicum optimum donabo, cum hac tamen exceptione, si ille non senserit.' Nunquam altiore somno ephebus obdormivit. Itaque primum implevi lactentibus papillis manus, mox basio inhaesi, deinde in unum omnia vota coniunxi. Mane sedere in cubiculo coepit atque expectare consuetudinem meam. Scis quanto facilius sit, columbas gallosque gallinaceos emere quam asturconem, et praeter hoc etiam timebam, ne tam grande munus suspectam faceret humanitatem meam. Ego aliquot horis spatiatus in hospitium reverti nihilque aliud quam puerum basiavi. At ille circumspiciens ut cervicem meam iunxit amplexu, ' rogo ' inquit ' domine, ubi est asturco? ' . . .

87   " Cum ob hanc offensam praeclusissem mihi aditum, quem feceram, iterum ad licentiam redii. Interpositis enim paucis diebus, cum similis casus nos in eandem fortunam rettulisset, ut intellexi stertere patrem, rogare coepi ephebum, ut reverteretur in gratiam mecum, id est ut pateretur satis fieri sibi, et cetera quae libido distenta dictat. At ille plane iratus nihil aliud dicebat nisi hoc: ' aut dormi, aut ego iam dicam patri.' Nihil est tam arduum, quod non improbitas extorqueat. Dum dicit: ' patrem excitabo,' irrepsi tamen et male repugnanti gaudium extorsi. At ille non indelectatus nequitia mea, postquam diu questus est deceptum se et derisum traductumque inter condiscipulos, quibus iactasset censum [2] meum, ' videris tamen ' inquit ' non ero

---

[1] *Müller deletes* dormienti.
[2] censum *P. Daniel and P. Pithoeus*: sensum.

him the full desirable union I will give the boy
to-morrow in return for this happiness a Macedonian
thoroughbred, on this condition only, that he has felt
nothing.' The boy never slept more soundly. So I
first filled my hands with his milk-soft breasts, next
was glued in a kiss, and then united all my desires
into one. Next morning he sat in his room waiting
for my company. You may imagine that doves and
cockerels are easier to be bought than a thoroughbred
horse; besides, I was also afraid lest so splendid a
present should make my kindness suspect. I therefore walked about for a few hours, and when I returned to my lodging gave the boy no more than a
kiss. He looked about, then threw his arms about
my neck, saying, ' Please sir, where's the thoroughbred?' . . .

   " This breach of my word closed against me the
approach I had made; but I found my chance again.
For not many days after, another festival brought us
into the same state as before. When I heard the
father snoring, I proceeded to beg the boy to be
friends again, that he would let me satisfy him, and
the sort of things that love delayed make you say.
But he was clearly angry, and returned no other
answer than ' Go to sleep, or I will tell my father at
once.' But there is nothing too hard for boldness
to extort. I crept on him and extorted my pleasure
in spite of a faint resistance, while he kept saying,
' I'll wake father!' He was not displeased with my
naughtiness, but with a long complaint that he was
cheated and laughed at and abused among his play-
fellows, to whom he had been boasting of my riches,
he said, ' You shall see that I will not be like you; do

tui similis. Si quid vis, fac iterum.' Ego vero
deposita omni offensa cum puero in gratiam redii
ususque beneficio eius in somnum delapsus sum.
Sed non fuit contentus iteratione ephebus plenae
maturitatis et annis ad patiendum gestientibus.
Itaque excitavit me sopitum et 'numquid vis?'
inquit. Et non plane iam molestum erat munus.
Utcunque igitur inter anhelitus sudoresque tritus,
quod voluerat, accepit, rursusque in somnum decidi
gaudio lassus; interposita minus hora pungere me
manu coepit et dicere: 'quare non facimus?' tum
ego totiens excitatus plane vehementer excandui et
reddidi illi voces suas: 'aut dormi, aut ego iam patri
dicam.' " . . .

88   Erectus his sermonibus consulere prudentiorem
coepi aetates tabularum et quaedam argumenta mihi
obscura simulque causam desidiae praesentis excu-
tere, cum pulcherrimae artes perissent, inter quas
pictura ne minimum quidem sui vestigium reliquisset.
Tum ille " pecuniae " inquit " cupiditas haec tropica
LO instituit. | Priscis enim temporibus, cum adhuc nuda
virtus placeret, vigebant artes ingenuae summumque
certamen inter homines erat, ne quid profuturum
saeculis diu lateret. Itaque herbarum omnium sucos
Democritus expressit, et ne lapidum virgultorumque
vis lateret, aetatem inter experimenta consumpsit.
Eudoxos quidem [1] in cacumine excelsissimi montis

---

[1] quidem *was omitted by L.*

---

[1] Greek of Abdera, c. 460–361 B.C., founder, with Leucippus,
of the theory that all things were made from collisions of in-
finitely small " atoms " (" uncuttables ")—though he did not
conceive of them as being nearly as small as " modern " atoms.

it again if you like.' And so we made it up and I
enjoyed his kindness and slipped off to sleep. But
the boy—of full maturity, his years being desirous of
submission—was not satisfied with repetition. So he
roused me out of my slumber and said ' Do you want
anything?' And by now it was indeed no unpleasant task. Anyhow, with gasps on my part and
sweat he got a pounding and so had what he all
along wanted, and again I fell asleep tired out with
joy; but it was less than an hour ere he was prob-
ing me with his hand and crying, ' Why aren't
we doing it?' Then I flew in a great passion to
be so often disturbed, and turned his own words
upon him—' Go to sleep, or I'll tell your father at
once.' " . . .

Encouraged by his conversation, I proceeded to
draw on his knowledge about the age of the pictures,
and about some of the stories which puzzled me, and
at the same time to discuss the decadence of the age,
since the fine arts had died, and painting, for instance, had left no trace of its existence behind.
" Love of money began this revolution," he replied.
" In former ages virtue was still loved for her own
sake, the noble arts flourished, and there were the
keenest struggles among mankind to prevent anything being long undiscovered which might benefit
posterity. So Democritus [1] extracted the juice of
every plant on earth, and spent his whole life in
experiments to discover the virtues of stones and
twigs. Eudoxos [2] grew old on the top of a very high

---

[2] Greek of Cnidus (c. 408–355 B.C.), astronomer, geometer,
and philosopher, of whose prose work *Phaenomena* the substance in a versification by Aratus survives.

consenuit, ut astrorum caelique motus deprehenderet, et Chrysippus, ut ad inventionem sufficeret,
ter elleboro animum detersit. Verum ut ad plastas
convertar, Lysippum statuae unius lineamentis inhaerentem inopia extinxit, et Myron, qui paene
animas hominum ferarumque aere comprehenderat,
non invenit heredem. At nos vino scortisque demersi
ne paratas quidem artes audemus cognoscere, sed
accusatores antiquitatis vitia tantum docemus et
discimus. Ubi est dialectica? Ubi astronomia?
Ubi sapientiae cultissima [1] via? Quis unquam venit
in templum et votum fecit, si ad eloquentiam per-
venisset? Quis, si philosophiae fontem attigisset?
Ac ne bonam quidem mentem aut bonam valetudinem
petunt, sed statim antequam limen Capitolii [2] tangant,
alius donum promittit, si propinquum divitem extu-
lerit, alius, si thesaurum effoderit, alius, si ad trecenties sestertium salvus pervenerit. Ipse senatus,
recti bonique praeceptor, mille pondo auri Capitolio
promittere solet, et ne quis dubitet pecuniam con-
cupiscere, Iovem quoque peculio exornat. Noli
ergo mirari, si pictura defecit, cum omnibus diis
hominibusque formosior videatur massa auri, quam
quicquid Apelles Phidiasque, Graeculi delirantes,

---

[1] cultissima *R*: consultissima *the rest*: occultissima *suggests*
Müller; consultis ⟨tritis⟩sima *Fraenkel*: consuetissima
Burman.

[2] *Fraenkel would delete* Capitolii.

---

[1] Greek of Soli in Cilicia in Asia Minor (280–206 B.C.),
a philosopher who did much to shape and develop Stoicism.

[2] Greek of Sicyon (fourth century B.C.) famous sculptor of
natural rather than idealized beauty in men. We have a
marble copy of his bronze Agias an athlete.

[3] Greek of Eleutherae (fifth century B.C.), renowned sculp-

mountain in order to trace the movements of the
stars and the sky, and Chrysippus [1] three times
cleared his wits with hellebore to improve his powers
of invention. If you turn to sculptors, Lysippus [2]
died of starvation as he brooded over the lines of a
single statue, and Myron,[3] who almost caught the
very soul of men and beasts in bronze, left no heir
behind him. But *we* are besotted with wine and
whores and cannot rise to understand even the arts
that are developed; we slander the past, and learn
and teach nothing but vices. Where is dialectic now,
or astronomy? Where is the exquisite way of wisdom? Who has ever been to a temple and promised
an offering should he attain to eloquence, or drink of
the waters of philosophy? Men do not even ask for
good sense or good health, but before they even
touch the threshold of the Capitol, one promises an
offering if he may bury his rich kinsman, another if he
may dig up a hid treasure, another if he may make
thirty millions in safety. Even the Senate, the
teachers of what is right and good, often promise a
thousand pounds in gold to the Capitol, and decorate
even Jupiter with pelf, that no one need be ashamed of
lusting for money. So there is nothing surprising in
the decadence of painting, when all the gods and men
think an ingot of gold more beautiful than anything
those poor crazy Greeks, Apelles and Phidias,[4] ever did.

tor. Of his " Discus-Thrower " and his " Marsyas " copies
survive. He is said to have had a son, Lycius.

[4] For Apelles, see above. Phidias of Athens (c. 490–432)
was perhaps the most celebrated of Greek sculptors, especially
in bronze and in gold-and-ivory. How far he was concerned
in the creation of the Parthenon and its stone sculptures is not
known.

PETRONIUS ARBITER

89 fecerunt.   Sed video te totum in illa haerere tabula,
quae Troiae halosin ostendit.   Itaque conabor opus
versibus pandere:

Iam decima maestos inter ancipites metus
Phrygas obsidebat messis et vatis fides
Calchantis atro dubia pendebat metu,
cum Delio profante caesi [1] vertices
Idae trahuntur scissaque in molem cadunt
robora, minacem quae figurabunt [2] equum.
Aperitur ingens antrum et obducti specus,
qui castra caperent.   Huc decenni proelio
irata virtus abditur, stipant graves
Danai recessus, in suo voto latent.
O patria, pulsas mille credidimus rates
solumque bello liberum: hoc titulus fero
incisus, hoc ad furta [3] compositus Sinon
firmabat et mens semper [4] in damnum potens.
   Iam turba portis libera ac bello carens
in vota properat.   Fletibus manant genae
mentisque pavidae gaudium lacrimas habet,

[1] ferro caesi *MSS.*; ferro *is rightly omitted by Sambucus and
by Scaliger in l and in his Catalecta.*
[2] figurabunt *Lachmann*: figurabant *and* figurabat.
[3] furta *Buecheler*: fata.
[4] mens semper *Pithoeus*: m̃ semper *cd. Autissiodurensis*:
mendacium semper *R*: mendacium *the other MSS.*: mendacio
Brassicanus: mendacii *Heinsius and in margin of Tornaesius'
edition.*

---

[1] The poem which follows largely summarizes in *senarii* the
first part of the 2nd book of the *Aeneid* of Virgil, of whom there
are various echoes.   These may be part of parody which seems
to pervade the poetry—a parody not of Virgil but of rhetorical
method, perhaps of messengers' speeches in classical tragedies.

" But I see your whole attention is riveted on that picture, which represents the fall of Troy. Well, I will try and explain the situation in verse: [1]

" ' It was now the tenth harvest of the siege of the Phrygians, who were worn with anxious fear, and the honour of Calchas the prophet hung wavering in dark dread, when at Apollo's bidding the wooded peaks of Ida were felled and dragged down, and the sawn planks fall into a heap—planks that will shape a threatening horse.[2] Within it a great hollow was opened, and a hidden cave that could shelter a camp. In this the warriors who chafed at a war ten years long were packed away; the baleful Greeks fill every corner, and lie waiting in their own votive offering. Ah! my country! we thought the thousand ships were beaten off, and the land released from strife. The inscription carved on this beast, Sinon's bearing, planned for deceit with this horse, and his spirit (ever powerful for evil it was) all strengthened our confidence.[3]

" 'Now a crowd hurries from the gate to worship, careless and free of the war. Their cheeks are wet with tears, and the joy of their trembling souls brings

[2] The Trojans were called Phrygians because they were in the Phrygian area of Asia Minor. According to story, Calchas the Greek foretold that the siege of Troy would last ten years; he was priest and prophet of the god Apollo (imagined as born in Delos island), who told the Greeks to make the wooden horse. King Laomedon of Troy had refused to pay the gods Apollo and Posidon (Neptune) for building the city walls of Troy—hence Apollo's hatred. Mount Ida is near Troy.

[3] Sinon was a Greek. He let himself be captured by the Trojans whom he convinced that the horse was a harmless votive offering. In fact it was packed with Greek soldiers.

quas metus abegit.   Namque Neptuno sacer
crinem solutus omne Laocoon replet
clamore vulgus.   Mox reducta cuspide
uterum notavit, fata sed tardant manus,
ictusque resilit et dolis addit fidem.
Iterum tamen confirmat invalidam manum
altaque bipenni latera pertemptat.   Fremit
captiva pubes intus et, dum murmurat,
roborea moles spirat alieno metu.
Ibat iuventus capta, dum Troiam capit,
bellumque totum fraude ducebat [1] nova.
Ecce alia monstra: celsa qua Tenedos mare
dorso replevit, tumida consurgunt freta
undaque resultat scissa tranquillo † minor † [2]
qualis silenti nocte remorum sonus
longe refertur, cum premunt classes mare
pulsumque marmor abiete imposita gemit.
Respicimus: angues orbibus geminis ferunt
ad saxa fluctus, tumida quorum pectora
rates ut altae lateribus spumas agunt.
Dat cauda sonitum, liberae ponto iubae
consentiunt luminibus, fulmineum [3] iubar
incendit aequor sibilisque undae fremunt.[4]
Stupuere mentes.   Infulis stabant sacri
Phrygioque cultu gemina nati pignora
Lauconte.   Quos repente tergoribus ligant

---

[1] *Nisbet suggests* cludebat.
[2] mari *J .Tollius*; *but see two lines above and below.   Perhaps*
tranquillo omine *or* t. Iove.
[3] alienum *Norden*.   [4] fremunt *Haupt*: tremunt.

to their eyes tears that terror had banished. Laocoon,[1] priest of Neptune, with hair unbound, stirs the whole assembly to cry aloud. Next, he drew back his spear and gashed the belly of the horse, but fate stayed his hand, the spear leaped back, and won us to trust the fraud. But he nerved his feeble hand a second time, and sounded the deep sides of the horse with an axe. The young soldiers shut within breathed loud, and while the sound lasted the wooden mass gasped with a terror that was not its own. The prisoned warriors went forward to make Troy prisoner, and waged all the war by a new subtlety.

" ' There followed further portents; where the steep ridge of Tenedos [2] blocks the sea, the billows rise and swell, and the shattered wave leaps back in calm † weather † with noise as of oars borne far through the silent night, when ships bear down the ocean, and the marble surface is stirred and splashes under the fir-wood keel. We look back: the tide carries two coiling snakes towards the rocks, their swollen breasts like tall ships throwing the foam from their sides. Their tails crash through the sea, their crests move free over the open water, fierce as their eyes; a brilliant beam kindles the waves, and the waters resound with their hissing. Our heartbeats stopped. The priests stood wreathed for sacrifice with the two sons of Laocoon in Phrygian raiment. Suddenly the gleaming snakes twine their bodies

---

[1] Laocoön, son of Priam King of Troy at the time of the war, had been a priest of Apollo whose temple he profaned, but became priest of Posidon (Neptune), who like Apollo hated Troy.

[2] An island near the coast of the Troad.

angues corusci.   Parvulas illi manus
ad ora referunt, neuter auxilio sibi,
uterque fratri: transtulit pietas vices
morsque ipsa miseros mutuo perdit metu.
Accumulat ecce liberum funus parens,
infirmus auxiliator.   Invadunt virum
iam morte pasti membraque ad terram trahunt.
Iacet sacerdos inter aras victima
terramque plangit.   Sic profanatis sacris
peritura Troia perdidit primum deos.
    Iam plena Phoebe candidum extulerat iubar
minora ducens astra radianti face,
cum inter sepultos Priamidas nocte et mero
Danai relaxant claustra et effundunt viros.
Temptant in armis se duces, veluti [1] solet
nodo [2] remissus Thessali quadrupes iugi
cervicem et altas quatere ad excursum iubas.
Gladios retractant, commovent orbes manu
bellumque sumunt.   Hic graves alius mero
obtruncat et continuat in mortem ultimam
somnos, ab aris alius accendit faces
contraque Troas invocat Troiae sacra." . . .

90 *L* | Ex is, qui in porticibus spatiabantur, lapides in
Eumolpum recitantem miserunt.   At ille, qui plausum ingenii sui noverat, operuit caput extraque tem-

---

[1] veluti *Krohn*: ceu vi *Lachmann*: ceu ubi, *as if for the
Homeric* ὡς (δ')ὅτε.
[2] nodo *Dousa*: nudo.

---

[1] The famous group in marble by the Rhodians Hagesander,
Polydorus, and Athenodorus (Pliny, XXXVI, 37–38), re-

round them.[1] The boys throw up their little hands
to their faces, neither helping himself, but each his
brother: such was the exchange of love, and death
himself slew both poor children by their unselfish
fear. Then before our eyes the father, a feeble
helper, laid his own body down upon his children's.
The snakes, now gorged with death, attacked the
man and dragged his limbs to the ground. The priest
lies a victim before his altars and thrashes the earth.
Thus the doomed city of Troy first lost her gods by
profaning their worship.

"'Now Phoebe[2] at the full lifted up her white
beam, and led forth the smaller stars with her glowing torch, and the Greeks unbarred the horse, and
poured out their warriors among Priam's sons[3]
drowned in darkness and wine. The leaders try
their strength in arms, as a steed untied from the
knot of a Thessalian[4] chariot will toss his head and
lofty mane as he rushes forth. They draw their
swords, brandish their shields, and begin the fight.
One slays Trojans heavy with drink and makes sleep
merge into death that endeth all, another lights
torches from the altars, and calls on the holy places
of Troy to fight against the Trojans.'" . . .

Some of the people who were walking in the colonnades threw stones at Eumolpus as he recited. But
he recognized this tribute to his genius, covered his

presenting Laocoön and his two sons in serpent-coils, survives
today. It is in the Vatican.

[2] The moon.

[3] Priam was King of Troy. The Greeks were called Danai
from the mythical founder of Argos.

[4] Thessaly with its plains was a land favourable to horses.

plum profugit. Timui ego, ne me poetam vocaret.[1]
Itaque subsecutus fugientem ad litus perveni, et ut
primum extra teli coniectum licuit consistere,
" Rogo " inquam " quid tibi vis cum isto morbo?
Minus quam duabus horis mecum moraris, et saepius
poetice quam humane locutus es. Itaque non miror,
si te populus lapidibus persequitur. Ego quoque
sinum meum saxis onerabo, ut quotiescunque
coeperis a te exire, sanguinem tibi a capite mittam."
Movit ille vultum et " O mi " inquit " adulescens,
non hodie primus auspicatus sum. Immo quoties
theatrum, ut recitarem aliquid, intravi, hac [2] me
adventicia excipere frequentia solet. Ceterum ne
[et] [3] tecum quoque habeam rixandum, toto die me
ab hoc cibo [4] abstinebo." " Immo " inquam ego
" si eiuras hodiernam bilem, una cenabimus " . . .

Mando aedicularum custodi cenulae officium . . .

91   Video Gitona cum linteis et strigilibus parieti appli-
citum tristem confusumque. Scires, non libenter
servire. Itaque ut experimentum oculorum caperem
⟨. . .⟩ [5] convertit ille solutum gaudio vultum et
" Miserere " inquit " frater. Ubi arma non sunt,
libere loquor. Eripe me latroni cruento et qualibet
saevitia paenitentiam iudicis tui puni. Satis magnum erit misero solacium, tua voluntate cecidisse."

---

[1] *Müller emends to* pro poeta mulcarent.
[2] hac *Dousa:* haec.
[3] *Deleted by Buecheler.*
[4] ab hoc cibo] *Ehlers would delete.*
[5] *Lacuna indicated by Buecheler.*

head, and fled out of the temple. I was afraid that he would call me also a poet. So I followed him in his flight, and came to the beach, and as soon as we were out of range and could stop, I said, " Tell me, cannot you get rid of your disease? You have been in my company less than two hours, and you have talked more often like a poet than like a man. I am not surprised that the crowd pursue you with stones. *I* shall load my pockets with stones too, and whenever you proceed to forget yourself I shall let blood from your head." His expression altered, and he said, " My dear young friend, I have taken notice of omens before to-day. I mean, whenever I go into the theatre to recite anything, this is the sort of come-if-you-wish gathering with which the house usually welcomes me. But I do not want to have anything to quarrel about with you [too], so I will keep off this food for a whole day." " Well," said I, " if you forswear your madness for to-day, we will dine together." . . .

I gave the house-porter orders about our supper. . . .

I saw Giton, with some towels and scrapers, hugging the wall in sad embarrassment. You could see he was not a willing slave. So to enable me to catch his eye . . . he turned round, his face softened with pleasure, and he said, " Forgive me, brother. As there are no deadly weapons here, I speak freely. Take me away from this bloody robber and punish me as cruelly as you like, your penitent judge.[1] It will be quite enough consolation for my misery to die

[1] The words refer to the phrase in Chapter 80 *commisi iudici* (sc. *Gitoni*) *litem*, where Encolpius left Giton to choose between himself and Ascyltos.

Supprimere ego querellam iubeo, ne quis consilia deprehenderet, relictoque Eumolpo—nam in balneo carmen recitabat—per tenebrosum et sordidum egressum extraho Gitona raptimque in hospitium meum pervolo. Praeclusis deinde foribus invado pectus amplexibus et perfusum os lacrimis vultu meo contero. Diu vocem neuter invenit; nam puer etiam singultibus crebris amabile pectus quassaverat. " O facinus " inquam " indignum, quod amo te quamvis relictus, et in hoc pectore, cum vulnus ingens fuerit, cicatrix non est. Quid dicis, peregrini amoris concessio? Dignus hac iniuria fui?" Postquam se amari sensit, supercilium altius sustulit ⟨. . .⟩[1]

" Nec amoris arbitrium ad alium iudicem detuli.[2] Sed nihil iam queror, nihil iam memini, si bona fide paenitentiam[3] emendas." Haec cum inter gemitus lacrimasque fudissem, detersit ille pallio vultum et " Quaeso " inquit " Encolpi, fidem memoriae tuae appello: ego te reliqui, an tu me prodidisti? Equidem fateor et prae me fero: cum duos armatos viderem, ad fortiorem confugi." Exosculatus pectus sapientia plenum inieci cervicibus manus, et ut facile intellegeret redisse me in gratiam et optima fide reviviscentem amicitiam, toto pectore adstrinxi.

92   Et iam plena nox erat mulierque cenae mandata curaverat, cum Eumolpus ostium pulsat. Interrogo ego: " quot estis?" obiterque per rimam foris speculari diligentissime coepi, num Ascyltos una venisset.

---

[1] *Lacuna indicated in Pithoeus's 2nd edition.*

[2] detuli *Buecheler*: tulit *and* tuli.

[3] praeterita *Müller*: praeteritam dementiam *suggests Fraenkel.*

because you wish it." I told him to stop his lamentation, for fear anyone should overhear our plans. We left Eumolpus behind—for he was reciting a poem in the bathroom—and I took Giton out by a dark, dirty exit, and flew with all speed to my lodgings. Then I shut the door and warmly embraced him, and rubbed my face against his cheek, which was wet with tears. For a time neither of us could utter a sound; the boy's dear breast shook with continuous sobs. "It is a shame and a wonder!" I cried, "You left me, and yet I love you, and no scar is left on my breast, where the wound was so deep. Have you any excuse for yielding your love to a stranger? Did I deserve this blow?" As soon as he felt that I loved him, he began to hold his head up. . . .

"I laid our love's cause before no other judge. But I make no complaint, I will forget all, if you improve your penitence by keeping your word." I poured out my words with groans and tears, but Giton wiped his face on his cloak, and said, "Now, Encolpius, I ask you, I appeal to your honest memory; did *I* leave you, or did *you* betray me? I admit, I confess it openly, that when I saw two armed men before me, I hurried to the side of the stronger." I pressed my lips to his dear wise breast, and put my arms round his neck, and hugged him close to me, to make it quite plain that I was in amity with him again, and that our friendship lived afresh in perfect confidence.

It was now quite dark, and the woman had seen to our orders for supper, when Eumolpus knocked at the door. I asked, "How many of you are there?" and began as I spoke to look carefully through a chink in the door to see whether Ascyltos had come with him.

Deinde ut solum hospitem vidi, momento recepi.
Ille ut se in grabatum reiecit viditque Gitona in
conspectu ministrantem, movit caput et " Laudo "
inquit " Ganymedem. Oportet hodie bene sit."
Non delectavit me tam curiosum principium timuique,
ne in contubernium recepissem Ascylti parem.
Instat Eumolpus, et cum puer illi potionem dedisset,
" Malo te " inquit " quam balneum totum " siccato-
que avide poculo negat sibi unquam acidius fuisse.
" Nam et dum lavor " ait " paene vapulavi, quia
conatus sum circa solium sedentibus carmen recitare,
et postquam de balneo tanquam de theatro [1] eiectus
sum, circuire omnes angulos coepi et clara voce
Encolpion clamitare. Ex altera parte iuvenis nudus,
qui vestimenta perdiderat, non minore clamoris
indignatione Gitona flagitabat. Et me quidem pueri
tanquam insanum imitatione petulantissima derise-
runt, illum autem frequentia ingens circumvenit cum
plausu et admiratione timidissima. Habebat enim
inguinum pondus tam grande, ut ipsum hominem
laciniam fascini crederes. O iuvenem laboriosum:
puto illum pridie incipere, postero die finire. Itaque
statim invenit auxilium; nescio quis enim, eques
Romanus ut aiebant [2] infamis, sua veste errantem
circumdedit ac domum abduxit, credo, ut tam magna
fortuna solus uteretur. At ego ne mea quidem vestimenta ab offici⟨ali dol⟩oso [3] recepissem, nisi notorem

---

[1] *Müller deletes* tamquam de theatro.
[2] aiebant *Dousa*: aiebat.
[3] officiali doloso *Fraenkel*: officioso⟨capsario⟩ *Müller in his*
2nd edition (an adscript of Scaliger gives capsarius). officioso *L*.

---

[1] See above, pp. 128–129.

When I saw that he was the only visitor, I let him in at once. He threw himself on a bed, and when he saw Giton before his eyes waiting at table, he wagged his head and said, "I like your Ganymede.[1] To-day should be a fine time for us." I was not pleased at this inquisitive opening; I was afraid I had let Ascyltos's double into companionship. Eumolpus persisted, and, when the boy brought him a drink, said, "I like you better than the whole bathful." He greedily drank the cup dry, and said he had never taken anything with a sharper tang in it. "Why, I was nearly flogged while I was washing," he cried, "because I tried to go round the bath and recite poetry to the people sitting in it, and when I was thrown out of the bathroom as if it were the theatre, I proceeded to look round all the corners, and shouted for Encolpius in a loud voice. In another part of the place a naked young man who had lost his clothes kept clamouring for Giton with equally noisy indignation. The boys laughed at me with saucy mimicry as if I were crazy, but a large crowd surrounded him, clapping their hands and humbly admiring. For the weight of groin which he had was so huge that you would have thought that the man himself was the flap of a prick-charm. Oh dear! What a hero of labours the young man is! I think he could start on the day before and end only on the day after. So he found an ally at once: some Roman knight or other, a low fellow they said, put his own clothes on him as he strayed round, and took him off home, I suppose, in order to enjoy so great a good fortune alone. I should never have got my own clothes back from the crafty attendant if I had not produced someone to

dedissem. Tanto magis expedit inguina quam
ingenia fricare." Haec Eumolpo dicente mutabam
ego frequentissime vultum, iniuriis scilicet inimici
mei hilaris, commodis tristis. Utcunque tamen,
tanquam non agnoscerem fabulam, tacui et cenae
ordinem explicui . . .

93   " Vile est, quod licet, et animus errori intentus [1]
iniurias diligit.

> Ales Phasiacis petita Colchis
> atque Afrae [2] volucres placent palato,
> quod non sunt faciles : at albus anser
> et pictis anas enotata [3] pennis
> plebeium sapit.   Ultimis ab oris
> attractus scarus atque arata [4] Syrtis,
> si quid naufragio dedit, probatur :
> mullus iam gravis est.   Amica vincit
> uxorem.   Rosa cinnamum veretur.
> Quicquid quaeritur, optimum videtur."

" Hoc est " inquam " quod promiseras, ne quem
hodie versum faceres ? per fidem, saltem nobis parce,

---

[1] errori intentus *Buecheler*: ⟨in⟩ errore lentus *and later*
animus errore inlectus *suggests Müller*: errore lentus.

[2] Afrae *Puteanus*: aeriae.

[3] enotata *Jungermann*: enovata *Pithoeus*: involuta *Busche*:
innotata *suggests Fraenkel*: elevata *thinks Müller in ed.
1*, involuta *in ed. 2*: renovata.

[4] taetra (tetra) *Jacobs*.

---

[1] The meaning seems to be that it is more important to stir
up one's sexual than one's mental powers.

[2] The bird is the pheasant, the name being derived, through
the Latin *phasianus* or *phasiana*, from the river Phasis (the
Rion) in Colchis east of the Black Sea into which the Rion
flows. From this region pheasants (still common there) were
first brought westwards. The reciter is Eumolpus.

vouch for me. So much the greater gain is it to rub groins than geniuses." [1] As Eumolpus told me all this, my expression kept changing, for of course I laughed at my enemy's straits and frowned on his fortune. But anyhow I kept quiet as if I did not know what the story was about, and set forth our bill of fare. . . .

"What we may have we do not care about; our minds are bent on folly and love what is troublesome.

"The bird [2] won from Colchis where Phasis flows, and fowls [3] from Africa, are sweet to taste because they are not easy to win; but the white goose and the duck with brightly marked wings have a homely savour. The wrasse drawn from far-off shores, and the yield of furrowed [4] Syrtis is praised if first it wrecks a ship: the mullet by now is a weariness. The mistress eclipses the wife, the rose bows down to the cinnamon. What men must seek after seems ever best."

"What about your promise, that you would not make a single verse today?" I said. "On your

---

[3] Guinea-fowl (particularly *Numida ptilorhyncha*) from north and north-west Africa, especially Numidia (Algeria).

[4] " ploughed " used of the surface of the sea, furrowed by voyaging ships, or of a beach scored by landing ships. But " ploughed " might be taken in the agricultural sense; and *arare Syrtes* (" to plough the Syrtes ") may have been used like *arare litus* (" to plough the sea-shore ") which would be useless labour. *Syrtis* properly meant a marine sandbank; but the name was used specially for two broad gulfs, with their shores, in North Africa—the *Syrtis maior*, the Gulf of Sirte (Sidri), Cyrenaica and Tripolitania, and the *Syrtis minor*, the Gulf of Gabès in Tunisia. Their desolate sandy beaches had the reputation of being very dangerous because of sand-clouds raised by wind.

219

qui te nunquam lapidavimus. Nam si aliquis ex is, qui in eodem synoecio potant, nomen poetae olfecerit, totam concitabit viciniam et nos omnes sub eadem causa obruet. Miserere et aut pinacothecam aut balneum cogita." Sic me loquentem obiurgavit Giton, mitissimus puer, et negavit recte facere, quod seniori conviciarer simulque oblitus officii mensam, quam humanitate posuissem, contumelia tollerem, multaque alia moderationis verecundiaeque verba, quae formam eius egregie decebant. . . .

94 LO | " O felicem " inquit " matrem tuam, quae te talem peperit: macte virtute esto. Raram fecit mixturam cum sapientia forma. Itaque ne putes te tot verba perdidisse, amatorem invenisti. Ego laudes tuas carminibus implebo. Ego paedagogus et custos etiam quo non iusseris, sequar. Nec iniuriam Encolpius accipit, alium amat." Profuit etiam Eumolpo miles ille, qui mihi abstulit gladium; alioquin quem animum adversus Ascylton sumpseram, eum in Eumolpi sanguinem exercuissem. Nec fefellit hoc Gitona. Itaque extra cellam processit, tanquam aquam peteret, iramque meam prudenti absentia extinxit. Paululum ergo intepescente saevitia " Eumolpe " inquam " iam malo vel carminibus loquaris, quam eiusmodi tibi vota proponas. Et ego iracundus sum, et tu libidinosus: vide, quam non conveniat his moribus. Puta igitur me furiosum esse, L cede insaniae, id est ocius foras exi." | Confusus hac denuntiatione Eumolpus non quaesiit iracundiae causam, sed continuo limen egressus adduxit re-

---

[1] There are echoes here of three passages of Virgil: *Aeneid,* I, 605–606; IX, 641–642, and V, 343–344. Codex *l* says that Eumolpus addresses Giton.

honour, spare us at least: we have never stoned you. If a single one of the people who are drinking in the same tenement with us scents the name of a poet, he will rouse the whole neighbourhood and ruin us all for the same reason. Spare us then, and remember the picture-gallery or the baths." Giton, the gentle boy, reproved me when I spoke thus, and said that I was wrong to rebuke my elders, and forget my duty so far as to spoil with my insults the dinner I had ordered out of kindness, with much more tolerant and modest advice which well became his beautiful self. . . .

"Happy was the mother who bore such a son as you," he said, "be good and prosper. Beauty and wisdom has made a rare conjunction.[1] So do not think that all your words have been wasted. In me you have found a lover. I will do justice to your worth in verse. I will teach and protect you, and follow you even where you do not bid me. I do Encolpius no wrong; he loves another."

That soldier who took away my sword did Eumolpus a good turn too; otherwise I would have appeased the wrath raised in me against Ascyltos with the blood of Eumolpus. Giton was not blind to this. So he went out of the room on a pretence of fetching water, and quenched my wrath by his tactful departure. Then, as my fury cooled a little, I said, "I would prefer even that you should talk poetry now, Eumolpus, rather than harbour such hopes. *I* am choleric, and *you* are lecherous: understand that these dispositions do not suit each other. Well, regard me as a maniac, yield to my infirmity, in short, get out quick." Eumolpus was staggered by this attack, and never asked why I was angry, but went out of the room at

pente ostium cellae meque nihil tale expectantem
inclusit, exemitque raptim clavem et ad Gitona
investigandum cucurrit.

Inclusus ego suspendio vitam finire constitui. Et
iam semicinctio ⟨lecti⟩ [1] stantis ad parietem spondam
vinxeram cervicesque nodo condebam,[2] cum reseratis
foribus intrat Eumolpus cum Gitone meque a fatali
iam meta revocat ad lucem. Giton praecipue ex dolore in rabiem efferatus tollit clamorem, me utraque
manu impulsum praecipitat super lectum, " erras "
inquit " Encolpi, si putas contingere posse, ut ante
moriaris. Prior coepi; in Ascylti hospitio gladium
quaesivi. Ego si te non invenissem, periturus per
praecipitia [3] fui. Et ut scias non longe esse quaeren-
tibus mortem, specta invicem, quod me spectare vo-
luisti." Haec locutus mercennario Eumolpi novaculam rapit et semel iterumque cervice percussa ante
pedes collabitur nostros. Exclamo ego attonitus,
secutusque labentem eodem ferramento ad mortem
viam quaero. Sed neque Giton ulla erat suspicione
vulneris laesus, neque ego ullum sentiebam dolorem.
Rudis enim novacula et in hoc retusa, ut pueris
discentibus audaciam tonsoris [4] daret, instruxerat
thecam. Ideoque nec mercennarius ad raptum
ferramentum expaverat, nec Eumolpus interpella-
verat mimicam mortem.

95 LO | Dum haec fabula inter amantes luditur, dever-
sitor cum parte cenulae intervenit, contemplatusque
foedissimam volutationem iacentium " rogo " inquit

---

[1] lecti *added by Buecheler.*   [2] indebam *Burman.*
[3] *For* per (*added in Tornaesius' edition*) praecipitia *Nisbet
proposes* praecipiti via.
[4] *Fraenkel would delete* tonsoris.

once and suddenly banged the door, taking me completely by surprise and shutting me in. He pulled out the key in a moment and ran off to look for Giton.

I was locked in. I made up my mind to hang myself and die. I had just tied a belt to the frame of a bed which stood by the wall, and was stowing my neck in the noose, when the door was unlocked, Eumolpus came in with Giton, and called me back to light from the very bourne of death. Nay, Giton passed from grief to raving madness, and raised a shout, pushed me with both hands and threw me on the bed, and cried, " Encolpius, you are wrong if you suppose you could possibly die before me. *I* thought of suicide first; I looked for a sword in Ascyltos's lodgings. If I had not found you I would have hurled myself to death over a precipice. I will show you that death stands close by those who seek him : behold in your turn the scene you wished me to behold."

With these words he snatched a razor from Eumolpus's servant, drew it once, twice across his throat, and tumbled down at our feet. I gave a cry of horror, rushed to him as he fell, and sought the road of death with the same steel. But Giton was not marked with any trace of a wound, and I did not feel the least pain. The razor was untempered, and specially blunted in order to give boy-pupils the courage of a barber, and so had provided its own sheath. So the servant had not been alarmed when the steel was snatched from him, and Eumolpus did not interrupt our death-scene.

While this lover's play was being performed, an inmate of the house came in with part of our little dinner, and after looking at us rolling in most filthy fashion on the ground he said, " Are you drunk,

" ebrii estis, an fugitivi, an utrumque ? Quis autem
grabatum illum erexit, aut quid sibi vult tam furtiva
molitio ? Vos mehercules ne mercedem cellae daretis,
fugere nocte in publicum voluistis. Sed non impune.
Iam enim faxo sciatis non viduae hanc insulam esse
sed M. Mannicii." Exclamat Eumolpus " etiam
minaris ? " simulque os hominis palma excussissima
pulsat. Ille tot hospitum potionibus † liberum † [1]
urceolum fictilem in Eumolpi caput iaculatus est
solvitque clamantis frontem et de cella se proripuit.
Eumolpus contumeliae impatiens rapit ligneum
candelabrum sequiturque abeuntem et creberrimis
ictibus supercilium suum vindicat. Fit concursus
familiae hospitumque ebriorum frequentia. Ego
autem nactus occasionem vindictae Eumolpum
excludo, redditaque scordalo vice sine aemulo scilicet
et cella utor et nocte.

Interim coctores insulariique mulcant exclusum et
alius veru extis stridentibus plenum in oculos eius
intentat, alius furca de carnario rapta statum proe-
liantis componit. Anus praecipue lippa, sordidissimo
praecincta linteo, soleis ligneis imparibus imposita,
canem ingentis magnitudinis catena trahit instigat-
que in Eumolpon. Sed ille candelabro se ab omni
periculo vindicabat. Videbamus nos omnia per fora-
96 men valvae, quod paulo ante ansa ostioli rupta laxa-

[1] *This and the other reading* liber *are corrupt and some words
may be missing. Read perhaps simply* libatum *or* tritum.

---

[1] So Heseltine: *liberum* if not corrupt might mean simply
" free " from so many drinkings: not being used any longer.

please, or run-away slaves, or both? Who put up the
bed there, and what do all these sneaking contri-
vances mean? I declare you meant to run off in the
dark into the public street rather than pay for your
room. But you shall pay for it. I will teach you
that this block of flats does not belong to a poor
widow, but to Marcus Mannicius." "What?"
shouted Eumolpus, "you dare threaten us." And as
he spoke he struck the man in the face with all the
force of his outstretched hand. The man hurled a
little earthenware pot, which was empty, all the
guests having drunk from it,[1] at Eumolpus's head,
broke the skin of his forehead in the midst of his
clamour, and rushed out of the room. Eumolpus
would not brook an insult; he seized a wooden candle
stick and followed the lodger out, and avenged his
bloody forehead with a rain of blows. All the household ran up, and a crowd of drunken lodgers. I had a
chance of punishing Eumolpus, and I shut him out,
and so got even with the brawler, and of course had
the room and the night to myself without a rival.

Meanwhile cooks and lodgers belaboured him now
that he was locked out, and one thrust a spit full of
hissing meat into his eyes, another took a fork from a
dresser and struck a fighting attitude. Above all, a
blear-eyed old woman with a very dirty linen wrap
round her, balancing herself on an uneven pair of
clogs, took the lead, brought up a dog of enormous
size on a chain, and set him on to Eumolpus. But
the candlestick was enough to protect him from all
danger.

We saw everything through a hole in the folding
doors, which had been made by the handle of the

verat, favebamque ego vapulanti. Giton autem non
oblitus misericordiae suae reserandum esse ostium
succurrendumque periclitanti censebat. Ego du-
rante adhuc iracundia non continui manum, sed caput
miserantis stricto acutoque [1] articulo percussi. Et
ille quidem flens consedit in lecto. Ego autem alter-
nos opponebam foramini oculos iniuriaque [2] Eumolpi

L | velut quodam cibo me replebam | advocationemque
LO commendabam, cum procurator insulae Bargates a
cena excitatus a duobus lecticariis in mediam rixam
perfertur; nam erat etiam pedibus aeger. Is ut
rabiosa barbaraque voce in ebrios fugitivosque diu
peroravit, respiciens ad Eumolpon " o poetarum " inquit " disertissime, tu eras? Et non discedunt ocius
nequissimi servi manusque continent a rixa? " . . .

L | " Contubernalis mea mihi fastum facit. Ita, si me
amas, maledic illam versibus, ut habeat pudorem " . . .

97   Dum Eumolpus cum Bargate in secreto loquitur,
intrat stabulum praeco cum servo publico aliaque
sane [3] modica frequentia, facemque fumosam magis
quam lucidam quassans haec proclamavit: " puer in
balneo paulo ante aberravit, annorum circa XVI,
crispus, mollis, formosus, nomine Giton. Si quis eum
reddere aut commonstrare voluerit, accipiet nummos

---

[1] *Nisbet would delete* acutoque.
[2] iniuriaque *Tornaesius's edition*: iniuriamque (iniuriam δ).
For the order of the next words see Müller and Buecheler.
[3] *After* sane *Pithoeus adds* ⟨non⟩.

---

[1] Nisbet's suggestion " with knuckles drawn " (like a
sword) is attractive, but need we delete *acutoque*? " Knuckles,
a sword drawn and sharp."

door being broken a short time before; and I was delighted to see him thrashed. But Giton clung to compassion, and said we ought to open the door and run to his help in peril. My indignation was still awake; I did not hold my hand, I rapped his compassionate head with my clenched sharp knuckles.[1] He cried and sat down on the bed. I put each eye to the chink by turns, and gorged myself on the miseries of Eumolpus like a dainty dish, and approved their prolongation. Then Bargates, the man in charge of the block of flats, was disturbed at his dinner, and two chairmen carried him right into the brawl; for he had gouty feet. In a furious vulgar voice he made a long oration against drunkards and escaped slaves, and then he looked at Eumolpus and said, " What, most learned bard, was it you? Get away quick, you damned slaves, and keep your hands from quarrelling." . . .

[2]" My mistress despises me. So curse her for me in rhyme, if you love me, and put shame into her." . . .

While Eumolpus was talking privately to Bargates, a crier came into the house with a municipal slave and quite a small crowd of other people, shook a torch which gave out more smoke than light, and made this proclamation: " Lost recently in the public baths, a boy aged about sixteen, hair curly, looks soft, of attractive appearance, answers to the name of Giton. A reward of a thousand pieces will be paid to any person willing to bring him back or indicate his where-

---

[2] The speaker is apparently Bargates. Codex *l* prefixes *Bargates procurator ad Eumolpum*, " Bargates the manager addressing Eumolpus."

mille." Nec longe a praecone Ascyltos stabat amictus discoloria veste atque in lance argentea indicium et fidem praeferebat. Imperavi Gitoni, ut raptim grabatum subiret annecteretque pedes et manus institis, [quibus sponda culcitam ferebat,] [1] ac sic [ut olim Vlixes pro ariete adhaesisset, extentus infra grabatum] [2] scrutantium eluderet manus. Non est moratus Giton imperium [3] momentoque temporis inseruit vinculo manus et Vlixem astu simillimo vicit. Ego ne suspicioni relinquerem locum, lectulum vestimentis implevi uniusque hominis vestigium ad corporis mei mensuram figuravi.

Interim Ascyltos ut pererravit omnes cum viatore cellas, venit ad meam, et hoc quidem pleniorem spem concepit, quo diligentius oppessulatas invenit fores. Publicus vero servus inserta [4] commissuris secure [5] claustrorum firmitatem [6] laxavit. Ego ad genua Ascylti procubui et per memoriam amicitiae perque societatem miseriarum petii, ut saltem ostenderet fratrem. Immo ut fidem haberent fictae preces, " scio te " inquam " Ascylte, ad occidendum me venisse. Quo enim secures attulisti ? Itaque satia

---

[1] *Müller deletes the clause* quibus . . . ferebat.
[2] *Fraenkel would delete the clause* ut olim . . . adhaesisset *and Müller continues the deletion through* grabatum. *For* pro ariete *Muncker proposed* imo ariete, *and Buecheler proposed* pro⟨. . .⟩arieti, *for example* pro⟨salute⟩arieti. *It may be that nothing is interpolated here but that* pro ariete *was written by Petronius after* grabatum " *under the bed in place of a ram* "; *that later* pro ariete *was misplaced in front of* adhaesisset; *and that we should read* ac sic ut olim Ulixes adhaesisset extentus

abouts." Ascyltos stood close by the crier in clothes of many colours, holding out the reward on a silver dish to prove his honesty. I told Giton to get under the bed at once, and hook his feet and hands into the girths which held up the mattress on the frame, and (as Ulysses of old clung tightly), stretched out under the bed instead of a ram,[1] evade the grasp of searchers. Giton obeyed orders at once, and in a second had slipped his hands into the webbing, and surpassed even Ulysses at his own tricks. I did not want to leave any room for suspicion, so I stuffed the bed with clothes, and arranged them in the shape of a man about my own height sleeping by himself.

Meanwhile Ascyltos went round all the rooms with a constable, and when he came to mine, his hopes swelled within him at finding the door bolted with especial care. The municipal slave put an axe into the joints, and loosened the bolts from their place. I fell at Ascyltos's feet, and besought him, by the memory of our friendship and the miseries we had shared, at least to show me my brother. Further to win belief in my sham prayers, I said, " I know you have come to kill me, Ascyltos. Else why have you brought an axe with you ? Well, satisfy your rage.

---

[1] For the story of how Odysseus escaped from the blinded Cyclops by clinging to a ram's belly underneath, see Homer, *Odyssey*, IX, 420 ff.

---

infra grabatum pro ariete scrutantium eluderet manus. *This I have translated. E. H. W.*

3 *Müller deletes* imperium.
4 inserta *Fraenkel*: insertans.
5 securem (*sc.* insertans) *Buecheler.*
6 firmitatem *Dousa*: infirmitatem.

iracundiam tuam: praebeo ecce cervicem, funde
sanguinem, quem sub praetextu quaestionis petisti."
Amolitur Ascyltos invidiam et se vero nihil aliud
quam fugitivum suum dixit quaerere, mortem nec[1]
hominis concupisse nec supplicis, utique eius quem[2]
98 post fatalem rixam habuit[3] carissimum. At non
servus publicus tam languide agit, sed raptam
cauponi harundinem subter lectum mittit omniaque
etiam foramina parietum scrutatur. Subducebat
Giton ab ictu corpus et reducto[4] timidissime spiritu
ipsos sciniphes ore tangebat . . .

Eumolpus autem, quia effractum ostium cellae neminem poterat excludere, irrumpit perturbatus et
" mille " inquit " nummos inveni; iam enim perse-
quar abeuntem praeconem et in potestate tua esse
Gitonem   meritissima   proditione[5]   monstrabo.
Genua ego perseverantis amplector, ne morientes
vellet occidere, et ´ merito " inquam " excan-
desceres, si posses perditum[6] ostendere. Nunc
inter turbam puer fugit, nec quo abierit, suspicari
possum. Per fidem, Eumolpe, reduc puerum et vel
Ascylto redde." Dum haec ego iam credenti persuadeo, Giton collectione spiritus plenus ter continuo
ita sternutavit, ut grabatum concuteret. Ad quem
motum Eumolpus conversus[7] salvere Gitona iubet.
Remota etiam culcita videt Vlixem, cui vel esuriens

---

[1] after nec Fuchs adds reasonably insontis.
[2] after quem Ernout adds etiam, rightly?
[3] habuerit Jacobs: habuisset Buecheler.
[4] retento Müller.
[5] proditione Pithoeus: propositione.

Here is my neck, shed my blood, the real object of
your pretended legal search." Ascyltos threw off his
resentment, and declared that he wanted nothing but
his own runaway slave, that he did not desire the
death of any man or any suppliant, much less of one
whom he loved very dearly now that their deadly dispute was over.

But the constable was not so deficient in energy.
He took a cane from the inn-keeper, and pushed it
under the bed, and poked into everything, even the
cracks in the walls. Giton twisted away from the
stick, drew in his breath very gently, and pressed his
lips even against the bugs in the bedding. . . . The
broken door of the room could not keep anyone out,
and Eumolpus rushed in in a fury, and cried, " I have
found a thousand pieces; for I mean to follow the
crier as he goes away, and betray you as you richly
deserve, and tell him that Giton is in your hands."
He persisted, I fell at his feet, besought him not to
kill a dying man, and said, " You might well be ex-
cited if you could reveal the lost one. As it is, the
boy has run away in the crowd, and I have not the
least idea where he has gone. As you love me,
Eumolpus, get the boy back, and give him to Ascyltos
if you like." I was just inducing him to believe me,
when Giton burst with holding his breath, and all at
once sneezed three times so that he shook the bed.
Eumolpus turned round at the stir, and said " Good
day, Giton." He pulled off the mattress, and saw an

---

[6] perditum *Jacobs*: abditum *Fraenkel*: quaesitum *Müller*
(*2nd edition*).

[7] conversus] *Fraenkel suggested deleting. Compare Chapter*
41.

Cyclops potuisset parcere. Mox conversus ad me
"quid est" inquit "latro? ne deprehensus quidem
ausus es mihi verum dicere. Immo ni deus quidam
humanarum rerum arbiter pendenti puero excussis-
set indicium, elusus circa popinas errarem " . . .

Giton longe blandior quam ego, primum araneis
oleo madentibus vulnus, quod in supercilio factum
erat, coartavit. Mox palliolo suo laceratam mutavit
vestem, amplexusque iam mitigatum osculis tanquam
fomentis aggressus est et "in tua" inquit "pater
carissime, in tua sumus custodia. Si Gitona tuum
amas, incipe velle servare. Utinam me solum inimicus ignis hauriret vel hibernum invaderet mare. Ego
enim omnium scelerum materia, ego causa sum. Si
perirem, conveniret inimicis " . . .

99   " ego sic semper et ubique vixi, ut ultimam quam-
que lucem tanquam non redituram consumerem " . . .

profusis ego lacrimis rogo quaesoque, ut mecum
quoque redeat in gratiam: neque enim in amantium
esse potestate furiosam aemulationem. Daturum
tamen operam, ne aut dicam aut faciam amplius, quo
possit offendi. Tantum omnem scabitudinem animo
tanquam bonarum artium magister delevet [1] sine
cicatrice. " Incultis asperisque regionibus diutius

---

[1] delevet *Fraenkel* (*Glotta, XXXVII, 1958, 312*): deleret.

---

[1] Codex *l* here prefixes Eumolpus as the speaker. In
Chapter 99 the reconciliation between Encolpius and Eumolpus
seems to complete the pacification begun in Chapter 98. Yet
suddenly all three pack up and go on board a ship (as arranged
by Eumolpus, Chapter 101) for a voyage for which the reason
and preparations have not been mentioned in the tradition;

Ulysses whom even a hungry Cyclops might have spared. Then he turned on me, " Now, you thief; you did not dare to tell me the truth even when you were caught. In fact, unless the God who controls man's destiny had wrung a sign from this boy as he hung there, I should now be wandering round the pot-houses like a fool." . . .

Giton was far more at ease than I. He first stanched a cut which had been made on Eumolpus's forehead with spider's webs soaked in oil. He then took off his torn clothes, and in exchange gave him a short cloak of his own, then put his arms round him, for he was now softening, poulticed him with kisses, and said, " Dearest father, we are in your hands, yours entirely. If you love your Giton, make up your mind to save him. I wish the cruel fire might engulf me alone, or the wintry sea assail me. I am the object of all his transgressions, I am the cause. If I were gone, you two might patch up your quarrel." . . .

[1]" At all times and in all places I have lived such a life that I spent each passing day as though that light would never return." . . .

I burst into tears, and begged and prayed him to be friends again with me too: a true lover was incapable of mad jealousy. At the same time I would take care to do nothing more in word or deed by which he could possibly be hurt. Only he must smooth off all irritation from his mind like a man of true culture, and leave no scar. " On the wild rough uplands the

I feel that the gap at the end of 98 is a large one in which came matters connected with the projected voyage, with Eumolpus not yet fully appeased.

233

nives haerent, ast ubi aratro domefacta tellus nitet,
dum loqueris, levis pruina dilabitur. Similiter [in
pectoribus] ira [considit] [1] feras quidem mentes
obsidet, eruditas praelabitur." " Ut scias " inquit
Eumolpus " verum esse, quod dicis, ecce etiam osculo
iram finio. Itaque, quod bene eveniat, expedite
sarcinulas et vel sequimini me vel, si mavultis,
ducite." Adhuc loquebatur, cum crepuit ostium
impulsum, stetitque in limine barbis horrentibus
nauta et " moraris " inquit " Eumolpe, tanquam
† propudium † [2] ignores." Haud mora, omnes con-
surgimus, et Eumolpus quidem mercennarium suum
iam olim dormientem exire cum sarcinis iubet. Ego
cum Gitone quicquid erat, in iter [3] compono et adora-
tis sideribus intro navigium . . .

100 " molestum est quod puer hospiti placet. Quid
autem? Non commune est, quod natura optimum
fecit? Sol omnibus lucet. Luna innumerabilibus
comitata sideribus [4] etiam feras ducit ad pabulum.
Quid aquis dici formosius potest? In publico tamen
manant. Solus ergo amor furtum potius quam praemium erit? Immo vero nolo habere bona, nisi quibus
populus inviderit. Unus, et senex, non erit gravis;
etiam cum voluerit aliquid sumere, opus anhelitu pro-
det." Haec ut infra fiduciam posui fraudavique

---

[1] in pectoribus *and* considit] *delete, says Fraenkel.*

[2] *Perhaps* pro pudor! *J. Sullivan thinks* prope diem *lurks
here.*

[3] in iter *Buecheler*: manticae *Fraenkel*: alt∽. *There are
various conjectures* impono *Fraenkel for* compono.

snow lies late, but when the earth is beautiful under the mastery of the plough, the light frost passes while you speak. Thus anger besieges savage minds, and glides over the man of learning." "There," said Eumolpus, "you see what you say is true. Behold, I banish my anger with a kiss. So good luck go with us. Get ready your luggage and follow me, or lead the way if you like." He was still talking, when a knock sounded on the door, and a sailor with a straggly beard stood at the entrance and said, "You hang about, Eumolpus, as if you did not know [—blast you] (?)." We all got up in a hurry, and Eumolpus ordered his paid servant, already asleep for some time, to come out with his baggage. Giton and I put together all we had for a journey; I asked a blessing of the stars, and went aboard. . .

" I am annoyed because the boy takes a stranger's fancy. But are not all the finest works of nature common property? The sun shines upon all men. The moon with countless troops of stars in her train leads even the beasts to their food. Can we imagine anything more lovely than water? yet it flows for all the world. Then shall love alone be stolen rather than enjoyed? The truth is that I do not care for possessions unless the common herd are jealous of them. One rival, and he too an old man, will not be troublesome; even if he wants to gain an advantage his shortness of breath will give him away." When I had made these points without any confidence,

---

4 *Fraenkel would delete* innumerabilibus c. sideribus. *The phrase may come, in prose-parody, from hexameter or elegiac poetry.*

animum dissidentem, coepi somnum obruto tunicula capite mentiri.

Sed repente quasi destruente fortuna constantiam meam eiusmodi vox super constratum puppis congemuit: " ergo me derisit ? " Et haec quidem virilis et paene auribus meis familiaris animum palpitantem percussit. Ceterum eadem indignatione mulier lacerata ulterius excanduit et " Si quis deus manibus meis " inquit " Gitona imponeret, quam bene exulem exciperem."[1] Uterque nostrum tam inexpectato ictus sono amiserat sanguinem. Ego praecipue quasi somnio quodam turbulento circumactus[2] diu vocem collegi tremebundisque manibus Eumolpi iam in soporem labentis laciniam et " Per fidem " inquam " pater, cuius haec navis est, aut quos vehat, dicere potes ? " Inquietatus ille moleste tulit et " Hoc erat " inquit " quod placuerat tibi, ut supra constratum[3] navis occuparemus secretissimum locum, nos patereris requiescere ? Quid porro ad rem pertinet, si dixero Licham Tarentinum esse dominum huiusce navigii, qui Tryphaenam exulem[4] Tarentum 101 ferat ? " Intremui post hoc fulmen attonitus, iuguloque detecto " aliquando " inquam " totum me, Fortuna, vicisti." Nam Giton quidem super pectus meum positus diu animam egit. Deinde ut effusus

---

[1] exciperem *in margin of Tornaesius's edition*: exciperent *Reiske*: exciperet *L*: acciperem *suggests Buecheler.*

[2] circumactus *Bongars*: circumamictus.

[3] *Fraenkel would delete* supra constratum.

[4] *Müller deletes* exulem.

deceiving my protesting spirit, I proceeded to cover
my head in my cloak and pretended to be asleep.

But suddenly, as though fate were in arms against
my resolution, a voice on the ship's deck said with a
groan, like this: " So he deceived me, then? "
These manly tones were somehow familiar to my ears,
and my heart beat fast as they struck me. But then
a woman torn by the same indignation broke out yet
more vehemently: " Ah, if the gods would deliver
Giton into my hands, what a fine welcome I would
give the runaway." The shock of these unexpected
sounds drove all the blood out of both of us. I
especially felt as if I were being hunted round in some
troubled dream; I was a long while finding my voice,
and then pulled Eumolpus's lappet with a shaking
hand, just as he was falling into a deep sleep, and said,
" Tell me the truth, father; can you say who owns
this ship, or who is on board? " He was annoyed at
being disturbed, and replied, " Was this why you
chose a very quiet corner on deck, to prevent us from
getting any rest? Further, what on earth is the use
of my telling you that Lichas of Tarentum is the
master of this boat, and is carrying Tryphaena to
Tarentum as under a sentence of banishment? "[1] I
was thunderstruck at this blow. I bared my throat,
and cried, " Ah, Fate, at last you have smitten me hip
and thigh." For Giton, who was sprawling over me,
had already fainted. Then the sweat broke out on us

[1] The name Tryphaena implies sexiness and good living.
Unless *exulem* means the same as applies to Giton just above—
" runaway ", " on the run ", the reason for her banishment
was probably told in some missing passage. We hear more
about her later.

sudor utriusque spiritum revocavit, comprehendi
Eumolpi genua et " Miserere " inquam " mori-
entium et pro consortio studiorum commoda manum;
mors venit, quae nisi per te ⟨non⟩ [1] licet, potest esse
pro munere." Inundatus hac Eumolpus invidia iurat
per deos deasque se neque scire quid acciderit, nec
ullum dolum malum consilio adhibuisse, sed mente
simplicissima et vera fide in navigium comites in-
duxisse, quo ipse iam pridem fuerit usurus. " Quae
autem hic insidiae sunt " inquit " aut quis nobiscum
Hannibal navigat? Lichas Tarentinus, homo vere-
cundissimus et non tantum huius navigii dominus,
quod regit, sed fundorum etiam aliquot et familiae
negotiantis, onus deferendum ad mercatum conducit.
Hic est Cyclops ille et [2] archipirata, cui vecturam
debemus; et praeter hunc Tryphaena, omnium
feminarum formosissima, quae voluptatis causa huc
atque illuc vectatur." " Hi sunt " inquit Giton
" quos fugimus " simulque raptim causas odiorum et
instans periculum trepidanti Eumolpo exponit. Confusus ille et consilii egens iubet quemque suam
sententiam promere et " Fingite " inquit " nos
antrum Cyclopis intrasse. Quaerendum est aliquod
effugium, nisi naufragium patimur et omni nos
periculo liberamus." [3] " Immo " inquit Giton " per-

[1] non *added* (*above the line*) *in* l.
[2] *Fraenkel would delete* Cyclops *and* et.
[3] patimur *Fuchs for* ponimus. liberamur *for* liberamus
Müller in his 2nd edition. Perhaps et omnino ⟨sic⟩ periculo
liberamur. *J. Sullivan proposes* facimus *for* ponimus.

and called us both back to life. I took Eumolpus by the knees, and cried, " Mercy on us! We are dead men. Help us, I implore you by our fellowship in learning; death is upon us, and we may come to welcome death, unless you prevent us from doing so."

Eumolpus was overwhelmed by this attack, and swore by gods and goddesses that he did not understand what had happened, and had no sinister intentions in his mind, but had taken us to share the voyage with him in perfect honesty and absolute good faith; he had been meaning to sail himself some time before. " Is there any trap here? " he said, " and who is the Hannibal[1] we have on board? Lichas of Tarentum is a respectable person. He is not only owner and captain of this ship, but has several estates and some slaves in business. He is carrying a cargo consigned to a market. This is the [ogre and][2] pirate king to whom we owe our passage; and besides, there is Tryphaena, loveliest of women, who sails from one place to another in the cause of pleasure." " It is these two we are running away from," said Giton, and poured out the story of our feud, and explained our imminent danger, till Eumolpus shook. He became muddled and helpless, and asked us each to put forward our views. " I would have you imagine that we have entered the ogre's den," he said. " We must find some way out, unless we suffer shipwreck and free ourselves from all danger." " No," said Giton,

[1] Hannibal, the great Carthaginian enemy of Rome in the third century B.C., was undeservedly regarded by Rome as cruel and faithless.

[2] A Cylops was taken from mythology as a type of horrid cruelty.

suade gubernatori, ut in aliquem portum navem
deducat, non sine praemio scilicet, et affirma ei
impatientem maris fratrem tuum in ultimis esse.
Poteris hanc simulationem et vultus confusione et
lacrimis obumbrare, ut misericordia permotus gubernator[1] indulgeat tibi." Negavit hoc Eumolpus
fieri posse, " quia ⟨nec⟩[2] magna " inquit " navigia
portubus se curvatis[3] insinuant, nec tam cito fratrem
defecisse veri simile erit. Accedit his, quod forsitan
Lichas officii causa visere languentem desiderabit.
Vides, quam valde nobis expediat, ultro dominum ad
fugientes accersere.[4] Sed finge navem ab ingenti
posse cursu deflecti et Licham non utique circumit-
urum aegrorum cubilia: quomodo possumus egredi
nave, ut non conspiciamur a cunctis? Opertis
capitibus, an nudis? Opertis, et quis non dare
manum languentibus volet? Nudis, et quid erit
102 aliud quam se ipsos proscribere?" " Quin potius "
inquam ego " ad temeritatem confugimus et per
funem lapsi descendimus in scapham praecisoque
vinculo reliqua fortunae committimus? Nec ego
in hoc periculum Eumolpon arcesso. Quid enim
attinet innocentem alieno periculo imponere? Contentus sum, si nos descendentes adiuverit" [casus][5].
" Non imprudens " inquit " consilium " Eumolpos
" si aditum haberet. Quis enim non euntes notabit?
Utique gubernator, qui pervigil nocte siderum quoque motus custodit. Et utcunque ⟨ei⟩[6] imponi

---

[1] *Nisbet would delete* gubernator.
[2] nec *added by Müller.*
[3] contractis *Müller in his 2nd edition. Perhaps* curtis.
[4] accersere *Buecheler*: arcessere *Jacobs*: accedere.
[5] *Deleted by Fuchs.*   [6] ei *added by Fuchs.*

" persuade the helmsman to run the boat into some harbour. Pay him well, of course, and tell him your brother cannot stand the sea, and is at his last gasp. You will be able to hide your deception by the confused look and the tears on your face. You will touch the helmsman's heart, and he will do you a favour." Eumolpus declared that this was impossible: "For large boats don't steer into landlocked [?] harbours, and it is incredible that our brother should collapse so soon. Besides, Lichas may perhaps ask to see the sick man as a matter of kindness. You realize what a fine turn we should do ourselves by leading the master up to his runaways with our own hands. But supposing the ship could be turned aside from her long passage, and Lichas will not after all go round the patients' beds; how could we leave the ship without being seen by every one? Cover our heads, or bare them? Cover them and every one will want to lend his arm to the poor sick man! Bare them, that is nothing more or less than advertising ourselves." " No," I said, " I should prefer to take refuge in boldness, slip down a rope into the boat,[1] cut the painter, and leave the rest to luck. I do not invite Eumolpus to share the risk. It is not fair to load an innocent person with another's troubles. I am satisfied if chance [?] will help us to get down." " It is a clever plan," said Eumolpus, " if there were any way of starting it. But every one will see you going: especially the helmsman, who watches all night long, and keeps guard even over the motions of the stars. Of course you might elude his unsleeping watchful-

---

[1] A single boat towed behind the ship.

nihil[1] dormienti posset, si per aliam partem navis fuga quaereretur: nunc per puppim, per ipsa gubernacula delabendum est [, a quorum regione funis descendit, qui scaphae custodiam tenet].[2] Praeterea illud miror, Encolpi, tibi non succurrisse, unum nautam stationis perpetuae interdiu noctuque iacere in scapha, nec posse inde custodem[3] nisi aut caede expelli aut praecipitari viribus. Quod an fieri possit, interrogate audaciam vestram. Nam quod ad meum quidem comitatum attinet, nullum recuso periculum, quod salutis spem ostendit. Nam sine causa [quidem][4] spiritum tanquam rem vacuam impendere ne vos quidem existimo velle. Videte, numquid hoc placeat: ego vos in duas iam pelles coniciam vinctosque loris inter vestimenta pro sarcinis[5] habebo, apertis scilicet aliquatenus labris, quibus et spiritum recipere possitis et cibum. Conclamabo deinde nocte servos poenam graviorem timentes praecipitasse se in mare. Deinde cum ventum fuerit in portum, sine ulla suspicione pro sarcinis vos efferam." " Ita vero " inquam ego " tanquam solidos alligaturus, quibus non soleat venter iniuriam facere? An tanquam eos qui sternutare non soleamus nec stertere? An quia hoc genus furti semel [mea][6] feliciter cessit? Sed finge una die vinctos posse durare: quid ergo, si diutius aut tranquillitas nos tenuerit aut adversa tempestas?

[1] nihil *Buecheler*: vel. *Fuchs deletes* vel dormienti.
[2] *Deleted by Müller*
[3] *Fraenkel would delete* custodem.
[4] *Deleted by Buecheler.*
[5] *Fraenkel would delete* pro sarcinis.

ness, if you wanted to escape off another part of the ship; but as it is, you want to slip off the stern close to the helm itself [where the rope which holds the boat safe hangs just by]. Again, I am surprised that it did not occur to you, Encolpius, that one sailor is always on duty night and day lying in the boat, and you cannot turn this sentry out except by killing him, or throw him out except by force. You must ask your own bold heart whether that can be done. As far as my coming with you goes, I do not shirk any danger which offers a chance of safety. But I suppose that even you do not wish to squander your lives like a vain trifle without any reason. Now see whether you approve of this. I will roll you in two bales, tie you up, and put you among my clothes as luggage, of course leaving the ends a bit open, so that you can get your breath and your food. Then I will raise the cry that my slaves have jumped overboard in the dark, being afraid of some heavier punishment. Then after we have arrived in harbour, I will carry you out like baggage, without arousing any suspicion." "What," I cried, "tie us up like wholly solid people whose stomachs never make them unhappy? Like people who never sneeze nor snore? Or just because this kind of trick turned out a success just once[1]? But even supposing we could endure one day tied up: what if we were detained longer by a calm or by rough weather? What should we do?

---

[1] Cleopatra had herself conveyed wrapped up in a carpet to Julius Caesar at Alexandria, Plutarch: *Life of Caesar*, c. 49.

---

[6] mea *deleted by Scaliger*: mihi *cod. Lambeth.*: antea *Schoppius*: ante *Müller in his 2nd edition*.

Quid facturi sumus? Vestes quoque diutius vincta
ruga consumit, et chartae alligatae mutant figuram
Iuvenes adhuc laboris expertes statuarum ritu
patiemur pannos et vincla?" . . .
" Adhuc aliquod iter salutis quaerendum est. Inspi
cite, quod ego inveni. Eumolpus tanquam litterarum
studiosus utique atramentum habet. Hoc ergo re
medio mutemus colores a capillis usque ad ungues
Ita tanquam servi Aethiopes et praesto tibi erimus
sine tormentorum iniuria hilares, et permutato colore
imponemus inimicis." " Quidni? " inquit Giton
" etiam circumcide nos, ut Iudaei videamur, et per-
tunde aures, ut imitemur Arabes, et increta facies, ut
suos Gallia cives putet: tanquam hic solus color
figuram possit pervertere et non multa una oporteat
consentiant ⟨ut⟩ omni ratione mendacium [1] constet.
Puta infectam medicamine faciem diutius durare
posse; finge nec aquae asperginem imposituram
aliquam corpori maculam, nec vestem atramento
adhaesuram, quod frequenter etiam non accersito
ferrumine infigitur: [2] age, numquid et labra possumus tumore taeterrimo implere? Numquid et crines
calamistro convertere? Numquid et frontes cicatri-
cibus scindere? Numquid et crura in orbem pandere? Numquid et talos ad terram deducere?
Numquid et barbam peregrina ratione figurare?
Color arte compositus inquinat corpus, non mutat.

[1] *The tradition for the whole passage here has*: pervertere et
non multa una oportet consentiant et non natione (ratione
Pithoeus's 2nd edition) mendacium constet. *On Fraenkel's
authority Müller in his 1st edition deletes the first* et non *and*

Even clothes that are tied up too long get creased and spoilt, and papers in bundles lose their shape. Are we young fellows who never worked in our lives to put up with ropes and dirty rags as if we were statues? . . . No, we still have to find some way of salvation. Look at what *I* thought of. Eumolpus, as a man of learning, is sure to have some ink. Let us use this medicine to dye ourselves, hair, nails, everything. Then we will stand by you with pleasure like Aethiopian slaves, without undergoing any tortures, and our change of colour will take in our enemies."

" Oh! yes," said Giton, " and please circumcise us too so that we look like Jews, and bore our ears to imitate Arabians, and chalk our faces till Gaul takes us for her own sons; as if this colour alone could alter our shapes, and it were not needed that many things act in unison to make a good lie on all accounts. Suppose the stain of dye on the face could last for some time; imagine that never a drop of water could make any mark on our skins, nor our clothes stick to the ink, which often clings to us without the use of any cement: but, tell me, can we also make our lips swell to a hideous thickness? Or transform our hair with curling-tongs? Or plough up our foreheads with scars? Or walk bow-legged? Or bend our ankles over to the ground? Or trim our beards in a foreign cut? Artificial colours dirty one's body without

---

una; *and he also deletes* et non natione. *In his 2nd edition he revises his opinion, and reads* pervertere et non multa una oporteat consentiant ut omni ratione mendacium. (oporteat *taken with* tamquam *above Heinsius*): ut omni *Crusius for the second* et non.

² *Stephanie West would delete the clause* quod . . . infigitur.

PETRONIUS ARBITER

Audite, quid amenti[1] succurrerit: praeligemus vesti-
103 bus capita et nos in profundum mergamus." " Nec
istud dii hominesque patiantur" Eumolpus exclamat " ut vos tam turpi exitu vitam finiatis. Immo
potius facite, quod iubeo. Mercennarius meus, ut ex
novacula comperistis, tonsor est: hic continuo radat
utriusque non solum capita, sed etiam supercilia.
Sequar ego frontes notans inscriptione sollerti,
ut videamini stigmate esse puniti. Ita eaedem litterae
et suspicionem declinabunt quaerentium et vultus
umbra supplicii tegent."

Non est dilata fallacia, sed ad latus navigii furtim
processimus capitaque cum superciliis[2] denudanda
tonsori praebuimus. Implevit Eumolpus frontes
utriusque ingentibus litteris et notum fugitivorum
epigramma per totam faciem liberali manu duxit.
Unus forte ex vectoribus, qui acclinatus lateri navis
exonerabat stomachum nausea gravem, notavit sibi
ad lunam tonsorem intempestivo inhaerentem ministerio, execratusque omen, quod imitaretur naufra-
gorum ultimum votum, in cubile reiectus est. Nos[3]
dissimulata nauseantis devotione ad † ordinem †[4]
tristitiae redimus, silentioque compositi reliquas
noctis horas male soporati consumpsimus . . .
104 " Videbatur mihi secundum quietem Priapus di-

[1] amenti *Buecheler*: menti *suggests Fraenkel*: timenti *l*:
dementi *cod. Lambeth. Perhaps* tamen.
[2] *Fraenkel would delete* cum superciliis.
[3] nos *Dousa*: non.
[4] ordinem *seems to be corrupt. Perhaps* turbinem.

---

[1] People threatened by shipwreck dedicated pieces of their
hair or beard to sea-gods.

altering it. Listen, I have thought of this in a crazy mood. Let us tie our heads in our clothes, and plunge into the deep."

" God and man forbid," cried Eumolpus, " that you should make such a vile conclusion of your lives. No, better take my advice. My slave, as you learned by his razor, is a barber. Let him shave the head of each of you this minute, and your eyebrows as well. Then I will come and mark your foreheads with some neat inscription, so that you look like slaves punished by branding. These letters will divert inquisitive people's suspicions, and at the same time conceal your faces with the shadow of punishment." We tried the trick at once, and walked cautiously to the side of the ship, and yielded up our heads and eyebrows to the barber to be shorn. Eumolpus covered both our foreheads with enormous letters, and scrawled the usual mark of runaway slaves all over our faces with a generous hand. But one of the passengers, who was extremely seasick, happened to be leaning over the side of the ship to relieve his stomach, and observed the barber in the moonlight busy with his ill-timed work. The man cursed this for an omen, because it looked like the last offering of a doomed crew,[1] and then threw himself back into his bunk. We pretended not to hear the sea-sick man, and went back to our process of gloom, and then lay down in silence and passed the remaining hours of the night in uneasy sleep. . . .

[2]" I thought I heard Priapus say in my dream: ' I

[2] Codex *l* here prefixes Lichas as the speaker. For Priapus, see p. 27.

cere: ' Encolpion quod [1] quaeris, scito a me in navem tuam esse perductum.' " Exhorruit Tryphaena et " Putes " inquit " una nos dormiisse; nam et mihi simulacrum Neptuni, quod Baiis in tetrastylo [2] notaveram, videbatur dicere: ' in nave Lichae Gitona invenies.' " " Hinc scies " inquit Eumolpus " Epicurum esse hominem divinum, qui eiusmodi ludibria facetissima ratione condemnat " ⟨. . .⟩ [3]

ceterum Lichas ut Tryphaenae somnium expiavit,[4] " quis " inquit " prohibet navigium scrutari, ne videamur divinae mentis opera damnare? " ⟨. . .⟩ [5] Is qui nocte miserorum furtum deprehenderat, Hesus nomine [6] subito proclamat: " Ergo illi qui [7] sunt qui nocte ad lunam [8] radebantur pessimo medius fidius exemplo? Audio enim non licere cuiquam mortalium in nave neque ungues neque capillos 105 deponere, nisi cum pelago ventus irascitur." Excanduit Lichas hoc sermone turbatus et " Itane " inquit " capillos aliquis in nave praecidit, et hoc nocte intempesta? Attrahite ocius nocentes in medium, ut sciam, quorum capitibus debeat navigium lustrari." " Ego " inquit Eumolpus " hoc iussi. Nec in [9] eodem futuro navigio auspicium mihi feci, sed quia

---

[1] quem *suggests Fraenkel.*

[2] Baiis in tetrastylo *Buecheler*: Baistor asylo. *Perhaps* Baiis pro asylo. *Heinsius proposed* in peristylo, *J. F. Gronov* in peristylio.

[3] *Lacuna indicated by Buecheler.*

[4] *Nisbet suggests* expiaret.

[5] *Lacuna indicated by Buecheler.*

[6] laesus omine *in margin of Tornaesius's edition. Fraenkel suggests* offensus omine.

[7] *Segebade deletes* qui.

tell you that Encolpius—to answer your inquiry—
has been led by me on board your ship.'" Tryphaena
shuddered and said, "You would think we had
slept together; I also dreamed that a likeness of
Neptune, which I noticed in a gallery at Baiae, said
to me: ' You will find Giton on board Lichas's ship.'"
" This shows you," said Eumolpus, "That Epicurus[1]
was a superhuman creature; he condemns jokes of
this kind in a very witty fashion." . . . However,
Lichas first prayed that Tryphaena's dream might
mean no harm, and then said, " There is no objection
to searching the ship to show that we do not despise
the workings of Providence." . . . Then the man who
had caught us at our wretched tricks the night before,
whose name was Hesus, suddenly shouted, " Then
who are those fellows who were being shaved in the
dark by moonlight? A mighty bad precedent, I
swear. I am told that no man alive ought to shed a
nail or a hair on board ship, unless winds and waves
are raging." At this speech Lichas fired up in alarm,
and said, " What, has anyone cut his hair on board my
ship, and at dead of night too? Quick, bring the
villains out here. I want to know what persons are
to be punished to give us a clear voyage." " Oh,"
said Eumolpus, " I gave those orders. I was not
doing anything unlucky, considering that I had to

---

[1] Epicurus, c. 342–270 B.C., the famous philosopher, who
taught that freedom from pain was the highest good. But
the allusion here is obscure.

---

[8] *Müller deleted* ad lunam *in his 1st edition, but retains the
words in his 2nd.*
[9] *in* Buecheler: non.

nocentes [1] horridos longosque habebant capillos, ne
viderer de nave carcerem facere, iussi squalorem
damnatis auferri; simul ut notae quoque litterarum
non adumbratae [2] comarum praesidio totae [3] ad
oculos legentium acciderent. Inter cetera apud
communem amicam consumpserunt pecuniam meam,
a qua illos proxima nocte extraxi mero unguentisque
perfusos. Ad summam, adhuc patrimonii mei
reliquias olent " . . .

itaque ut tutela navis expiaretur, placuit quadra-
genas utrique plagas imponi. Nulla ergo fit mora;
aggrediuntur nos furentes nautae cum funibus
temptantque vilissimo sanguine tutelam placare. Et
ego quidem tres plagas Spartana nobilitate concoxi.
Ceterum Giton semel ictus tam valde exclamavit, ut
Tryphaenae aures notissima voce repleret. [4] Non
solum era [5] turbata est, sed ancillae etiam omnes
familiari sono inductae ad vapulantem decurrunt.
Iam Giton mirabili forma exarmaverat nautas coe-
peratque etiam sine voce saevientes rogare, cum
ancillae pariter proclamant: " Giton est, Giton,
inhibete crudelissimas manus; Giton est, domina,
succurre." Deflectit aures Tryphaena iam sua
sponte credentes raptimque ad puerum devolat.
Lichas, qui me optime noverat, tanquam et ipse vocem

---

[1] *Fraenkel would delete* nocentes.

[2] *Fraenkel suggested deleting* adumbratae. *Müller in his 2nd
edition reads* obumbratae *with Buecheler.*

[3] tectae *Müller (1st edition):* tutae *Fraenkel:* totae, *retained
by Müller in his 2nd edition.*

[4] *Since Petronius would hardly end a sentence* vōcĕ rĕplērĕt,
Müller reads compleret, *Fraenkel* impleret. *Perhaps* repleret
voce.

share the voyage myself. It was because these ruffians had long, dirty hair. I did not want to turn the ship into a prison, so I ordered the filth to be cleared off the brutes. Besides, I did not want the marks of branding to be screened and covered by their hair. They ought to show a full length for every one to read. Furthermore, they squandered my money on a certain lady friend of ours; I pulled them away from her the night before, reeking with wine and scent. In fact, they still stink of the shreds of my inheritance." . . .

So it was decided that forty stripes should be inflicted on each of us to appease the guardian angel of the ship. So not a moment was lost; the angry sailors advanced upon us with ropes-ends, and tried to soften their guardian angel's heart with our miserable blood. *I* indeed digested three full blows with Spartan pride. But Giton cried out so lustily the moment he was touched, that his familiar voice filled Tryphaena's ears. Not only was the mistress in a flutter, but all her maids were drawn by the well-known tones, and came running to the victim. Giton's loveliness had already disarmed the sailors; even without speaking he had appealed to his tormentors. Then all the maids screamed out together: " It is Giton, it is: stop beating him, you monsters. Help, ma'am, Giton is here." Tryphaena had already convinced herself, and inclined her ear to them, and flew on wings to the boy. Lichas, who knew me intimately, ran up as though he had heard my voice

---

⁵ era *Buecheler*: ergo⟨ea⟩ *Novák*: ergo. *Müller reads* nec solum ea conturbata est.

audisset, accurrit et nec manus nec faciem meam consideravit, sed continuo ad inguina mea luminibus deflexis [1] movit [2] officiosam manum et " Salve " inquit
" Encolpi." Miretur nunc aliquis Vlixis nutricem
post vicesimum annum cicatricem invenisse originis [3]
indicem, cum homo prudentissimus [4] confusis omnibus
corporis orisque lineamentis [5] ad unicum fugitivi
argumentum tam docte pervenerit. Tryphaena
lacrimas effudit decepta supplicio [6]—vera enim stig-
mata credebat captivorum frontibus impressa—
sciscitarique submissius coepit, quod ergastulum
intercepisset errantes, aut cuius tam crudeles manus
in hoc supplicium durassent. Meruisse quidem con-
tumeliam aliquam fugitivos,[7] quibus in odium bona
sua venissent ⟨. . .⟩ [8]

106 concitatus iracundia prosiliit Lichas et " O te " inquit
" feminam simplicem, tanquam vulnera ferro praepa-
rata litteras biberint. Utinam quidem hac se inscriptione frontis [9] maculassent; haberemus nos extremum solacium. Nunc mimicis [10] artibus petiti sumus
et adumbrata inscriptione derisi."
Volebat Tryphaena misereri, quia non totam voluptatem perdiderat, sed Lichas memor adhuc uxoris

---

[1] *Fraenkel was inclined to delete* luminibus deflexis.
[2] admovit *Müller in his 1st edition only.*
[3] *Fraenkel would delete* originis.
[4] pudentissimus *Dousa*: imprudentissimus *Schoppius.*
[5] *Müller deletes the clause* confusis . . . lineamentis *in
which Buecheler reads* orisque *for* indiciorumque.
[6] *Fraenkel suggested deleting* decepta supplicio.
[7] *P. George would delete* fugitivos.

too, and did not glance at my hands or face, at once looking down applied a busy hand to my groin, and said, " How are you, Encolpius ? " No one need be surprised that Ulysses's nurse discovered the scar[1] which revealed his identity after twenty years, when a clever man hit upon the one test of a runaway so brilliantly, though every feature of his face and body was blurred. Tryphaena, thinking that the marks on our foreheads were real prisoners' brands, cried bitterly over our supposed punishment, and proceeded to inquire more gently what prison had stayed us in our wanderings, and what hand had been so ruthless as to inflict such marks upon us. " But, of course," she said, " runaway slaves who come to hate their own happiness, do deserve some chastisement." . . .

Lichas leaped forward in a transport of rage and cried, " You silly woman, as if these letters were made by the scars of the branding-iron. I only wish they had defiled their foreheads with that kind of inscription; we should have some consolation left. As it is, we have been assailed by an actor's tricks, and befooled by a mere outline of an inscription."

Tryphaena besought him to have pity, because she had not lost all her desire for Giton, but the seduction of his wife and the insults offered to him in the Porch

---

[1] Odysseus' old nurse Euryclea recognized him, despite his age and disguise, by a scar on his leg—Homer, *Odyssey*, XIX, 467 ff.

---

8 *Lacuna indicated by Buecheler.*
9 *Müller deletes* frontis.
10 mimicis *Pithoeus*: inimici.

corruptae contumeliarumque, quas in Herculis porticu acceperat, turbato vehementius vultu proclamat: " Deos immortales rerum humanarum agere curam, puto, intellexisti, o Tryphaena. Nam imprudentes noxios in nostrum induxere navigium, et quid fecissent, admonuerunt pari somniorum consensu. Ita vide, ut possit illis ignosci, quos ad poenam ipse deus deduxit. Quod ad me attinet, non sum crudelis, sed vereor, ne quod remisero, patiar." Tam superstitiosa oratione Tryphaena mutata negat se interpellare supplicium, immo accedere etiam iustissimae ultioni. Nec se minus grandi vexatam iniuria quam Licham,[1] cuius pudoris dignitas [2] in contione proscripta sit . . .

107   " Me, ut puto, hominem non ignotum, elegerunt ad hoc officium [legatum] [3] petieruntque, ut se reconciliarem aliquando amicissimis. Nisi forte putatis iuvenes casu in has plagas incidisse, cum omnis vector nihil prius quaerat, quam cuius se diligentiae credat. Flectite ergo mentes satisfactione lenitas, et patimini liberos homines ire sine iniuria, quo destinarunt.[4] Saevi quoque implacabilesque domini crudelitatem suam impediunt, si quando paenitentia fugitivos reduxit, et dediticiis hostibus parcimus. Quid ultra petitis aut quid vultis ? In conspectu vestro supplices

---

[1] *Fraenkel would delete* Licham.
[2] *Buecheler conjectures* pudor et dignitas: [pudoris] dignitas *Fraenkel*: uxoris dignitas *Jacobs.*
[3] *Omitted by Pithoeus and cod. Lambeth.*
[4] destinarunt *Buecheler*: destinant.

of Hercules[1] were still in Lichas's mind, and he cried out with a look of still more profound agitation, " Tryphaena, I believe you admit that the Gods in Heaven take some trouble about men's affairs. They brought these sinners on board my boat without their knowledge, and told us what they had done by a coincidence in dreams. Then do consider; how can we possibly pardon people whom a God himself has handed over to us for punishment? As for me, I am not a bloodthirsty man, but personally I am afraid that if I let them off anything it will fall on me." Tryphaena veered round at this appeal to superstition, declined to interfere with the punishment, and declared that she approved of this most proper vengeance. She had been just as gravely wronged as Lichas, considering that her reputation for chastity had been publicly and adversely shown up. . . .

[2] " I believe I am a man of some reputation, and they have chosen me for this duty, and begged me to make it up between them and their old friends. I suppose you do not imagine that these young men have fallen into the snare by chance, when the first care of every one who goes a voyage is to find a trustworthy person to depend on. So unbend the sternness which has been softened by revenge, and let the men go free without hindrance to their destination. Even a harsh and unforgiving master reins in his cruelty if his runaways are at last led back by penitence, and we all spare an enemy who surrenders. What do you want or wish for more? These free and

---

[1] This incident presumably occurred in a lost passage of Petronius.

[2] Codex *l* adds Eumolpus as the speaker.

iacent iuvenes ingenui, honesti, et quod utroque
potentius est, familiaritate vobis aliquando coniuncti.
Si mehercules intervertissent pecuniam vestram, si
fidem proditione laesissent, satiari tamen potuissetis
hac poena, quam videtis. Servitia ecce in frontibus [1]
eernitis et vultus ingenuos voluntaria poenarum lege
proscriptos." Interpellavit deprecationem supplicii [2]
Lichas et " Noli " inquit " causam confundere, sed
impone singulis modum. Ac primum omnium, si
ultro venerunt, cur nudavere crinibus capita ?
Vultum enim qui permutat, fraudem parat, non
satisfactionem. Deinde, si gratiam te [3] legato molie-
bantur, quid ita omnia fecisti, ut quos tuebaris,
absconderes ? Ex quo apparet casu incidisse noxios
in plagas et te artem quaesisse, qua nostrae animad-
versionis impetum eluderes. Nam quod invidiam
facis nobis ingenuos honestosque clamando, vide, ne
deteriorem facias confidentia causam. Quid debent
laesi facere, ubi rei ad poenam confugiunt ? At enim
amici fuerunt nostri: eo maiora meruerunt [4] sup-
plicia; nam qui ignotos laedit, latro appellatur, qui
amicos, paulo minus quam parricida." Resolvit
Eumolpos tam iniquam declamationem et " Intellego " inquit " nihil magis obesse iuvenibus miseris,
quam quod nocte deposuerunt capillos: hoc argu-
mento incidisse videntur in navem, non venisse.[5]
Quod velim tam candide ad aures vestras perveniat,

---

[1] servilia ecce in frontibus ⟨stigmata⟩ *Jacobs. There are
other suggestions;* servitii indicia *Burman.*

[2] supplicii *Buecheler:* supplicis, *omitted in Tornaesius's
edition and Pithoeus's 1st and cd. Lambeth.: Müller deletes.*

[3] te *Buecheler:* a.

[4] *Fraenkel suggests, because of the clausula,* meruere.

[5] *Müller deletes the whole sentence* hoc . . . venisse.

respectable young men lie prostrate before your eyes, and what is more important than either, they were once bound to you by close friendship. I take my oath that if they had embezzled your money, or hurt you by betraying your confidence, you might still be satisfied with the punishment you have seen inflicted. Look, you see slavery on their foreheads, and their free faces defiled under a self-imposed sentence of punishment." Lichas interrupted this plea for mercy, saying, "Do not go confusing the issue, but let each single point have its place. And first of all, if they came of their own accord, why have they stripped all the hair off their heads? A man who disguises himself wants to play a trick, not to make amends. Again, if they were contriving some act of grace with you as mediator, why did you do everything in your power to hide your protégés away? All this makes it clear that the ruffians fell into the net by accident, and that you hunted for some device to avoid the force of our displeasure. When you try to prejudice us by calling them free and respectable, mind you do not spoil your case by impudence. What should an injured party do, when the guilty run into punishment? Oh! you say, they were once our friends! Then they deserve the harsher treatment. A person who injures a stranger is called a robber, but a man who hurts his friends is practically a parricide." Eumolpus put an end to this unfair harangue by saying, "I know that nothing is more against the poor young men than their cutting their hair at night. This looks like a proof that they came by chance upon the ship and did not come on purpose. Now I want the plain truth to come to your ears just

quam simpliciter gestum est. Voluerunt enim
antequam conscenderent, exonerare capita molesto
et supervacuo pondere, sed celerior ventus distulit
curationis propositum. Nec tamen putaverunt ad
rem pertinere, ubi inciperent, quod placuerat ut
fieret, quia nec omen nec legem navigantium nove-
rant." " Quid " inquit Lichas " attinuit supplices
radere? Nisi forte miserabiliores calvi solent esse.
Quamquam quid attinet veritatem per interpretem
quaerere? quid dicis tu, latro? quae [sola][1] sala-
mandra supercilia tua exussit? cui deo crinem vovisti?
pharmace, responde."

108 Obstupueram ego supplicii metu pavidus, nec quid
in re manifestissima dicerem inveniebam turbatus
⟨. . .⟩[2] et deformis praeter spoliati capitis dedecus
superciliorum etiam aequalis cum fronte calvities, ut
nihil nec facere deceret nec dicere. Ut vero spongia
uda facies plorantis detersa est et liquefactum per
totum os atramentum omnia scilicet[3] lineamenta
fuliginea nube confudit, in odium se ira convertit.
⟨. . .⟩[4] Negat Eumolpus passurum se, ut quisquam
ingenuos contra fas legemque contaminet, interpel-
latque saevientium minas non solum voce sed etiam
manibus. Aderat interpellanti[5] mercennarius comes
et unus alterque infirmissimus vector, solacia magis
litis quam virium auxilia. Nec quicquam pro me de-

---

[1] *deleted by Pithoeus.*
[2] *Lacuna indicated by Buecheler.*
[3] *Fuchs would delete* scilicet.
[4] *Lacuna indicated by Fraenkel.*
[5] ei [interpellanti] *Müller.*

as simply as it happened. They wanted to relieve their heads of the troublesome and useless weight before they came aboard, but the wind got up and postponed their scheme of treatment. They never thought that it made any difference where they began what they had decided to do; they were quite ignorant of sailors' omens and sea-law." "But why should they shave themselves to excite pity?" said Lichas, "Unless of course bald people are naturally more pitiable. But what is the use of trying to discover the truth through a third person? Now *you* speak up, you ruffian! Who was the salamander[1] that singed off your eyebrows? What God had the promise of your hair? Answer me, poisonous fellow!"

I was dumb with terror of being punished, and too upset to find a word to say, for the case was only too clear. . . . We were in no position to speak, or do anything, for to say nothing of the disgrace of our heads both unseemly and shaven, our eyebrows were as bald as our pates. But when a wet sponge was wiped down my doleful contenance, and the ink ran over all my face and of course blotted out every feature in a cloud of smut, anger passed into loathing. . . . Eumolpus cried out that he would not allow anyone to disfigure free young men without right or reason, and cut short the angry sailors' threats not only by argument but by force. His slave stood by him in his protest, and one or two of the most feeble passengers; but they merely gave him moral support in the dispute, not an increase in his strength. For

---

[1] There was a belief that if you touched a salamander you lost all your hair. Lichas here speaks to Encolpius.

precabar, sed intentans in oculos Tryphaenae manus
usurum me viribus meis clara liberaque voce clamavi,
ni abstineret a Gitone iniuriam mulier damnata et
in toto navigio sola verberanda. Accenditur audacia
mea iratior Lichas, indignaturque quod ego relicta
mea causa tantum pro alio clamo. Nec minus
Tryphaena contumelia saevit accensa totiusque
navigii turbam diducit in partes. Hinc mercennarius
tonsor [1] ferramenta sua nobis et ipse armatus distri-
buit, illinc Tryphaenae familia nudas expedit manus,
ac ne ancillarum quidem clamor aciem destituit, uno
tantum gubernatore relicturum se navis ministerium
denuntiante, si non desinat rabies libidine perditorum
collecta. Nihilo minus tamen perseverat dimi-
cantium furor, illis pro ultione, nobis pro vita pug-
nantibus. Multi ergo utrinque sine morte [2] labuntur,
plures cruenti vulneribus referunt veluti ex proelio [3]
pedem, nec tamen cuiusquam ira laxatur. Tunc
fortissimus Giton ad virilia sua admovit novaculam
infestam, minatus se abscisurum tot miseriarum
causam, inhibuitque Tryphaena tam grande facinus
non dissimulata missione. Saepius ego cultrum
tonsorium super iugulum meum posui, non magis me
occisurus, quam Giton, quod minabatur, facturus.
Audacius tamen ille tragoediam implebat, quia sciebat se illam habere novaculam, qua iam sibi cervicem
LO praeciderat. | Stante ergo utraque acie, cum ap-

---

[1] *Burman deletes* tonsor.

[2] sine morte *deleted by Delz and Nisbet, rightly?* sine mora
Pflug.

[3] *Fraenkel would delete* veluti ex proelio.

my part I shirked nothing. I shook my fist in Tryphaena' face, and declared in a loud open voice that I
would use violence to her if she did not leave off hurt-
ing Giton, for she was a wicked woman and the only
person on the ship who deserved flogging. Lichas's
wrath blazed hotter at my daring, and he taunted me
with throwing up my own case and only shouting for
somebody else. Tryphaena was equally hot and
angry and abusive, and divided the whole ship's company into factions. On our side, the hireling [barber]
handed out his blades to us, and kept one for himself,
on the other side Tryphaena's slaves were ready with
bare fists, and even the cries of women were not un-
heard on the field. The helmsman alone swore that
he would give up minding the ship if this madness,
which had been stirred up to suit a pack of scoundrels,
did not stop. None the less, the fury of the com-
batants persisted, the enemy fighting for revenge and
we for dear life. Many fell on both sides without
fatal results, still more got bloody wounds and retired
in the style of a real battle, and still we all raged im-
placably. Then the gallant Giton turned a razor
against his genitals and threatened to put an end to
our troubles by self-mutilation, and Tryphaena
averted the horrible disaster by an effort to free us
from our troubles which she made in all sincerity. I
lifted a barber's knife to my throat several times,
no more meaning to kill myself than Giton meant
to do what he threatened. Still he filled the tragic
part more recklessly, because he knew that he was
holding the very razor with which he had already
made a cut on his throat. Both sides were drawn
up in battle array, and it was plain that the fight

pareret futurum non tralaticium bellum, aegre
expugnavit gubernator, ut caduceatoris more Tryphaena indutias faceret. Data ergo acceptaque ex
more patrio fide praetendit ramum oleae a tutela
navigii raptum, atque in colloquium venire ausa

" Quis furor " exclamat " pacem convertit in arma ?
Quid nostrae meruere manus ?   Non Troius heros [1]
hac in classe vehit decepti pignus Atridae,
nec Medea furens fraterno sanguine pugnat.
Sed contemptus amor vires habet.   Ei mihi, fata
hos inter fluctus quis raptis evocat armis ?
Cui non est mors una satis ?   Ne vincite pontum
gurgitibusque feris alios imponite fluctus."

109   Haec ut turbato clamore mulier effudit, haesit
paulisper acies, revocataeque ad pacem manus inter-
misere bellum.   Utitur paenitentiae occasione dux
Eumolpos et castigato ante vehementissime Licha
tabulas foederis signat, quis [2] haec formula erat : " Ex
tui animi sententia, ut tu, Tryphaena, neque iniuriam
tibi factam a Gitone quereris, neque si quid ante hunc
diem factum est, obicies vindicabisve aut ullo alio
genere persequendum curabis ; ut tu nihil imperabis
puero repugnanti, non amplexum, non osculum, non
coitum venere constrictum, nisi pro qua re praesentes
numeraveris denarios centum.   Item, Licha, ex tui

---

[1] heros *cod. Autissiodurensis and O*; hostis: hospes *Wehle.*
[2] cuius *conjectures Buecheler.*

---

[1] Paris who carried off to Troy from Sparta Helen, wife of
King Menelaus (son of Atreus) and so caused the Trojan war.
[2] In Greek mythology Absyrtus, Medea's brother, and son of
Aietes King of Colchis, plotted against Jason, who had come

would be no ordinary affair, when the helmsman with difficulty induced Tryphaena to conclude a truce like a herald with staff. So the usual formal undertakings were exchanged, and she waved an olive-branch which she took from the ship's figure-head, and ventured to come up and talk to us: " What madness," she cried, " is turning peace into war? What have our hands done to deserve it? No Trojan hero[1] carries the bride of the cuckold son of Atreus in this fleet, nor does frenzied Medea[2] fight her foe by slaying her brother. But love despised is powerful. Ah! who courts destruction among these waves by drawing the sword? Who does not find a single death enough? Do not strive to outdo the sea and heap fresh waves upon its savage floods."

The woman poured out these words in a loud ex-cited voice, the fighting died away for a little while, our hands were recalled to the way of peace, and dropped the war. Our leader Eumolpus seized the occasion of their relenting, and after making a warm attack on Lichas, signed the deed of treaty, which ran as follows: " Agreed on your part, Tryphaena, that you will not complain of any wrong done to you by Giton, and if any has been done to you before this date will not bring it up against him or punish him or take steps to follow it up in any other way whatso-ever; that you will give the boy no orders which he dislikes, for a hug, a kiss, or a lover's close embrace, without paying a hundred pieces for it cash down. Furthermore, it is agreed on your part, Lichas, that

seeking the Golden Fleece. While fleeing with Jason, his mistress Medea cut Absyrtus into pieces and dropped them overboard to delay the pursuers.

animi sententia, ut tu Encolpion nec verbo contume-
lioso insequeris nec vultu, neque quaeres ubi nocte
dormiat, aut si quaesieris,[1] pro singulis iniuriis nume-
rabis praesentes denarios ducenos." In haec verba
L foederibus compositis arma deponimus, | et ne residua
in animis etiam post iusiurandum ira remaneret, praeterita aboleri osculis placet. Exhortantibus universis
odia detumescunt, epulaeque ad certamen prolatae
LO conciliant hilaritatem [concilium].[2] | Exsonat ergo can-
tibus totum navigium, et quia repentina tranquillitas
intermiserat cursum, alius exultantes quaerebat[3]
fuscina pisces, alius hamis blandientibus convellebat
praedam repugnantem. Ecce etiam per antemnam
pelagiae consederant volucres, quas textis harundinibus peritus artifex tetigit; illae viscatis illigatae
viminibus deferebantur ad manus. Tollebat plumas
aura volitantes, pinnasque per maria inanis spuma
torquebat.

Iam Lichas redire mecum in gratiam coeperat, iam
Tryphaena Gitona extrema parte potionis spargebat,
cum Eumolpus et ipse vino solutus dicta voluit in
calvos stigmososque iaculari, donec consumpta
frigidissima urbanitate rediit ad carmina sua coepitque capillorum elegidarion dicere:

"Quod solum[4] formae decus est, cecidere capilli,
vernantesque comas tristis abegit hiemps.
Nunc umbra nudata sua iam tempora maerent,

---

[1] *Müller deletes* si quaesieris.

[2] hilaritatem *Jacobs*: hilaritate. *For* concilium (*or* consilium), *which Jacobs deletes, Buecheler proposes* concordiam,
keeping hilaritate. *Another suggestion is* convivium.

you will not pursue Encolpius with insulting words or
grimaces, nor inquire where he sleeps at night, or if
you do inquire will pay two hundred pieces cash down
for every injurious act done to him." Peace was
made on these terms, and we laid down our arms, and
for fear any vestige of anger should be left in our
minds, even after taking the oath, we decided to wipe
out the past with a kiss. There was applause all
round, our hatred died down, and a feast which had
been brought for the fight made us one in joviality.
Then the whole ship rang with songs; and a sudden
calm having stayed us in our course, one man pursued the leaping fish with a spear, another pulled in
his struggling prey on alluring hooks. Besides all
this, some sea-birds settled on one of the yards, and a
clever sportsman took them in with a jointed rod of
reeds, they were snared by these limed twigs and
brought down into our hands. The breeze carried
off their flitting down, and light foam whirled their
feathers about when they were cast into the waves.

Lichas was just beginning to be friendly with me
again, Tryphaena was just pouring the dregs of a
drink over Giton, when Eumolpus, who was unsteady
with drink himself, tried to aim some satire at bald
persons and branded criminals, and after exhausting
his chilly wit, went back to his poetry and proceeded
to declaim a little dirge on Hair:

" The hair that is the whole glory of the body is
fallen, dull winter has carried away the bright locks of
spring. Now the temples are bare of their shade

---

³ *Müller suggests* petebat.
⁴ summum *Florilegia*.

areaque attritis ridet [1] adusta [2] pilis.
O fallax natura deum: quae prima dedisti   5
aetati nostrae gaudia, prima rapis."

⟨. . .⟩ [3]

" Infelix, modo crinibus nitebas   7
Phoebo pulchrior et sorore Phoebi.
At nunc levior aere vel rotundo
horti tubere, quod creavit unda,[4]   10
ridentes fugis et times puellas.
Ut mortem citius venire credas,
scito iam capitis perisse partem."

110   Plura volebat proferre, credo, et ineptiora praeteri-
tis, cum ancilla Tryphaenae Gitona in partem navis
inferiorem ducit corymbioque dominae pueri adornat
caput. Immo supercilia etiam profert de pyxide
sciteque iacturae lineamenta secuta totam illi formam suam reddidit. Agnovit Tryphaena verum
Gitona, lacrimisque turbata tunc primum bona fide
L puero basium dedit. | Ego etiam si repositum in
pristinum decorem puerum gaudebam, abscondebam
tamen frequentius vultum intellegebamque me non
tralaticia deformitate esse insignitum, quem alloquio
dignum ne Lichas quidem crederet.   Sed huic tristitiae eadem illa succurrit ancilla, sevocatumque [5] me

[1] ardet *Birt*: sordet *or* aret *Iunius*.
[2] adulta *suggests Buecheler*.
[3] *lacuna indicated by cod. Lambeth., Tornaesius's edition, and Pithoeus's 1st edition. Before Turnebus and Sambucus re-*

and are downcast, and the scorched space on my old head shines where the hair is worn away. Ye Gods that love to cheat us; ye rob us first of the first joys ye gave to our youth. . . .

"Poor wretch, a moment ago thy hair shone bright and more beautiful than Phoebus[1] and the sister of Phoebus. Now thou art smoother than bronze or the round garden truffle that is born in rain, and turnest in dread from a girl's mockery. To teach thee how quickly death shall come, know that a part of thine head hath died already."

He wanted to produce some more lines even more silly than the last, I believe, when one of Tryphaena's maids took Giton below decks, and ornamented the boy's head with some of her mistress's clustered curls. Further, she also took some eyebrows out of a box, and by cunningly following the lines where he was defaced she restored his proper beauty complete. Tryphaena recognized the true Giton, there was a storm of tears, and she then for the first time gave the boy a kiss with real affection. Of course, I was glad to see him clothed again in his former loveliness, but still I kept hiding my own face continually, for I realized that I was marked with no common ugliness, since not even Lichas considered me fit to speak to. But the same maid came and rescued me from gloom,

---

[1] The god of the sun, Apollo, whose twin sister was Phoebe, goddess of the moon, Artemis-Diana.

---

arranged lines 7–13 of this poem, they were in the order 7, 9, 11, 8, 10, 12, 13.

4 imber *Jahn.*

5 sevocatumque *Goldast*: evocatumque.

non minus decoro exornavit capillamento; immo commendatior vultus enituit, quia flavum [1] corymbion erat . . .

LO | Ceterum Eumolpos, et periclitantium advocatus et praesentis concordiae auctor, ne sileret sine fabulis hilaritas, multa in muliebrem levitatem coepit iactare: quam facile adamarent, quam cito etiam filiorum obliviscerentur, nullamque esse feminam tam pudicam, quae non peregrina libidine usque ad furorem averteretur. Nec se tragoedias veteres curare aut nomina saeculis nota, sed rem sua memoria factam, quam expositurum se esse, si vellemus audire. Conversis igitur omnium in se vultibus auribusque sic orsus est:

111 '' Matrona quaedam Ephesi tam notae erat pudicitiae, ut vicinarum quoque gentium feminas ad spectaculum sui evocaret. Haec ergo cum virum extulisset, non contenta vulgari more funus passis prosequi crinibus aut nudatum pectus in conspectu frequentiae plangere, in conditorium etiam prosecuta est defunctum positumque in hypogaeo Graeco more [2] corpus custodire ac flere totis noctibus diebusque coepit. Sic afflictantem se ac mortem inedia persequentem non parentes potuerunt abducere, non propinqui; magistratus ultimo repulsi abierunt, complorataque singularis exempli femina ab omnibus quintum iam diem

---

[1] flavum *in margin of Tornaesius's edition*: flaucorum. *There are other suggestions.*

[2] Graeco more *perhaps should be deleted* (*Fraenkel*).

called me aside, and decked me with equally becoming curls. Indeed, my face shone with a greater glory. My curls were golden! . . .

Then Eumolpus, our spokesman in peril and the begetter of our present peace, to save our jollity from falling dumb for want of good stories, proceeded to hurl many taunts at the fickleness of women; how easily they fell in love, how quickly they forgot even their children, how no woman was so chaste that she could not be led away into utter madness by a passion for a stranger. He was not thinking of old tragedies or names notorious in history, but of an affair which happened in his lifetime. He would tell it us if we liked to listen. So all eyes and ears were turned upon him, and he began as follows:[1]

" There was a married woman in Ephesus of such famous virtue that she drew women even from the neighbouring states to gaze upon her. So when she had buried her husband, the common fashion of following the procession with loose hair, and beating the naked breast in front of the crowd, did not satisfy her. She followed the dead man even to his resting-place, and proceeded to watch and weep night and day over the body, which was laid in an underground vault in the Greek fashion. Neither her parents nor her relations could divert her from thus torturing herself, and courting death by starvation; the officials were at last rebuffed and left her; every one mourned for her as a woman of unique character, and she was

---

[1] The story which follows was one of the " Milesian Tales " which became popular by the first century B.C. We find it first in Phaedrus. It has been specially famous since the twelfth century.

sine alimento trahebat. Assidebat aegrae fidissima
ancilla, simulque et lacrimas commodabat [1] lugenti, et
quotienscunque defecerat positum in monumento
lumen renovabat. Una igitur in tota civitate fabula
erat, solum illud affulsisse verum pudicitiae amorisque
exemplum omnis ordinis homines confitebantur, cum
interim imperator provinciae latrones iussit crucibus
affigi secundum illam casulam, in qua recens cadaver
matrona deflebat. Proxima ergo nocte, cum miles,
qui cruces asservabat, ne quis ad sepulturam corpus
detraheret, notasset sibi [et] [2] lumen inter monu-
menta clarius fulgens et gemitum lugentis audisset,
vitio gentis humanae concupiit scire, quis aut quid
faceret. Descendit igitur in conditorium, visaque
pulcherrima muliere primo quasi quodam monstro
infernisque imaginibus turbatus substitit. Deinde ut
et corpus iacentis conspexit et lacrimas consideravit
faciemque unguibus sectam, ratus scilicet id quod
erat, desiderium extincti non posse feminam pati,
attulit in monumentum cenulam suam coepitque
hortari lugentem, ne perseveraret in dolore supervacuo ac nihil profuturo gemitu pectus diduceret:
omnium eundem esse exitum [sed] [3] et idem domicilium, et cetera quibus exulceratae mentes ad sanitatem revocantur. At illa ignota [4] consolatione per-

---

[1] commodabat *Rittershusius*: commendabat.
[2] *Deleted by Buecheler.*
[3] *Deleted by Orelli.*
[4] *For* ignota, *which seems wrong, Rittershusius proposed*

now passing her fifth day without food. A devoted maid sat by the failing woman, shed tears in sympathy with her woes, and at the same time filled up the lamp, which was placed in the tomb, whenever it sank. So there was but one opinion throughout the city, every class of person admitting this was the one true and brilliant example of chastity and love. At this moment the governor of the province gave orders that some robbers should be crucified near the small building where the lady was bewailing her recent loss. So on the next night, when the soldier who was watching the crosses, to prevent anyone taking down a body for burial, observed a light shining plainly among the tombs and heard a mourner's groans, a very human weakness made him curious to know who it was and what he was doing. So he went down into the vault, and on seeing a very beautiful woman, at first halted in confusion, as if he had seen a portent or some ghost from the world beneath. But afterwards noticing the dead man lying there, and watching the woman's tears and the marks of her nails on her face, he came to the correct conclusion, that she found her regret for the lost one unendurable. He therefore brought his supper into the tomb, and proceeded to urge the mourner not to persist in useless grief, and break her heart with unprofitable sobs; for all men made the same end and found the same resting-place, and so on with the other platitudes which restore wounded spirits to health. But she took no notice [?] of his sympathy, struck and tore

---

inopinata. *Nisbet proposes* ingrata, *and for* percussa *suggests* praeclusa.

cussa laceravit vehementius pectus ruptosque[1] crines
super corpus[2] iacentis imposuit. Non recessit
tamen miles, sed eadem exhortatione temptavit dare
mulierculae cibum, donec ancilla vini certum habeo[3]
odore corrupta primum ipsa porrexit ad humanitatem
invitantis victam manum, deinde refecta potione et
cibo expugnare dominae pertinaciam coepit et ' Quid
proderit ' inquit ' hoc tibi, si soluta inedia fueris, si te
vivam sepelieris, si antequam fata poscant, indemna-
tum spiritum effuderis?

Id cinerem aut manes credis sentire sepultos?

Vis tu reviviscere? Vis discusso muliebri errore,
quam diu licuerit, lucis commodis frui? Ipsum te
iacentis corpus commonere[4] debet, ut vivas.' Nemo
invitus audit, cum cogitur [aut cibum sumere aut][5]
vivere. Itaque mulier aliquot dierum abstinentia
sicca passa est frangi pertinaciam suam, nec minus
avide replevit se cibo quam ancilla, quae prior victa
112 est. Ceterum scitis, quid plerumque soleat temptare humanam satietatem. Quibus blanditiis im-
petraverat miles, ut matrona vellet vivere, isdem
etiam pudicitiam eius aggressus est. Nec deformis
aut infacundus iuvenis castae videbatur, conciliante
gratiam ancilla ac subinde dicente:

[1] raptosque *John of Salisbury*.
[2] corpus *Nodot*: pectus.
[3] certum habeo *John of Salisbury*: certum ab eo *B, with*
certum *altered to* certo: certe ab eo *P*, δ: ab eo certo *R*.
The doubtful words are omitted by l and the Florilegia.
[4] ammonere *B, R*. commovere *other MSS*.

her breast more violently than ever, wrenched out her hair, and laid it on the dead body. Still the soldier did not retire, but tried to give the poor woman food with similar encouragements, until the maid, who was—I'm sure of it—seduced by the smell of his wine, first gave in herself, and put out her hand at his kindly invitation, and then, refreshed with food and drink, proceeded to assail her mistress's obstinacy, and say, ' What will you gain by all this, if you faint away with hunger, if you bury yourself alive, if you breathe out your undoomed soul before Fate calls for it ? " Believest thou that the ashes or the spirit of the buried dead can feel thy woe ? "[1] Will you not begin life afresh ? Will you not shake off this womanish failing, and enjoy the blessings of the light so long as you are allowed ? Your poor dead husband's body itself here ought to persuade you to keep alive.' People are always ready to listen when they are urged to [take a meal or to] keep alive. So the lady, being thirsty after several days' abstinence, allowed her resolution to be broken down, and filled herself with food as greedily as the maid who had been the first to yield.

" Well, you know which temptation generally assails a man on a full stomach. The soldier used the same insinuating phrases which had persuaded the lady to consent to live, to conduct an assault upon her virtue. Her modest eye saw in him a young man, handsome and eloquent. The maid begged her to be

---

[1] Virgil, *Aeneid*, IV, 34, with *curare* altered to *sentire*.

---

[5] *Deleted by Fraenkel.*

PETRONIUS ARBITER

' Placitone etiam pugnabis amori?
[Nec venit in mentem, quorum consederis arvis? '][1]

quid diutius moror? ne hanc quidem partem [corporis][2] mulier abstinuit, victorque miles utrumque
persuasit. Iacuerunt ergo una non tantum illa
nocte, qua nuptias fecerunt, sed postero etiam ac
tertio die, praeclusis videlicet conditorii foribus, ut
quisquis ex notis ignotisque ad monumentum venisset, putaret expirasse super corpus viri pudicissimam uxorem. Ceterum delectatus miles et forma
mulieris et secreto, quicquid boni per facultates
poterat, coemebat et prima statim nocte in monumentum ferebat. Itaque unius cruciarii parentes
ut viderunt laxatam custodiam, detraxere nocte
pendentem supremoque mandaverunt officio. At
miles circumscriptus dum desidet, ut postero die
vidit unam sine cadavere crucem, veritus supplicium,
mulieri quid accidisset exponit: nec se exspectaturum iudicis sententiam, sed gladio ius dicturum
ignaviae suae. Commodaret ergo illa perituro locum
et fatale conditorium ⟨unum⟩[3] familiari ac viro
faceret. Mulier non minus misericors quam pudica
' nec istud ' inquit ' dii sinant, ut eodem tempore

---

[1] *Intruded from Virgil into the O-tradition and thence into the
L-tradition; omitted by the Florilegia (which go back to λ independently of the rest of the L-tradition—see introduction, pp. xxiv–xxv) and deleted in cod. Lambeth.*

[2] *Fraenkel would add* in *before* hanc; *and with Jacobs would
delete* corporis. *But Müller also wonders whether either change
is needed.*

[3] unum *added by Müller in his 2nd edition.*

---

[1] Virgil, *Aeneid*, IV, 38–39.

gracious, and then said, ' Wilt thou fight love even
when love pleases thee ? [Or dost thou never remember in whose lands thou art resting ? '[1]] I need
hide the fact no longer. The woman did not hold
back even this part,[2] and the conquering hero won
her over on both counts. So they passed not only
their wedding night together, but the next and a
third, of course shutting the door of the vault, so
that any friend or stranger who came to the tomb
would imagine that a most virtuous lady had breathed
her last over her husband's body. Well, the soldier
was delighted with the woman's beauty, and his
stolen pleasure; he bought up all the fine things his
means permitted, and carried them to the tomb the
moment darkness fell. So the parents of one of the
crucified, seeing that the watch was ill-kept, took
their man down in the dark and administered the last
rite to him. The soldier was eluded while he was off
duty, and next day, seeing one of the crosses without
its corpse, he was in terror of punishment, and explained to the lady what had happened. He declared
that he would not wait for a court-martial, but would
punish his own neglect with a thrust of his sword. So
she had better get ready a place for a dying man, and
make one gloomy vault for both her husband and her
lover. The lady's heart was tender as well as pure.
' Heaven forbid,' she replied, ' that I should look at

---

[2] I feel that *corporis* is an addition (put before *partem* in the
L-tradition, and after *partem* in the O-tradition) but the word
may be Petronius's, whereby he may make Eumolpus use
abstineo transitively and probably point at Tryphaena. The
other matter in which the soldier won over the matron was
accepting food and drink, Chapter 111.

duorum mihi carissimorum hominum duo funera
spectem. Malo mortuum impendere quam vivum
occidere.' Secundum hanc orationem iubet ex arca
corpus mariti sui tolli atque illi, quae vacabat, cruci
affigi. Usus est miles ingenio prudentissimae feminae, posteroque die populus miratus est, qua ratione
mortuus isset in crucem."

113   Risu excepere fabulam nautae, [et] [1] erubescente
non mediocriter Tryphaena vultumque suum super
cervicem Gitonis amabiliter ponente. At non Lichas
risit, sed iratum commovens caput " Si iustus " inquit
" imperator fuisset, debuit patris familiae corpus in
monumentum referre, mulierem affigere cruci."

Non dubie redierat in animum Hedyle [2] expilatum-
que libidinosa migratione navigium. Sed nec foederis verba permittebant meminisse, nec hilaritas,
quae occupaverat mentes, dabat iracundiae locum.
Ceterum Tryphaena in gremio Gitonis posita modo
implebat osculis pectus, interdum concinnabat spolia-
L tum [3] crinibus vultum. | Ego maestus et impatiens
foederis novi non cibum, non potionem capiebam,
sed obliquis trucibusque oculis utrumque spectabam.
Omnia me oscula vulnerabant, omnes blanditiae,
quascunque mulier libidinosa fingebat. Nec tamen
adhuc sciebam, utrum magis puero irascerer, quod
amicam mihi auferret, an amicae, quod puerum
corrumperet: utraque inimicissima oculis meis et
captivitate praeterita tristiora. Accedebat huc,

[1] *omitted in the L-tradition.*
[2] Hedyle *suggests Buecheler*: hedile *or* edile.
[3] *Perhaps* spoliati.

the same moment on the dead bodies of two men whom I love. No, I would rather make a dead man useful, than send a live man to death.' After this speech she ordered her husband's body to be taken out of the coffin and fixed up on the empty cross. The soldier availed himself of this far-seeing woman's device, and the people wondered the next day by what means the dead man had ascended the cross.''

The sailors received this tale with a laugh; Tryphaena blushed deeply, and laid her face caressingly on Giton's neck. But there was no laugh from Lichas; he shook his head angrily and said: " If the governor of the province had been a just man, he should have put the dead husband back in the tomb, and hung the woman on the cross."

No doubt he was thinking once more of Hedyle[1] and how his ship had been pillaged on her passionate elopement. But the terms of our treaty forbade us to bear grudges, and the joy which had filled our souls left no room for wrath. Tryphaena was now lying in Giton's lap, covering his breast with kisses one moment, and sometimes caressing his shaven head. I was gloomy and uneasy about our new terms, and did not touch food or drink, but kept shooting angry looks askance at them both. Every kiss was a wound to me, every pleasing wile that the wanton woman conjured up. I was not yet sure whether I was more angry with the boy for taking away my mistress, or with my mistress for leading the boy astray: both of them were hateful to my sight and more depressing than the bondage I had escaped.

[1] Presumably Lichas' wife. The incident was doubtless in a lost part of Petronius.

quod neque Tryphaena me alloquebatur tanquam familiarem et aliquando gratum sibi amatorem, nec Giton me aut tralaticia propinatione dignum iudicabat, aut quod minimum est, sermone communi vocabat, credo, veritus, ne inter initia coeuntis gratiae recentem cicatricem rescinderet. Inundavere pectus lacrimae dolore paratae,[1] gemitusque suspirio tectus animam paene submovit . . .

In partem voluptatis temptabat admitti, nec domini supercilium induebat, sed amici quaerebat obsequium . . .

" Si quid ingenui sanguinis habes, non pluris illam facies, quam scortum.[2] Si vir fueris, non ibis ad spintriam " [3] . . .

Me nihil magis pudebat [4] quam ne Eumolpus sensisset, quicquid illud fuerat, et homo dicacissimus carminibus vindicaret . . .

Iurat Eumolpus verbis conceptissimis . . .

114 Dum haec taliaque iactamus, inhorruit mare nubesque undique adductae obruere tenebris diem. Discurrunt nautae ad officia trepidantes velaque tempestati subducunt. Sed nec certos [5] fluctus ventus impulerat, nec quo destinaret cursum, gubernator sciebat. † Siciliam modo ventus dabat, saepissime

---

[1] *Müller in his second edition conjectures* partae.

[2] scortum *Putsch*: sportam *l* (spurcam *in margin*): sportum *cod. Lambeth.*

[3] spurcam *in Tornaesius's edition, but also* spinthriam *in margin*: spuicam *l* (spingem *in margin*): spintam *cod. Lambeth.*

[4] pungebat *Buecheler*: urebat *Dousa.*

[5] certus *Jungermann*: cer⟨tus commo⟩tos *suggests Müller.*

And besides all this, Tryphaena did not address me like a friend whom she was once pleased to have for a lover, and Giton did not think fit to drink my health in the ordinary way, and would not even so much as include me in general conversation. I suppose he was afraid of reopening a tender scar just as friendly feeling began to draw it together. My unhappiness moved me till tears overflowed my heart, and the groan I hid with a sigh almost stole my life away. . . .

He tried to gain admission to share their joys, not wearing the proud look of a master, but begging him to yield as a friend. . . .

[1] " If you have a drop of honest blood in you you will think no more of her than of a whore. If you are going to be a man, you won't go to a pansy-boy." . . .

Nothing shamed me more than the fear that Eumolpus might have got some idea of whatever was going on, and might employ his powers of speech in attacking me in verse. . . .

Eumolpus swore an oath in most formal language. . . .

While we talked over this matter and others, the sea rose, clouds gathered from every quarter, and overwhelmed the day in darkness. The sailors ran to their posts in terror, and furled the sails before the storm. But the wind did not drive the waves in any one direction, and the helmsman was at a loss which way to steer. One moment the wind † set towards Sicily, very often the north wind blew onto the Italian

---

[1] Codex *l* and (in margin) *cod. Lambeth* prefix: *ancilla Tryphaenae ad Encolpium* " handmaid of Tryphaena speaking to Encolpius."

[in oram] Italici litoris † [1] aquilo possessor convertebat huc illuc obnoxiam ratem,[2] et quod omnibus pro-
cellis periculosius erat, tam spissae repente tenebrae
lucem suppresserant, ut ne proram quidem totam
gubernator videret.   Itaque hercules postquam maris
ira infesta [3] convaluit, Lichas trepidans ad me
supinas porrigit manus et " tu " inquit " Encolpi,
succurre periclitantibus et [4] vestem illam divinam
sistrumque redde navigio. Per fidem, miserere,
quemadmodum quidem soles."

Et illum quidem vociferantem in mare ventus
excussit, repetitumque infesto gurgite procella
circumegit atque hausit.   Tryphaenam autem prope
iam [5] fidelissimi rapuerunt servi, scaphaeque im-
positam cum maxima sarcinarum parte abduxere
certissimae morti ⟨. . .⟩ [6]

Applicitus cum clamore flevi et " Hoc " inquam
" a diis meruimus, ut nos sola morte coniungerent?
Sed non crudelis fortuna concedit. Ecce iam ratem
fluctus evertet, ecce iam amplexus amantium iratum
dividet mare. Igitur, si vere Encolpion dilexisti,
da oscula, dum licet, ultimum hoc gaudium fatis

---

[1] *In his 1st edition Müller deleted* Siciliam, *marked* ventus
dabat *as corrupt, added* Siciliae *after* in oram (*these two last
words were added in Tornaesius's edition*), *and deleted* huc illuc
after convertebat; *and suggests* modo v⟨iol⟩ent⟨er nŏt⟩us (*so
Jacobs for* ventus) flabat.   *In his 2nd edition Müller conjectures*
modo ⟨a⟩ Sicilia ventus ⟨Africus⟩ flabat, saepissime [in oram]
Italici . . .

[2] ratem *Goddast*: partem. *In the margin of Tornaesius's
edition is written* proram.

coast,† [1] mastered the ship which was at its mercy and twisted her in every direction; and what was more dangerous than any squall, such thick darkness had suddenly blotted out the light that the steersman could not even see the whole prow. Then for a wonder, as the hostile fury of the storm gathered, Lichas trembled and stretched out his hands to me imploringly, and said, " Help us in our peril, *you,* Encolpius; let the ship have the goddess's robe again and her holy rattle.[2] Be merciful, I impore you, as your way is."

But even as he shouted the wind blew him into the water, a squall whirled him round and round repeatedly in a fierce whirlpool, and sucked him down. Tryphaena's faithful slaves carried her off almost . . ., put her in the boat with most of her luggage, and so rescued her from certain death. . . .

I embraced Giton, and wept and cried aloud: " Did we deserve this from the gods, that they should unite us only when they slay? But cruel Fate does not grant us even this. Look! even now the waves will upset the boat; even now the angry sea will sunder a lover's embrace. So if you ever really loved Encolpius, kiss him while you may, and snatch this last joy

---

[1] The text is a muddle here.
[2] Sacred emblems of Isis which Encolpius had probably stolen.

---

[3] maris ira infesta *suggested by Buecheler: There are other suggestions:* manifesta.
[4] et *Buecheler:* id est *rightly?* = ' that is ' = ' I mean.'
[5] *after* iam *Buecheler suggests* exanimatam *or the like, rightly? Perhaps for* iam *we might read* inanimam.
[6] *lacuna indicated in Pithoeus's 2nd edition.*

properantibus rape." Haec ut ego dixi, Giton
vestem deposuit meaque tunica contectus exeruit
ad osculum caput. Et ne sic cohaerentes malignior
fluctus distraheret, utrumque zona circumvenienti
praecinxit et " Si nihil aliud, certe diutius " inquit
" iuncta nos mors [1] feret, vel si voluerit ⟨mare⟩ [2]
misericors ad idem litus expellere, aut praeteriens
aliquis tralaticia humanitate lapidabit, aut quod
ultimum est iratis etiam fluctibus, imprudens harena
componet." Patior ego vinculum extremum, et
veluti lecto funebri aptatus exspecto mortem iam
non molestam. Peragit interim tempestas mandata
fatorum omnesque reliquias navis expugnat. Non
arbor erat relicta, non gubernacula, non funis aut
remus, sed quasi rudis atque infecta materies ibat
cum fluctibus . . .

Procurrere piscatores parvulis expediti navigiis
ad praedam rapiendam. Deinde ut aliquos viderunt, qui suas opes defenderent, mutaverunt crudelitatem in auxilium . . .

115   Audimus murmur insolitum et sub diaeta magistri
quasi cupientis exire beluae gemitum. Persecuti
igitur sonum invenimus Eumolpum sedentem mem-
branaeque ingenti versus ingerentem. Mirati ergo,
quod illi vacaret in vicinia mortis poema facere,
extrahimus clamantem iubemusque bonam habere
mentem. At ille interpellatus excanduit et " Sinite
me " inquit " sententiam explere; laborat carmen
in fine." Inicio ego phrenetico manum iubeoque

----

[1] iuncta nos mors *L*: iuncta nos sors *suggests Fraenkel*:
iunctos nos mare *P. du Faur.*

[2] *added by Müller.*

as Fate swoops down upon you." As I spoke Giton took off his clothes, and I covered him with my shirt as he put up his head to be kissed. And that no envious wave should pull us apart as we clung to each other, he put on his belt—it went round us both—and tied it tight, saying, " Whatever happens to us, at least for a long while a common death will carry us along or if the sea has pity and will cast us up on the same shore, some one may come by and put stones over us out of ordinary human kindness, or the last work of the waves even in their wrath will be to cover us with the unconscious sand." I submitted thus to a final bond, and then waited, like a man dressed for his death-bed, for an end that had lost its bitterness. Meanwhile by Fate's decree the storm rose to its height, and took by violence all that was left of the ship. No mast, no helm, no rope or oar remained on her. She drifted on the waves like a rough and un-shapen lump of wood. . . .

Some fishermen in handy little boats put out to seize their prey. When they saw some men alive and ready to fight for their belongings, they altered their savage plans and came to the rescue. . . .

We heard a strange noise, and a groaning like a wild beast wanting to get out, coming from under the master's cabin. So we followed the sound, and found Eumolpus sitting there inscribing verses on a great parchment. So we were surprised at his having time to write poetry with death close at hand, and we pulled him out, though he protested, and implored him to be sensible. But he was furious at our inter-ruption, and cried: " Let me complete my thought; the poem halts at the close." I laid hands on the

Gitona accedere et in terram trahere poetam mugien-
tem . . .

Hoc opere tandem elaborato casam piscatoriam
subimus maerentes, cibisque naufragio corruptis
utcunque curati tristissimam exegimus noctem.
Postero die, cum poneremus consilium,[1] cui nos
regioni crederemus, repente video corpus humanum
circumactum levi vertice ad litus deferri. Substiti
ergo tristis coepique umentibus [2] oculis maris fidem
inspicere et " Hunc forsitan " proclamo " in aliqua
parte terrarum secura exspectat uxor, forsitan
ignarus tempestatis filius aut pater; [3] utique reliquit
aliquem, cui proficiscens osculum dedit. Haec sunt
consilia mortalium, haec vota magnarum cogitationum.[4] En homo quemadmodum natat." Adhuc
tanquam ignotum deflebam, cum inviolatum os
fluctus convertit in terram, agnovique terribilem
paulo ante et implacabilem Licham pedibus meis
paene subiectum. Non tenui igitur diutius lacrimas,
immo percussi semel iterumque manibus pectus et
" Ubi nunc est" inquam " iracundia tua, ubi impo-
tentia tua? nempe piscibus beluisque expositus es,
et qui paulo ante iactabas vires imperii tui, de tam
magna nave ne tabulam quidem naufragus habes.
Ite nunc mortales, et magnis cogitationibus pectora
implete. Ite cauti, et opes fraudibus captas per [5]

---

[1] *Fraenkel suggests* proponeremus consilia.

[2] humentibus (*with other readings*) *in margin of Tornaesius's
edition*: urentibus *Lips:* viventibus.

[3] pater *Buecheler, who also conjectured* fratrem *and put it in
his text*: patrem. *Fraenkel suggests* patrem⟨aut⟩.

maniac, and told Giton to help me to drag the bellow-
ing bard ashore. . . .

When this business was at last completed, we came
sadly to a fisherman's cottage, refreshed ourselves
more or less with food spoilt by sea-water, and
passed a very miserable night. Next morning, as we
were trying to decide into what part of the country
we should venture, I suddenly saw a man's body
caught in a gentle eddy and carried ashore. I
stopped gloomily, and, with moist eyes, proceeded to
reflect upon the treachery of the sea. " Maybe,"
I cried, " there is a wife waiting cheerfully at home
for this man in a far-off land, or a son or a father,
maybe, who know nothing of this storm; he is sure
to have left some one behind whom he kissed before
he went. So much for mortal men's plans, and the
prayers of high ambition. Look how the man floats."
I was still crying over him as a perfect stranger,
when a wave turned his face towards the shore without a mark upon it, and I recognized Lichas, but a
while ago so fierce and so relentless, now thrown
almost under my feet. Then I could restrain my
tears no longer; I beat my breast again and again,
and cried, " Where is your temper and your hot head
now? Behold! you are a prey for fish and savage
beasts. An hour ago you boasted the strength of
your command, and you have not one plank of your
great ship to save you. Now let mortal men go and
fill their hearts with proud imaginations. Let misers
make arrangements for a thousand years about the

---

4 *Fraenkel would delete* magnarum cogitationum.
5 *Nisbet conjectures* in.

mille annos disponite. Nempe hic proxima luce
patrimonii sui rationes inspexit, nempe diem etiam,
quo venturus esset in patriam, animo suo fixit.[1] Dii
deaeque, quam longe a destinatione sua iacet. Sed
non sola mortalibus maria hanc fidem praestant.
Illum bellantem arma decipiunt, illum diis vota
reddentem penatium suorum ruina sepelit. Ille
vehiculo lapsus properantem spiritum excussit, cibus
avidum strangulavit, abstinentem frugalitas. Si
bene calculum ponas, ubique naufragium est. At
enim fluctibus obruto non contingit [2] sepultura. Tanquam intersit, periturum corpus quae ratio con-
sumat, ignis an fluctus an mora.[3] Quicquid feceris,
omnia haec eodem ventura sunt. Ferae tamen
corpus lacerabunt. Tanquam melius ignis accipiat;
immo hanc poenam gravissimam credimus, ubi servis
irascimur. Quae ergo dementia est, omnia facere,
ne quid de nobis relinquat sepultura? " . . .

Et Licham quidem rogus inimicis collatus manibus
adolebat. Eumolpus autem dum epigramma mortuo
facit, oculos ad arcessendos sensus longius mittit . . .

116 Hoc peracto libenter officio destinatum carpimus
iter ac momento temporis in montem sudantes con-
scendimus, ex quo haud procul impositum arce sub-
limi oppidum cernimus. Nec quod esset, sciebamus
errantes, donec a vilico quodam Crotona esse cognovimus, urbem antiquissimam et aliquando Italiae

---

[1] fixit *Oevering*: finxit.
[2] contingit *Goldast*: contigit. continget *Barth*.
[3] terra *Crusius*. *Buecheler suggests* aura.

---

[1] Now Crotona, originally a Greek colony, in South Italy.

gains they win by fraud. Lo! this man but yesterday looked into the accounts of his family property,
and even settled in his own mind the very day when
he would come home again. Lord, Lord, how far he
lies from his consummation! But it is not the waves
of the sea alone that thus keep faith with mortal men.
The warrior's weapons fail him; another pays his
vows to Heaven, and his own house falls and buries
him in the act. Another slips from his coach and
dashes out his eager soul: the glutton chokes at
dinner, the sparing man dies of want. Make a fair
reckoning, and you find shipwreck everywhere. You
tell me that for those the waters whelm there is no
burial. As if it mattered how our perishable flesh
comes to its end, by fire or water or the lapse of time!
Whatever you may do, all these things achieve the
same goal. But beasts will tear the body, you say,
as though fire would give it a more kindly welcome!
When we are angry with our slaves, we consider
burning their heaviest punishment. Then what madness to take such trouble to prevent the grave from
leaving aught of us behind! " . . .

So Lichas was burned on a pyre built by his
enemy's hands. Eumolpus proceeded to compose
an epitaph on the dead man, and looked about in
search of some far-fetched ideas. . . .

We gladly performed this last office, and then took
up our proposed way, and in a short while came
sweating to a mountain top, from which we saw, not
far off, a town set on a high hill. We had lost ourselves, and did not know what it was, until we
learned from a farm-bailiff that it was Croton,[1] a
town of great age, and once the first city in Italy.

primam. Cum deinde diligentius exploraremus, qui homines inhabitarent nobile solum, quodve genus negotiationis praecipue probarent post attritas bellis frequentibus opes, "O mi" inquit "hospites, si negotiatores estis, mutate propositum aliudque vitae praesidium quaerite. Sin autem urbanioris notae homines sustinetis semper mentiri, recta ad lucrum curritis. In hac enim urbe non litterarum studia celebrantur, non eloquentia locum habet, non frugalitas sanctique mores laudibus [1] ad fructum perveniunt, sed quoscunque homines in hac urbe videritis, scitote in duas partes esse divisos. Nam aut captantur aut captant. In hac urbe nemo liberos tollit, quia quisquis suos heredes habet, non ad cenas,[2] non ad spectacula admittitur, sed omnibus prohibetur commodis, inter ignominiosos latitat. Qui vero nec uxorem [3] unquam duxerunt nec proximas necessitudines habent, ad summos honores perveniunt, [id est soli militares,] [4] soli fortissimi atque etiam innocentes habentur. Adibitis" inquit "oppidum tanquam in pestilentia campos, in quibus nihil aliud est nisi cadavera, quae lacerantur, aut corvi, qui lacerant" . . .

117　prudentior Eumolpus convertit ad novitatem rei mentem genusque id venationis [5] sibi non displicere confessus est. Iocari ego senem poetica levitate credebam, cum ille "Utinam quidem sufficeret lar-

---

[1] *P. George would delete* laudibus.
[2] coenas *Bongars*: scenas.
[3] uxorem *prefers Buecheler*: uxores.
[4] *Fraenkel deletes.*

288

When we went on to inquire particularly what men lived on such honoured soil, and what kind of business pleased them best, now that their wealth had been brought low by so many wars, the man replied, " My friends, if you are business men, change your plans and look for some other safe way of life. But if you profess to be men of a superior stamp and thorough-paced liars, you are on the direct road to wealth. For in this city the pursuit of learning is not esteemed, eloquence has no place, economy and a pure life do not win their reward in honour: know that the whole of the men you see in this city are divided into two classes. They are either the prey of legacy-hunting or legacy-hunters themselves. In this city no one brings up children, because anyone who has heirs of his own stock is never admitted to dinner or the theatre; he is deprived of all advantages, and lies in obscurity among the base-born. But those who have never married, and have no near relations, reach the highest positions; they alone are considered gallant, or even good. Yes," he went on, " you will go into a town that is like a plague-stricken plain, where there is nothing but carcasses to be torn to pieces, and crows to tear them." . . .

Eumolpus was more cautious, and directed his attention to the novelty of the case, declaring that that kind of hunting did not make him uneasy. I thought the old man was joking with the light heart of a poet, but then he said, " I only wish I had a more

---

⁵ id venationis *Müller (2nd edition)*: invitationis *Nisbet*: id invitationis *Haase*: dilationis *Dousa*: divinationis.

PETRONIUS ARBITER

gior scaena, id est [1] vestis humanior, instrumentum
lautius,[2] quod praeberet mendacio fidem : non mehercules † penam † [3] istam differrem, sed continuo vos
ad magnas opes ducerem. Atquin promitto, quicquid exigeret, dummodo placeret vestis, rapinae
comes, et quicquid Lycurgi villa grassantibus prae-
buisset. Nam nummos in praesentem usum deum
matrem pro fide sua reddituram " ⟨. . .⟩ [4]

" Quid ergo " inquit Eumolpus " cessamus mimum
componere ? Facite ergo me dominum, si negotiatio
placet." Nemo ausus est artem damnare nihil
auferentem. Itaque ut duraret inter omnes tutum
mendacium, in verba Eumolpi [sacramentum] [5]
iuravimus : uri, vinciri, verberari ferroque necari, et
quicquid aliud Eumolpus iussisset. Tanquam legiti-
mi gladiatores domino corpora animasque religiosis-
sime addicimus. Post peractum sacramentum ser-
viliter ficti [6] dominum consalutamus, elatumque ab
Eumolpo filium pariter condiscimus, iuvenem ingentis eloquentiae et spei, ideoque de civitate sua
miserrimum senem exisse, ne aut clientes sodalesque
filii sui aut sepulcrum quotidie causam lacrimarum
cerneret. Accessisse huic tristitiae proximum naufragium, quo amplius vicies sestertium amiserit ; nec

[1] *Fraenkel suggested deleting* id est *here as elsewhere; but it
seems a favourite phrase with Petronius.*
[2] lautius *Gulielmius*: latius.
[3] penam *l*: poenam *cod. Lambeth.*: spem *Jacobs*: scenam
J. F. Gronov: operam *Iunius*: penuriam *P. George*: peram
(= πεῖραν) *Pithoeus*: *in his 1st edition Müller conjectures* pug-
nam, *in his 2nd*, praedam.
[4] *Lacuna indicated by Buecheler.*
[5] *Fraenkel deletes.*

ample background, I mean a more gentlemanly dress, and finer ornaments, to lend colour to my strange tale; I declare I would not put off the business [?], I would bring you into great wealth in a moment. Anyhow, I promise to do whatever my fellow-robber demands, so long as my clothes were satisfactory, and whatever we found in Lycurgus's country-house when we broke in.[1]   For I am sure that our mother of the gods for her honour's sake will pay up some coin to use for present needs." . . . " Well then," said Eumolpus, " Why shouldn't we make up a farce ? Now appoint me your master, if you like the business." No one dared to grumble at this harmless device.   So to keep the lie safe among us all, we took an oath to obey Eumolpus; to endure burning, bondage, flogging, death by the sword, or anything else that Eumolpus ordered. We pledged our bodies and souls to our master most solemnly, like regular gladiators. When the oath was over, we posed like slaves and saluted our master, and learned all together that Eumolpus had lost a son, a young man of great eloquence and promise, and that the poor old man had left his own country for this reason, to escape seeing his son's dependants and friends, or the tomb which was the source of his daily tears. His grief had been increased by a recent shipwreck, in which he lost over two million sesterces: it was not

---

[1] This adventure is missing. The mother of the gods is Cybele introduced from Asia to Rome and then worshipped as *Magna Mater.*

---

[6] *Fraenkel denied the correctness of* ficti. cincti *suggests Müller in his 2nd edition*: vestiti *Nisbet.*

illum iactura moveri, sed destitutum ministerio non
agnoscere dignitatem suam. Praeterea habere in
Africa trecenties sestertium fundis nominibusque
depositum; nam familiam quidem tam magnam per
agros Numidiae esse sparsam, ut possit vel Cartha-
ginem capere. Secundum hanc formulam impera-
mus Eumolpo, ut plurimum tussiat, ut sit [modo] [1]
solutioris stomachi cibosque omnes palam damnet;
loquatur aurum et argentum fundosque mendaces et
perpetuam terrarum sterilitatem; sedeat praeterea
quotidie ad rationes tabulasque testamenti omnibus
⟨mensibus⟩ [2] renovet. Et ne quid scaenae deesset,
quotiescunque aliquem nostrum vocare temptasset,
alium pro alio vocaret, ut facile appareret dominum etiam eorum meminisse, qui praesentes non
essent.

His ita ordinatis, " quod bene feliciterque eveniret " [3] precati deos viam ingredimur. Sed neque
Giton sub insolito fasce durabat, et mercennarius
Corax, detrectator ministerii, posita frequentius
sarcina male dicebat properantibus affirmabatque
se aut proiecturum sarcinas aut cum onere fugiturum.
" Quid vos " inquit " iumentum me putatis esse aut
lapidariam navem? Hominis operas locavi, non
caballi. Nec minus liber sum quam vos, etiam si
pauperem pater me reliquit." Nec contentus male-
dictis tollebat subinde altius pedem et strepitu
obsceno simul atque odore viam implebat. Ridebat
contumaciam Giton et singulos crepitus eius pari
clamore prosequebatur . . .

---

[1] *Deleted by Casaubon*: ⟨modo astrictioris⟩modo *Wehle.*
[2] *Added by Buecheler.*
[3] *Nisbet suggests deleting the clause* quod . . . eveniret.

the loss that troubled him, but with no servant to wait upon him he could not recognize his own importance. Besides, he had thirty millions invested in Africa in estates and bonds; such a horde of his slaves was scattered over the fields of Numidia[1] that he could positively have taken Carthage. Under this scheme we asked Eumolpus to cough frequently, to complain about loose bowels, and to find fault openly with all his food; he must talk of gold and silver and his disappointing farms and the obstinate barrenness of the soil; further, he must sit over his accounts daily, and revise the sheets of his will every month. To make the setting quite complete, he was to use the wrong names whenever he tried to call one of us, so that it would clearly look as though our master had also in his mind some servants who were not present. This was all arranged; we offered a prayer to Heaven for a prosperous and happy issue, and started on our journey. But Giton was not used to a burden and could not bear it, and hireling Corax, a shirker of work, kept putting down his bundle and cursing our hurry, and declaring that he would either throw the baggage away or run off with his load. "You seem to think I am a beast of burden or a ship for carrying stones," he cried. "You paid for the services of a man, not a horse. I am just as free as you are, although my father did leave me a poor man." Not satisfied with curses, he kept lifting his leg up and filling the whole road with a disgusting noise and smell. Giton laughed at his impudence and matched every noise he made. . . .

---

[1] Numidia, in north Africa, corresponds with Algeria to-day.

118 *LO* | " Multos, inquit Eumolpos, o[1] iuvenes, carmen
decepit. Nam ut quisque versum pedibus intruxit
sensumque teneriorem[2] verborum ambitu intexit,
putavit se continuo in Heliconem venisse. Sic
forensibus ministeriis exercitati frequenter ad carminis tranquillitatem tanquam ad portum feliciorem[3]
refugerunt, credentes facilius poema exstrui posse,
quam controversiam sententiolis vibrantibus pictam.
Ceterum [neque][4] generosior spiritus sanitatem[5]
amat, neque concipere[6] aut edere partum mens
potest nisi ingenti flumine litterarum inundata.
Refugiendum est ab omni verborum, ut ita dicam,
vilitate et sumendae voces a plebe semotae,[7] ut fiat
‘ odi profanum vulgus et arceo.’[8] Praeterea curan-
dum est, ne sententiae emineant extra corpus orationis expressae,[9] sed intexto vestibus colore niteant.
Homerus testis et lyrici Romanusque Vergilius et
Horatii curiosa felicitas. Ceteri enim aut non
viderunt viam, qua iretur ad carmen, aut visam[10]
timuerunt calcare. Ecce belli civilis ingens opus
quisquis attigerit, nisi plenus litteris, sub onere
labetur. Non enim res gestae versibus comprehen-

---

[1] *Buecheler deletes* inquit Eumolpus *O. Cod. l and cod.
Lambeth. and the Florilegia omit* inquit Eumolpus *but codd. l
and (in margin) Lambeth. have* Eumolpus *before* multos. δ
omitted o. *The Florilegia have* multos nimirum carmen,
omitting inquit . . . iuvenes.

[2] teneriore *B:* teretiore *suggests Müller in his 2nd edition.*

[3] feliciorem *cod. Messanensis (now destroyed):* faciliorem.
Müller deletes.

[4] neque *deleted on Fraenkel's suggestion.*

[5] vanitatem *cod. Messanensis. Sullivan suggests* inanita-
tem.

[6] concipere *l in margin:* conspicere *l, cod. Lambeth.:* con-
spici *O.* [7] semotae *I. B. Pius:* summotae.

" Yes, my young friends," said Eumolpus, " poetry has led many astray. As soon as a man has shaped his verse in feet and woven into it a more delicate meaning with an ingenious circumlocution, he thinks that forthwith he has scaled Helicon.[1] In this fashion people who are tired out with forensic oratory often take refuge in the calm of poetry as in some happier haven, supposing that a poem is easier to construct than a declamation adorned with quivering epigrams. But nobler souls love wholesomeness, and the mind cannot conceive or bring forth its fruit unless it is steeped in the vast flood of literature. One must flee away from all diction that is, so to speak, cheap, and choose words divorced from popular use, putting into practice, ' I hate the common herd and hold it afar.'[2] Besides, one must take care that the thoughts do not stand out from the body of the speech: they must shine with a brilliancy that is woven into the material. Homer proves this, and the lyric poets, and Roman Virgil, and the studied felicity of Horace. The others either did not see the path that leads to poetry, or saw it and were afraid to walk in it. For instance, anyone who attempts the vast theme of the civil war will sink under the burden unless he is full of literature. It is not a question

---

[1] Mount Helicon is Zagara, in Boeotia, sacred in ancient times to Apollo and the Muses.
[2] Horace, *Odes*, III, 1, 1.

---

[8] *Perhaps we should delete* ut . . . arceo, *as Fraenkel has suggested.*
[9] *Fraenkel would delete* expressae.
[10] visam *N. Lefèvre*: versu *Anton*: versum.

dendae sunt, quod longe melius historici faciunt, sed
per ambages deorumque ministeria et fabulosum [1]
sententiarum † tormentum † [2] praecipitandus est liber
spiritus, ut potius furentis animi vaticinatio appareat
quam religiosae orationis sub testibus fides: tanquam
si placet hic impetus, etiam si nondum recepit
ultimam manum " . . .

119   " Orbem iam totum victor Romanus habebat,
qua mare, qua terrae, qua sidus currit utrumque.
Nec satiatus erat.   Gravidis freta pulsa carinis
iam peragebantur; si quis sinus abditus ultra,
si qua foret tellus, quae fulvum mitteret aurum,
hostis erat, fatisque in tristia bella paratis
quaerebantur opes.   Non vulgo nota placebant
gaudia, non usu plebeio trita voluptas.
Aes Ephyreiacum [3] laudabat miles in unda; [4]
quaesitus tellure nitor certaverat ostro;   10
hinc Numidae † accusant † [5] illinc nova vellera Seres,
atque Arabum populus sua despoliaverat arva.

    [1] *Perhaps* fabulosarum.
    [2] torrentem *Barth.   Perhaps* tonitrum.   *Fraenkel suggests*
fragosum sententiarum torrentem.
    [3] aes Ephyreiacum *Heinsius*: aes Ephyrae coctum *Müller*,
2nd edition: perhaps aes Pyrenaeum (Pirenaeum *Mössler*). *There
are many other suggestions.   The MSS vary* (aesepyre cum *B*).
    [4] ima *Goldast.*
    [5] accusant *l*: accusatius *B*, δ: accusati *P*: crustas *Scaliger.*
Perhaps ecce satūs.   *Cf. Chapter 117 per agros Numidiae.*

    [1] This poem, very long as part of the present novel, very
short as an epic, is a problem.   See Additional Note. pp.
380–384, and W. H. Stubbe, *Die Verseinlagen im Petron,*
Leipzig, 1933, (*Philol.* suppl. XXV, 2); and W. H. Friedrich,
in *Hermes,* LXXIII, 1937, 393.   Cf. Heseltine's remarks on p. xi.
    [2] A great exaggeration, of course; but the Romans' power

of recording real events in verse; historians can do
that far better. The free spirit of genius must
plunge headlong into allusions and divine interpositions, and rack [?] itself for great thoughts
coloured by mythology, so that what results seems
rather the prophecies of an inspired seer than the
exactitude of a statement made on oath before witnesses: the following effusion will show what I mean,
if it take your fancy, though it has not yet received
my final touches. . . .

¹" The conquering Roman now held the whole
world,² sea and land and the course of sun and moon.
But he was not satisfied. Now the waters were
stirred and troubled by his loaded ships; if there
were any hidden bay beyond, or any land that promised a yield of yellow gold, that place was Rome's
enemy, fate stood ready for the sorrows of war, and
the quest for wealth went on. There was no happiness in familiar joys, or in pleasures dulled by the
common man's use. The soldier out at sea would
praise the bronze of Corinth;³ bright colours dug from
earth rivalled the purple; from this side the
African † ⁴ . . .; † from that side the Chinaman had
plundered his marvellous silks,⁵ and the Arabian
people had stripped their own fields bare.

was indeed supreme in all regions surrounding the Mediterranean sea.
   ³ For Corinthian bronze, see note on Chapter 50. Ephyra
was an ancient name of Corinth.
   ⁴ The reading leaves it uncertain what the Numidians
provided. Their agriculture was of some importance; and
Numidian marble was admired.
   ⁵ Chinese silk was now reaching the Roman Empire in some
quantity. The Arabians sent frankincense above all.

PETRONIUS ARBITER

Ecce aliae clades et laesae vulnera pacis.
Quaeritur in silvis auro [1] fera, et ultimus Hammon
Afrorum excutitur, ne desit belua dente
ad mortes pretiosa; fames [2] premit advena classes,
tigris et aurata [3] gradiens vectatur in aula,
ut bibat humanum populo plaudente cruorem.
Heu, pudet effari perituraque prodere fata,
Persarum ritu male pubescentibus annis   20
surripuere viros exsectaque viscera ferro
in venerem fregere, atque ut fuga nobilis aevi
circumscripta mora properantes differat annos,
quaerit se natura nec invenit.   Omnibus ergo
scorta placent fractique enervi corpore gressus
et laxi crines et tot nova nomina vestis,
quaeque virum quaerunt.   Ecce Afris eruta terris
citrea mensa greges servorum ostrumque renidens
ponitur ac maculis imitatur vilius [4] aurum
quae sensum trahat.   Hoc sterile ac male nobile
    lignum   30
turba sepulta mero circum venit, omniaque orbis
praemia correptis [5] miles vagus esurit armis.
Ingeniosa gula est.   Siculo scarus aequore mersus
ad mensam vivus perducitur, atque Lucrinis
eruta litoribus vendunt conchylia cenas,

[1] circo *Iunius*: Tauri *Busche.*
[2] fremens *Brouhier.*   Perhaps canes; *or* chama et (*lynx*).
[3] aerata *Broukhusius.*
[4] vilius *J. F. Gronov*: vilibus.
[5] corruptis *Bourdelot*: contentis *Burman.*

[1] Or Ammon a shrine of Jupiter at the oasis Siwah in Libya.

" Yet again more destruction, and peace hurt and bleeding. The wild animal is searched out in the woods at a great price, and men trouble Hammon[1] far away in Africa to supply the beast[2] whose tusks make him precious even to the deaths of men; strange ravening creatures freight the fleets, and the padding tiger is wheeled in a gilded palace to drink the blood of men while the crowd applauds.

" I shrink from speaking plain and betraying our destiny of ruin; real men whose years of puberty have hardly begun are kidnapped, and the powers the knife has shown are forced in the Persian way to the service of lust, and in order that the passing of man's finest age may be hedged round with delay and hold back the hurrying years, Nature seeks for herself, and finds herself not. So all take their pleasure in harlotry, and the halting steps of a feeble body, and in flowing hair and numberless clothes of new names, everything that finds manhood missing.

" Tables of citrus-wood—see!—are dug out of the soil of Africa and set up, the spots on them resembling gold which is cheaper than they, their polish reflecting hordes of slaves and purple clothes, to lure the senses. Round this barren and low-born wood there gathers a crowd drowned in drink, and the soldier of fortune having taken up his arms hungers for all the prizes of the world.

" Gluttony is a fine art. The wrasse is brought alive to table in sea-water from Sicily, and the oysters torn from the banks of the Lucrine lake[3] make a dinner saleable, in order to renew men's hunger by

---

[2] The elephant, important for ivory.
[3] Lago Lucrino, a salt-water lake near Baia.

ut renovent per damna famem.   Iam Phasidos unda
orbata est avibus, mutoque in litore tantum
solae [1] desertis adspirant frondibus aurae.
Nec minor in campo furor est, emptique Quirites
ad praedam strepitumque lucri suffragia vertunt.   40
Venalis populus, venalis curia patrum,
est favor in pretio.   Senibus quoque libera virtus
exciderat, sparsisque opibus conversa potestas
ipsaque maiestas auro corrupta iacebat.
Pellitur a populo victus Cato; tristior ille est,
qui vicit, fascesque pudet rapuisse Catoni.
[Namque—hoc dedecoris populo morumque ruina—][2]
non homo pulsus erat, sed in uno victa potestas
Romanumque decus.   Quare tam perdita Roma
ipsa sui merces erat et sine vindice praeda.   50
Praeterea gemino deprensam gurgite plebem [3]
faenoris ingluvies [4] ususque exederat aeris.
Nulla est certa domus, nullum sine pignore corpus,
sed veluti tabes tacitis concepta medullis
intra membra furens curis latrantibus errat.
Arma placent miseris, detritaque commoda luxu
vulneribus reparantur.   Inops audacia tuta est.
Hoc mersam caeno Romam somnoque iacentem

---

[1] surdae ("*voiceless*") *suggests Nisbet.*
[2] *Broukhusius deleted this line.*
[3] plebem *Burman*: praedam.
[4] ingluvies *Palmier*: illuvies.

---

[1] Pheasants; see note on chapter 93.
[2] *Quirites*: an old name for Roman citizens of Rome itself.
See Fragment XXII.
[3] Marcus Porcius Cato the younger (95–46 B.C.) was the
honest but obstinate defender of Republican Government as

their extravagance. All the birds[1] are now gone from the waters of Phasis; the shore is quiet; only the empty air breathes on the lonely leaves.

" The same madness is in public life, the true-born Roman[2] is bought, and changes his vote for plunder and the cry of gain. The people are corrupt, the house of senators is corrupt, their support hangs on a price. The freedom and virtue of the old men had decayed, their power was swayed by largesse, even their dignity was stained by money and trodden in the dust.

" Cato[3] is beaten and driven out by the mob; his conqueror[4] is more unhappy than he, and is ashamed to have torn the rods of office from Cato. [For—and the shame of the nation and the fall of their character lay in this—] There was not only one man's defeat. In his person the power and glory of Rome was humbled. So Rome in her deep disgrace was herself price and prize, and despoiled herself without an avenger. Moreover greed for usury and the handling of money had caught the common people in a double whirlpool, and destroyed them. Not a house is safe, not a man but is mortgaged; the madness spreads through their limbs, and trouble bays and hounds them down like some disease sown in the dumb marrow. In despair they turn to violence, and bloodshed restores the good things lost by luxury. A beggar can risk everything in safety. Could the spell of healthful reason stir Rome from the

he knew it; he took his own life at Utica in N. Africa rather than submit to Julius Caesar in the Civil War. In Lucan's *Pharsalia* he is a great hero.

[4] Julius Caesar who became supreme.

quae poterant artes sana ratione movere,
ni furor et bellum ferroque excita [1] libido?   60
120   Tres tulerat Fortuna duces, quos obruit omnes
armorum strue diversa feralis Enyo.
Crassum Parthus habet, Libyco iacet aequore
   Magnus,
Iulius ingratam perfudit sanguine Romam,
et quasi non posset tot tellus ferre sepulcra,
divisit cineres.   Hos gloria reddit honores.
   Est locus exciso penitus demersus hiatu
Parthenopen inter magnaeque Dicarchidos arva,
Cocyti perfusus aqua; nam spiritus, extra
qui furit effusus,[2] funesto spargitur aestu.   70
Non haec autumno tellus viret aut alit herbas
caespite laetus ager, non verno persona cantu
mollia discordi strepitu virgulta locuntur,
sed chaos et nigro squalentia pumice saxa
gaudent ferali circum tumulata cupresso.
Has inter sedes Ditis pater extulit ora
bustorum flammis et cana sparsa favilla,
ac tali volucrem Fortunam voce lacessit:

      [1] excita *Iunius*: accincta *Heinsius*: excisa, excissa.
      [2] *Nisbet reasonably suggests* expulsus.

---

    [1] Gnaeus Pompeius Magnus (106–48 B.C.), Marcus Licinius Crassus (c. 115–53 B.C.) and Gaius Julius Caesar (102–44 B.C.).
    [2] Ἐννώ, in Latin Bellona.
    [3] Crassus in 55 B.C. received Syria as his province and was defeated by the Parthians at Carrhae in Mesopotamia in 53.
    [4] After his defeat by Caesar at Pharsalus, Pompeius fled to Egypt and was there murdered on the orders of King Ptolemy XII, 48 B.C.
    [5] Julius Caesar was murdered in Rome in 44 B.C.
    [6] An old Greek name for the Greek city Νεάπολις (" New

filth where she rolled in heavy sleep, or only madness and war and the lust wakened by the sword?

" Fortune brought forth three generals,[1] and the goddess of War[2] and Death buried them all, each beneath a pile of arms. The Parthian has Crassus in keeping,[3] Pompey the Great lies by the Libyan water,[4] Julius stained ungrateful Rome[5] with his blood; as though the earth could not endure the burden of so many graves, she has separated their ashes. These are the wages paid by fame.

" Between Parthenope[6] and the fields of the great town[7] of Dicarchis there lies a spot[8] plunged deep in a cloven chasm, wet with the water of Cocytus:[9] for the air that rushes furiously outward is laden with that baleful spray. The ground here is never green in autumn, the field does not prosper or nurture herbage on its turf, the soft thickets never ring nor are loud in springtime with the songs of rival birds, but chaos is there, and gloomy rocks of black pumice-stone lie happy in the gloom of the cypresses that mound them about. From this place father Dis[10] lifted his head, lit with funeral flames and flecked with white ashes, and provoked winged Fortune with these words:

Town "), Napoli, Naples, apparently founded on the site of an older city Parthenope.

[7] Puteoli, now Pozzuoli, called also, when it was a Greek city, Dicarchis or Dicaearchia from its reputed founder Dicaearchus.

[8] The Phlegraean Plain, now Solfatara between Pozzuoli and Naples.

[9] " Wailing River " one of the six rivers of the underworld in Greek mythology.

[10] The Greek god Pluto, ruler of the underworld.

' Rerum humanarum divinarumque potestas,
Fors, cui nulla placet nimium secura potestas,[1]   80
quae nova semper amas et mox possessa relinquis,
ecquid Romano sentis te pondere victam,
nec posse ulterius perituram extollere molem ?
Ipsa suas vires odit Romana iuventus
et quas struxit opes, male sustinet.   Aspice late
luxuriam spoliorum et censum in damna furentem.
Aedificant auro sedesque ad sidera mittunt,
expelluntur aquae saxis, mare nascitur arvis,
et permutata rerum statione rebellant.
En etiam mea regna petunt.   Perfossa dehiscit   90
molibus insanis tellus, iam montibus haustis
antra gemunt, et dum vanos [2] lapis invenit usus,
inferni manes caelum sperare fatentur.
Quare age, Fors, muta pacatum in proelia vultum
Romanosque cie ac nostris da funera regnis.
Iam pridem nullo perfundimus ora cruore,
nec mea Tisiphone sitientis perluit artus,
ex quo Sullanus bibit ensis et horrida tellus
extulit in lucem nutritas sanguine fruges.'
121   Haec ubi dicta dedit, dextrae coniungere dextram
conatus rupto tellurem solvit hiatu.   101
Tunc Fortuna levi defudit pectore voces :
' O genitor, cui Cocyti penetralia parent,

---

[1] *The lost codex* δ *omitted this line; but it may be that it is
line 79 instead which ought to be omitted or transposed.*
[2] vanos *Flor.*: varios *l and cd. Lambeth.* (vanos *in margin*):
varius *Scaliger (Catalecta)*: vanus *O.*

---

[1] Of the three Furies in Greek mythology, Tisiphone was
" Avenger of Murder," Allecto and Megaera her sisters being
the others.

304

" ' Disposer of life in earth and heaven, Chance,
always angry against power too firmly seated, everlasting lover of change and quick forsaker of thy con-
quests, dost not thou feel thy spirit crushed under the
weight of Rome, and that thou canst not further raise
up the mass that is doomed to fall? The youth of
Rome contemns its own strength, and groans under
the wealth its own hands have heaped up. See,
everywhere they squander their spoils, and the mad
use of wealth brings its own loss. They have
buildings of gold and homes raised to the stars,
they drive out the waters with their stone piers, the
sea springs forth amid the fields: rebellious man
turns creation's order upside down. Aye, they grasp
even at my kingdom. The earth is hewn through for
their madmen's foundations and gapes wide, now the
mountains are hollowed out until the caves groan,
and while men turn nature's stone to their empty
purposes, the ghosts of hell declare their hopes of
winning heaven. Arise, then, Chance, change thy
looks of peace to war, harry the Roman, and let my
kingdom have the dead. It is long now since my
lips were wet with blood, and never has my loved
Tisiphone[1] bathed her thirsty limbs since the sword
of Sulla[2] drank deep, and the earth stood thick
with corn, and thrust up, into the light, grain
fattened on blood.'

" He spoke and ended, and strained to take her
hand in his, till he broke and clove the earth asunder.
Then Fortune poured forth words from her fickle
heart: ' Father, whom the inmost places of Cocytus

---

[2] In 82 B.C., when supreme in Rome, Lucius Cornelius Sulla
(138–78 B.C.) massacred the supporters of Marius.

si modo vera mihi fas est impune profari,
vota tibi cedent; nec enim minor ira rebellat
pectore in hoc leviorque exurit flamma medullas.
Omnia, quae tribui Romanis arcibus, odi
muneribusque meis irascor.   Destruet istas
idem, qui posuit, moles deus.   Et mihi cordi
quippe cremare viros et sanguine pascere luxum. 110
Cerno equidem gemina iam stratos morte Philippos
Thessaliaeque rogos et funera gentis Hiberae.
[Iam fragor armorum trepidantes personat aures.] [1]
Et Libyae cerno tua, Nile, gementia claustra
Actiacosque sinus et Apollinis arma timentes.
Pande, age, terrarum sitientia regna tuarum
atque animas accerse novas.   Vix navita [2] Porthmeus
sufficiet simulacra virum traducere cumba;
classe opus est.   Tuque ingenti satiare ruina,
pallida Tisiphone, concisaque vulnera mande :   120
ad Stygios manes laceratus ducitur orbis.'
122   Vixdum finierat, cum fulgure rupta corusco
intremuit nubes elisosque abscidit ignes.

---

[1] *I think Müller was right in proposing in his 1st edition
deletion of this line, which is transferred elsewhere by other
scholars.*
[2] tenvia *Müller in his 2nd edition.*

---

[1] It is sometimes supposed that Petronius alludes to the
Battle of Pharsalus where Pompeius was defeated by Caesar
in 48 B.C. as well as the Battle of Philippi where Brutus and
Cassius were defeated in 42 by Octavian (future emperor
Augustus) and Antony.   But the Battle of Philippi itself was
a double battle.
[2] Pharsalus is in Thessaly.
[3] Spain, where Julius Caesar campaigned against the
Pompeians in 49 and 45 B.C.

bey, thy prayer shall prosper, if at least I may fore-
ell the truth without fear; for the anger that rises in
ny heart is stern as thine, and the flame that burns
leep in my bones as fierce. I hate all the gifts I have
nade to towering Rome, and am angry at my own
dlessings. The god that raised up those high palaces
shall destroy them too. It will be my delight also to
ourn the men and feed my lust with blood. Lo,
already I see Philippi's field strewn with the dead of
two battles,[1] and the blazing pyres of Thessaly[2] and
the burial of the people of Iberia.[3] [Already the
crash of arms rings in my trembling ears.] And in
Libya I see the barriers of you, o Nile[4] groan, and the
people in terror at the gulf of Actium and the army
loved by Apollo.[5] Open, then, the thirsty realms of
thy dominion, and summon fresh souls. The old
sailor, the Ferryman,[6] will scarcely have strength to
carry over the ghosts of the men in his boat; a whole
fleet is needed. And thou, pale Tisiphone,[7] take thy
fill of wide destruction, and tear the bleeding wounds;
the whole world is rent in pieces and drawn down to
the Stygian[8] shades.'

"She had scarcely ceased to speak when a cloud
shook and was riven by a gleam of lightning, and
flashed forth a moment's burst of flame. The father[9]

[4] Because of Julius Caesar's campaigns in Egypt in 48–
47 B.C.
[5] The emperor Augustus ascribed his victory over Antony
and Cleopatra at Actium (La Punta in Albania) in 31 B.C. to
Apollo.
[6] Charon who ferried dead souls across the River Styx in the
underworld.
[7] See note on p. 304.   [8] See note 6.
[9] Pluto = Dis. See p. 303, n. 10.

Subsedit pater umbrarum, gremioque reducto
telluris pavitans fraternos palluit ictus.
Continuo clades hominum venturaque damna
auspiciis patuere deum.   Namque ore cruento
deformis Titan [1] vultum caligine texit:
civiles acies iam tum spectare [2] putares.
Parte alia plenos extinxit Cynthia vultus   130
et lucem sceleri subduxit.   Rupta tonabant
verticibus lapsis montis iuga, nec vaga passim
flumina per notas ibant morientia ripas.
Armorum strepitu caelum furit et tuba Martem
sideribus tremefacta ciet, iamque Aetna voratur
ignibus insolitis et in aethera fulmina mittit.
Ecce inter tumulos atque ossa carentia [3] bustis
umbrarum facies diro stridore minantur.[4]
Fax stellis comitata novis incendia ducit,
sanguineoque recens descendit Iuppiter imbre.   140
Haec ostenta brevi solvit deus.   Exuit omnes
quippe moras Caesar, vindictaeque actus amore
Gallica proiecit, civilia sustulit arma.

  Alpibus aeriis, ubi Graio numine [5] pulsae
descendunt rupes et se patiuntur adiri,

---

[1] Titan *cd. Vat. lat. 1671*: titubans.
[2] spectare *Anton*: spirare (spitare *B before alteration*):
veritum spectare *Crusius*.
[3] carentia *B, R*: calentia *J. F. Gronov*: arentia.
[4] minantur *Goldast*: minatur.
[5] numine *Burman*: nomine.

---

[1] Zeus, Latin Jupiter.
[2] The sun.
[3] The moon.   Artemis = Diana was supposed to have been
born on Mt. Cynthus in Delos island.
[4] By crossing in 49 B.C. the little river Rubicon, the bound-

of darkness sank down, closed the chasm in earth's bosom, and grew white with terror at the stroke of his brother.[1]   Straightway the slaughter of men and the destruction to come were made plain by omens from on high.   For Titan[2] was disfigured and dabbled in blood, and veiled his face in darkness: thou hadst thought that even then he gazed on civil strife.   In another quarter Cynthia[3] darkened her full face, and denied her light to the crime.   The mountain-tops slid down and the peaks broke in thunder, the wandering streams were dying, and no more ranged abroad between their familiar banks.   The sky is loud with the clash of arms, the trumpet shakes to the stars and rouses the War God, and at once Aetna is the prey of unaccustomed fires, and casts her light-nings high into the air.   The faces of the dead are seen visible among the tombs and the unburied bones, gibbering in dreadful menace.   A blazing light girt with unknown stars leads the way for the flames of cities, and the sky rains down fresh showers of blood. In a little while God made these portents plain.   For now Caesar shook off all his lingering, and, spurred by the passion of revenge, threw down his arms against Gaul and took them up against Rome.[4]

" In the high Alps, where the rocks trodden by a Greek god[5] slope downward and allow men to ap-proach them, there is a place sacred to the altars of

ary between Italy proper and Cisalpine Gaul (northern Italy). He had been campaigning in Gaul proper (France) and neighbouring lands since 59–58 B.C.

[5] Hercules (Heracles) was in mythology said to have been the first to cross the Alps, after killing Geryon in Spain.   See also p. 454, n. 1.

est locus Herculeis aris sacer: hunc nive dura
claudit hiemps canoque ad sidera vertice tollit.
Caelum illinc cecidisse [1] putes: non solis adulti [2]
mansuescit radiis, non verni temporis aura,
sed glacie concreta rigent [3] hiemisque pruinis: 150
totum ferre potest umeris minitantibus orbem.
Haec ubi calcavit Caesar iuga milite laeto
optavitque [4] locum, summo de vertice montis
Hesperiae campos late proxpexit et ambas
intentans cum voce manus ad sidera dixit:
' Iuppiter omnipotens, et tu,[5] Saturnia tellus,
armis laeta meis olimque onerata [6] triumphis,
testor, ad has acies invitum accersere Martem,
LO invitas me ferre manus.   Sed vulnere cogor,
pulsus ab urbe mea, dum Rhenum sanguine tingo,
dum Gallos iterum Capitolia nostra petentes   161
Alpibus excludo, vincendo certior exsul.
Sanguine Germano sexagintaque triumphis [7]

---

[1] tetigisse *Müller in his 2nd edition*: illic sedisse *J. F. Gronov.*

[2] adulti *Scaliger (Catalecta)*: adusti.

[3] rigent *Lips, it seems*: riget *B, R*: rigens.

[4] optavitque *in margin of l (from Sambucus)*: oravitque.

[5] tu *L*: eu *B*: heu *R, P, δ. Buecheler proposed* te.

[6] ornata *Wernsdorf.* oneranda *or* ornanda *Burman.*

[7] *Nisbet suggests* tropaeis. *Perhaps* sescentis ("*countless* ") atque.

---

[1] Italy, land of the west. Ἕσπερος was the planet Venus as the evening star.

[2] Again Italy, land of Saturnus, mythical king of Latium and the providing god of agriculture and civilization.

[3] Caesar would fall victim to accusations from political opponents if he were to be without official command. He wished to pass straight from his Gallic command to a consulship without having to obey the rule that he should canvass

Hercules: the winter seals it with frozen snow, and
heaves it up on its white top to the sky.   It seems as
though the sky had fallen away from there: the
beams of the full sun do not soften the air, nor the
breezes of the springtime, but the soil stands stiff with
ice and winter's frost: its frowning shoulders could
support the whole globe.   When Caesar with his
exultant army trod these heights and chose a place, he
looked far over the fields of Hesperia[1] from the high
mountain-top, and lifted his voice and both hands to
the stars and said: ' Jupiter, Lord of all, and thou
land of Saturn,[2] once proud of my victories and
loaded with my triumphs, I call you to witness that
I do not willingly[3] summon the War God to these
hosts, and that my hand is not raised willingly to
strike.   But I am driven on by injury, by banishment
from my own city, while I dyed the Rhine[4] with blood
and cut off the Gauls from the Alps on their second
march to our Capitol.[5]   Victory makes my exile
doubly sure.   My rout of the Germans and my sixty
triumphs[6] were the beginning of my offences.   Yet

for this in Rome as a private citizen.   The senatorial government refused to grant his request.

[4] Caesar in 58 B.C. defeated the German King Ariovistus
who had crossed the Rhine; and in 55, when the Usipetes and
the Tencteri crossed the lower Rhine, Caesar massacred them,
built a bridge across the river, and made a demonstration of
force on the right bank.

[5] Caesar claims that his campaigns against the Gauls had
prevented an inroad of Gauls such as had devastated even
Rome itself in 390 or 387 B.C.

[6] Cf. note 4.   After an important victory a Roman general
could be granted a *triumphus*—a splendid entry into Rome.
That Caesar should claim sixty " triumphs " is absurd, less so
if the word here means simply victories.   Cf. line 157.

esse nocens coepi. Quanquam quos gloria terret,
aut qui sunt qui bella vetent? [1] Mercedibus emptae
ac viles operae, quorum est mea Roma noverca.
At [2] reor, haud impune, nec hanc sine vindice dextram
vinciet ignavus. Victores ite furentes, [3]
ite mei comites, et causam dicite ferro.
Namque omnes unum crimen vocat, omnibus una 170
impendet clades. Reddenda est gratia vobis,
non solus vici. Quare, quia poena tropaeis
imminet et sordes meruit victoria nostra,
iudice Fortuna cadat alea. Sumite bellum
et temptate manus. Certe mea causa peracta est:
inter tot fortes armatus nescio vinci.'
Haec ubi personuit, de caelo Delphicus ales
omina [4] laeta dedit pepulitque meatibus auras.
Nec non horrendi nemoris de parte sinistra
insolitae voces flamma sonuere sequenti. 180
Ipse nitor Phoebi vulgato laetior orbe
crevit et aurato praecinxit fulgure vultus.
123 Fortior ominibus movit Mavortia signa
Caesar et insolitos gressu prior occupat ausus.
Prima quidem glacies et cana vincta pruina
non pugnavit humus mitique horrore quievit.
Sed postquam turmae nimbos fregere ligatos
et pavidus quadrupes undarum vincula rupit,
incaluere nives. Mox flumina montibus altis

---

[1] vetent *Mössler*: vetant *J. F. Gronov*: iubent *Gulielmius*:
cient *Reiske*: vident.
[2] at *cd. P.*: ut.
[3] furentes *A*: ferentes. *In the margin of Tornaesius's
edition* frequentes.
[4] omina *A and l, Iunius*: omnia *O and cd. Lambeth*.

who is it that fears my fame, who are the men that forbid me make war? Base hirelings bought at a price, to whom my native Rome is a step-mother. But I think that no coward shall bind my strong arm unhurt without a blow in return. Come, men, to victory while anger is hot, come, my comrades, and plead our cause with the sword. For we are all summoned under one charge, and the same doom hangs over us all. My thanks are your due, my victory is not mine alone. Wherefore, since punishment threatens our trophies, and disgrace is the meed of conquest, let Chance decide how our lot shall fall. Raise the standard and prove your strength. My pleading at least is accomplished; armed amid so many warriors I cannot know defeat.' As he spoke these words aloud, the Delphic bird[1] in the sky gave a happy omen, and beat the air as it flew about. And from the left quarter of a gloomy grove strange voices sounded and fire flashed thereafter. Even Phoebus[2] glowed with orb brighter than his wont, and set a burning halo of gold about his face.

" Heartened by these omens, Caesar advanced the standards of war, and marched first to open this strange tale of daring. At first indeed the ice and the ground fettered with white frost did not fight against them, and lay quiet in the kindly cold. But then the regiments broke the close-bound clouds, the trembling horses shattered the frozen bonds of the waters, and the snows melted. Soon new-born rivers

---

[1] The raven, supposed to have a gift of prophecy and therefore imagined to be the bird of Apollo, god of Prophecy.
[2] The sun.

313

undabant modo nata, sed hae quoque—iussa
    putares—   190
stabant, et vincta fluctus stupuere ruina,[1]
et paulo ante lues iam concidenda iacebat.
Tum vero male fida prius vestigia lusit
decepitque pedes; pariter turmaeque virique
armaque congesta strue deplorata iacebant.
Ecce etiam rigido concussae flamine nubes
exonerabantur, nec rupti turbine venti
derant aut tumida confractum grandine caelum.
LO Ipsae iam nubes ruptae super arma cadebant,
et concreta gelu ponti velut unda ruebat.   200
Victa erat ingenti tellus nive victaque caeli
sidera, victa suis haerentia flumina ripis;
nondum Caesar erat, sed magnam nixus in hastam
horrida securis frangebat gressibus arva,
qualis Caucasea decurrens arduus arce
Amphitryoniades, aut torvo Iuppiter ore,
cum se verticibus magni demisit Olympi
et periturorum disiecit [2] tela Gigantum.

    Dum Caesar tumidas iratus deprimit arces,
interea volucer motis conterrita pinnis   210
Fama volat summique petit iuga celsa Palati
atque hoc † Romano †[3] tonitru ferit omnia signa[4] †:
iam classes fluitare mari totasque per Alpes

---

[1] ruina *Reiske*: pruina. *Perhaps* vincti . . . pruina.
[2] disiecit *Gulielmius*: deiecit.   [3] rumoris *Helm*.
[4] *Corrupt?*

---

[1] Hercules (Heracles) when he liberated Prometheus
chained to the Caucasus by Zeus. Amphitryon of Tiryns was

rolled from the mountain heights, but they, too, stood
still as if by some command, and the waves stopped
numb with ruining floods enchained, and the water
that ran a moment before now halted, hard enough to
cut. But then, treacherous before, it mocked their
steps and failed their footing; horses and men and
arms together fell heaped in misery and ruin. Lo!
too, the clouds were shaken by a freezing wind, and
let fall their burden, and round the army were gusts
of whirlwind and a sky broken by swollen hail. Now
the clouds themselves burst and fell on the armed
men, and a mass of ice showered upon them like a
wave of the sea. Earth was overwhelmed in the deep
snow, and the stars of heaven, and the rivers that
clung to their banks. But Caesar was not yet overwhelmed; he leaned on his tall spear and crushed the
rough ground with fearless tread, like the son of
Amphitryon[1] hastening down from a high peak of
Caucasus, or the fierce countenance of Jupiter, when
he descended from the heights of great Olympus and
scattered the arms of the doomed Giants.[2]

" While Caesar treads down the swelling peaks in
his wrath, Rumour flies swift in terror with beating
wings, and seeks out the lofty top of the tall Palatine
hill.[3] Then she strikes all the images of the gods
with her message of Roman thunder: how ships are
now sweeping the sea, and the horsemen red with

reputed father of Heracles by his wife Alcmene who was
visited by Zeus.

[2] The snake-legged giants born of Ge, Earth, tried to
climb Mount Olympus, the seat of the gods. They were
struck by Zeus's lightning and buried under Mount Aetna.

[3] At Rome. The readings in the next sentence are doubtful.

fervere Germano perfusas sanguine turmas.
Arma, cruor, caedes, incendia totaque bella
ante oculos volitant.   Ergo pulsata tumultu
pectora perque duas scinduntur territa causas.
Huic fuga per terras, illi magis unda probatur
et patria pontus iam tutior.   Est magis arma
qui temptare velit fatisque iubentibus uti.   220
[Quantum quisque timet, tantum fugit.   Ocior ipse][1]
hos inter motus populus, miserabile visu,
quo mens icta iubet, deserta ducitur urbe.
Gaudet Roma fuga, debellatique Quirites
rumoris sonitu maerentia tecta relinquunt.
Ille manu pavida natos tenet, ille penates
occultat gremio deploratumque relinquit
limen et absentem votis interficit hostem.
Sunt qui coniugibus maerentia pectora iungant,
grandaevosque patres onerisque ignara iuventus   230
id pro quo metuit, tantum trahit.   Omnia secum
hic vehit imprudens praedamque in proelia ducit:
ac velut ex alto cum magnus inhorruit auster
et pulsas evertit aquas, non arma ministris,
non regimen prodest, ligat alter pondera pinus,
alter tuta sinus [2] tranquillaque litora quaerit:
hic dat vela fugae Fortunaeque omnia credit.
Quid tam parva queror?   Gemino cum consule
    Magnus,
ille tremor Ponti saevique repertor Hydaspis

----

[1] *Deleted by Mössler.*   [2] sinus *Bursian*: sinu.

German[1] blood pouring hotly over the range of the
Alps. Battle, blood, slaughter, fire, and the whole
picture of war flits before their eyes. Thus hearts
shake in confusion, and are fearfully divided between
two counsels. One man chooses flight by land, another trusts rather to the water, and the open sea now
safer than his own country. Some prefer to attempt
a fight and turn Fate's decree to use; [each flies as
far as his fear is deep;] in this turmoil [2] the people,
a woeful sight, are led out of the deserted city,
whither their stricken heart drives them. Rome
is glad to flee, her true sons are cowed by war, and
at a rumour's breath leave their houses to mourn.
One holds his children with a shaking hand, one hides
his household gods in his bosom, and weeping, leaves
his door and calls down death on the unseen enemy.
Some clasp their wives to them in tears, youths carry
their aged sires, and, unused to burdens, take with
them only what they dread to lose. The fool drags
all his goods after him, and marches laden with booty
to the battle: and all now is as when on high the rush
of a strong south wind tumbles and drives the waters,
and neither rigging nor helm avail the crews, and one
girds together the heavy planks of pine, another
heads for safe inlets and a waveless shore: he sets
sail and flees, and trusts all to Chance. But why
sorrow for these petty ills? Pompey the Great,
who made Pontus[3] tremble and explored fierce

---

[1] The word has a double meaning here—(i) "German," as
in line 163; and (ii) "germane "—that is, related—the blood
of civil war.

[2] This part of the poem is like Lucan, *Pharsalia*, I, 490 ff.

[3] In 63 B.C. Pompeius brought the struggles with the great
Mithridates VI of Pontus to a successful end for Rome.

et piratarum scopulus, modo quem ter ovantem   240
Iuppiter horruerat, quem fracto gurgite Pontus
et veneratus erat submissa Bosporos unda,
pro pudor, imperii deserto nomine fugit,
ut Fortuna levis Magni quoque terga videret.

124   Ergo tanta lues divum quoque numina vicit,[1]
consensitque fugae caeli timor.   Ecce per orbem
mitis turba deum terras exosa furentes
deserit atque hominum damnatum avertitur agmen.
Pax prima ante alias niveos pulsata lacertos
abscondit galea [2] victum caput atque relicto   250
orbe fugax Ditis petit inplacabile regnum.
Huic comes it submissa Fides et crine soluto
Iustitia ac maerens lacera Concordia palla.
At contra, sedes Erebi qua rupta dehiscit,
emergit late Ditis chorus, horrida Erinys
et Bellona minax facibusque armata Megaera
Letumque [3] Insidiaeque et lurida Mortis imago.
Quas inter Furor, abruptis ceu liber habenis,

---

[1] vicit *Jacobs, G. Hermann*: fundit *Bourdelot*: vidit.
[2] palla *Schrader, Jacobs.*
[3] *It is unnecessary to alter* Letum *to some other personification, as some scholars wish.*

---

[1] The river Jhelum in north India.   The Romans liked to represent their great achievements as rivalling greater ones. Alexander the Great had defeated the Indian Porus in 326 B.C. on the Hydaspes; and here Pompeius, who did not go farther than the Euphrates, is none the less represented as a Roman Alexander.
[2] In 67 B.C., with a great fleet and exceptional authority, Pompeius cleared the Mediterranean of powerful pirates centred round Crete and the coast of Cilicia in Asia Minor.
[3] Pompeius passed over these waters in 66 B.C. in his cam-

Hydaspes,[1] the rock that broke the pirates,[2] who of late, in his three triumphs, shook the heart of Jupiter, to whom the troubled waters of Pontus and the conquered Sea of Bosporus[3] bowed, flees shamefully with the two consuls[4] and lets his imperial title drop, that fickle Chance might see the back of great Pompey himself turned in flight.

" Thus so great a calamity broke the power of the gods also, and dread in heaven swelled the rout. A host of gentle deities throughout the world abandon the frenzied earth in loathing, and turn aside from the doomed army of mankind.

" Peace first of all, with her snow-white arms bruised, hides her vanquished head beneath her helmet, and leaves the world and turns in flight to the inexorable realm of Dis. At her side goes humble Faith and Justice with loosened hair, and Concord weeping with her cloak rent in pieces. But where the hall of Erebus is open and gapes wide, the dreadful company of Dis ranges forth, the grim Fury, and threatening Bellona, Megaera[5] whirling her torches, and Destruction, and Treachery, and the pale presence of Death. And among them Madness, like a steed loosed when the reins snap, flings up her

paign against Mithridates. His first triumphal entry into Rome was in 81 B.C. after he defeated the Marians in Africa; his second was on the last day of 71 after victory in Spain; and his third was in 61 as conqueror of Spain, Africa, and Asia.

[4] C. Claudius Marcellus and L. Cornelius Lentulus, 49 B.C.

[5] For Dis, see p. 303, n. 10. Erebus: god of darkness, son of Chaos; the darkness through which souls passed to Hades in the Underworld. Erinys: a Fury. Bellona: goddess of War, wife of Mars. Megaera: see p. 304, n. 1.

sanguineum late tollit caput oraque mille
vulneribus confossa cruenta casside velat;   260
haeret detritus laevae Mavortius umbo
innumerabilibus telis gravis, atque flagranti
stipite dextra minax terris incendia portat.
    Sentit terra deos mutataque sidera pondus
quaesivere suum; namque [1] omnis regia caeli
in partes diducta ruit.   Primumque Dione
Caesaris arma [2] sui ducit, comes additur illi
Pallas et ingentem quatiens Mavortius hastam.
Magnum [3] cum Phoebo soror et Cyllenia proles
excipit ac totis [4] similis Tirynthius actis.   270
    Intremuere tubae ac scisso Discordia crine
extulit ad superos Stygium caput.   Huius in ore
concretus sanguis, contusaque lumina flebant,
stabant aerati [5] scabra rubigine dentes,
tabo lingua fluens, obsessa draconibus ora,
atque inter torto laceratam pectore vestem
LO sanguineam tremula [6] quatiebat lampada dextra.
Haec ut Cocyti tenebras et Tartara liquit,
alta petit gradiens iuga nobilis Appennini,
unde omnes terras atque omnia litora posset   280
aspicere ac toto fluitantes orbe catervas,

---

[1] iamque *suggests Nisbet*.
[2] arma *Passerat*: acta.
[3] Magnum *Gevaerts*: magnaque.
[4] tantis *suggests Nisbet*.
[5] aerati *cd. Lambeth., and in margin of Tornaesius's edition
and in Pithoeus's editions*: atrati *Burman*: irati.
[6] sanguinea tremulam *suggests Sambucus*.

---

[1] Venus, though properly Dione is the mother of Venus.
Caesar by convention was descended from her through Iulus
and Aeneas.

bloody head and shields her face, scarred by a thousand wounds, with a blood-stained helm; her left hand grips her worn martial shield, heavy with countless spear-points, her right waves a blazing brand and carries fire through the world.

" Earth felt the gods in action, the stars were shaken, and swung seeking their former poise; for the whole palace of the sky broke and tumbled to ruin. And first Dione[1] champions the arms of Caesar, and Pallas[2] joins her side, and the child of Mars,[3] who brandishes his tall spear. Phoebus, and his sister[4] with him, and the son of Cyllene[5] and the hero of Tiryns,[6] like to him in all his deeds, receive Pompey the Great.

" The trumpets quavered, and Discord with dishevelled hair raised her Stygian head to the upper sky. Blood had dried on her face, tears ran from her bruised eyes, her teeth were mailed with a scurf of rust, her tongue was dripping with foulness and her face beset with snakes, her clothes were torn before her writhen breasts, and she waved a blood-red torch in her quivering hand. When she had left behind the darkness of Cocytus and Tartarus,[7] she strode forward to the high ridges of proud Apennine, whence she could gaze down upon all the earth and all its shores, and the armies streaming over the whole

[2] Minerva, here as goddess of war.
[3] Romulus, a son of Mars.
[4] Apollo and Diana.
[5] Mercury, son of Maia and Zeus, born on Mount Cyllene in the Peloponnese.
[6] Hercules, who lived at Tiryns while he served Eurystheus.
[7] Coeytus was one of the mythical rivers in the underworld (Tartarus). See note on chapter 120, line 69.

atque has erumpit furibundo pectore voces:
' Sumite nunc gentes accensis mentibus arma,
sumite et in medias immittite lampadas urbes.
Vincetur, quicunque latet; non femina cesset,
non puer aut aevo iam desolata senectus;
ipsa tremat tellus lacerataque tecta rebellent.
Tu legem, Marcelle, tene. Tu concute plebem,
Curio. Tu fortem ne supprime, Lentule, Martem.
Quid porro tu, dive, tuis cunctaris in armis,⠀⠀⠀290
non frangis portas, non muris oppida solvis
thesaurosque rapis? Nescis tu, Magne, tueri
Romanas arces?[1] Epidamni moenia quaere
Thessalicosque sinus humano[2] sanguine tingue.' "
[Factum est in terris, quicquid Discordia iussit.]

Cum haec Eumolpos ingenti volubilitate verborum[3]
effudisset, tandem Crotona intravimus. Ubi quidem
parvo deversorio recepti,[4] postero die amplioris fortunae domum quaerentes incidimus in turbam here-
dipetarum sciscitantium, quod genus hominum aut
unde veniremus. Ex praescripto ergo consilii com-

---

[1] arces *Passerat:* acies.
[2] Romano *Cornelissen:* *The next line is probably spurious.*
[3] *Fraenkel proposes* voce *for* volubilitate verborum *in view
of* verborum volubilitate *two sentences later.*
[4] recepti *Müller:* refecti. *In his 2nd edition he also reads*
parvo quidem *for* quidem parvo.

---

[1] One of the two consuls of 49 B.C. (see p. 319, n. 4). But
it was his brother who was responsible for the Senate's decree
in 49 that Julius Caesar must give up his command and his
army and return to Rome as a private citizen.
[2] C. Scribonius Curio was a strong supporter of Caesar,
acting as his agent in Rome.

globe; then these words were wrung from her angry soul: ' To arms now, ye peoples, while your spirit is hot, to arms, and set your torches to the heart of cities. He that would hide him shall be lost: let no women halt, nor children, nor the old who are now wasted with age; let the earth herself quake, and the shattered houses join the fight. Thou, Marcellus,[1] hold fast the law. Thou, Curio,[2] make the rabble quail. Thou, Lentulus,[3] give brave Mars no check. And thou, divine Caesar, why art thou a laggard with thine arms? Crash down the gates, strip towns of their walls and seize their treasure. So Magnus[4] knows not how to hold the hills of Rome? Let him take the bulwarks of Epidamnus[5] and dye the bays of Thessaly[6] with the blood of men.' [Then all the commands of Discord were fulfilled upon the earth.]'[7]

Eumolpus poured out these lines with immense fluency, and at last we came into Croton. There indeed we were received in a little inn, but on the next day we went to look for a house of greater pretensions, and fell in with a crowd of fortune-hunters, who inquired what kind of men we were, and where we had come from. Then, as arranged by our com-

---

[3] The other consul of 49 B.C. (p. 319, n. 4).

[4] Pompeius Magnus was now in command against Caesar.

[5] Dyrrachium (Durazzo) by the Adriatic where Pompeius tried to establish himself after evacuating Italy in the face of Caesar.

[6] Where Pharsalus was, the scene of Pompeius' final defeat.

[7] This line is a summing up substitute for the rest of the civil war, and is probably an interpolation. No lacuna is indicated after the line.

munis exaggerata verborum volubilitate, unde aut [1]
qui essemus, haud dubie credentibus indicavimus.

L | Qui statim opes suas summo cum certamine in
Eumolpum congesserunt. ⟨. . .⟩ [2]

Certatim omnes heredipetae [3] muneribus gratiam
Eumolpi sollicitant . . .

125 dum haec magno tempore Crotone aguntur ⟨. . .⟩ [4]
et Eumolpus felicitate plenus prioris fortunae esset
oblitus statum [5] adeo, ut superbius [6] iactaret, neminem gratiae suae ibi posse resistere impuneque suos,
si quid deliquissent in ea urbe,[7] beneficio amicorum
laturos.   Ceterum ego, etsi quotidie magis magisque
superfluentibus bonis saginatum corpus impleveram
putabamque a custodia mei removisse vultum [8]
Fortunam, tamen saepius tam consuetudinem meam
cogitabam quam causam, et " quid " aiebam " si
callidus captator exploratorem in Africam miserit
mendaciumque deprehenderit nostrum ?   Quid, si
etiam mercennarius [Eumolpi] [9] praesenti felicitate
lassus indicium ad amicos detulerit totamque falla-
ciam invidiosa [10] proditione detexerit ?   Nempe rursus
fugiendum erit et tandem expugnata paupertas nova
mendicitate revocanda.   Dii deaeque, quam male est

----

[1] et *Strelitz.*
[2] *Lacuna indicated by Buecheler.*
[3] heredipetae *omitted by cd. Lambeth. and Pithoeus's editions.*
[4] *Buecheler deletes* dum . . . aguntur.
[5] *P. George would delete* statum.
[6] superbius *suggests Fraenkel:* subinde *Jacobs:* suis.
[7] *Müller deletes* in ea urbe.

mon council, a torrent of ready words burst from us,
and they gave easy credence to our account of ourselves or our country. They at once quarrelled
fiercely in their eagerness to heap their own riches on
Eumolpus. . . .[1]

The fortune-hunters all competed to win Eumolpus's favour with presents. . . .

This went on for a long while in Croton, . . .
Eumolpus was flushed with success, and so far forgot
the former state of his fortunes as to boast very arro-
gantly that no one there could cross his good pleasure,
and that his own dependants would escape un-
punished by the kindness of his friends if they committed any crime in that city. But though I had
lined my stuffed body well every day with the ever-
growing supply of good things, and believed that
Fortune had turned away her face from keeping a
watch on me, still I again and again thought over my
past habits as much as the cause of it all, and kept
saying to myself, " Supposing some cunning legacy-
hunter sends a spy over to Africa and finds out our
lies ? Or supposing the servant grows weary of his
present luck and gives his friends a hint, or betrays us
out of spite, and exposes the whole plot ? Of course
we shall have to run away again; we must start
afresh as beggars, and call back the poverty we have
now at last driven out. Ah! gods and goddesses! the

---

[1] Buecheler proposed a lacuna here. But the preceding
sentence and the next one seem to be alternative to each other.

---

[8] *After* vultum *Fraenkel suggests adding* meam.
[9] *Added in l.*
[10] *Nisbet suggests* insidiosa.

extra legem viventibus: quicquid meruerunt, semper
exspectant " . . .

126 " Quia nosti venerem tuam, superbia ⟨lucru⟩m [1]
captas vendisque amplexus, non commodas. Quo
enim spectant flexae pectine comae, quo facies medicamine attrita et oculorum quoque mollis petulantia,
quo incessus arte [2] compositus et ne vestigia quidem
pedum extra mensuram aberrantia, nisi quod formam
prostituis, ut vendas? [3] Vides me: nec auguria novi
ned mathematicorum caelum curare soleo, ex vultibus
tamen hominum mores colligo, et cum spatiantem
vidi, quid cogitet [4] scio. Sive ergo nobis [5] vendis
quod peto, mercator paratus est, sive quod humanius
est, commodas, effice ut beneficium debeam.[6] Nam
quod servum te et humilem fateris, accendis desiderium aestuantis. Quaedam enim feminae sordibus
calent, nec libidinem concitant, nisi aut servos
viderint aut statores altius cinctos. Harena aliquas [7]
accendit aut perfusus pulvere mulio aut histrio
scaenae ostentatione traductus.[8] Ex hac nota
domina est mea: usque ab orchestra quattuordecim
transilit et in extrema plebe quaerit quod diligat."
Itaque oratione blandissima plenus " rogo "

---

[1] superbia ⟨lucru⟩m *is Fraenkel's suggestion*: superbiam *L*:
superbia me *Heinsius*: *Nisbet suggests* iactas *for* captas.
[2] arte *Dousa*: delicate *Fraenkel*: scite *Heinsius*: astute
Jacobs: tute.
[3] *Fraenkel would delete* ut vendas.
[4] cogitet *Burman*: cogites.
[5] *Fraenkel suggested deleting* nobis.
[6] *Anton suggested* debeamus, *Jungermann* debeat (*sc. Circe*).
[7] alias *Buecheler*.
[8] *Perhaps* traductas.

outlaw has a hard life; he is always waiting to get what he deserves." . . .

[1] " Because you know your beauty, you haughtily hunt after gain, and do not bestow your embraces, but sell them. What is the object of your nicely combed hair, your face plastered with dyes, and the soft fondness even in your glance, and your walk arranged by art so that never a footstep strays from its place? It means of course that you offer your comeliness freely for sale. Look at me; I know nothing of omens, and I never attend to the astrologer's sky, but I read character in a man's face, and when I see him walk I know his thoughts. So if you will sell us what I want, there is a buyer ready: if you will be more gracious and bestow it upon us, let me be indebted to you for a favour. For when you admit that you are a slave of low degree, you fan the passion of a lady who burns for you. Some women kindle for vile fellows, and cannot rouse any desire unless they have a slave or a servant in short garments in their eye. Some burn for a gladiator, or a muleteer smothered in dust, or an actor disgraced by exhibiting himself on the stage. My mistress is of this class; she skips fourteen [2] rows away from the orchestra, and hunts for something to love among the low people at the back."

With my ears full of her winning words I then said,

[1] Codex *l* adds here *Chrysis ancilla Circes ad Pollienum* (for *Polyaenum*): " Chrysis, handmaid of Circe, speaking to Polyaenus "—that is Encolpius who assumed this name at Croton.

[2] By the *Lex Roscia* of 67 B.C. the fourteen rows just behind those allotted to Senators (the government-class) in the theatre were reserved for the Equites (Knights—the moneyed business class).

327

inquam " numquid illa, quae me amat, tu es ? "
Multum risit ancilla post tam frigidum schema et
" nolo " inquit " tibi tam valde placeas. Ego adhuc
servo nunquam succubui, nec hoc dii sinant, ut
amplexus meos in crucem mittam. Viderint matronae, quae flagellorum vestigia osculantur; ego
etiam si ancilla sum, nunquam tamen nisi in equestri-
bus sedeo." Mirari equidem tam discordem libidinem coepi atque inter monstra numerare, quod
ancilla haberet matronae superbiam et matrona
ancillae humilitatem.

LO | Procedentibus deinde longius iocis rogavi ancillam,
ut in platanona perduceret dominam. Placuit puellae
consilium. Itaque collegit altius tunicam flexitque
se in eum daphnona, qui ambulationi adhaerebat.[1]
Nec diu morata dominam [2] producit e latebris lateri-
que meo applicat, mulierem omnibus simulacris
emendatiorem. Nulla vox est quae formam eius
possit comprehendere, nam quicquid dixero, minus
erit. Crines ingenio suo flexi per totos se umeros
effuderant, frons minima et quae radices capillorum
retro flexerat, supercilia usque ad malarum scriptu-
ram [3] currentia et rursus confinio luminum [4] paene
permixta, oculi clariores stellis extra [5] lunam fulgenti-
bus, nares paululum inflexae et osculum quale

---

[1] adhaerebat *Nisbet*: haerebat.
[2] *Fraenkel would delete* dominam.
[3] suturam *suggests Nisbet*: curvaturam *Fraenkel*: purpuram
Müller in his 2nd edition. There are other suggestions.
[4] *Fraenkel suggested deleting* luminum.
[5] *Nisbet suggests* citra; *but cf.* extra nubem *at beginning of
Chapter 127.*

---

[1] The castaways are posing as Eumolpus's slaves.

" It is not you, I suppose, who love me so ? " The handmaid laughed loudly at such a clumsy turn of speech, and said, " Pray do not be so conceited. I never yielded to a slave [1] yet, and God forbid that I should throw my arms round a gallows-bird. The married women may see to that, and kiss the scars of a flogging ; I may be only a lady's maid, for all that I never sit down in any seats but the knights '." I proceeded to marvel at their contrary passions, and to count them as portents, the handmaid having the pride of a married lady, and the married lady the low tastes of a handmaid.

Then as our jokes proceeded further, I asked the maid to bring her mistress into the grove of plane-trees. The plan pleased the girl. So she gathered her skirts up high, and turned into the laurel grove which grew close to our path. She was not long away before she led the lady out of her hiding-place, and brought her to my side. The woman was more perfect than any artist's dream. There are no words that can include all her beauty, and whatever I write must fall short of her. Her hair grew in natural waves and flowed all over her shoulders, her forehead was small, and the roots of her hair curved back from it, her brows ran to the outline of her cheekbones and almost met again near her eyes, and those eyes were brighter than stars when there is no moon,[2] and her nose had a little curve, and her little

[2] *extra lunam*, " outside the moon " suggests simply " farther away than the moon." But compare *extra nubem* at the beginning of Chapter 127, where " outside any cloud " seems to mean " cloudless." If we accept *citra*, " this side of " as Nisbet suggests, in both places, the meaning is still " cloudless."

329

Praxiteles habere Dianam [1] credidit. Iam mentum,
iam cervix, iam manus, iam pedum candor intra auri
gracile vinculum positus: Parium marmor exstinxe-
rat. Itaque tunc primum Dorida vetus amator
contempsi . . .

> Quid factum est, quod tu proiectis, Iuppiter, armis
>   inter caelicolas fabula muta iaces? [2]
> Nunc erat a torva submittere cornua fronte,
>   nunc pluma canos dissimulare tuos.
> Haec vera est Danae. Tempta modo tangere
>   corpus,
>   iam tua flammifero membra calore fluent . . .

127   Delectata illa risit tam blandum, ut videretur mihi
plenum os [3] extra nubem luna proferre. Mox digitis
gubernantibus vocem "Si non fastidis" inquit
"feminam ornatam et hoc primum anno virum
expertam, concilio tibi, o iuvenis, sororem. Habes tu
quidem et fratrem, neque enim me piguit inquirere,
sed quid prohibet et sororem adoptare? Eodem
gradu venio. Tu tantum dignare et meum osculum,
cum libuerit, agnoscere." "Immo" inquam ego
"per formam tuam te rogo, ne fastidias hominem

---

[1] *Jahn suggested* Cnidiam *and* (*less likely*) Dionen, *which is
poetic, as* Dionaeam *also would be.* Dionam *Meyer.*
[2] iaces *Fraenkel:* taces.
[3] *For* plenum os *l'has* caput.

---

[1] Diana was the Roman counterpart of the Greek goddess
Artemis. The renowned sculptor Praxiteles of the fourth
century B.C. made for the city Mantinea a group of Leto with
Apollo and Artemis, a statue of Artemis Brauronia for Athens,
and an Artemis for the city Ancyra. But since he also made
a famous statue of Aphrodite (Venus) for the city Cnidus in

mouth was the kind that Praxiteles dreamed Diana[1] had. And her chin and her neck, and her hands, and the gleam of her foot under a light band of gold! She had turned the marble of Paros[2] dull. So then at last I put my old passion for Doris to despite. . . .

" What is come to pass, Jupiter,[3] that thou hast cast away thine armour, and now liest silent in heaven and become an idle tale? Now were a time for thee to let the horns sprout on thy lowering forehead, or hide thy white hair under a swan's feathers. This is the true Danaë. Dare only to touch her body, and all thy limbs shall be loosened with fiery heat." . . .

She was delighted, and smiled so sweetly that I thought a cloudless moon was showing me her face full. Then she said, letting her fingers guide her words, " If you do not despise a rich woman who has known a man first this very year, dear youth, I will give you a new sister.[4] True, you have a brother, too, for I made bold to inquire, but why should you not take to yourself a sister as well? I will come as the same kind of relation. Deign only to recognize my kiss also when it is your good pleasure."

" I should rather implore you by your beauty," I replied, " not to scorn to enrol a stranger among your

Caria in Asia Minor, Jahn suggested reading here *Cnidiam*, " the Cnidian goddess," or else *Dionen*, Dione being in mythology the mother of Venus and also, but in poetry, Venus herself.

[2] The white marble of Paros island was famous.

[3] When Zeus (Jupiter) loved Europa, Leda, and Danaë, he appeared to them as a bull, a swan, and a shower of gold respectively.

[4] " sister," as in the next sentence " brother," means sexual lover.

peregrinum inter cultores admittere. Invenies re-
ligiosum, si te adorari permiseris. Ac ne me iudices ad
hoc templum [Amoris] [1] gratis accedere, dono tibi
fratrem meum." " Quid? Tu " [2] inquit illa " donas
mihi eum, sine quo non potes vivere, ex cuius osculo
pendes, quem sic tu amas, quemadmodum ego te
volo? " Haec ipsa cum diceret, tanta gratia concili-
abat vocem loquentis, tam dulcis sonus pertemptatum
mulcebat aëra, ut putares inter auras canere Sirenum
concordiam. Itaque miranti [et] [3] toto mihi caelo
clarius nescio quid relucente libuit deae nomen
quaerere. " Ita " inquit " non dixit tibi ancilla
mea me Circen vocari? Non sum quidem Solis pro-
genies, nec mea mater, dum placet, labentis mundi
cursum detinuit. Habebo tamen quod caelo impu-
tem, si nos fata coniunxerint. Immo iam nescio quid
tacitis cogitationibus deus agit. Nec sine causa
Polyaenon Circe amat: semper inter haec nomina
magna fax surgit. Sume ergo amplexum, si placet.
Neque est quod curiosum aliquem extimescas: longe
ab hoc loco frater est." Dixit haec Circe, implici-
tumque me bracchiis mollioribus pluma deduxit in
terram vario gramine indutam.

---

[1] amoris *B, P, om. R, δ, L: Fraenkel deletes.*
[2] quid tu *Pithoeus's 2nd edition*: quid ni.
[3] *Probably to be deleted (Fraenkel).*

---

[1] In Greek mythology, a sorceress, daughter of the sun
(*Phoebēïa Circe* in Chapter 134). As related in Book X of
Homer's *Odyssey*, lines 230–240, she turned the bodies (not the
minds) of Odysseus's companions into those of pigs for a time.
[2] Encolpius (see p. 277, n. 1). Polyaenus occurs elsewhere

worshippers. You will find me a true votary, if you allow me to kneel before you. And do not think that I would enter this shrine [of Love] without an offering; I will give you my own brother."

"What," she said, "you give me the one without whom you cannot live, on whose lips you hang, whom you love as I would have you love me?" Even as she spoke grace made her words so attractive, the sweet noise fell so softly upon the listening air, that one seemed to have the harmony of the Sirens ringing in the breeze. So as I marvelled, and all the light of the sky somehow fell brighter upon me, I was moved to ask my goddess her name. "Then my maid did not tell you that I am called Circe?"[1] she said. "I am not the Sun-child indeed, and my mother has never stayed the moving world in its course while she will. But I shall have a debt to pay to Heaven if fate brings you and me together. Surely now, the Gods with their quiet thoughts have some plan in the making. Circe does not love Polyaenus[2] without good reason; when these two names meet, a great fire is always set ablaze. Then take me in your embrace if you like. You need have no fear of any spy; your brother is far away from here."

Circe was silent, folded me in two arms softer than a bird's wing, and drew me to the ground on a varied carpet of grass.

also as a proper name. The epithet πολύαινος ("much-praise") was given to Odysseus by the virgin-faced sweet-singing birds, the Sirens (Homer, *Odyssey*, XII, 184). It is found elsewhere in Homer, always as an epithet of Odysseus. Circe was imagined to dwell near the headland and town Circeii (Circello) in Latium, the Sirens along the south coast of Italy, especially near Naples.

Idaeo quales fudit de vertice flores
terra parens, cum se concesso [1] iunxit amori
Iuppiter et toto concepit pectore flammas:
emicuere rosae violaeque et molle cyperon,
albaque de viridi riserunt lilia prato:
talis humus Venerem molles clamavit in herbas,
candidiorque dies secreto favit amori.

In hoc gramine pariter compositi mille osculis lusi-
mus, quaerentes voluptatem robustam . . .

128 L ¡ " Quid est? " inquit " numquid te osculum meum
offendit? Numquid spiritus ieiunio marcens? [2]
Numquid alarum ⟨sum⟩ negligens [sudor puto]? [3] Si
haec non sunt, numquid Gitona times? " Perfusus
ego rubore manifesto etiam si quid habueram virium,
perdidi, totoque corpore velut luxato [4] " quaeso "
inquam " regina, noli suggillare miserias. Veneficio
contactus sum " . . .

" Dic, Chrysis, sed verum: numquid indecens
sum? Numquid incompta? Numquid ab aliquo
naturali vitio formam meam excaeco? Noli decipere
dominam tuam. Nescio quid peccavimus." Rapuit
deinde tacenti speculum, et postquam omnes vultus
temptavit, quos solet inter amantes risus [5] fingere,[6]

---

[1] concesso *Sambucus*: confesso.

[2] marcens *Buecheler*: marcet *in margin of l*: acet *Wouweren*: macet *Gruter*: macer.

[3] *Fraenkel suggests adding* sum *and deleting* sudor puto.
This seems simplest. But Nisbet's neglegens odor *might be
right. In his second edition Müller proposes* neglegens sudor?
si ⟨ut⟩ puto haec. *Lips proposed* sudor putet, *Burman*
sudorem puteo, *Anton* sudore puteo.

[4] luxato *Jungermann*: laxato.

[5] *Müller conjectures* lusus, *Buecheler* usus, *Dousa* nisus.

[6] fingere *Cuperus*: frangere.

SATYRICON

" Such flowers as Earth, our mother, spread on Ida's top when Jupiter embraced her[1] in lawful love, and all his heart was kindled with fire: roses glowed there, and violets, and the tender flowering rush; and white lilies laughed from the green meadow: such a soil summoned Venus to the soft plants, and the day grew brighter and looked kindly on their hidden pleasure."

We lay together there on this grass and exchanged a thousand light kisses, but we looked for sterner pleasure. . . .

[2]" Tell me," she cried, " do you find some offence in my kiss? In my breath that faints with hunger? Am I careless about my armpits?[3] If it is none of these, are you afraid of Giton? " I crimsoned with blushes under her eyes, and lost any strength I might have had before, and cried as though there were no whole part in my body, " Dear lady, have mercy, do not mock my grief. Some poison has infected me." . . .

[4] " Speak to me, Chrysis, tell me true: am I ugly or untidy? Is there some natural blemish that darkens my beauty? Do not deceive your own mistress. I have sinned somehow or other." She then snatched a mirror from the silent girl, and after trying every look that raises a smile to most lovers' lips, she

---

[1] Juno (Greek, Hera) his sister. (See Homer, *Iliad*, XIV, 346 ff.) If *concesso* is right, it stresses that for gods sexual union of brother and sister was not incest.

[2] Codex *l* adds *Circe ad Polyaenum.*

[3] [*sudor puto*] " sweat, I think," is most likely a remark intruded by a scribe. Yet Anton's suggestion *sudore puteo* is reasonable.

[4] *l* indicates Circe as the speaker.

excussit vexatam solo vestem raptimque aedem
Veneris intravit. Ego contra damnatus et quasi
quodam visu in horrorem perductus interrogare
animum meum coepi, an vera voluptate fraudatus
essem.

LO | Nocte soporifera veluti cum somnia ludunt
errantes oculos effossaque protulit aurum
in lucem tellus: versat manus improba furtum
thesaurosque rapit, sudor quoque perluit ora [1]
et mentem timor altus habet, ne forte gravatum
excutiat gremium secreti conscius auri:
mox ubi fugerunt elusam gaudia mentem
veraque forma redit, animus, quod perdidit, optat
atque in praeterita se totus imagine versat . . .

L | " Itaque hoc nomine tibi gratias ago, quod me
Socratica fide diligis. Non tam intactus Alcibiades
in praeceptoris sui lecto iacuit " . . .

129 " Crede mihi, frater, non intellego me virum esse,
non sentio. Funerata est illa pars corporis, qua
quondam Achilles eram " . . .

Veritus puer, ne in secreto deprehensus daret sermonibus locum, proripuit se et in partem aedium
interiorem fugit . . .

LO | cubiculum autem meum Chrysis intravit codicil-

[1] *Buecheler deletes this line.*

---

[1] Giton speaks to Encolpius—so Codex *l* indicates.
[2] Plato in his *Symposium*, 217–219, represents the young
profligate politician and general Alcibiades (born c. 450 B.C.)

shook out the cloak the earth had stained, and hurried into the temple of Venus. But I was lost and horror-stricken as if I had seen a ghost, and proceeded to inquire of my heart whether I was cheated of my true delight.

As when dreams deceive our wandering eyes in the heavy slumber of night, and under the spade the earth yields gold to the light of day: our greedy hands finger the spoil and snatch at the treasure, sweat too runs down our face, and a deep fear grips our heart that maybe some one will shake out our laden bosom, where he knows the gold is hid: next, when these pleasures flee from the brain they mocked, and the true shape of things comes back, our mind is eager for what is lost, and moves with all its force among the shadows of the past. . . .

[1]" So in his name I give you thanks for loving me as true as Socrates. Alcibiades[2] never lay so unspotted in his master's bed." . . .

[3]" I tell you, brother, I do not realize that I am a man, I do not feel it. That part of my body where I was once an Achilles[4] is dead and buried." . . .

The boy was afraid that he might give an opening for scandal if he were caught in a quiet place with me, and tore himself away and fled into an inner part of the house. . . .

Crysis came into my bedroom and gave me a letter

as loved by the philosopher Socrates, his friend and teacher, in a completely " platonic " manner, in spite of every opportunity.

[3] Encolpius speaks to Giton, as Codex *l* indicates.

[4] That is, young and strong, like the famous Greek hero Achilles at Troy.

337

losque mihi dominae suae reddidit, in quibus haec
erant scripta: " Circe Polyaeno salutem. Si libidinosa essem, quererer decepta; nunc etiam languori
tuo gratias ago. In umbra voluptatis diutius lusi.
Quid tamen agas, quaero, et an tuis pedibus per-
veneris domum; negant enim medici sine nervis
homines ambulare posse. Narrabo tibi, adulescens,
paralysin cave. Nunquam ego aegrum[1] tam magno
periculo vidi; medius fidius[2] iam peristi. Quod si
idem frigus genua manusque temptaverit tuas, licet
ad tubicines mittas. Quid ergo est? Etiam si
gravem iniuriam accepi, homini tamen misero non
invideo medicinam. Si vis sanus esse, Gitonem roga.[3]
Recipies, inquam, nervos tuos, si triduo sine fratre
dormieris. Nam quod ad me attinet, non timeo, ne
quis inveniatur cui minus placeam. Nec speculum
mihi nec fama mentitur. Vale, si potes."

Ut intellexit Chrysis perlegisse me totum convicium " Solent " inquit " haec fieri, et praecipue in
hac civitate, in qua mulieres etiam lunam deducunt
. . . itaque huius quoque rei cura agetur. Rescribe
modo blandius dominae animumque eius candida
humanitate restitue. Verum enim fatendum est: ex
qua hora iniuriam accepit, apud se non est." Libenter quidem parui ancillae verbaque codicillis talia
130 imposui: " Polyaenos Circae salutem. Fateor me,
domina, saepe peccasse; nam et homo sum et

---

[1] *Fuchs adds* in *after* aegrum.
[2] *P. Thomas would delete* fidius.
[3] relega *Delz.*

from her mistress, who wrote as follows: " Circe greets Polyaenus. If I were a passionate woman, I should feel betrayed and hurt: as it is I can be thankful even for your coldness. I have amused myself long with the shadow of pleasure. But I should like to know how you are, and whether your feet carried you safely home; the doctors say that people who have lost their sinews cannot walk. I tell you what, young man, you must beware of paralysis. I have never seen a sick person in such grave danger; I declare you are as good as dead. If the same mortal chill attacks your knees and hands, you may send for the funeral trumpeters. And what about me? Well, even if I have been deeply wounded, I do not grudge a poor man a cure. If you want to get well, ask Giton. I think you will recover your sinews if you sleep for three days without your brother. So far as I am concerned, I am not afraid of finding anyone who dislikes me more. My looking-glass and my reputation do not lie. Keep as well as you can."

When Chrysis saw that I had read through the whole of this complaint, she said: " These things often happen, especially in this town, where the women can even draw down the moon from the sky, . . . and so attention will be paid to this matter also. Only do write back sweetly to my mistress, and restore her spirits by your frank kindness. For I must tell you the truth: she has never been herself from the moment you insulted her."

I obeyed the girl with pleasure and wrote on a tablet as follows: " Polyaenus greets Circe. Dear lady, I admit my many failings; for I am human, and

adhuc iuvenis. Nunquam tamen ante hunc diem
usque ad mortem deliqui. Habes confitentem reum :
quicquid iusseris, merui. Proditionem feci, hominem
occidi, templum violavi : in haec facinora quaere
supplicium. Sive occidere placet,[1] ferro meo venio,
sive verberibus contenta es, curro nudus ad dominam.
Illud unum memento, non me sed instrumenta
peccasse. Paratus miles arma non habui. Quis hoc
turbaverit, nescio. Forsitan animus antecessit corporis moram, forsitan dum omnia concupisco voluptatem tempore consumpsi. Non invenio, quod feci.
Paralysin tamen cavere iubes : tanquam ea [2] maior
fieri possit, quae abstulit mihi, per quod etiam te
habere potui. Summa tamen excusationis meae
haec est : placebo tibi, si me culpam emendare
permiseris " . . .

L | Dimissa cum eiusmodi pollicitatione Chryside
curavi diligentius noxiosissimum corpus, balneoque
praeterito modica unctione usus, mox cibis validiori-
bus pastus, id est bulbis cochlearumque sine iure
cervicibus, hausi parcius merum. Hinc ante somnum
levissima ambulatione compositus sine Gitone cubiculum intravi. Tanta erat placandi cura, ut timerem,
131 ne latus meum frater convelleret. Postero die, cum
sine offensa corporis animique consurrexissem, in
eundem platanona descendi, etiam si locum inauspi-
catum timebam, coepique inter arbores ducem
itineris exspectare Chrysidem. Nec diu spatiatus
consederam, ubi hesterno die fueram, cum illa intus

---

[1] *Buecheler adds* cum *before* ferro.
[2] ea *Buecheler*: iam.

still young. But never before this day have I committed deadly sin. The culprit confesses to you; I have deserved whatever you may order. I have been a traitor, I have destroyed a man, and profaned a temple: demand my punishment for these crimes. If you decide on execution, I will come with my sword; if you let me off with a flogging, I will run naked to my lady. Remember that one thing—that not I but my tools went wrong. A soldier ready I was but had no weapons. Who upset me so I know not. Perhaps my will ran on while my body lagged behind, perhaps I wasted all my pleasure in delay by desiring too much. I cannot discover what I did. But you tell me to beware of paralysis: as if the disease could grow worse, which has taken away from me the means of making you my own. But my apology amounts to this—I will do your pleasure if you allow me to mend my fault." . . .

Chrysis was sent off with this promise, and I paid great attention to my offending body, and after omitting my bath anointed myself in moderation, and then fed on strong foods, onions, I mean, and snails' necks without sauce, and drank sparingly of wine. I then settled myself with a gentle walk before bed, and went into my room without Giton. I was so anxious to please her that I was afraid my brother might take away my strength. Next day I got up sound in mind and body, and went down to the same grove of plane-trees, though I was rather afraid of the unlucky place, and proceeded to wait among the trees for Chrysis to lead me on my way.

After walking up and down a short while, I sat where I had been the day before, and Chrysis came

venit [1] comitem aniculam trahens. Atque ut me consalutavit, " Quid est " inquit " fastose, ecquid bonam mentem habere coepisti ? "

Illa de sinu licium protulit varii coloris filis intortum cervicemque vinxit meam. Mox turbatum sputo pulverem medio sustulit digito frontemque repugnantis signavit ⟨. . .⟩ [2]

Hoc peracto carmine ter me iussit exspuere terque lapillos conicere in sinum, quos ipsa praecantatos purpura involverat, admotisque manibus temptare coepit inguinum vires. Dicto citius nervi paruerunt imperio manusque aniculae ingenti motu repleverunt. At illa gaudio exsultans " Vides " inquit " Chrysis mea, vides, quod ⟨aiunt⟩ [3] aliis leporem excitavi ? " . . .

LO | Nobilis aestivas platanus diffuderat umbras
et bacis redimita Daphne tremulaeque cupressus
et circum tonsae trepidanti vertice pinus.
Has inter ludebat aquis errantibus amnis
spumeus et querulo vexabat rore lapillos.
Dignus amore locus : testis silvester aëdon [4]
atque urbana Procne, quae circum gramina fusae
ac molles violas cantu sua furta [5] colebant . . .

---

[1] intus venit *Buecheler*: intervenit.
[2] *lacuna indicated by Boschius.*
[3] *I accept Nisbet's addition of* aiunt.
[4] silvester aedon *Pius*: silvesterisdon *B*: silvester iasdon *RP*: silvestris hirundo *l and cod. Lambeth.*
[5] furta *Buecheler*: rura *l, R, δ*: iura *cod. Lambeth. The readings and meaning of the whole line are in dispute.*

---

[1] Proselenos (see Chapter 132), a sorceress. Her Greek name means " before the moon," " older than the moon."
[2] Laurel, into which was changed Daphne, daughter of a river god.

under the trees, bringing an old woman[1] with her.
When she had greeted me, she said, " Well, dis-
dainful lover, have you gone so far as to come to your
senses ? " Then the old woman took a twist of
threads of different colours out of her dress, and
tied it round my neck. Then she mixed some
dust with spittle, and took it on her middle finger,
and made a mark on my forehead despite my
protest. . . .

After this chant she ordered me to spit three
times and throw stones into my bosom three times,
after she had said a spell over them and wrapped
them in purple, and laid her hands on me and proceeded to try the force of her charm on the powers of
my groin. Before you could say a word, my sinews
obeyed her command and filled the old woman's
hands with a huge upstir. Then she, triumphant
with joy, " Do you see, my dear Chrysis ? " she said,
—" I have put up a hare for other people, as they
say." . . .

The stately plane-tree, and Daphne[2] decked with
berries, and the quivering cypresses, and the swaying
tops of the shorn pines, cast a summer shade.
Among them played the straying waters of a foamy
river, lashing the pebbles with its chattering flow.
The place was proper to love; so the nightingale of
the woods bore witness, and Procne[3] from the
town, as they hovered about the grasses and the
tender violets, and pursued their stolen loves with a
song. . . .

[3] Swallow, into which was changed Procne, daughter of
Pandion a traditional King of Athens, and sister of Philomela,
who was changed into a nightingale.

Premebat illa resoluta marmoreis cervicibus aureum torum myrtoque florenti quietum ⟨aera⟩ [1] verberabat.[2] Itaque ut me vidit, paululum erubuit, hesternae scilicet iniuriae memor; [3] deinde ut remotis omnibus secundum invitantem consedi, ramum super oculos meos posuit, et quasi pariete interiecto audacior facta " Quid est " inquit " paralytice? ecquid hodie totus venisti? " " Rogas " inquam ego " potius quam temptas? " Totoque corpore in amplexum eius immissus non praecantatis usque ad satietatem osculis fruor . . .

132 *L* | (Ipsa corporis pulchritudine me ad se vocante [4] trahebat ad venerem. Iam pluribus osculis collisa labra crepitabant, iam implicitae manus omne genus amoris invenerant, iam alligata mutuo ambitu corpora animarum quoque mixturam fecerant.) . . .

Manifestis matrona contumeliis verberata [5] tandem ad ultionem decurrit vocatque cubicularios et me iubet catomizari.[6] Nec contenta mulier tam gravi iniuria mea convocat omnes quasillarias familiaeque sordidissimam partem ac me conspui iubet. Oppono ego manus oculis meis, nullisque effusis precibus, quia sciebam quid meruissem, verberibus sputisque [7] extra ianuam eiectus sum. Eicitur et Proselenos,

---

[1] aera *added by Ernout.*
[2] *Müller suggests* ventilabat.
[3] *Müller deletes* hesternae . . . memor.
[4] *Fraenkel would delete* ad se vocante.
[5] *Buecheler conjectures* exacerbata, *Nisbet* vexata.
[6] catomizari *Saumaise:* catorogare. *There are various suggestions.*
[7] *Müller deletes* verberibus sputisque. *Buecheler adds* ⟨obrutus⟩ *after* sputisque.

344

She was stretched out there with her marble neck pressed on a golden bed, vigorously fanning the still air with a spray of myrtle in flower. So when she saw me she blushed a little, of course remembering my rudeness the day before; then, when they had all left us, she asked me to sit by her, and I did; she laid the sprig of myrtle over my eyes, and then growing bolder, as if she had put a wall between us, "Well, poor paralytic," she said, "have you come here to-day a whole man?" "Do not ask me," I replied, "try me." I threw myself eagerly into her arms, and enjoyed her kisses unchecked by any magic until I was tired. . . .

(The mere loveliness of his[1] body called to me and drew us into love. There was the sound of a rain of kisses as our lips met, our hands were clasped and discovered all the ways of love, then our bodies were held and bound by our embrace until even our souls were made as one soul.) . . .

My open taunts lashed the lady; at last she ran to avenge herself, and called her chamber grooms, and ordered me to be hoisted on their shoulders for flogging. Not content with this black insult, the woman called up all her low spinsters, and the very dregs of her slaves, and invited them to spit upon me. I put my hands to my eyes and never poured forth any appeal, for I knew my deserts, and was beaten and spat upon and thrown out of doors. Proselenos

---

[1] Not "her" because Codex *l* prefixes to this sentence *Encolpius de Endymione puero,* "Encolpius speaking about a boy Endymion." This indicates that this passage is intruded here out of its proper place because what precedes and what comes after it concern the love-affair of Encolpius and Circe.

Chrysis vapulat, totaque familia tristis inter se mussat quaeritque, quis dominae hilaritatem confuderit . . .

Itaque pensatis vicibus animosior verberum notas arte contexi, ne aut Eumolpus contumelia mea hila-
LO rior fieret aut tristior Giton. | Quod solum igitur salvo pudore poteram, contingere [1] languorem simulavi, conditusque lectulo totum ignem furoris in eam converti, quae mihi omnium malorum causa fuerat:

ter corripui terribilem manu bipennem,
ter languidior coliculi repente thyrso
ferrum timui, quod trepido male dabat usum.
Nec iam poteram, quod modo conficere libebat;
namque illa metu frigidior rigente bruma
confugerat in viscera mille operta rugis.
Ita non potui supplicio caput aperire,
sed furciferae mortifero timore lusus
ad verba, magis quae poterant nocere, fugi.

Erectus igitur in cubitum hac fere oratione contumacem vexavi: " Quid dicis " inquam " omnium hominum deorumque pudor? Nam ne nominare quidem te inter res serias fas est. Hoc de te merui,
L ut me in caelo positum ad inferos traheres? | Ut traduceres annos primo florentes vigore senectaeque ultimae mihi lassitudinem imponeres? Rogo te, mihi apodixin ⟨non⟩ [2] defunctoriam redde." Haec ut iratus effudi,

[1] *Palmier deletes* contingere.
[2] non *added by Müller in his second edition.*

was thrown out too, Chrysis was flogged, and all the slaves muttered gloomily to themselves, and asked who had upset their mistress's spirits. . . . So after considering my position I took courage, and carefully hid the marks of the lash for fear Eumolpus should exult or Giton be depressed at my disgrace. Therefore as the only way to hide my shame, I began to pretend that sickness was affecting me; and having got in bed, turned the whole fire of my madness against that which had been the cause of all my misfortunes, and "Thrice I seized in hand the dreaded axe, thrice, fainter than a little cabbage stalk, I feared the steel, that served me ill in my panic. So what I would like to have done, just before, by now I could not do. For that thing, colder from fear than freezing mid-winter, had retracted into my flesh covered with a thousand wrinkles. So I couldn't uncover its head for execution. But, mere baffled plaything of the deadly fear of that rascal, I fled for refuge in words which could hurt more."

Then raising myself on my elbow, in this or like manner I reproached the sullen impotent: "What have you to say, thou shame of heaven and man, that canst not be seriously mentioned? Have I deserved from you, that when I was in heaven you dragged me down to hell? To have a scandal fixt on the very prime and vigour of my years, and to be reduced to the weakness of extreme old age? I beseech you sir, give no mere perfunctory show of your quality," but though I upbraided it thus,[1] it stayed there turned

---

[1] What follows is from Virgil, *Aeneid*, VI, 469 (the whole line); *Eclogue*, V, 16 (*lenta salix*); *Aeneid*, IX, 436 (*lassove papavera collo*).

LO | illa solo fixos oculos aversa tenebat,
nec magis incepto vultum sermone movetur
quam lentae salices lassove papavera collo.

Nec minus ego tam foeda obiurgatione finita paenitentiam agere sermonis mei coepi secretoque rubore perfundi, quod oblitus verecundiae meae cum ea parte corporis verba contulerim, quam ne ad cognitionem quidem admittere severioris notae homines solerent, Mox perfricata diutius fronte " Quid autem ego " inquam " mali feci, si dolorem meum naturali convicio exoneravi? Aut quid est quod in corpore humano ventri male dicere solemus aut gulae capitique etiam, cum saepius dolet? Quid? Non et *L* Vlixes cum corde litigat suo, | et quidam tragici oculos suos tanquam audientes castigant? Podagrici pedibus suis male dicunt, chiragrici manibus, lippi oculis, et qui offenderunt saepe digitos, quicquid doloris habent, in pedes deferunt:

LO | Quid me constricta spectatis fronte Catones
damnatisque novae simplicitatis opus?
Sermonis puri non tristis gratia ridet,
quodque facit populus, candida lingua refert.
Nam quis concubitus, Veneris quis gaudia nescit?
Quis vetat [1] in tepido membra calere toro?
Ipse pater veri doctos [2] Epicurus amare [3]
iussit, et hoc vitam dixit habere τέλος " . . .

[1] vetat *Dousa*: petat *and* petit.
[2] doctos *W. Canter*: doctus.
[3] amare *W. Canter*: in arte *and* in arce.

---

[1] In the line τέτλαθι δή, κραδίη. καὶ κύντερον ἄλλο ποτ' ἔτλης. Homer, *Odyssey*, XX, 18.

away with eyes fixed on the ground and at this unfinished speech its looks were no more stirred than
pliant willows are or poppies on their tired stalky
necks.

Nor less after this disgraceful objurgation did I
repent of what I had said, and with a secret blush
proceeded to think how unaccountable it was, that
forgetting all shame, I should argue with that part of
me that all men of severer brand reckon not worth
their thoughts.

Then, after rubbing my forehead for a long while, I
said, " But what harm have I done if I have relieved
my sorrow with some free abuse ?   And then there is
the fact that of our bodily members we often damn
our guts, our throats, even our heads, when they
often ache.   Did not Ulysses argue with his own
heart,[1] while some tragedians curse their eyes as if
they could hear ?   Gouty people damn their feet,
people with chalk-stones their hands, blear-eyed
people their eyes, and men who have often hurt their
toes put down all their ills to their poor feet:

" Why do ye, Cato's[2] disciples, look at me with
wrinkled foreheads, and condemn a work of fresh simplicity ?   A cheerful kindness laughs through my
pure speech, and my clean mouth reports whatever
the people do.   All men born know of mating and the
joys of love; all men are free to let their limbs glow
in a warm bed.   Epicurus himself,[3] the true father of
truth, bade wise men be lovers, and said that therein
lay the goal of life." . . .

---

[2] This would be Marcus Porcius Cato the Elder (234–149
B.C.), a man of austere severity, not he of Chapter 119.

[3] See note on page 249.

L | " Nihil est hominum inepta persuasione falsius
nec ficta severitate ineptius " . . .

133 *LO* | Hac declamatione finita Gitona voco et " Narra
mihi " inquam " frater, sed tua fide: ea nocte, qua te
mihi Ascyltos subduxit, usque in iniuriam vigilavit,
an contentus fuit vidua pudicaque nocte ? " Tetigit
puer oculos suos conceptissimisque iuravit verbis sibi
ab Ascylto nullam vim factam . . .

Positoque in limine genu sic deprecatus sum
numen aversum: [1]

" Nympharum Bacchique comes, quem pulchra Dione
divitibus silvis numen dedit, inclita paret
cui Lesbos viridisque Thasos, quem Lydus adorat
† semper   flavius † [2]   templumque   suis [3]   imponit
   Hypaepis:
huc ades o [4] Bacchi tutor Dryadumque voluptas,
et timidas admitte preces.   Non sanguine tristi
perfusus venio, non templis impius hostis
admovi dextram, sed inops et rebus egenis
attritus facinus non toto corpore feci.
Quisquis peccat inops, minor est reus.   Hac prece
   quaeso,
exonera mentem culpaeque ignosce minori,
et quandoque mihi fortunae arriserit hora,
non sine honore tuum patiar decus.   Ibit ad aras,

---

[1] numen aversum *is someone's conjecture recorded by Bur-*
man: numina versu.

[2] semper flavius *B:* semperfluus *R:* septifluus *most other*
MSS.: vestifluus *Turnebus:* sertifluus *Reiske:* semper ovans
Buecheler which Heseltine translated.

[3] suis *Iunius:* tuis.

[4] o *Scaliger (Catalecta):* et.

There is nothing more insincere than people's silly persuasions, or more silly than their sham morality. . . .

When my speech was over, I called Giton, and said, " Now tell me, brother, but on your honour. That night when Ascyltos took you away from me, did he keep awake until he had wronged you, or was he satisfied with spending the night decently alone ? " The boy touched his eyes and swore a most precise oath that Ascyltos had used no force to him. . . .

I kneeled down on the threshold and thus entreated the god whose face was turned away:

" Comrade[1] of the Nymphs[2] and Bacchus, whom lovely Dione[3] set as god over the wide forests, whom famous Lesbos and green Thasos[4] obey, whom the Lydian worships † in perpetual celebration,† whose temple he has set in his own city of Hypaepa:[5] come hither, o guardian of Bacchus and the Dryads'[6] delight, and hear my humble prayer. I come not to thee stained with dark blood, I have not laid hands on a temple like a wicked enemy, but when I was poor and worn with want I sinned, yet not with my whole body. There is less guilt in a poor man's sin. This is my prayer; take the load from my mind, forgive a light offence; and whenever fortune's season smiles upon me, I will not leave thy glory without

[1] Priapus, god of procreation.
[2] Half-goddesses of various outdoor places—woods, trees, mountains, and waters, fresh and salt.
[3] Venus.
[4] Islands in the northern Aegean Sea.
[5] A small town in Lydia in Asia Minor, at the foot of Mt. Aepa.
[6] Wood-nymphs.

$B(O)$ sancte tuas hircus, pecoris pater, ibit ad aras [1]
  LO corniger et querulae fetus [2] suis, hostia lactens.
    Spumabit pateris hornus liquor, et ter ovantem
    circa delubrum gressum feret ebria pubes " . . .

    Dum haec ago curaque sollerti deposito meo caveo,
    intravit delubrum anus laceratis crinibus nigraque
    veste deformis, extraque vestibulum me iniecta manu
    duxit . . .

134 L " Quae striges comederunt nervos tuos, aut quod
    purgamentum [in] [3] nocte calcasti in trivio aut
    cadaver? Ne [4] a puero quidem te vindicasti, sed
    mollis, debilis, lassus tanquam caballus in clivo, et
    operam et sudorem perdidisti. Nec contentus ipse
    peccare, mihi deos iratos excitasti " [5] . . .

  LO | Ac me iterum in cellam sacerdotis nihil recu-
    santem perduxit impulitque super lectum et harundi-
    nem ab ostio rapuit iterumque nihil respondentem
    mulcavit. Ac nisi primo ictu harundo quassata
    impetum verberantis minuisset, forsitan etiam
    brachia mea caputque fregisset. Ingemui ego utique
    propter mascarpionem, lacrimisque ubertim mananti-
    bus obscuratum dextra caput super pulvinum
    inclinavi. Nec minus illa fletu confusa altera parte
    lectuli sedit aetatisque longae moram tremulis voci-
    bus coepit accusare, donec intervenit sacerdos. $\langle \ldots \rangle$ [6]

---

[1] *Only B has this line.*
[2] fetus *Iunius*: festus.   [3] *Deleted by Goldast.*
[4] ne *Buecheler*: nec.   [5] excitasti *Wouweren*: extricasti.
      [6] *Lacuna indicated by Buecheler.*

---

[1] Proselenos.
[2] Codex *l* and (in margin) codex Lambethanus here indicate
that the speaker is the old woman Proselenos addressing
Encolpius.

worship. A goat shall walk to thine altars, most holy one, yes, a horned goat that is father of the flock, shall walk to thine altars and the young of a squealing sow, a tender sacrifice. The new wine of the year shall foam in the bowls, and the young men full of wine shall trace their joyous steps three times round thy sanctuary." . . .

As I was doing this and making clever plans to guard my trust, the old woman[1] in ugly black clothes, with her hair down, came into the shrine, laid hands on me, and drew me out through the porch. . . .

[2] " What screech-owls have eaten your nerve away, what foul thing or corpse have you trodden on at a cross-road in the dark? Never even in boyhood could you hold your own, but you were weakly, feeble, tired, and like a cab-horse on a hill you wasted your efforts and your sweat. And not content with failing yourself, you have roused the gods to wrath against me." . . .

And she took me unresisting into the priestess's room again, and pushed me over the bed, and took a cane off the door and beat me again when I remained unresponsive. And if the cane had not broken at the first stroke and lessened the force of the blow, I daresay she would have broken my head and my arm outright. Anyhow I groaned at her "hand-grasping," and wept abundantly, and covered my head with my right arm, and leaned against the pillow. She was upset, and cried too, and sat on another piece of the bed, and began to curse the delays of old age in a quavering voice, when the priestess[3] came in. . . .

[3] Oenothea, a priestess of Priapus; see below. Her name means " wine-goddess."

"Quid vos" inquit "in cellam meam tanquam
O ante recens bustum venistis? | Utique die feriarum,
quo etiam lugentes rident." ⟨. . .⟩ ¹
LO |"O" inquit "Oenothea, hunc adulescentem
quem vides: malo astro natus est; nam neque puero
L neque puellae bona sua vendere potest. | Nunquam tu
hominem tam infelicem vidisti: lorum in aqua, non
LO inguina habet. | Ad summam, qualem putas esse, qui
L de Circes toro sine voluptate surrexit?" | His auditis
Oenothea inter utrumque consedit motoque diutius
capite "Istum" inquit "morbum sola sum quae
emendare scio. Et ne putetis perplexe agere, rogo
ut adulescentulus mecum nocte dormiat ⟨. . .⟩ ²
nisi illud tam rigidum reddidero quam cornu:

LO | Quicquid in orbe vides, paret mihi. Florida tellus,
cum volo, siccatis arescit languida sucis,
cum volo, fundit opes, scopulique atque horrida
saxa
Niliacas iaculantur aquas. Mihi pontus inertes
submittit fluctus, zephyrique tacentia ponunt
ante meos sua flabra pedes. Mihi flumina parent
Hyrcanaeque tigres et iussi stare dracones.³
Quid leviora loquor? Lunae descendit imago
carminibus deducta meis, trepidusque furentes
flectere Phoebus equos revoluto cogitur orbe.
[Tantum dicta valent. Taurorum flamma quiescit

---

¹ *Lacuna indicated by Buecheler.*
² *Lacuna indicated by Buecheler.*
³ dracones *O*; leones *L*.

---

¹ Here codex Lambethanus in margin has *Proselenos ad
Enotheam sacerdotem Priapi de Encolpio.* "Proselenos
speaking to Oenothea, priestess of Priapus, about Encolpius."

" Why have you come into my room as if you were
visiting a fresh-made grave ? " she said. " Especially
on a holiday, when even mourners smile." . . .
" Ah,[1] Oenothea," said the woman, " this young man
was born under a bad star; he cannot sell his treasure
to boys or girls either. You never beheld such an
unlucky creature : he is a piece of wash-leather; he
has no genitals. Just to show you, what do you think
of a man who can come away from Circe without a
spark of pleasure ? " When Oenothea heard this she
sat down between us, shook her head for some time,
and then said, " I am the only woman alive who knows
how to cure that disease. And, lest you think I'm
twisting, I ask that the young man sleep a night with
me . . . if I don't make that thing stiffer than horn :

" Whatever thou seest in the world is obedient to
me. The flowery earth, when I will, faints and
withers as its juices dry, and, when I will, pours forth
its riches, while rocks and rough crags spurt waters
wide as the Nile. The great sea lays its waves lifeless before me, and the winds lower their blasts in
silence at my feet. The rivers obey me, and
Hyrcanian[2] tigers, and serpents, whom I bid rise
upright. But I will not tell you of small things; the
shape of the moon is drawn down to me by my spells,
and Phoebus[3] trembles and must turn his fiery steeds
as I compel him back in his course. [So[4] great is the
power of words. The flaming spirit of bulls is

Codex *l* gives the same except that it has *Oenothean* and omits
de Encolpio.
[2] The Hyrcani dwelt round the southern part of the Caspian
Sea.
[3] The sun.
[4] The following lines seem not to belong here.

355

virgineis exstincta sacris, Phoebeia Circe
carminibus magicis socios mutavit Vlixis,
Proteus esse solet quicquid libet.   His ego callens
artibus Idaeos frutices in gurgite sistam
et rursus fluvios in summo vertice ponam."] [1]

135   Inhorrui ego tam fabulosa pollicitatione conterritus, anumque inspicere diligentius coepi ⟨. . .⟩ [2]
" Ergo " exclamat Oenothea " imperio parete "
⟨. . .⟩ [3] detersisque curiose manibus inclinavit se in
lectulum ac me semel iterumque basiavit . . .

L | Oenothea mensam veterem posuit in medio altari,
quam vivis implevit carbonibus, et camellam etiam [4]
vetustate ruptam pice temperata refecit.   Tum
clavum, qui detrahentem secutus cum camella lignea

LO fuerat, fumoso parieti reddidit. | Mox incincta quad-
rato pallio cucumam ingentem foco apposuit, simulque pannum de carnario detulit furca, in quo faba

L erat ad usum reposita | et sincipitis vetustissima par-

LO ticula mille plagis dolata. | Ut solvit ergo licio pan-
num, partem leguminis super mensam effudit iussitque me diligenter purgare.   Servio ego imperio
granaque sordidissimis putaminibus vestita curiosa
manu segrego.   At illa inertiam meam accusans † improba tollit,[5] dentibusque folliculos pariter spoliat
atque in terram veluti muscarum imagines despuit . . .

----

[1] *The last six lines were deleted by Wehle.*

[2] *Lacuna indicated by Buecheler.*

[3] *Lacuna indicated by Buecheler.*

[4] etiam *deleted by Jahn.   In his 2nd edition Müller reads*
[et] iam.

[5] *apparently corrupt.* ipsa fabas tollit *suggests Buecheler*:
[accusans] improbans ⟨fabas⟩ tollit *Fraenkel*: impigre fabas
Müller in edition 2.

quenched and calmed by a maiden's rites, and Circe, the child of Phoebus, transfigured Ulysses's crew with magic songs,[1] and Proteus[2] can take what form he will. And I, who am cunning in these arts, can plant the bushes on Mount Ida in the sea, or set rivers back on lofty peaks."]

I shrank in horror from her promised miracles, and proceeded to look at the old woman more carefully. . . . " Now," cried Oenothea, " obey my orders! " . . . and she wiped her hands carefully, leaned over the bed, and kissed me once, twice. . . .

Oenothea put up an old table in the middle of the altar, and covered it with live coals, and repaired a wine-cup that had cracked from age with warm pitch. Then she drove in once more on the smoky wall a nail which had come away with the wooden wine-cup when she took it down. Then she put on a square cloak, and laid an enormous cooking-pot on the hearth, and at the same time took off the meat-hooks with a fork a bag which had in it some beans put by for use, and some very mouldy piece of a pig's head smashed into a thousand fragments. After un-fastening the string of the bag she poured out some of the beans on the table, and told me to shell them carefully. I obeyed orders, and my careful fingers parted the kernels from their dirty covering of shell. But she, † the rascal, reproved me for lack of skill, snatched them up, tore off the shells with her teeth in a moment, and spat them on to the ground like the empty husks of flies. . . .

---

[1] See pp. **332–333**.
[2] A sea-god who could change his shape.

PETRONIUS ARBITER

Mirabar equidem paupertatis ingenium singula-
rumque rerum quasdam artes:

Non Indum fulgebat ebur, quod inhaeserat auro,
nec iam calcato radiabat marmore terra
muneribus delusa suis, sed crate saligna
impositum Cereris vacuae nemus et nova terrae
⟨. . .⟩[1]
pocula, quae facili vilis rota finxerat actu.   5
Hinc mollis tiliae lacus[2] et de caudice lento
vimineae lances maculataque testa Lyaeo.
At paries circa palea satiatus inani
fortuitoque luto clavos[3] numerabat agrestes,
et viridi iunco gracilis pendebat harundo.   10
Praeterea quae fumoso suspensa tigillo
conservabat opes humilis casa, mitia sorba
inter odoratas pendebant texta coronas
⟨. . .⟩[4]
et thymbrae veteres et passis uva racemis:
qualis in Actaea quondam fuit hospita terra,   15
digna sacris Hecale,[5] quam Musa loquentibus
annis
† Bachineas veteres mirando †[6] tradidit aevo . . .

---

[1] *Lacuna indicated by Buecheler.*
[2] mollis tiliae (*Pithoeus*) lacus (*Scaliger*): molli stillae latus.
I had thought of mellis stillati, *deleting* hinc.
[3] clavos *Sambucus*: clavus.   *There are other suggestions.*
[4] *Lacuna indicated by Iunius.*
[5] Hecale *Iunius*: Hecates.
[6] *Among other suggestions,* Battiadae vatis *P. Daniel:*

SATYRICON

I marvelled at the resources of poverty, and the art displayed in each particular. " No Indian ivory set in gold shone here, the earth did not gleam with marble now trodden upon and mocked for the gifts she gave, but the grove of Ceres[1] on her holiday was set round with hurdles of willow twigs and fresh cups of clay shaped by a quick turn of the lowly wheel. There was a basin of soft lime-wood, and wicker-work plates of pliant bark, and a jar dyed with the juice of Bacchus.[2] And the wall round was stuffed with light chaff and ready-to-hand clay; on it hung rows of rude nails and slim stalks of green rushes. Besides this, the little cottage roofed with smoky beams preserved their goods, the mellow service-berries hung entwined in fragrant wreaths, and dried savory and bunches of raisins; such a hostess was here as was once on Athenian[3] soil—Hecale worthy of worship of whom the Muse † testified for all ages to adore her, in the years when the poet of Cyrene sang." † [4] . .

[1] Goddess of agriculture, in particular of corn and of fruits.
[2] Lyaeus, the Releaser, a name of Bacchus; here wine.
[3] *Actaea terra = Attica terra.*
[4] Hecale was a poor old woman who, in legend, entertained King Theseus of Athens hospitably. The great poet Callimachus (died about 240 B.C.), a native of Cyrene in north Africa (founded it was said by one Aristotleles of Thera called Battus), wrote a famous but lost epic poem about her. The Latin text is corrupt here.

---

mirandam *someone recorded by Goldast. Buecheler, retaining the indicated lacunae, suggests re-ordering these 17 lines thus: 1, 2, 3, 4, 10, 8, 9, 6, 7, 5, 13, 11, 12, 14, 15, 16, 17. The L-tradition omitted line 12 but l added it in margin as if to put it between 10 and 11. Müller keeps the traditional order but interchanges 13 and 14, again on a suggestion of Buecheler.*

136 Dum illa carnis etiam paululum delibat ⟨. . .⟩[1]
et dum coaequale natalium suorum sinciput in carnarium furca reponit, fracta est putris sella, quae
staturae altitudinem adiecerat, anumque pondere
suo deiectam super foculum mittit. Frangitur ergo
cervix cucumulae ignemque modo convalescentem

L restinguit. | Vexat cubitum ipsa stipite ardenti |
LO faciemque totam excitato cinere perfundit. Consurrexi equidem turbatus anumque non sine risu
erexi ⟨. . .⟩[2]

L | Statimque, ne res aliqua sacrificium moraretur, ad
reficiendum ignem in viciniam cucurrit[3] ⟨. . .⟩[4]

O | Itaque ad casae ostiolum processi ⟨. . .⟩[5]

LO|L | cum ecce tres anseres sacri[6] | qui ut puto medio
LO die solebant ab anu diaria exigere, | impetum in
me faciunt foedoque ac veluti rabioso stridore
circumsistunt trepidantem. Atque alius tunicam
meam lacerat, alius vincula calceamentorum resolvit
ac trahit; unus etiam, dux ac magister saevitiae,
non dubitavit crus meum serrato vexare morsu.
Oblitus itaque nugarum pedem mensulae extorsi
coepique pugnacissimum animal armata elidere
manu. Nec satiatus defunctorio ictu, morte me
anseris vindicavi:

Tales Herculea Stymphalidas arte coactas
ad caelum fugisse reor, caenoque[7] fluentes

---

[1] *Lacuna here?* [2] *Lacuna indicated by Buecheler.*
[3] cucurrit *Schoppius*: cucurri.
[4] *Lacuna indicated by Buecheler.*
[5] *Lacuna indicated by Buecheler. See him and Müller on
this sentence.*
[6] *In his 2nd edition Müller deletes* sacri.
[7] caenoque *Krohn:* peneque *or the like.* sanieque *P.
Daniel. There are other guesses.*

While she [1] was having a small mouthful of meat as well, . . . and was replacing the pig's head, which must have been born on her own birthday, on the jack with her fork, the rotten stool which she was using to increase her height broke, and the old woman's weight sent her down on to the hearth. So the neck of the pot broke and put out the fire, which was just getting up. A glowing brand touched her elbow, and her whole face was covered with the ashes she scattered. I jumped up in confusion and put the old woman straight, not without a laugh. . . . She [2] ran off to her neighbours to see to reviving the fire, to prevent anything keeping the ceremony back. . . . So I went to the door of the house, . . . when all at once three sacred geese, who I suppose generally demanded their daily food from the old woman at mid-day, made a rush at me, and stood round me while I trembled, cackling horribly like mad things. One tore my clothes, another untied the strings of my sandals and tugged them off; the third, the ringleader and chief of the brutes, lost no time in attacking my leg with his jagged bill. Forgetting all mere trifles, I wrenched off a leg of the little table and proceeded to hammer the ferocious creature with this weapon in my hand. One simple blow did not content me. I avenged my honour by the death of the goose.

" Even so I suppose the birds of Stymphalus [3] fled into the sky when the power of Hercules compelled

[1] Proselenos.
[2] Oenothea.
[3] Heracles successfully dealt with some horrid birds of prey, which inhabited a mountain lake in the Stymphalian district of Arcadia, by banging on metal pots—according to one version.

Harpyias, cum Phineo maduere veneno
fallaces epulae.   Tremuit perterritus aether
planctibus insolitis, confusaque regia caeli . . .

L | Iam reliqui revolutam [1] passimque per totum effu-
sam pavimentum collegerant fabam, orbatique, ut
existimo, duce redierant in templum, cum ego praeda
simul [atque] ac [2] vindicta gaudens post lectum
occisum anserem mitto vulnusque cruris haud altum
aceto diluo.   Deinde convicium verens abeundi for-
mavi consilium, collectoque cultu meo ire extra
casam coepi.   Necdum superaveram [3] cellulae limen,
cum animadverto Oenotheam cum testo ignis pleno
venientem.   Reduxi igitur gradum proiectaque veste,
tanquam exspectaram morantem, in aditu steti.
Collocavit illa ignem cassis [4] harundinibus collectum,
ingestisque super pluribus lignis excusare coepit
moram, quod amica se non dimisisset nisi tribus
potionibus e lege siccatis.   " Quid " porro " tu "
inquit " me absente fecisti, aut ubi est faba ? "   Ego,
qui putaveram me rem laude etiam dignam fecisse,
ordine illi totum proelium exposui, et ne diutius tristis
esset, iacturae pensionem anserem obtuli.   Quem |
LO anus ut vidit, tam magnum † aeque † [5] clamorem

---

[1] evolutam *Müller in his 2nd edition*: resolutam *Jungermann*: devolutam *suggests Buecheler.*
[2] [atque] ac *Thielmann*: atque hac.   *Buecheler suggests
deleting* hac.   *Perhaps* aeque ac.
[3] superaveram *Turnebus*: liberaveram *l.*
[4] quassis *l perhaps rightly.*
[5] acremque *Cornelissen, rightly?* ea quoque *suggests Fraenkel.
Possibly* aeque *is an alternative for* tam magnum.

---

[1] The Harpyiae ('Αρπυιαι " snatchers ") were mythical
dirty creatures, birds with the faces of women which, according

them, and the Harpies[1] dripping filth when the
tantalizing food of Phineus ran with poison. The air
above trembled and shook with unwonted lamentation, and the palace of heaven was in an uproar." . . .

The remaining geese had now picked up the beans,
which were spilt and scattered all over the floor, and
having lost their leader had gone back, I think, to
the temple. Then I came in, proud of my prize and
my victory, threw the dead goose behind the bed,
and bathed the wound on my leg, which was not
deep, with vinegar. Then, being afraid of a scolding,
I made a plan for getting away, put my things together, and started to leave the house. I had not yet
got outside the room, when I saw Oenothea coming
with a jar full of live coals. So I drew back and threw
off my coat, and stood in the entrance as if I were
waiting for her slow return. She made up a fire
raised out of some dead reeds, and after heaping on
a quantity of wood, proceeded to apologize for her
delay, saying that her friend would not let her go
until the customary three glasses had been emptied.
"What did you do while I was away?" she went on,
"and where are the beans?" Thinking that I had
done something which deserved even a word of praise,
I described the whole of my fight in detail, and to put
an end to her depression I produced the goose as a
set-off to her losses. When the old woman saw the
bird, she raised such a great shriek that you would

to a legend, infested the dinner-table of Phineus, King of
Salmydessus in Thrace (because he had blinded his sons), and
stole or befouled his food whenever he sat down to eat, until
Zetes and Calaïs, two of the Argonauts, drove them away for
ever.

sustulit, ut putares iterum anseres limen intrasse.
Confusus itaque et novitate facinoris attonitus
quaerebam, quid excanduisset, aut quare anseris
137 potius quam mei misereretur. At illa complosis
manibus "Scelerate" inquit "etiam [1] loqueris?
Nescis quam magnum flagitium admiseris: occidisti
Priapi delicias, anserem omnibus matronis acceptissi-
mum. Itaque ne te putes nihil egisse, si magistratus
hoc scierint, ibis in crucem. Polluisti sanguine
domicilium meum ante hunc diem inviolatum, fecis-
tique ut me, quisquis voluerit inimicus, sacerdotio
pellat." . . .

L | "Rogo" inquam "noli clamare: ego tibi pro
ansere struthocamelum reddam" . . .

Dum haec me stupente in lectulo sedet anserisque
fatum complorat, interim Proselenos cum impensa
sacrificii venit, visoque ansere occiso sciscitata causam
[tristitiae] [2] et ipsa flere vehementius coepit meique
misereri, tanquam patrem meum, non publicum
anserem, occidissem. Itaque taedio fatigatus "rogo"
inquam "expiare manus pretio liceat [3] ⟨. . .⟩ [4]
si vos provocassem, etiam si homicidium fecissem.
Ecce duos aureos pono, unde possitis et deos et
anseres emere." Quos ut vidit Oenothea, "ignosce"
inquit "adulescens, sollicita sum tua causa. Amoris
est hoc argumentum, non malignitatis. Itaque
dabimus operam, ne quis hoc sciat. Tu modo deos
roga, ut illi facto tuo ignoscant."

---

[1] etiam *Dousa*: et.   [2] *Deleted by Müller, rightly.*
[3] liceat *Dousa*: licet.   [4] *Lacuna indicated by Buecheler.*

have thought that the geese had come back into the room again. I was astonished and shocked to find so strange a crime at my door, and I asked her why she had flared up, and why she should be more sorry for the goose than for me. But she beat her hands together and said, " You villain, you dare to speak ? Do you not know what a dreadful sin you have committed ? You have killed the darling of Priapus, the goose beloved of all married women. And do not suppose that it is not serious : if any magistrate finds out, on the cross you go. My house was spotless until to-day, and you have defiled it with blood, and you have given any enemy of mine who likes the power to turn me out of my priesthood." . . .

" Not such a noise, please," I said ; " I will give you an ostrich to replace the goose." . . .

I was amazed, and the woman sat on the bed and wept over the death of the goose, until Proselenos came in with materials for the sacrifice, and seeing that the goose was dead, inquired why this was so. When she found out she began to weep loudly, too, and to compassionate me as if I had killed my own father instead of a common goose. So I grew tired and disgusted, and said, " Please let me cleanse my hands by paying ; . . . it would be another thing if I had insulted you or even done a murder. Look, I will put down two gold pieces. You can buy both gods and geese for that." When Oenothea saw the money, she said, " Forgive me, young man, I am troubled on your account. I am showing my love and not my ill-will. So we will do our best to keep this secret. But pray the gods to pardon what you have done."

LO | Quisquis habet nummos, secura navigat [1] aura
    fortunamque suo temperat [2] arbitrio.
Uxorem ducat Danaen ipsumque licebit
    Acrisium iubeat credere quod Danaen.
Carmina componat, declamet, concrepet omnes
    et peragat causas sitque Catone prior.
Iurisconsultus " parret, non parret " [3] habeto
    atque esto quicquid Servius et Labeo.
Multa loquor: quod vis, nummis praesentibus opta,
    et veniet.   Clausum possidet arca Iovem [4] . . .

L | Infra manus meas camellam vini posuit, et cum
digitos pariter extensos porris apioque lustrasset,
abellanas nuces cum precatione mersit in vinum.   Et
sive in summum redierant, sive subsederant, ex hoc [5]
coniecturam ducebat.[6] Nec me fallebat inanes
scilicet ac sine medulla ventosas [7] nuces in summo
umore consistere, graves autem et plenas [8] integro
fructu ad ima deferri . . .

Recluso pectore extraxit fartissimum [9] iecur et
inde mihi futura praedixit.

Immo, ne quod vestigium sceleris superesset,

[1] navigat *Vincentius*: naviget.
[2] temperat *B*: temperet.
[3] parret non parret *B*: paret non paret.
[4] *The O-tradition ends with* Iovem.
[5] hoc *Goldast*: hac.
[6] coniecturam ducebat *Dousa*: coniectum dicebat *Wouweren*: coniectura dicebat.
[7] *Müller deleted* inanes . . . medulla *in his 1st edition. In his 2nd he deletes* ac sine medulla ventosas *instead.*
[8] *Müller deletes* et plenas.

" Whoever has money sails in a fair wind, and directs his fortune at his own pleasure. Let him take Danaë to wife, and he can tell Acrisius himself to believe what he told Danaë.[1] Let him write poetry, make speeches, snap his fingers at the world, win his cases and outdo Cato.[2] A lawyer, let him have his ' Proven ' and his ' Not proven,' and be all that Servius and Labeo[3] were. I have said enough: with money about you, wish for what you like and it will come. Your safe has Jupiter shut up in it." . . .

She stood a jar of wine under my hands, and made me stretch all my fingers out, and rubbed them with leeks and celery, and threw filberts into the wine with a prayer. She drew her conclusions from them according as they rose to the top or sank. I noticed that the nuts which were empty and had no kernel, but were filled with air, stayed on the surface, while the heavy ones, which were ripe and full, were carried to the bottom. . . .

She cut the goose open, drew out a very fat liver, and foretold the future to me from it. Further, to remove all traces of my crime, she ran the goose right

---

[1] Acrisius a traditional King of Argos was warned that he would be killed by a son of his daughter Danaë whom he therefore shut up in a tower of bronze. But, after Zeus in the form of a shower of gold visited her, she bore Perseus, who later killed Acrisius unintentionally.

[2] Probably the Younger (cf. Chapters 119 and 132).

[3] Servius Sulpicius Rufus, a famous lawyer of the first century B.C. (c. 106–43) and Q. Antistius Labeo, another eminent lawyer 54 B.C.–A.D. 17.

---

[9] fartissimum *Heinsius*: sordidissimum *Cuper*: fortissimum.

totum anserem laceratum verubus confixit epulas-
que etiam lautas paulo ante, ut ipsa dicebat, perituro
paravit. ⟨. . .⟩ [1]

Volabant inter haec potiones meracae . . .

138   Profert Oenothea scorteum fascinum, quod ut oleo
et minuto pipere atque urticae trito circumdedit
semine, paulatim coepit inserere ano meo. ⟨. . .⟩ [2]

Hoc crudelissima anus spargit subinde umore femina mea . . .

Nasturcii sucum cum habrotono miscet perfusisque
inguinibus meis viridis urticae fascem comprehendit
omniaque infra umbilicum coepit lenta manu cae-
dere . . .

Aniculae quamvis solutae mero ac libidine essent,
eandem viam tentant et per aliquot vicos secutae
fugientem " Prende furem " clamant. Evasi tamen
omnibus digitis inter praecipitem decursum cruenta-
tis . . .

" Chrysis, quae priorem fortunam tuam oderat,
hanc vel cum periculo capitis persequi destinat " . . .

" Quid huic formae aut Ariadne habuit aut Leda
simile? Quid contra hanc Helene, quid Venus posset? Ipse Paris, dearum litigantium [3] iudex, si hanc
in comparatione vidisset tam petulantibus oculis, et
Helenen huic [4] donasset et deas. Saltem si permit-

---

[1] *Lacuna indicated by Buecheler.*
[2] *Lacuna indicated by Buecheler.*
[3] litigantium *Dousa*: licitantium *Lips*: lividantium *Gruter*:
libidinantium.
[4] *Fraenkel would delete* huic.

---

[1] Apparently Proselenos.
[2] In legend, Ariadne, daughter of King Minos of Crete,
rescued Theseus of Athens from the labyrinth, went away with

through with a spit, and made quite a fine meal for me, though I had been at death's door a moment ago, as she told me. . . .

Cups of neat wine went swiftly round with it. . . .

Oenothea, drawing out a leathern prick, dipped it in a medley of oil, small pepper, and the bruised seed of nettles, and proceeded by degrees to direct its passage through my hinder parts. . . . With this mixture the old woman [1] barbarously sprinkled my thighs; . . . and with the juice of cresses and southern-wood washing my loins, she took a bunch of green nettles and began to strike gently all the vale below my navel. . . .

Though the poor old things were silly with drink and passion they tried to take the same road, and pursued me through several streets, crying " Stop thief! " But I escaped, with all my toes running blood in my headlong flight. . . .

" Chrysis, who despised your lot before, means to follow you now even at peril of her life." . . .

" Ariadne and Leda [2] had no beauty like hers. Helen and Venus would be nothing beside her. And Paris himself, who decided the quarrel of the goddesses, [3] would have made over Helen besides the goddesses too to her, if his eager gaze had seen her to compare with them. If only I were allowed a kiss, or

him, was deserted by him and became the bride of the god Dionysus, Leda was mother of Helen, Castor, and Pollux, by the god Zeus.

[3] Paris judged the claims of Hera, Aphrodite, and Athena to the golden apple ascribed " To the fairest," which Eris threw among the guests at the wedding of Peleus and Thetis, and awarded it to Aphrodite after she had promised him the most beautiful woman in the world—Helen.

teretur osculum capere, si illud caeleste ac divinum
pectus amplecti forsitan rediret hoc corpus ad vires
et resipiscerent partes veneficio, credo, sopitae. Nec
me contumeliae lassant: quod verberatus sum,
nescio; quod eiectus sum, lusum puto. Modo redire
in gratiam liceat " . . .

139   Torum frequenti tractatione [1] vexavi, amoris mei
quasi quandam imaginem . . .

" Non solum me numen et implacabile fatum
persequitur. Prius Inachia Tirynthius ora
exagitatus onus caeli tulit, ante profanam
Laomedon gemini satiavit numinis iram,
Iunonem Pelias sensit, tulit inscius arma
Telephus et regnum Neptuni pavit [2] Vlixes.
Me quoque per terras, per cani Nereos aequor
Hellespontiaci sequitur gravis ira Priapi " . . .

Quaerere a Gitone meo coepi, num aliquis me
quaesisset. " Nemo " inquit " hodie. Sed hesterno
die mulier quaedam haud inculta ianuam intravit,
cumque diu mecum esset locuta et me accersito sermone lassasset, ultimo coepit dicere, te noxam
meruisse daturumque serviles poenas, si laesus in
querella perseverasset " . . .

----

[1] iactatione *Jungermann.*
[2] pavit *Pithoeus's 2nd edition*: cavit.

----

[1] Heracles = Hercules, hated by Hera, wife of Zeus
Inachian means Greek, from Inachus, traditionally the first
King of Argos.
[2] Strong Heracles relieved, for a little, Atlas, who carried
the world on his shoulders.
[3] He refused to pay the gods Apollo and Poseidon (Neptune)
for building the walls of Troy.

could put my arms round the breast that is heaven's own self, maybe my body would come back to its strength, and the parts of me that were drowsed with poison, I believe, might be themselves again. No insult turns me back; I forget my floggings, and I think it fine sport to have been flung out of doors. Only let her be kind to me again." . . .

I plagued the bed again and again with my writhing, as if I sought for a sort of ghost of my love. . . .

" I am not the only one whom God and an inexorable doom pursues. Before me the son[1] of Tiryns was driven from the Inachian shore and bore the burden of heaven,[2] and Laomedon before me satisfied the ominous wrath of two gods.[3] Pelias[4] felt Juno's power, Telephus[5] fought in ignorance, and Ulysses was in awe of Neptune's kingdom.[6] And me too the heavy wrath of Hellespontine Priapus follows over the earth and over the waters of hoary Nereus."[7] . . .

I proceeded to inquire of Giton whether anyone had asked for me. " No one to-day," he said, " but yesterday a rather pretty woman came in at the door, and talked to me for a long while, till I was tired of her forced conversation, and then proceeded to say that you deserved to be hurt and would have the tortures of a slave, if your adversary persisted with his complaint." . . .

[4] Pelias, King of Iolcus, offended Hera (Juno) by killing, at her altar, his mother's step-mother.
[5] The allusion is unknown. Telephus was a traditional King of Mysia in Asia Minor. He fought with Greeks driven ashore on the way to Troy, where he was wounded by Achilles.
[6] Odysseus' sea-wanderings as told in Homer's *Odyssey* were caused by the anger of Posidon (Neptune).
[7] Nereus was a sea-god.

Nondum querellam[1] finieram, cum Chrysis intervenit amplexuque effusissimo me invasit et " Teneo
te " inquit " qualem speraveram: tu desiderium
meum, tu voluptas mea, nunquam finies hunc ignem,
nisi sanguine exstinxeris " . . .

Unus ex noviciis servulis subito accurrit et mihi
dominum iratissimum esse affirmavit, quod biduo iam
officio defuissem. Recte ergo me facturum, si excusa-
tionem aliquam idoneam praeparassem. Vix enim
posse fieri, ut rabies irascentis sine verbere consi-
deret . . .

140   Matrona inter primas honesta, Philomela nomine,
quae multas saepe hereditates officio aetatis extorse-
rat, tum anus et floris exstincti, filium filiamque ingerebat orbis senibus, et per hanc successionem artem
suam perseverabat extendere. Ea ergo ad Eumolpum venit et commendare liberos suos eius prudentiae
bonitatique . . . credere se et vota sua. Illum esse
solum in toto orbe terrarum, qui praeceptis etiam
salubribus instruere iuvenes quotidie posset. Ad
summam, relinquere se pueros in domo Eumolpi, ut
illum loquentem audirent . . . quae sola posset here-
ditas iuvenibus dari. Nec aliter fecit ac dixerat,
filiamque speciosissimam cum fratre ephebo in cubiculo reliquit simulavitque se in templum ire ad vota
nuncupanda. Eumolpus, qui tam frugi erat ut illi
etiam ego puer viderer, non distulit puellam invitare

[1] *Fraenkel suggested deleting* querellam.

---

[1] Eumolpus. Encolpius and Giton at Croton are still the
pretended attendants on Eumolpus.

I had not finished grumbling, when Chrysis came in, ran up and warmly embraced me, and said, " Now I have you as I hoped; you are my desire, my pleasure, you will never put out this flame unless you quench it in my blood." . . .

One of the new slaves suddenly ran up and said that my master[1] was furious with me because I had now been away from work two days; the best thing I could do would be to get ready some suitable excuse. For it was hardly possible that his savage wrath would abate without a flogging for me. . . .

A very venerable matron, her name Philomela, who by the well-managed virtues of her younger age had often extorted legacies, now grown old, and past her blooming years, had a mind to thrust her son and daughter upon childless old men, and hoped by this succession to continue the use of her art. Accordingly she came to Eumolpus, and addressing herself to him, . . . commends her children to his conduct, affirming, that she committed herself and all her hopes to his wisdom and goodness; that he was the only person in the world who could instruct the young people with wholesome principles day by day. In short, that she would leave her children there in the house of Eumolpus, to hear his discourse, which was the only portion she could give them. Nor was she worse than her word; and leaving in the chamber a lovely daughter, with her brother, already a young man, she went out under pretence of paying heaven public thanks in the temple for the favours she had received. Eumolpus, who was so temperate that he thought even me a boy, did not hesitate to invite the

373

ad † pigiciaca [1] † sacra. Sed et podagricum se esse lumborumque solutorum omnibus dixerat, et si non servasset integram simulationem, periclitabatur totam paene tragoediam evertere. Itaque ut constaret mendacio fides, puellam quidem exoravit, ut sederet super [2] commendatam bonitatem, Coraci autem imperavit, ut lectum, in quo ipse iacebat, subiret positisque in pavimento manibus dominum lumbis suis commoveret. Ille lente [3] parebat imperio puellaeque [4] artificium pari motu remunerabat. Cum ergo res ad effectum spectaret, clara Eumolpus voce exhortabatur Coraca, ut spissaret officium. Sic inter mercennarium amicamque positus senex veluti oscillatione ludebat. Hoc semel iterumque ingenti risu, etiam suo, Eumolpus fecerat. Itaque ego quoque, ne desidia consuetudinem perderem, dum frater sororis suae automata per clostellum miratur, accessi temptaturus, an pateretur iniuriam. Nec se reiciebat a blanditiis doctissimus puer, sed me numen inimicum ibi quoque invenit . . .

"Dii maiores sunt, qui me restituerunt in integrum. Mercurius enim, qui animas ducere et reducere solet, suis beneficiis reddidit mihi, quod manus irata praeciderat, ut scias me gratiosiorem esse quam Protesilaum aut quemquam alium antiquorum."

---

[1] physica *or* Aphrodisiaca *suggests Buecheler*: *in his 2nd edition Müller accepts* Aphrodisiaca. Isiaca *Valesius*: πυγησιακὰ *in margin of l.*

[2] super *Buecheler*: supra.

[3] lente *Schoppius*: lento.　　　[4] puellaque *Cuperus*.

---

[1] Protesilaus, leader of the Thessalians in the war against Troy, was the first man to be killed there. He was allowed

girl to a lesson in † rump-ritual? †. Well he always
gave himself out to everyone as a victim of gout and
relaxed loins, and if he could not keep up all his pretence he ran the risk of upsetting the applecart. So
to secure faith in his deception, he begged the girl to
sit on top of the recommended " goodness," but
ordered Corax to get into the bed in which he himself
was lying, and, putting his hands on the floor, to stir
up his master with his buttocks. He obeyed this
order in slow motion, and presented the girl's artistry
with a similar movement. So, when the business
looked like approaching completion, Eumolpus in
loud tones urged Corax to pile on the job faster. In
this way Eumolpus, the older man, placed between
the servant and the girl-friend, sported in a sort of
swinging to and fro between one and the other.
This Eumolpus did not only once but again amid
huge laughter including his own. So I also, so as not
to lose practice through slackness, while her brother
was watching his sister's robots through the key-
hole, came up to try whether he would submit to an
assault by me. The clever clever boy was not deaf
to my flatteries, but very adverse fortune still
attended me. . . .

" But there are greater gods, who have restored me
to my strength. For Mercury, that conveys and
reconveys our soul, by his favours has restored to me
what his anger had taken away. So you may know
me to be more in favour than Protesilaus[1] or any
other of the ancient heroes." With these words I

by Hermes (Roman counterpart: Mercurius), who was a guide
of souls on the way to Hades, to revisit the earth once after
his death because of his widow's plea.

Haec locutus sustuli tunicam Eumolpoque me totum
approbavi.   At ille primo exhorruit, deinde ut plurimum crederet, utraque manu deorum beneficia
tractat . . .

"Socrates, deorum hominumque ⟨. . .⟩[1] gloriari
solebat, quod nunquam neque in tabernam conspexerat nec ullius turbae frequentioris concilio
oculos suos crediderat.   Adeo nihil est commodius
quam semper cum sapientia loqui." ⟨. . .⟩[2]

"Omnia" inquam "ista vera sunt; nec ulli enim
celerius homines incidere debent in malam fortunam,
quam qui alienum concupiscunt.   Unde plani autem
unde levatores viverent, nisi aut locellos aut sonantes
aere sacellos pro hamis in turbam mitterent?   Sicut
muta animalia cibo inescantur, sic homines non cape-
rentur nisi spei[3] aliquid morderent" . . .

141   "Ex Africa navis, ut promiseras, cum pecunia tua
et familia non venit.   Captatores iam exhausti
liberalitatem imminuerunt.   Itaque aut fallor, aut
fortuna communis coepit redire ad paenitentiam
suam"[4] . . .

"Omnes, qui in testamento meo legata habent,
praeter libertos[5] meos hac condicione percipient, quae
dedi, si corpus meum in partes conciderint et astante
populo comederint" . . .

"Apud quasdam gentes scimus adhuc legem ser-
vari, ut a propinquis suis consumantur defuncti, adeo
quidem, ut obiurgentur aegri frequenter, quod
carnem suam faciant peiorem.   His admoneo amicos

---

[1] *L indicates a gap here.   Rutgers suggests adding* iudicio
sapientissimus.   *Scaliger thought that a Greek word was needed.*

376

lifted my tunic and offered my whole self for the approbation of Eumolpus. At first he was terrified, then so as to believe as far as possible he felt with both hands the favour of the gods. . . .

" Socrates, the friend of God and man, used to boast that he had never peeped into a shop, or allowed his eyes to rest on any large crowd. So nothing is more blessed than always to converse with wisdom." . . .

" All that is very true," I said, " and no one deserves to fall into misery sooner than the covetous. But how would cheats or pickpockets live, if they did not expose little boxes or purses jingling with money, like hooks, to collect a crowd? Just as dumb creatures are snared by food, human beings would not be caught unless they had a nibble of hope." . . .

" The ship from Africa with your money and slaves that you promised does not arrive. The fortune-hunters are tired out, and their generosity is shrinking. So that unless I am mistaken, our usual luck is on its way back to its repentance." . . .

" All those who come into money under my will, except my own freedmen will get what I have left them on one condition, that they cut my body in pieces and eat it up in sight of the crowd." . . .

" We know that in some countries a law is still observed, that dead people shall be eaten by their relations, and the result is that sick people are often blamed for spoiling their own flesh. So I warn my

---

² *Lacuna indicated by Buecheler.*   ³ spei *Buecheler*: spe.
⁴ tuam *suggests Buecheler.*
⁵ liberos *cod. Lambeth., Tornaesius, Pithoeus.*

meos, ne recusent quae iubeo, sed quibus animis
devoverint spiritum meum, eisdem etiam corpus
consumant " . . .

Excaecabat pecuniae ingens fama [1] oculos animosque miserorum.

Gorgia paratus erat exsequi . . .

" De stomachi tui recusatione non habeo quod
timeam. Sequetur imperium, si promiseris illi pro
unius horae fastidio multorum bonorum pensationem.
Operi modo oculos et finge te non humana viscera sed
centies sestertium comesse. Accedit huc, quod aliqua
inveniemus blandimenta, quibus saporem mutemus.
Neque enim ulla caro per se placet, sed arte quadam
corrumpitur [2] et stomacho conciliatur averso. Quod
si exemplis quoque vis probari consilium, Saguntini
obsessi [3] ab Hannibale humanas edere carnes, nec
hereditatem exspectabant. Petelini [4] idem fecerunt
in ultima fame, nec quicquam aliud in hac epulatione
captabant, nisi tantum ne esurirent. Cum esset
Numantia a Scipione capta, inventae sunt matres,
quae liberorum suorum tenerent semesa in sinu corpora " . . .

[1] fames *Boschius*.

[2] *Fraenkel suggests* conditur *or* convertitur, *Müller (in his
1st edition)* commendatur.

[3] obsessi *Rittershusius*: oppressi.

[4] Petelini *Puteanus*: Petavii.

friends not to disobey my orders, but to eat my body as heartily as they damned my soul." . . .

His great reputation for wealth dulled the eyes and brains of the fools. Gorgias was ready to manage the funeral. . . .

" I am not at all afraid of your stomach turning. You will get it under control if you promise to repay it for one unpleasant hour with heaps of good things. Just shut your eyes and dream you are eating up a solid million instead of human flesh. Besides, we shall find some kind of sauce which will change the taste. For no flesh at all is pleasant in itself, it has to be artificially disguised and reconciled to the unwilling digestion. But if you also wish the plan to be supported by precedents, the people of Saguntum,[1] when Hannibal besieged them, ate human flesh without any legacy in prospect. The people of Petelia[2] did likewise in the extremities of famine, and gained nothing by the diet, except of course that they were no longer hungry. And when Numantia was stormed by Scipio,[3] some mothers were found holding the half-eaten bodies of their children in their bosoms." . . .

[1] Saguntum (Murviedro) in Spain was besieged by the Carthaginian Hannibal and taken in 219 B.C. after an eight months' siege. This led to the outbreak of war between Rome and Carthage.
[2] A town in the territory of the Bruttii in south Italy. It was subdued by Rome during the third century B.C.
[3] Numantia (Garray) in Spain was taken in 133 B.C. after a fifteen months' blockade by Lucius Cornelius Scipio Aemilianus, who thereby established in Spain the supremacy of Rome.

ADDITIONAL NOTE

The poem on the civil war in Petronius 119–124

The question of a connection between this poem and
the extant poem of Lucan may be set out as follows.

Both Petronius and Lucan died through the enmity
of Nero, and both by the same cause and in effect at
the same time. Petronius was accused of friendship
with Flavius Scaevinus a member of Piso's ill-fated
plot against Nero in A.D. 65, and because of this took
his own life in 66. Marcus Annaeus Lucanus, born
in A.D. 39, was involved in the same conspiracy and
because of this had killed himself in A.D. 65.

Petronius in the *Satyricon*, chapter 118, makes the
old poet Eumolpus utter in prose a severe warning
to would-be poets, especially if they feel an urge to
compose such an *ingens opus* (' a huge work ') as a
bellum civile. Such a subject in epic poetry, says
Eumolpus, demands a rich knowledge of literature;
mere recording of events should not be attempted in
verse because historians do that better (in prose);
in an historical epic poem such as one on civil war
there should be mythology and interpositions by the
gods, and the poet should sound like an inspired
prophet rather than an utterer of facts as if on oath.
Then Petronius makes Eumolpus recite a miniature
epic (lacking, says E., the final touches) in hexameters
on the civil strife between Pompeius (and his sur-

vivors) and Caesar, B.C. 49–45. Lucan at his death left unfinished an incomparably larger epic in ten books of hexameters on the same struggle.

Petronius's poem has no title, but we may conclude from chapter 118 that it can be called *Bellum Civile*. Lucan's poem has the title *Bellum Civile* in the best MSS, the title *Pharsalia* (from Pharsalus, scene of the final defeat of Pompeius by Caesar) in others.

Petronius's novel must have been finished, or left unfinished, before A.D. 66 or early in that year. Lucan had completed (and perhaps published) three books in A.D. 61, five years before Petronius's death, covering thus far the same events as Petronius does in his poem as a whole. Lucan's poem, so far as it goes in the ten books, has more than 8000 lines, the war as far as the evacuation of Italy by Pompeius being contained in the first two books (695 + 736 = 1431 lines)): Book I: Evils of War. Causes of the Civil War. Roman luxury (lines 158–182 only, on the latter). Characters of Caesar and Pompeius. Caesar invades Italy. Fear at Rome. Pompeius flees. Book II: Alarm at Rome. Earlier turmoil of Marius and Sulla. Brutus and Cato. Caesar occupies all Italy which Pompeius successfully leaves. Book III: Caesar enters Rome. Goes to Massilia. Pompeius collects men from Greece and Asia (762 lines). Book IV: Caesar in Spain. Curio's fate in Africa. Book V: Caesar returns to Rome. His dictatorship. Caesar and the country Epirus. Pompeius's wife Cornelia. Book VI: Operations at Dyrrachium, etc. Both armies go to Thessaly. Book VII: Battle of Pharsalus. Victory of Caesar. Book VIII: Flight of Pompeius by way of W. Asia

Minor to Egypt where he is murdered. Book IX: Cato in N. Africa. Caesar reaches Egypt. Book X: Caesar in Alexandria. Lucan's epic, concerned with recent history, is written on historical lines, a sort of chronicle in verse; and has no superstructure of participating gods, herein disobeying, as none had before, one of the " laws " or customs of Latin historical epic poetry established by Ennius from the model of Homer in Greek. In Lucan, all is on an inflated scale of rhetorical art with every power and weakness of rhetoric.

Petronius's poem as we have it contains less than 300 lines: 1–44 Luxury of omnipotent Rome. 45–60 Cato is rejected. Madness of Rome. 61–66 Three great generals, Crassus, Pompeius, Caesar. 67–101 The god Dis stirs up Fortuna to harry Rome. 102–121 Fortuna replies and foresees the Battle of Pharsalus (48 B.C.), the Battles of Philippi (42 B.C.) and Civil War in Spain (49 and 45 B.C.), and Egypt (48–47 B.C.), and the Battle of Actium (31 B.C.); and slaughter. 122–141 Turmoil in heaven and earth. 141–176 Caesar crosses the Alps from Gaul, addresses Jupiter, justifies his act, and appeals to his soldiers. 177–208 Further turmoil in earth and sky as Caesar advances. 209–237 Rumour, panic and chaos at Rome. 238–244 Worse still—Pompeius, once conqueror in Asia, retreats. 245–263 The gentle deities, including Peace, seek the underworld; and the warlike ones, including Death and Madness, come out. 264–270 Some gods take sides. 271–287 Discord, all hideous comes from below and standing on the Apennine Mountains, stirs up peoples to war; 288–294 in particular Marcellus, Curio, Lentulus, and

Caesar. Pompeius must leave Italy. [295 Discord's commands are obeyed.]

Petronius's poem is not a connected narrative. The first 60 lines (about one-fifth of the whole poem) consist of moralising on the degeneracy of Rome, the rest being largely a series of comments, in part jumbled, and imaginary turmoil of gods and men, there being really only two real scenes—Caesar's crossing of the Alps and the resulting panic in Rome. Petronius takes the war's events hardly as far as the evacuation of Italy by Pompeius, mention of later events being merely forecasts. There are passages which have a likeness to Lucan, for example the panic of Rome which like the first advance of Caesar as a rebel comes in Lucan in that part of his poem which he had completed in A.D. 61. But this can lead to no conclusions. Petronius's poem seems to present a programme as much as one or more parodies; it is not very good either in itself or in consistent parody and is no model even for a miniature epic. But it may possibly include (i) parody of a widespread idea of anti-imperial epic, favoured perhaps by the so-called Stoic opposition to the Emperors, and "in the air" so to speak, during Petronius's lifetime, with Lucan in fact working on such an epic; what we have after all in Petronius is an effusion from the mouth of the rhetor and inferior poet Eumolpus, himself ready to burst into poetry at any time; (ii) parody of several features of rhetorical poetry such as messengers' speeches in tragedies, and imaginary actions of gods.

It is highly probable that Petronius knew Lucan as a friend and knew that Lucan was composing an

epic on the last days of the free Roman republic—
" *Ecce belli civilis ingens opus* " says Eumolpus, the
word *ecce*, " look now ", suggesting a definite example; Petronius may well have read Lucan's first
three books completed in A.D. 61, or heard recitations
from them, and may have disapproved in part; for
Lucan's epic is (i) a record of events (and of people's
feelings) in verse and (ii) lacks the divine activities of
deities; and both (i) (the method) and (ii) (the lack)
are criticised in chapter 118 of Petronius, and their
contraries are illustrated in Petronius's poem itself.
We might conclude that Petronius not only thought
that Lucan would turn out to be ' prosy ' but also
disapproves of Eumolpus's kind of poetry here as he
does elsewhere in the *Satyricon*. I feel that Petronius
criticises Lucan at work but parodies what is largely
others' poetry. He probably did not know all that
Lucan had written by the year 65. Certain it is
that Petronius's poem is not a comment on a completed work of Lucan.

FRAGMENTS

FRAGMENTA

I

Servius ad Vergili Aen. III 57: auri sacra fames]
sacra id est exercrabilis. Tractus est autem sermo ex
more Gallorum. Nam Massilienses quotiens pestilentia laborabant, unus se ex pauperibus offerebat
alendus anno integro publicis ⟨sumptibus⟩ [1] et purio-
ribus cibis. Hic postea ornatus verbenis et vestibus
sacris circumducebatur per totam civitatem cum
exsecrationibus, ut in ipsum reciderent mala totius
civitatis, et sic proiciebatur. Hoc autem in Petronio
lectum est

II

*Servius ad Vergili Aen. XII 159 de feminino nominum
in* TOR *exeuntium genere:* Si autem a verbo non venerint, communia sunt. Nam similiter et masculina et
femininia in TOR exeunt, ut hic et haec senator, hic et
haec balneator, licet Petronius usurpaverit " balneatricem " dicens

---

[1] sumptibus *added by Buecheler.*

FRAGMENTS

I

Servuis on Virgil, Aeneid III, 57: " The sacred hunger for gold." " Sacred " means " accursed." This expression is derived from a Gallic custom. For whenever the people of Massilia were burdened with pestilence, one of the poor would volunteer to be fed for an entire year out of public funds on food of special purity. After this period he would be decked with sacred herbs and sacred robes, and would be led through the whole state while people cursed him, in order that the sufferings of the whole state might fall upon him; and so he was cast out. This account has been given in Petronius.[1]

II

Servius on Virgil, Aeneid XII, 159, on the feminine gender of nouns ending in -tor: But if they are not derived from a verb they are common in gender. For in these cases both the masculine and the feminine end alike in -tor, for example, senator, a male or female senator, balneator, a male or female bath attendant, though Petronius makes an exception in speaking of a " *bath-woman* " (*balneatricem*).

[1] Perhaps in the story Encolpius was at Massilia. Cf. Fragm. IV.

PETRONIUS ARBITER

III

Pseudacro ad Horati epod. 5, 48: Canidia rodens pollicem] habitum et motum Canidiae expressit furentis. Petronius ut monstraret furentem, " pollice " ait " usque ad periculum roso "

IV

Sidonius Apollinaris, Carmen XXIII:

> quid vos eloquii canam Latini, 145
> Arpinas, Patavine, Mantuane ?—
> Et te Massiliensium per hortos 155
> sacri stipitis, Arbiter, colonum
> Hellespontiaco parem Priapo ?

V

Priscianus institutionum VIII 16 p. 381 et XI 29 p. 567 Hertzii inter exempla quibus deponentium verborum participia praeteriti temporis passivam significationem habere declarat: Petronius " animam nostro amplexam pectore "

V b

Boethius in Porphyrium a Victorino translatum dialogo II extremo p. 45 exemplarium Basiliensium: Ego faciam, inquit, libentissime. Sed quoniam iam matutinus, ut ait Petronius, sol tectis arrisit, surgamus, et si quid est illud, diligentiore postea consideratione tractabitur

FRAGMENTS

III

Pseud-Acro on Horace, Epodes 5, 48: " Canidia[1] biting her thumb ": He expressed the appearance and movements of Canidia in a rage. Petronius, wishing to portray a furious person, says " *his thumb bitten to the quick.*"

IV

Sidonius Apollinaris, Carmen XXIII, 145, 155: Why should I hymn you, tuneful Latin writers, thou of Arpinum, thou of Patavium, thou of Mantua?[2] And thou, Arbiter, who in the gardens of the men of Massilia findest a home on the hallowed tree-trunk as the peer of Hellespontine Priapus?

V

Priscian Institutiones VIII, 16 and XI, 29 (pp. 381, 567 ed. Hertz) among the examples by which he shows that the past participles of deponent verbs have a passive meaning: Petronius, " *the soul locked (amplexam) in our bosoms.*"

V[b]

Boethius on Victorinus's translation of Porphyry, Dialogue II (p. 45 ed. Basle): I shall be very glad to do it, he said. But since *the morning sun*, in Petronius's words, *has now smiled upon the roofs*, let us get up, and if there is any other point, it shall be treated later with more careful attention.

---

[1] A sorceress.
[2] The writers are Cicero, Livy, Virgil. Cf. Fragm. I.

PETRONIUS ARBITER

VI*

Fulgentius mythologiarum I p. 12 Helm: Nescis
. . . quantum saturam matronae formident. Licet
mulierum verbialibus undis et causidici cedant nec
grammatici muttiant, rhetor taceat et clamorem
praeco compescat, sola est quae modum imponit
furentibus, licet Petroniana subet [1] Albucia

VII*

*Fulgentius mythologiarum III 8 p. 73 ubi sucum
myrrhae valde fervidum esse dixit:* Unde et Petronius
Arbiter ad libidinis concitamentum myrrhinum se
poculum bibisse refert

VIII*

*Fulgentius in expositione Virgilianae continentiae p.
98:* Tricerberi enim fabulam iam superius exposui-
mus in modum iurgii forensisque litigii positam.
Unde et Petronius in Euscion ait " Cerberus forensis
erat causidicus " [2]

[1] subet *Buecheler:* subit.
[2] *Buecheler suggests deleting* causidicus.

---

[1] Codex Par. 7975 of the eleventh century by guesswork
attributes this fragment to Book XIV of Petronius and to a
context in Chapter 20 where Quartilla says, " Did Encolpius
drink up the whole of our loving cup? " The incident
naturally does not occur anywhere because nowhere does
Petronius speak of himself. But at least the words *myrrhinum
poculum* can be genuine. The expression would mean not a
cup of myrrh, but a " myrrhine cup," that is, one made either
of best agate or of fluor-spar. In Book XXXVII, 18–22 of his

FRAGMENTS

VI

Fulgentius Mythologiae I (p. 12 ed. Helm): You do not know . . . how women dread satire. Lawyers may retreat and scholars may not utter a syllable before the flood of a woman's words, the rhetorician may be dumb and the herald may stop his cries; satire alone can put a limit to their madness, though it be Petronius's *Albucia* who is in heat.

VII

Fulgentius Mythologiae III, 8 (p. 73). (where he remarked that essence of myrrh is very strong): Hence too Petronius Arbiter says *that he drank a myrrhine cup* [1] *in order to excite his passion.*

VIII

Fulgentius in his Treatise on the Contents of Virgil's works (p. 98): For we have already explained above the application of the myth of Cerberus [2] with Three Heads to quarrels and litigation in the courts. Hence too Petronius says against *Euscios*, " *The barrister was a Cerberus of the courts.*" C.f. Fragm. XI and p. 81.

Natural History, Pliny describes the costly " myrrhina," the description on 21 and 22 suiting fluor-spar, one of its merits being its smell, probably caused by hot resin in which the fluor-spar was soaked to prevent it from falling to pieces when it was worked. In 20 Pliny says that Titus Petronius, when he was about to die, broke, to spite Nero, a myrrhine dipper which Petronius had bought for 300,000 sesterces, so that he thus far disinherited Nero's table. See also p. xxxvii.

[2] This monster guarding the gates of Hades had, according to one myth, a hundred heads.

PETRONIUS ARBITER

IX*

Fulgentius in expositione sermonum antiquorum 42 p. 122: Ferculum dicitur missum carnium. Unde et Petronius Arbiter ait " postquam ferculum allatum est "

X*

Fulgentius ibidem 46 p. 123: Valgia vero sunt labellorum obtortiones in supinatione factae. Sicut et Petronius ait " obtorto valgiter labello "

XI*

Fulgentius ibidem 52 p. 124: Alucinare dicitur vana somniari, tractum ab alucitis, quos nos conopes dicimus. Sicut Petronius Arbiter ait " nam contubernalem [1] alucitae molestabant "

XII*

Fulgentius ibidem 60 p. 126: Manubies dicuntur ornamenta regum. Unde et Petronius Arbiter ait " tot regum manubies penes fugitivum repertae "

XIII*

Fulgentius ibidem 61 p. 126: Aumatium dicitur locum secretum publicum sicut in theatris aut in circo.

---

[1] contubernalem *Buecheler*: contum vernali me *the better MSS. There are various conjectures.*

FRAGMENTS

IX

Fulgentius in his Explanation of Old Words, 42 (p. 122): Ferculum means a dish of flesh. Hence too Petronius Arbiter says, " *After the dish of flesh (ferculum) was brought in.*" [1]

X

Fulgentius ibid. 46 (p. 123): Valgia really means the twisting of the lips which occurs in vomiting. As Petronius also says, " *With lips twisted as in a vomit (valgiter).*"

XI

Fulgentius ibid. 52 (p. 124): Alucinare means to dream nonsense, and is derived from *alucitae*, which we call *conopes* (mosquitoes). As Petronius Arbiter says, " *For the mosquitoes (alucitae) were troubling my companion.*"

XII

Fulgentius ibid. 60 (p. 126): Manubies is a term used for the ornaments of kings. Hence Petronius Arbiter also says, " *So many kingly ornaments (manubies, manubiae) found in the possession of a runaway.*"

XIII

Fulgentius ibid. 61 (p. 126): Aumatium means a private place in a public spot such as theatres or the

---

[1] Probably a dish of food in one of the courses of Trimalchio's dinner.

PETRONIUS ARBITER

Unde et Petronius Arbiter ait " in aumatium memet ipsum conieci "

XIV

Isidorus originum V 26, 7: Dolus est mentis calliditas ab eo quod deludat: aliud enim agit, aliud simulat. Petronius aliter existimat dicens " quid est, iudices, dolus? Nimirum ubi aliquid factum est quod legi dolet. Habetis dolum: accipite nunc malum "

XV

Glossarium S. Dionysii: Petaurus genus ludi. Petronius " petauroque iubente modo superior " [1]

XVI

Petronius " satis constaret eos nisi inclinatos non solere transire cryptam Neapolitanam " *ex glossario S. Dionysii*

XVII* [2]

In alio glossario:

> Suppes suppumpis, hoc est supinis pedibus.
> Tullia, media vel regia.

---

[1] *Housman adds* ⟨modo inferior⟩.
[2] Wrongly attributed to Petronius by Pithoeus through misunderstanding a marginal\note of Scaliger.

FRAGMENTS

circus. Hence Petronius Arbiter also says, "*I hurled myself into the privy-place (aumatium).*"

XIV

Isidorus Origines V, 26, 7: Dolus [1] is mental cunning and is derived from the fact that the mind " deludes ": for it does one thing and pretends another. Petronius takes a different view when he says, "*What is a device (dolus), gentlemen? It occurs of course whenever anything offensive to (dolet) the law is done. You understand what a device is; now take a bad device . . . .*". Cf. *Fragm. VIII.*

XV

Glossary of St. Dionysius: The spring-board is a kind of game. Petronius, "*Now lifted high at the will of the spring-board.*" See Chapters 53–54.

XVI

From the Glossary of St. Dionysius: Petronius, "*It was quite certainly their usual plan to go through the Grotto of Naples only with backs bent double.*"

XVII

Another Glossary:

> *Suppes suppumpis, that is with feet bent backwards.
> Tullia, mediator (?) or princess.*

---

[1] *Dolus* originally meant a *device* without moral connotation; hence the legal term for *fraud* was *dolus malus,* and the use of *dolus* alone in a bad sense is later.

PETRONIUS ARBITER

XVIII* 1

Nicolaus Perottus Cornu copiae p. 200, 26 editionis Aldinae anni 1513: Cosmus etiam excellens unguentarius fuit, a quo unguenta dicta sunt Cosmiana. Idem [*Iuvenalis 8, 86*] " et Cosmi toto mergatur aheno." Petronius " affer nobis, inquit, alabastrum Cosmiani "

XIX

Terentianus Maurus de metris (in Keilii Grammaticis VI p. 399):

> Horatium videmus
> versus tenoris huius
> nusquam locasse iuges,
> at Arbiter disertus
> libris suis frequentat.
> Agnoscere haec potestis,
> cantare quae solemus:
> " Memphitides puellae
> sacris deum paratae."
> " Tinctus colore noctis
> manu puer loquaci "

Marius Victorinus III 17 (in Keilii grammaticis VI p. 138): Huius tenoris ac formae quosdam versus poetas lyricos carminibus suis indidisse cognovimus, ut et apud Arbitrum invenimus, cuius exemplum

> " Memphitides puellae
> sacris deum paratae."
> " Tinctus colore noctis "
> " Aegyptias choreas "

FRAGMENTS

XVIII

Nicolaus Perottus in the Cornucopia (p. 200, 26 in the Aldine Edition of 1513): Cosmus too was a superb perfumer, and ointments are called Cosmian after him. The same writer (Juvenal 8, 86) says, " and let him be plunged deep in a bronze vase of Cosmus." Petronius, " *Bring us, he said, an alabaster box of Cosmus ointment.*"

XIX

Terentianus Maurus on Metre (Keil, Grammatici, VI, 399):

We see that Horace nowhere employed verse of this [1] rhythm continuously, but the learned Arbiter uses it often in his works. You can recognize these lines, which we are used to sing: " *The maidens of Memphis, made ready for the rites of the Gods.*" " *The boy coloured deep as the night with speaking gestures.*"

Marius Victorinus III, 17 (Keil, Grammatici, VI, 138):

We know that the lyric poets inserted some lines of this rhythm and form in their works, as we find too in Arbiter, for example: " *The maidens of Memphis,*[2] *made ready for the rites of the Gods,*" and again " *Coloured deep as the night.*" " *⟨Dancing⟩ Egyptian Dances.*"

[1] " Anacreontic," used by Maurus here.
[2] A famous Egyptian city south of Cairo.

---

[1] Not by Petronius.

PETRONIUS ARBITER

XX

Terentianus Maurus de metris (in Keilii Grammaticis VI 409):

> Nunc divisio, quam loquemur, edet
> metrum, quo memorant Anacreonta
> dulces composuisse cantilenas.
> Hoc Petronius invenitur usus,
> Musis cum lyricum refert eundem
> consonantia verba cantitasse,
> et plures alii. Sed iste versus
> quali compositus tome sit, edam.
> " Iuverunt segetes meum laborem."
> " Iuverunt " caput est id hexametri—
> quod restat " segetes meum laborem,"
> tale est ceu " triplici vides ut ortu
> Triviae rotetur ignis
> volucrique Phoebus axe
> rapidum pererret orbem "

XXI

Diomedes in arte III p. 518 Keilii: Et illud hinc est comma quod Arbiter fecit tale

> " Anus recocta vino
> trementibus labellis "

---

[1] Greek lyric poet of the sixth century B.C., born in Teos.
[2] I.e. as the new, the full, or the waning moon. Phoebus is the sun, Trivia the moon whose goddess Diana or Hecate was often worshipped where three roads meet.
[3] Proselenos? Or Oenothea? See pp. 342, 353 ff.

FRAGMENTS

XX

Terentianus Maurus on Metre (Keil, VI, 409):

Now the analysis, which we will explain, will give us the metre in which they say that Anacreon [1] wrote his sweet old songs. We find that Petronius, as well as many others, used this metre, when he says that this same lyric poet sang in words harmonious to the Muses. But I will explain with what kind of caesura this verse is written. In the line " *Iuverunt segetes meum laborem* " (" *The cornfields have lightened my labour* "), the word " *iuverunt* " is the beginning of a hexameter: the remaining words " *segetes meum laborem* " are in the same metre as

> " *triplici vides ut ortu*
> *volucrique Phoebus axe*
> *Triviae rotetur ignis*
> *rapidum pererret orbem* "

(" *You see how the fire of Trivia spins round from her threefold rising,*[2] *and Phoebus on his winged wheel traverses the hurrying globe.*")

XXI

Diomede on Grammar III (Keil p. 518): Hence arises the caesura which Arbiter employed thus:

> " *Anus recocta vino*
> *trementibus labellis* "

(" *An old woman* [3] *soaked in wine, with trembling lips* ")

399

PETRONIUS ARBITER

XXII

Servius in artem Donati p. 432, 22 Keilii: Item Quirites dicit numero tantum plurali.   Sed legimus apud Horatium hunc Quiritem, ut sit nominativus hic Quiris.   Item idem Horatius " quis te Quiritem? " cuius nominativus erit hic Quirites, ut dicit Petronius

Pompeius in commento artis Donati p. 167, 9 K: Nemo dicit " hic Quirites " sed " hi Quirites," licet legerimus hoc.   Legite in Petronio, et invenietis de nominativo singulari hoc factum.   Et ait Petronius " hic Quirites "

XXIII

Grammaticus de dubiis nominibus p. 578, 23 K: Fretum generis neutri et pluraliter freta, ut Petronius " freta Nereidum "

XXIV*

Hieronymus in epistula ad Demetriadem CXXX 19 p. 995 Vallarsii: Cincinnatulos pueros et calamistratos et peregrini muris olentes pelliculas, de quibus illud Arbitri est

" Non bene olet qui bene semper olet,"

quasi quasdam pestes et venena pudicitiae virgo devitet

---

[1] Sea-nymphs, the fifty daughters of Nereus.
[2] The words occur in Martial (II, xii, 4) who may have quoted Petronius.   But they may have been a common saying.

400

FRAGMENTS

XXII

Servius on the Grammar of Donatus (Keil p. 432, 22):
Again, he uses " Quirites " (" Roman citizens ") only
in the plural number. But we read in Horace the
accusative " hunc Quiritem " (" this Roman citizen ")
making the nominative " hic Quiris." Again, the
same Horace says " Quis te Quiritem ?" and there
the nominative will be " *hic Quirites*," as Petronius
says.

*Pompeius in his Commentary on the Grammar of
Donatus (Keil p. 167, 9):* No one says " this Roman
citizen," but " these Roman citizens," although we
find the former in books. Read Petronius, and you
will find this use of the nominative singular. And
Petronius says " *Hic Quirites* " (" *this Roman citizen* ").

XXIII

*A Grammarian on Nouns of uncertain gender (Keil
p. 578, 23):* Fretum (" a strait ") is of the neuter
gender, and its plural is freta, as Petronius says
" *Freta Nereidum* " (" *The straits of the Nereids* ").[1]

XXIV

*Hieronymus in a Letter to Demetriades CXXX, 19
(Vallarsius p. 995):* Boys with hair curled and crimped
and skins smelling like foreign rats, about whom
Arbiter wrote the words, " *To smell good always is not
to smell good*,"[2] showing how the virgin may avoid
certain plagues and poisons of modesty.

PETRONIUS ARBITER

XXV*

Fulgentius mythologiarum II 6 p. 45 Helm de Pro-
metheo: Quamvis Nicagoras . . . quod vulturi iecur
praebeat, livoris quasi pingat imaginem.   Unde et
Petronius Arbiter ait

> " qui voltur iecur intimum pererrat
> pectusque eruit [1] intimasque fibras,
> non est quem lepidi [2] vocant poetae,
> sed cordis ⟨mala⟩ [3] livor atque luxus "

[1] pectusque eruit *suggests Nisbet:* et querit pectus.
[2] lepidi *Pithoeus:* trepidi *or* timidi *Scaliger:* tepidi.
[3] *Added in cod. Mediolan. ann.* 1498.

FRAGMENTS

XXV

Fulgentius Mythologiae II, 6 (p. 45, on Prometheus):
Although Nicagoras . . . represents his yielding his
liver to a vulture, as an allegorical picture of envy.
Hence too Petronius Arbiter says: "*The vulture which
explores our inmost liver, and drags out our heart and inmost nerves, is not the bird of whom our dainty poets talk,
but those evils of the soul, envy and wantonness.*"

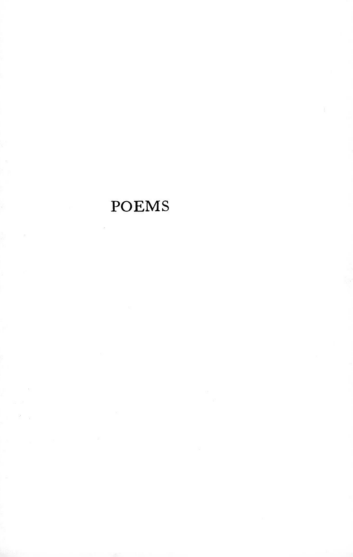

POEMS

INTRODUCTION

Of the poems which follow, 1–17 are found in the
cod. Vossianus L. Q. 86, a MS. of the ninth century.
They follow a number of epigrams attributed to
Seneca and are not attributed by the MS. to Petronius. But 3, 1 and 13, 6–9 are quoted by Fulgentius
(*Myth.* I, 1, p. 17, 3; III, 9, p. 74) as from Petronius,
while the general resemblance to Petronius led
Scaliger to attribute the remainder to the same
author. Though absolute proof of the correctness
of this attribution is lacking, most readers will feel
little doubt that Scaliger was right.

18–29[1] were contained in a MS. once at Beauvais
and now lost. The contents of this codex Bellovacensis were published by Claude Binet in 1579. The
last two poems were not, according to Binet, given to
Petronius by the MS., and I have included them with
some hesitation. But as Binet saw, the resemblance
to the style and tone of Petronius is considerable,
and they are therefore given here. The six poems
which followed in this MS. are given by Baehrens
(*P.L.M.* iv. 103–8) to Petronius. But they have no
particular affinity with the work of Petronius, and as
they have inserted among them in Binet's book a

---

[1] No. 20 is also contained in cod. Paris. 10318 (Salma-
sianus), cod. Vossianus *L.Q.* 86, cod. Paris. 8071 (Thua-
neus).

number of poems which are admittedly by Luxorius
(see Baehrens, *op. cit.* App. Crit. on *P.L.M.* iv. 104),
they are not included here.

The remaining two poems are found in cod. Vossianus L.F. 111, a MS. of the ninth century. They
are attributed to Petronius by the MS., and follow two
poems found in the MSS. of the novel (c. 14 and c.
83). Their general resemblance would betray their
authorship.   H. E. Butler.

For a discussion of these MSS. see Baehrens,
Poetae Latini Minores, vol. iv, pp. 11, 13, and 19.
Also p. 36 ff. Cf. also Adalaide Wegner, " The
Sources of the Petronius Poems in the *Catalecta* of
Scaliger," in *T.A.P.A.*, LXIV, 1933, p. lxvii. It is
likely that certain Petronian and other poems were
in the presumed archetype of the *Satyricon*-tradition
(see p. xix).

SIGLA [1]

Cod. Voss. L.Q. 86 = *V.*
Cod. Bellovacensis (now lost) = *W.*
Cod. Voss. L.F. 111 = *E.*

[1] At the head of any poem, B. followed by a number indicates the position in Buecheler's Petronius.

POEMATA

74 *Poet. Lat. Min.* iv, ed. Baehrens.   B. XXXV.
1 Inveniet quod quisque velit: non omnibus unum est
    quod placet: hic spinas colligit, ille rosas.

75 *P.L.M.*   B. XXXVIII.
2 Iam nunc algentes autumnus fecerat [1] umbras
  atque hiemem tepidis spectabat Phoebus habenis,
  iam platanus iactare comas, iam coeperat uvas
  adnumerare suas defecto palmite vitis:
  ante oculos stabat quidquid promiserat annus.

76 *P.L.M. Fragment* XXVII *Müller.*   B. XXXVII.
3 Primus in orbe deos fecit timor, ardua caelo
  fulmina cum caderent discussaque moenia flammis
  atque ictus flagraret Athos; mox Phoebus ab ortu [2]
  lustrata devectus [3] humo, Lunaeque senectus
  et reparatus honos; hinc signa effusa per orbem
  et permutatis disiunctus mensibus annus.
  Profecit [4] vitium iamque [5] error iussit inanis
  agricolas primos Cereri dare messis honores,

---

[1] algentes . . . fecerat *Baehrens*: ardentes . . . fregerat *V*.
[2] ab ortu *Butler*: ad ortus *V*.
[3] devectus *Heinsius*: deiectus *V*.
[4] proficit *anon.*: proiecit *V*.

408

POEMS

Every man shall find his own desire; there is no
one thing which pleases all: one man gathers thorns
and another roses.

Now autumn had brought its chill shades, and
Phoebus[1] was looking winterwards with cooler reins.
Now the plane-tree had begun to shed down her
leaves, now the young shoots had withered on the
vine, and she had begun to number her grapes: the
whole promise of the year was standing before our
eyes.

It was fear first created gods in the world, when the
lightning fell from high heaven, and the ramparts of
the world were rent with flame, and Athos was smitten
and blazed. Next 'twas Phoebus sank to earth, after
he had traversed earth from his rising; the Moon
grew old and once more renewed her glory; next the
starry signs were spread through the firmament, and
the year divided into changing seasons. The folly
spread, and soon vain superstition bade the labourer
yield to Ceres the harvest's chosen firstfruits, and

---

[1] The sun.

[5] iamque *Buecheler*: atque *V*.

palmitibus plenis Bacchum vincire, Palemque
pastorum gaudere manu; † nutat obrutus † [1] omnis
Neptunus demersus aqua; Pallasque [2] tabernas
vindicat; et voti reus et qui vendidit orbem,[3]
iam sibi quisque deos avido certamine fingit.

77 *P.L.M.*   B. XXXIII.

4 Nolo ego semper idem capiti suffundere costum
    nec noto [4] stomachum conciliare mero.
Taurus amat gramen mutata carpere valle
    et fera mutatis sustinet ora cibis.
Ipsa dies ideo nos grato perluit haustu,
    quod permutatis hora recurrit equis.

78 *P.L.M.*   B. XXXIV.

5 Uxor legitimus [5] debet quasi census amari.
    Nec censum vellem semper amare meum.

79 *P.L.M.*

6 Linque tuas sedes alienaque litora quaere,
o [6] iuvenis: maior rerum tibi nascitur ordo.
Ne succumbe malis: te noverit ultimus Hister,
te Boreas gelidus securaque regna Canopi,
quique renascentem Phoebum cernuntque cadentem:
maior in externas fit qui [7] descendit harenas.

---

[1] nutat obrutus *corrupt*. *Perhaps* nautae obvenit omni Neptunus *or* nautae obvenit omnis Neptuno.
[2] Pallasque *Scaliger*: pallidasque *V*.
[3] orbem *perhaps corrupt*: orbam *Barth*: urbem *Pithoeus'* 2nd ed.
[4] noto *Palmier*: toto *V*.
[5] legis onus *Baehrens*: inus *V*.

garland Bacchus with the fruitful vine-branch, and made Pales [1] to rejoice in the shepherd's work; Neptune . . . wholly plunged beneath the waters of the world, Pallas watches over shops, and the man who wins his prayer or has betrayed the world for gold now strives greedily to create gods of his own.

I would not always steep my head with the same sweet nard, nor strive to win my stomach with familar wine. The bull loves to enjoy his pasture by a change of valley, and the wild beast maintains his zest by change of food. Even to be bathed in the light of day is pleasant only because the night-hour races with altered steeds.

A wife should be loved like a fortune got legally. But I would not wish to love even my fortune for ever.

Leave thine home, O youth, and seek out alien shores: a larger range of life is ordained for thee. Yield not to misfortune; the far-off Danube shall know thee, the cold North-wind, and the untroubled kingdoms of Canopus,[2] and the men who gaze on the new birth of Phoebus or upon his setting: he that disembarks on distant sands, becomes thereby the greater man.

[1] Goddess of cattle and of shepherds.
[2] Egypt, from Canopus on the coast by the western mouth of the Nile.

---

[6] o *added by Scaliger, omitted by* V.
[7] fit qui *Baehrens*: itacui V.

80 *P.L.M.* B. XXXVI.

7 Nam nihil est, quod non mortalibus afferat usum;
    rebus in adversis quae iacuere iuvant.
Sic rate demersa fulvum deponderat aurum,
    remorum levitas naufraga membra vehit.
Cum sonuere tubae, iugulo stat divite ferrum
    barbaricum: tenuis praebia pannus habet.[1]

81 *P.L.M.* B. L

8 Parvula securo tegitur mihi culmine sedes
uvaque plena mero fecunda pendet ab ulmo.
Dant rami cerasos, dant mala rubentia silvae,
Palladiumque nemus pingui se vertice frangit.
Iam qua diductos potat levis area fontes,
Corycium mihi surgit olus malvaeque supinae
et non sollicitos missura papavera somnos.
Praeterea sive alitibus contexere fraudem
seu magis imbelles libuit circumdare cervos
aut tereti lino pavidum subducere piscem,
hos tantum novere dolos mea sordida rura.
I nunc et vitae fugientis tempora vende
divitibus cenis. Me si manet exitus idem,
his precor inveniat consumptaque tempora poscat.

82 *P.L.M.* B. XXXII.

9 Non satis est quod nos mergit [2] furiosa iuventus
    transversosque rapit fama sepulta probris?

---

[1] barbaricum *Baehrens*, tenuis *Butler*, praebia *Baehrens*:
barbara contempnit praelia *V, retaining which* hebes *for*
habet *Scaliger*, raraque contemptus proelia pannus habet
Reiske.

[2] mergis *V corr. Buecheler*.

For there is naught that may not serve the need of mortal men, and in adversity despised things help us. So when a ship sinks, yellow gold weighs down its possessor, while a flimsy oar bears up the shipwrecked body. When the trumpets sound, the savage's knife stands drawn at the rich man's throat; the poor man's rags wear the amulet of safety.

My little house is covered by a roof that fears no harm, and the grape swollen with wine hangs from the fruitful elm. The boughs yield cherries, the orchards ruddy apples, and the trees sacred to Pallas [1] break under the wealth of their branches. And now where the light soil drinks from the runnels of the spring, Corycian kale [2] springs up for me and creeping mallows, and the poppy with promise of untroubled sleep. Moreover, if my pleasure is to lay snares for birds, or if I choose rather to entrap the timid deer, or draw out the quivering fish on slender line, so much deceit is all that is known to my humble fields. Go, then, and barter the hours of flying life for rich banquets. My prayer is that since at the last the same end waits for me, it may find me here, here call me to account for the time that I have spent.

Is it not enough that mad youth engulfs us, and our good name is sunk in reproach and sweeps us

[1] The olive, which she (= Athena) gave to Athens. By this gift, which the Gods considered more useful than the horse given by Poseidon, she became the presiding deity of the city.
[2] Corycus (Khorgos) in Asia Minor was famous for saffron, but the poet here alludes to the happy simple old man of Corycus described by Virgil, *Georgics*, IV, 116–138.

413

En [1] etiam famuli cognataque faece caterva [2]
  inter conrasas [3] luxuriantur opes.
Vilis servus habet regni bona, cellaque capti
  deridet Vestam Romuleamque casam.
Idcirco virtus medio iacet obruta caeno,
  nequitiae classes candida vela ferunt.

83 *P.L.M.*   B. XXXIX.

10 Sic et membra solent auras includere ventris,[4]
quae penitus mersae cum rursus abire laborant,
verberibus rimantur iter; nec desinit ante
frigidus, adstrictis [5] qui regnat in ossibus, horror
quam tepidus laxo manavit corpore sudor.

84 *P.L.M.*

11 O litus vita mihi dulcius, o mare! felix
  cui licet ad terras ire subinde meas!
O formosa dies! hoc quondam rure solebam
  Naiadas [6] alterna sollicitare manu!
Hic fontis lacus est, illic sinus egerit algas:
  haec statio est tacitis fida [7] cupidinibus.
Pervixi; neque enim fortuna malignior unquam
  eripiet nobis quod prior hora [8] dedit.

85 *P.L.M.*   B. XL.

12 Haec ait et tremulo deduxit vertice canos
consecuitque genas; oculis nec defuit imber,

---

[1] en L. *Müller*: an *V.*
[2] caterva *Baehrens*: sepulti *V.*
[3] inter conrasas *Baehrens*: intesta merassas *V.*
[4] ventis *V, corr. Riese.*
[5] et frigidus strictis *V., corr. Reiske.*

astray? Behold! even bondmen and the rabble that is kindred to the mire wanton amid our gathered hoards! The low slave enjoys the treasure of a kingdom, and the captive's room shames Vesta [1] and the cottage of Romulus. So goodness lies obscured in the deep mud, and the fleet of the unrighteous carries snowy sails.

So, too, the body will shut in the belly's wind, which, when it labours to come forth again from its deep dungeon, prises forth a way by sharp blows: and there is no end to the cold shiver which rules the cramped frame, till a warm sweat bedews and loosens the body.

O sea-shore and sea more sweet to me than life! Happy am I who may come at once to the lands I love. O beauteous day! In this country long ago I used to rouse the Naiads [2] with my hands' alternate stroke. Here is the fountain's pool, there a bay washes up its sea-weeds: here is a sure haven for unspoken pleasures. I have had life in full; for never can harder fortune take away what was given us in time overpast.

With these words he tore the white hair from his trembling head, and rent his cheeks; his eyes filled

---

[1] Goddess of the hearth.   [2] Nymphs of fresh waters.

---

[6] Naiadas *Lindenbrog*: Iliadas *V*   alterna . . . manu
B: amatas . . . manus *V*.
[7] fida *Pithoeus*: victa *V*.
[8] prior hora *Scaliger*: priora *V*.

sed qualis rapitur per vallis improbus amnis,
cum gelidae periere nives et languidus auster
non patitur glaciem resoluta vivere terra,
gurgite sic pleno facies manavit et alto
insonuit gemitu turbato murmure pectus.

86 *P.L.M. Fragment XXVIII Müller.* B. XXVIII.
13 Nam citius flammas mortales ore [1] tenebunt
quam secreta tegant. Quicquid dimittis in aula,
effluit et subitis rumoribus oppida pulsat.
Nec satis est vulgasse fidem. Cumulatius exit
proditionis opus famamque onerare laborat.
Sic commissa verens avidus reserare [2] minister
fodit humum regisque latentes prodidit aures.
Concepit nam terra sonos calamique loquentes
incinuere Midam,[3] qualem narraverat [4] index.

87 *P.L.M.*
14 Illic alternis depugnat pontus et aer,
    hic rivo tenui pervia ridet humus.
Illic demersas [5] complorat navita puppes,
    hic pastor miti perluit amne pecus.
Illic immanes mors obdita [6] solvit hiatus,
    hic gaudet curva falce recisa Ceres.

[1] ore *Scaliger*: ora.
[2] verens reserare *Fulgentius*: ferens . . . seruare *V.*
[3] incinuere *Saumaise*: invenere *Fulgentius*: inuenerem *V.*
Midam *Fulgentius*: idem *V.*
[4] conceperat *Fulgentius*: conspexerat *Muncker.*
[5] demersas *Baehrens*: divisas *V.*
[6] obdita *Baehrens*: oblita *V.*

with tears, and as the impetuous river sweeps down the valleys when the cold snow has perished, and the gentle south-wind will not suffer the ice to live on the thawed out earth, so was his face wet with a full stream, and his heart rang with the troubled murmur of deep groaning.

For sooner will men hold fire in their mouths than keep a secret. Whatever you let escape you in your hall flows forth and beats at city walls in sudden rumours. Nor is it enough to have made promised secrecy common knowledge. The work of betrayal issues forth with increase, and strives to add weight to the report. So was it that the greedy slave, who feared to unlock his knowledge, dug in the ground and betrayed the secret of the king's hidden ears. For the earth brought forth sounds, and the whispering reeds sang how Midas was even such an one as the tell-tale had revealed.[1]

There sea and sky struggle and buffet each other, here the tiny stream runs through smooth and smiling country. There the sailor laments for his sunken ship, here the shepherd dips his flock in the gentle river. There death confronts and chokes the vast gape of greed, here the corn delights to be cut down by the curved sickle. There, with water everywhere,

---

[1] Midas, a traditional King of Phrygia, judged Pan to be a better musician than Apollo, who turned Midas's ears into a donkey's. Midas hid them under his hat, but the servant who cut his hair discovered and spread abroad Midas' secret.

Illic inter aquas urit sitis arida fauces,
  hic data periuro [1] basia multa viro.
Naviget et fluctus lasset mendicus Vlixes,
  in terris vivet candida Penelope.

88 *P.L.M.* B. LII.

15 Qui nolit properare [2] mori nec cogere fata
   mollia praecipiti rumpere fila manu,
hactenus irarum mare noverit.   Ecce refuso
   gurgite securos obluit unda pedes.
Ecce inter virides iactatur mytilus algas
   et rauco trahitur lubrica concha sinu.
Ecce recurrentes qua versat fluctus arenas,
   discolor attrita calculus exit humo.
Haec quisquis calcare potest, in litore tuto
   ludat et hoc solum iudicet esse mare.

89 *P.L.M.* B. XXXI.

16 Non est forma satis nec quae vult bella videri [3]
   debet vulgari more placere sibi.
Dicta, sales, lusus, sermonis gratia, risus
   vincunt naturae candidioris opus.
Condit enim formam quicquid consumitur artis,
   et nisi velle subest, [4] gratia nuda perit.

90 *P.L.M. Fragment XXVI Müller.*   B. XXVI.

17 Sic contra rerum naturae munera notae [5]
   corvus maturis frugibus ova refert.

---

  [1] data *Wernsdorf*: da *V*: periuro *probably corrupt*: *perhaps*
quaeque suo *Butler*.
  [2] nolit *Oudendorp*: moluit *V*: properare *Tollius*: propare *V*.

dry thirst burns the throat, here kisses are given in plenty to faithless man. Let Ulysses go sail and weary the waters in beggar's rags: the chaste Penelope [1] will be living on land.

The man that would not haste to die, nor force the Fates to snap the tender threads with impetuous hand, should know only this much of the sea's anger. Lo! where the tide flows back, and the wave bathes his feet without peril! Lo! where the mussel is thrown up among the green sea-weed, and hoarsely the whorl of the slippery shell is rolled along! Lo! where the wave turns the sands to rush back in the eddy, there pebbles of many a hue appear on the wave-worn floor. Let the man who may have these things under his feet, play safely on the shore, and count this alone to be the sea.

Outward beauty is not enough, and the woman who would appear fair must not be content with any common manner. Words, wit, play, sweet talk, and laughter surpass the work of too simple nature. For all expense of art seasons beauty, and bare loveliness is wasted all in vain, if it have not the will to please.

So, contrary to the known operations of nature, the raven lays her eggs when the crops are ripe. So the

---

[1] Odysseus' (Ulysses') faithful wife.

[3] *The first couplet is to be found in Fulgentius, Myth, I, 12, p. 44.*
[4] velle subest *probably corrupt*: sal suberit *Baehrens.*
[5] nota *Binet.*

Sic format lingua fetum cum protulit ursa
    et piscis nullo iunctus amore parit.
Sic Phoebea chelys partu [1] resoluta favente [2]
    Lucina [3] tepidis naribus ova fovet.
Sic sine concubitu textis apis excita ceris
    fervet et audaci milite castra replet.
Non uno contenta valet natura tenore,
    sed permutatas gaudet habere vices.

91 *P.L.M.*   B. XLI.

18 Indica purpureo genuit me litore tellus,
    candidus accenso qua redit orbe dies.
Hic ego divinos inter generatus honores
    mutavi Latio barbara verba sono.
Iam dimitte tuos, Paean o Delphice, cycnos:
    dignior haec vox est, quae tua templa colat.

92 *P.L.M.*   B. XLII.

19 Naufragus eiecta nudus rate quaerit eodem
    percussum telo, cui sua fata fleat.[4]
Grandine qui segetes et totum perdidit annum,
    in simili deflet tristia fata sinu.
Funera conciliant miseros, orbique parentes
    coniungunt gemitus et facit hora pares.
Nos quoque confusis feriemus sidera verbis;
    fama est coniunctas [5] fortius ire preces.

---

[1] partu *Müller (2nd edition).   In his 1st edition he suggests*
nixu: nutu *Butler*: vinclo *Binet*: victo *W.*
[2] favente *Müller (2nd edition)*: parentis.
[3] Lucina *Müller (2nd edition)*: Lucinae.
[4] fleat *Jacobs*: legat *W.*
[5] fama est coniunctas *Butler*: et fama est constans *W.*

she-bear shapes her cubs with her tongue when she has brought them forth, and the fish is ignorant of love's embrace, yet brings forth young. So the tortoise, sacred to Phoebus, heats with her warm nostrils the eggs delivered in laying by the favour of Lucina.[1] So the bee, begotten without wedlock from the woven cells, throbs with life and fills her camp with bold soldiery. The strength of nature lies not in holding on one even way, but she loves to change the fashion of her laws.

My [2] birthplace was India's glowing shore, where the day returns in brilliance with fiery orb. Here I was born amid the worship of the gods, and exchanged my barbaric speech for the Latin tongue. O healer [3] of Delphi, now dismiss thy swans; here is a voice more worthy to dwell within thy temple.

The sailor, naked from the shipwreck, seeks out a comrade stricken by the same blow to whom he may bewail his fate. The farmer who has lost his crops and the whole year's fruits in the hail, weeps his sad lot on a bosom wounded like his own. Death draws the unhappy together; bereaved parents utter their groans with one voice, and the moment makes them equal. We too will strike the stars with words in unison; the saying is that prayers travel more valiantly when united.

---

[1] Goddess of " bringing to light "; of childbirth. The point here is obscure.

[2] A parrot is speaking.

[3] Apollo.

93 *P.L.M.*   B. XLIII.

20 Aurea mala mihi, dulcis mea Martia, mittis,
    mittis et hirsutae munera castaneae.
Omnia grata putem, sed si magis ipsa venire
    ornares donum, pulcra puella, tuum.
Tu licet apportes stringentia mala palatum,
    tristia mandenti est melleus ore sapor.
At si dissimulas, multum mihi cara, venire,
    oscula cum pomis mitte; vorabo libens.

94 *P.L.M.*   B. XLIV.

21 Si Phoebi soror es, mando tibi, Delia, causam,
    scilicet ut fratri quae peto verba feras:
" Marmore Sicanio struxi tibi, Delphice, templum
    et levibus calamis candida verba dedi.
Nunc si nos audis atque es divinus, Apollo,
    dic mihi, qui nummos non habet, unde petat."

95 *P.L.M.*   B. XLV.

22 Omnia quae miseras possunt finire querellas,
    in promptu voluit candidus esse deus.
Vile holus et duris haerentia mora rubetis
    pungentis [1] stomachi composuere famem.
Flumine vicino stultus sitit, et riget [2] euro
    cum calidus tepido consonat igne focus.[3]
Lex armata sedet circum fera limina nuptae:
    nil metuit licito fusa puella toro.
Quod satiare potest dives natura ministrat;
    quod docet infrenis [4] gloria fine caret.

[1] pungentis *Dousa*: pugnantis *W.*
[2] et riget *Binet*: effugit *W.*
[3] focus *Buecheler*: rogus *W.*
[4] infrenis *Binet*: inferius *W.*

You send me golden apples, my sweet Martia, and you send me the fruit of the shaggy chestnut. Believe me, I would love them all; but should you choose rather to come in person, lovely girl, you would beautify your gift. Come, if you will, and lay sour apples to my tongue, the sharp flavour will be like honey as I bite. But if you feign you will not come, dearest, send kisses with the fruit; then gladly will I devour them.

If you are sister to Phoebus, Delia,[1] I entrust my petition to you, that you may carry to your brother the words of my prayer. "God of Delphi, I have built for you a temple of Sicilian marble, and have given you fair words of song from a slender pipe of reed. Now if you hear us, Apollo, and are indeed divine, tell me where a man who has no money is to seek it."

Honest Heaven ordained that all things which can end our wretched complaints should be ready to hand. Common green herbs and the berries that grow on rough brambles allay the gnawing hunger of the belly. A fool is he who goes thirsty with a river close by, and shivers in the east wind while a blazing fire roars on the warm hearth. The law sits armed by the threshold of a wanton bride; the girl who lies on a lawful bed knows no fear. The wealth of nature gives us enough for our fill: that which unbridled vanity teaches us to pursue has no end to it.

[1] "Of Delos," that is Artemis = Diana, sister of Phoebus, here Apollo. Both were imagined as born on the island Delos.

96 *P.L.M.*   B. XLVI.

23 Militis in galea nidum fecere columbae:
    apparet Marti quam sit amica Venus.

97 *P.L.M.*   B. XLVII.

24 Iudaeus licet et porcinum numen adoret
    et caeli summas advocet auriculas,
ni tamen et ferro succiderit inguinis oram
    et nisi nodatum solverit arte caput,
exemptus populo sacra [1] migrabit ab urbe
    et non ieiuna sabbata lege premet.[2]

98 *P.L.M.*

25 Una est nobilitas argumentumque coloris
    ingenui timidas non habuisse manus.

99 *P.L.M.*   B. XLVIII.

26 Lecto compositus vix prima silentia noctis
    carpebam et somno lumina victa dabam,
cum me saevus Amor prensat [3] sursumque capillis
    excitat et lacerum pervigilare iubet.
" Tu famulus meus," inquit, " ames cum mille puellas,
    solus, io, solus, dure, iacere potes ? "
Exsilio et pedibus nudis tunicaque soluta
    omne iter ingredior,[4] nullum iter expedio.
Nunc propero, nunc ire piget, rursumque redire
    paenitet, et pudor est stare via media.
Ecce tacent voces hominum strepitusque viarum
    et volucrum cantus fidaque turba canum;

[1] sacra *Beuhrens*: graia *W.*
[2] premet *W.*, *perhaps corrupt*: tremet *Buecheler.*
[3] prensat *Oudendorp*: prensum *W.*
[4] ingredior *Riese*: impedio *W.*

POEMS

Doves have made a nest in the soldier's helmet:
see how Venus loveth Mars.[1]

The Jew may worship his pig-god [2] and clamour in
the ears of high heaven, but unless he also cuts back
with a knife the region of his groin, and unless he
unlooses by art the knotted head, he shall go forth
from the holy city cast forth from the people, and
transgress the sabbath by breaking the law of fasting.

This is the one nobility and proof of honourable
strain, that a man's hands have shown no fear.

At rest in bed, I had scarce begun to enjoy the first
silence of night, and to give up my conquered eyes
to sleep, when fierce Love took hold of me and drew
me up by the hair, and tore me, bidding me watch
till day. " Ah, my slave," he said, " thou lover of
a thousand girls, canst thou lie alone here, alone oh
hard of heart? " I leaped up, and with bare feet and
disordered raiment started on every path and found
a way by none. Now I run, now to move is weariness:
I repent of turning back, and am ashamed to halt in
the midst of the road. Lo, the voices of men and the
roar of the streets, the singing of birds and the faithful company of watchdogs are all silent. I alone of

---

[1] An allusion to the story, told by Homer, of the love-
affair of the deities Aphrodite (who was wife of Hephaetus) =
Venus and Ares = Mars.

[2] It was believed that the abstention of the Jews from
eating pork must be due to a belief that the pig has some
sacred character.

solus ego ex cunctis paveo somnumque torumque,
  et sequor imperium, magne Cupido, tuum.

100 *P.L.M.* B. XLIX.
27 Sit nox illa diu nobis dilecta, Nealce,
  quae te prima meo pectore composuit:
sit torus et lecti genius secretaque lampas,[1]
  quis tenera in nostrum veneris arbitrium.
Ergo age duremus, quamvis adoleverit aetas,
  utamurque annis quos mora parva teret.
Fas et iura sinunt veteres extendere amores;
  fac cito quod coeptum est, non cito desinere.

101 *P.L.M.*
28 Foeda est in coitu et brevis voluptas
et taedet Veneris statim peractae.
Non ergo ut pecudes libidinosae
caeci protinus irruamus illuc
(nam languescit amor peritque flamma);
sed sic sic sine fine feriati
et tecum iaceamus osculantes.
Hic nullus labor est ruborque nullus:
hoc iuvit, iuvat et diu iuvabit;
hoc non deficit incipitque semper.

102 *P.L.M.*
29 Accusare et amare tempore uno
ipsi vix fuit Herculi ferendum.

120 *P.L.M. Fragment* XXIX *Müller.* B. XXIX.
30 Fallunt nos oculi vagique sensus
oppressa ratione mentiuntur.

all men dread both sleep and my bed, and follow thy command, great Lord of desire.

Long may that night be dear to us, Nealce, that first laid you to rest upon my heart. Dear be the bed and the genius of the couch, and the secret lamp that all saw you come gently to do our pleasure. Come, then, let us endure though we have grown older, and employ the years which a brief delay will blot out. It is lawful and right to prolong an old love: grant that what we began in haste may not hastily be ended.

The pleasure of the act of love is gross and brief, and love once consummated brings loathing after it. Let us then not rush blindly thither straightway like lustful beasts, for love sickens and the flame dies down; but even so, even so, let us keep eternal holiday, and lie with thy lips to mine. No toil is here and no shame: in this, delight has been, and is, and long shall be; in this there is no diminution, but a beginning everlastingly.

To love and accuse at one time were a labour Hercules himself could scarce have borne.

Our eyes deceive us, and our wandering senses weigh down our reason and tell us falsehoods. For

---

[1] lampas *Buecheler*: longa *W.*

Nam turris prope quae quadrata surgit,
detritis procul angulis rotatur.
Hyblaeum refugit satur liquorem
et naris casiam frequenter odit.
Hoc illo magis aut minus placere
non posset nisi lite destinata
pugnarent dubio tenore sensus.

121 *P.L.M. Fragment XXX Müller.* B. XXX.
31 Somnia quae mentes ludunt volitantibus umbris,
non delubra deum nec ab aethere numina mittunt,
sed sibi quisque facit. Nam cum prostrata sopore
urget membra quies et mens sine pondere ludit,
quidquid luce fuit tenebris agit. Oppida bello
qui quatit et flammis miserandas eruit urbes,
tela videt versasque acies et funera regum
atque exundantes profuso sanguine campos.
Qui causas orare solent, legesque forumque
et pavidi cernunt inclusum chorte [1] tribunal.
Condit avarus opes defossumque invenit aurum.
Venator saltus canibus quatit. Eripit undis
aut premit eversam periturus navita puppem.
Scribit amatori meretrix, dat adultera munus:
et canis in somnis leporis vestigia lustrat.
In noctis spatium miserorum vulnera durant.

[1] chorte *Mommsen*: corde *E.*

the tower which stands almost four-square has its
corners blunted at a distance and becomes rounded.
The full stomach turns from the honey of Hybla,[1] and
the nose often hates the scent of cinnamon.   One
thing could not please us more or less than another,
unless the senses strove in set conflict with wavering
balance.

It is not the shrines of the gods, nor the powers of
the air, that send the dreams which mock the mind
with flitting shadows; each man makes dreams for
himself.   For when rest lies about the limbs subdued
by sleep, and the mind plays with no weight upon
it, it pursues in the darkness whatever was its task
by daylight.   The man who makes towns tremble in
war, and overwhelms unhappy cities in flame, sees
arms, and routed hosts, and the deaths of kings, and
plains streaming with outpoured blood.   They whose
life is to plead cases have statutes and the courts
before their eyes, and look with terror upon the
judgment-seat surrounded by a throng.   The miser
hides his gains and discovers buried treasure.   The
hunter beats the woods with his dogs.   The sailor
snatches his shipwrecked bark from the waves, or
grips it in death-agony.   The prostitute writes to her
lover, the adulteress yields herself: and the dog
follows the tracks of the hare as he sleeps.   The
wounds of the unhappy endure into the night-season.

[1] A flowery hill with town on the southern slopes of Mt.
Aetna in Sicily.

Note on Chapter **34** of Petronius *super scorpionem . . . super aquarium* (see pp. 62–63).

For this part of Petronius the L tradition is available as well as H, but L does not give 1 and 2.

1. scorpionem *H only*: *Scheffer proposed* scorpionem ⟨scorpionem⟩, *Gaselee* scorpionem ⟨locustam⟩ *approved by K. Rose* † *and J. Sullivan*: scorpionem σκορπίον *Studer*.

Then:

2. pisciculum marinum *H only*: *Jacobs deletes* marinum *as a gloss, Gaselee both words*; *Rose and Sullivan approve Gaselee. For both 1 and 2 there are other proposals.*

Then:

3. (*both H and L being available*) super sagitarium oclopetam *H*: super sagittarium odopetam *l*: super sagittarium odepotam *cd. Vat. Lat. 11428 and cd. Lambeth. There were other readings and there are various conjectures.* oculatam *Rose and Sullivan which I accept; it was probably the fish now known as the oblade*: oclopectam *Heraeus*.

Then:

4. super capri cornua *l* (capricornum *Scaliger in margin of l*): super capricornum in quo cornua erant *H, of which* in . . . erant *look like a gloss on something*: *Gaselee suggested* super capricornum ⟨capri cornua⟩. *Rose and Sullivan propose* super capricornum ⟨caprum et cornutam⟩ ' *a boar-fish and a horned fish* '.

Then:

5. locustam marinam *L*: locusta marina *H*. *Here* marina(m) *might be a late gloss on* locustam *because for the Romans of Petronius's times the crustacean would not need the epithet. Gaselee suggested deleting both words here and Rose and Sullivan approve Gaselee.*

SENECAE
ΑΠΟΚΟΛΟΚΥΝΤΩΣΙΣ DIVI CLAUDII

INTRODUCTION

As a literary form, this piece belongs to the class called *Satura Menippea*, satiric medley in prose and verse. It is ascribed to Seneca by ancient tradition; it is impossible to prove that it is his, and impossible to prove that it is not. Of the MSS. (see below) which provide us with a Latin text, the best—Codex Sangallensis 569—gives the title as Ἀποθέωσις *Annaei Senecae per saturam*. Of the two next best codices, Codex Valentianensis 411 gives the title as *Ludus de Morte Claudi*, Codex Londiniensis suppl. 11983 as *Ludus de Morte Claudii Caesaris*. Of the later inferior manuscripts, many have *Ludus* simply, or *Ludus de morte Claudii*; several give the title as *de obitu Claudii*, several as *Satira de Claudio*. There are some other titles. But one MS., Codex. Vat. lat. 4498 (of the end of the fifteenth century) has *Senecae* Ἀποκολοκύντωσις which depends on the statement made by Dio Cassius of the third century A.D. (Epit. LX, 35) that Seneca composed what he called ἀποκολοκύντωσις as if for ἀποθανάτισις. The real title might be Ἀποκολοκένωσις or Ἀπορραφανίδωσις with gross undertones. But we can accept the title Ἀποκολοκύντωσις and treat *Ludus de Morte Claudii* as the alternative.

H. MacL. Currie, " The purpose of the Apocolocyntosis," in *L'Antiquité Classique*, XXXI, 1962, 91–97, feels reasonably that the work is indeed by

INTRODUCTION

Seneca who wished to get his own back, so to speak, on Claudius. E. Cizek, " L'Apocoloquintose," in *Acta Antiqua Philippopolitana*, 295, 303, suggests that the literary efforts of Agrippina are attacked. Note also that it is she who was priestess in charge of the cult of the deified Claudius. Cf. Currie in *Rhein. Mus.*, CV, 1962, 187–188. C. F. Russo, *Divi Claudii* ᾽Αποκολοκύντωσις edition 4,1964, pp. 7 ff., especially 8, 14–19, 131–132.

THE TEXT OF SENECA'S APOCOLOCYNTOSIS

From one lost archetype which we may call [a] is derived all the material of the *Apocolocyntosis* given by extant manuscripts. Of the three best manuscripts, Codex Sangallensis 569 (of which the leaves containing this work appear to belong to the tenth century) called S seems to be a copy of the archetype; whereas Codex Valentianensis (Valenciennensis) 411, formerly 393, of the late ninth or early tenth century, and called V, and Codex Londiniensis suppl. 11983, of the end of the eleventh or the beginning of the twelfth century, and called L, appear both to be derived from a lost intermediary (which we may call [β]) between them and [a]. The relevant material in all other extant MSS. is not only derived from one or other of the best three, S, V, L, but is also inferior. Cf. Russo's 4th edition, pp. 19–33, 133–34.

BIBLIOGRAPHY

Since the Editio princeps *Lucii Annaei Senecae in morte Claudii Caesaris Ludus*, C. Sylvanus Germanicus,

Rome, 1513, there have been published many other editions and also many translations. The following are specially noteworthy:

Divi Claudii Ἀποκολοκύντωσις. *Eine Satire des Annaeus Seneca*, F. Buecheler, *Symbola Philologorum Bonnensium.* Leipzig, 1864–1867, pp. 31–89.

Petronii Saturae et liber Priapeorum, ed. F. Buecheler, Berlin, 1862, was supplemented (as recorded above in the bibliography for Petronius) in its 2nd edition, 1871, by material from other writers, including the " *Satura* " of Seneca (*Senecae* Ἀποκολοκύντωσις *Divi Claudii*); edition 3, 1882; edition 4, 1904; edition 5, revision by W. Heraeus, 1912; and edition 6, revision and augmentation by W. Heraeus, 1922.

L. Annaei Senecae Divi Claudii Apotheosis . . ., ed. O. Rossbach, Bonn, 1926.

Sénèque, L'Apocoloquintose du divin Claude, R. W. Waltz, text and French translation and notes. Budé, Paris, 1934.

Seneca, Apokolokyntosis (Inzuccatura) del divo Claudio. Text and Italian translation A. Rostagni, Turin, 1944.

Senecae Apokolokyntosis. Text, critical notes, and Italian translation. A Ronconi, Milan, 1947.

L. Annaei Senecae Divi Claudii Ἀποκολοκύντωσις, C. F. Russo. Biblioteca di Studi Superiori III. Filologia Latina. " La Nuova Italia " Editrice, Florence (1st edition 1948), 4th edition 1964. Introduction, text, and critical notes,

Italian translation, and copious commentary, bibliography, and (1964) appendix. This work contains much information.

A new text by P. Eden is expected.

The English translation (with accompanying largely plain text) by W. H. D. Rouse in the Loeb Classical Library (with Heseltine's Petronius) was published in 1913; and R. Graves appended a translation to his *Claudius the God*, London 1935. *The Satire of Seneca on the Apotheosis of Claudius* . . . A. P. Ball, New York, 1902, has introduction, notes, and translation.[1] Cf. also *Senecas Apocolocyntosis* . . . Einführung, Analyse, und Untersuchungen. O. Weinreich, Berlin, 1923 (with German translation).

Bibliographical surveys: M. Coffey, Seneca, Apocol. 1922–1958, in *Lustrum* VI, 1961, 239–271. This survey succeeds that of Münscher in *Bursians Jahresbericht* 1922, 148–154. C. F. Russo's 4th edition (see above), pp. 34–40, 134.

---

[1] In W. B. Sedgwick, *The Cena Trimalchionis of Petronius together with Seneca's Apocolocyntosis*, Oxford 1925, edition 2 (a revision) 1950 (see p. xxx) the notes on the Seneca are limited in scope. Sedgwick advises for various allusions to read also some account of Claudius. That advice indeed is good.

SENECAE

APOCOLOCYNTOSIS DIVI CLAUDII

1   Quid actum sit in caelo ante diem III idus Octobris
anno novo, initio saeculi felicissimi, volo memoriae
tradere.   Nihil nec offensae nec gratiae dabitur.
Haec ita vera si quis quaesiverit unde sciam, primum, si noluero, non respondebo.   Quis coacturus
est?   Ego scio me liberum factum, ex quo suum
diem obiit ille, qui [1] verum proverbium fecerat, aut
regem aut fatuum nasci oportere.   Si libuerit respondere, dicam quod mihi in buccam venerit.   Quis
unquam ab historico iuratores exegit?   Tamen si
necesse fuerit auctorem producere, quaerito ab eo qui
Drusillam euntem in caelum vidit: idem Claudium
vidisse se dicet iter facientem " non passibus aequis."
Velit nolit, necesse est illi omnia videre, quae in caelo
aguntur: Appiae viae curator est, qua scis et divum
Augustum et Tiberium Caesarem ad deos isse.

---

[1] *After* qui *Mommsen suggested adding* bis.

---

[1] On 13 October A.D. 54 Claudius died, and the Senate
decided that for his merits he should be added to the gods with
the title " *divus Claudius*," as we might say " the (late
lamented) deified Claudius."   He had reigned since A.D. 41.

[2] Not Livia Drusilla, wife of Augustus Emperor (30 B.C.–

SENECA

THE PUMPKINIFICATION OF CLAUDIUS

I wish to place on record the proceedings in heaven October 13 last,[1] of the new year which begins this auspicious age. It shall be done without malice or favour. Ask if you like the source of my knowledge of these events which are so true; to begin with, I am not bound to please you with my answer. Who will compel me? I know the same day made me free, which was the last day for him who made the proverb true—One must be born either a Pharaoh or a fool. If I choose to answer, I will say whatever trips off my tongue. Who has ever made the historian produce witness to swear for him? But if an authority must be produced, ask of the man who saw Drusilla [2] translated to heaven: the same man will aver he saw Claudius on the road, dot and carry one.[3] Will he nill he, all that happens in heaven he needs must see. He is custodian of the Appian Way; by that route, you know, both Tiberius and Augustus went up to the

Virg.
Aen. ii,
724

A.D. 14) but Julia Drusilla, sister of Emperor Gaius Caligula (A.D. 37–41). When she died in A.D. 38, Gaius insisted on her deification. In support of its accomplishment one Livius Geminius swore that he saw her going up to heaven.

[3] The Latin means walking " with his steps not equal " as did little Iulus when in escaping from Troy he followed his father (Virgil, *Aeneid*, II, 724). But here the sting lies in the fact that Claudius was lame in his right foot.

Hunc si interrogaveris, soli narrabit: coram pluribus
nunquam verbum faciet. Nam ex quo in senatu
iuravit se Drusillam vidisse caelum ascendentem et
illi pro tam bono nuntio nemo credidit, quod viderit,[1]
verbis conceptis affirmavit se non indicaturum, etiam
si in medio foro hominem occisum vidisset. Ab hoc
ego quae tum audivi, certa clara affero, ita illum
salvum et felicem habeam.

2   Iam Phoebus breviore via contraxerat arcum [2]
     lucis, et obscuri crescebant tempora somni,
     iamque suum victrix augebat Cynthia regnum,
     et deformis hiemps gratos carpebat [3] honores
     divitis autumni, iussoque [4] senescere Baccho
     carpebat raras serus vindemitor uvas.

Puto magis intellegi, si dixero: mensis erat October,
dies III idus Octobris. Horam non possum certam
tibi dicere, facilius inter philosophos quam inter horo-
logia conveniet, tamen inter sextam et septimam
erat. Nimis rustice! Adquiescunt [5] omnes poetae,
non contenti ortus et occasus describere ut etiam

---

[1] *Gruter advised deleting* quod *or* quid viderit *because inferior
tradition omits the words. Gertz reads* quod viderat.

[2] arcum *P. Eden:* orbem *Fromond:* ortum.

[3] *Because of* carpebat *again two lines below several alterations
have been suggested.* turpabat *Haupt.*

[4] visoque *inferior tradition.*

[5] *This sentence has been variously altered by scholars.*

---

[1] Emperor Augustus, not Emperor Tiberius, was added to
the gods as *divus.* Since both died in Campania, Augustus at
Nola, Tiberius at Misenum, both were brought to Rome by the
Appian Way.

gods.[1] Question him, he will tell you the tale when you are alone; before company he is dumb. You see he swore in the Senate that he beheld Drusilla mounting heavenwards, and all he got for his good news was that everybody gave him the lie: since when he solemnly swears he will never bear witness again to what he has seen, not even if he had seen a man murdered in open market. What he told me I report plain and clear, as I hope for his health and happiness.

Now had the sun with shorter course drawn in his
    orbit's light,
And by equivalent degrees grew the dark hours of
    night:
Victorious Cynthia [2] now held sway over a wider
    space,
Grim winter drove rich autumn out, and now usurped
    his place;
And now the fiat had gone forth that Bacchus [3] should
    grow old,
The few last clusters of the vine were gathered ere
    the cold:

I shall make myself better understood, if I say the month was October, the day was the thirteenth. What hour it was I cannot certainly tell you; philosophers will agree more often than clocks; but it was between midday and one after noon. Very yokellike! All the poets are in agreement, not content to describe sunrise and sunset, and now they even dis-

[2] The moon. See note on Petronius 122.
[3] The grapes on the vines.

medium diem inquietent, tu sic transibis horam tam bonam?

Iam medium curru Phoebus diviserat orbem
et propior nocti fessas quatiebat habenas
obliquo flexam deducens tramite lucem:

3 Claudius animam agere coepit nec invenire exitum poterat. Tum Mercurius, qui semper ingenio eius delectatus esset, unam e tribus Parcis seducit et ait: " Quid, femina crudelissima, hominem miserum torqueri pateris? Nec unquam tam diu cruciatus cesset?[1] Annus sexagesimus [et][2] quartus est, ex quo cum anima luctatur. Quid huic et rei publicae invides? Patere mathematicos aliquando verum dicere, qui illum, ex quo princeps factus est, omnibus annis, omnibus mensibus efferunt. Et tamen non est mirum si errant et horam eius nemo novit; nemo enim unquam illum natum putavit. Fac quod faciendum est:

' Dede neci, melior vacua sine regnet in aula.' "

Sed Clotho " ego mehercules " inquit " pusillum temporis adicere illi volebam, dum hos pauculos, qui

[1] cesset *Iunius*: exiet *Haase*: quiescet *Birt*: esset.
[2] *Omitted by inferior tradition, rightly?*

---

[1] God of cleverness and eloquence, so this remark is ironical. Equated with the Greek god Hermes, he was guide or escort of dead souls on the way to Hades.
[2] Clotho (Κλωθώ) " Spinner," Lachesis (Λάχεσις) " she who allots " and Atropos ("Ατροπος) " Inflexible," " Not to be turned."

turb the midday siesta. Will *you* thus neglect so
good an hour?

Now the sun's chariot had gone by the middle of his
 way;
Half wearily he shook the reins nearer to night than
 day,
And led the light along the slope that down before
 him lay.

Claudius began to breathe his last, and could not
make an end of the matter. Then Mercury,[1] who had
always been much pleased with his wit, drew aside
one of the three Fates,[2] and said: "Cruel beldame,
why do you let the poor wretch be tormented? After
all this torture cannot he have a rest? Four and sixty
years it is now since he began to pant for breath.
What grudge is this you bear against him and the
whole empire? Do let the astrologers tell the truth
for once; since he became emperor, they have never
let a year pass, never a month, without laying him
out for his burial. Yet it is no wonder if they are
wrong, and no one knows his hour. Nobody ever believed he was really quite born.[3] Do what has to be
done: 'Kill him, and let a better man rule in his
empty court.'"[4]

Clotho[5] replied: "Upon my word, I did wish to
give him another hour or two, until he should make
Roman citizens of the half dozen who are still out-

Virg.
Georg.
iv, 90

---

[3] A proverb for a nobody, as Petron. 58 *qui te natum non
putat.*
[4] Virgil's advice to beekeepers—if a hive has two kings
(queens), kill the worse one.
[5] See above on the Fates.

supersunt, civitate donaret (constituerat enim omnes
Graecos, Gallos, Hispanos, Britannos togatos videre),
sed quoniam placet aliquos peregrinos in semen relin-
qui et tu ita iubes fieri, fiat." Aperit tum capsulam
et tres fusos profert: unus erat Augurini, alter
Babae,[1] tertius Claudii. " Hos " inquit " tres uno
anno exiguis intervallis temporum divisos mori iubebo, nec [2] illum incomitatum dimittam. Non oportet
enim eum, qui modo se tot milia hominum sequentia
videbat, tot praecedentia, tot circumfusa, subito
solum destitui. Contentus erit his interim con-
victoribus."

4   Haec ait et turpi convolvens stamina fuso
    abrupit stolidae regalia tempora vitae.
    At Lachesis redimita comas, ornata capillos,
    Pieria crinem lauro frontemque coronans,
    candida de niveo subtemina vellere sumit
    felici moderanda manu, quae ducta colorem
    assumpsere novum. Mirantur pensa sorores :

        [1] Babae *Muret*: badae.
        [2] ne *Wehle*.

---

[1] As Roman citizens, even though they were dwellers in the
Roman provinces—that is, lands governed by Rome, but
outside Italy. Even before Claudius's reign, natives of Gallia
Narbonensis (Southern France), of Spain, and of Africa had
been admitted even to the Roman Senate and magistracies.
He extended the privilege to the whole Gallic tribe the Aedui.
In A.D. 43 began the conquest of Britain.

[2] Augurinus (if indeed a real person is meant) is otherwise
unknown. Baba: Seneca, *Epist.*, XV, 9. The name seems

siders. (He made up his mind, you know, to see the whole world in the toga,[1] Greeks, Gauls, Spaniards, Britons, and all.) But since it is your pleasure to leave a few foreigners for seed, and since you command me, so be it." Then she opened her box and brought out three spindles. One was for Augurinus, one for Baba,[2] one for Claudius. "These three," she says, "I will cause to die within one year and at no great distance apart, and I will not dismiss *him* unattended. Think of all the thousands of men he was lately wont to see following after him, thousands going before, thousands all crowding about him; and it would never do to leave him alone on a sudden. These boon companions will satisfy him for the nonce."

This said, she twists the thread around his ugly
    spindle once,
Snaps off the last bit of the life of that Imperial
    dunce.
But Lachesis,[3] her hair adorned, her tresses neatly
    bound,
Pierian laurel on her locks, her brows with garlands
    crowned,
Plucks me from out the snowy wool new threads as
    white as snow,
Which handled with a happy touch change colour as
    they go,
Not common wool, but golden work; the Sisters won-
    dering gaze,

to indicate the type of utter fools. The alphabetic order of the names (A, B, C) may have satiric significance.
[3] See above on the Fates.

443

mutatur vilis pretioso lana metallo,
aurea formoso descendunt saecula filo.
Nec modus est illis, felicia vellera ducunt
et gaudent implere manus, sunt dulcia pensa.
Sponte sua festinat opus nulloque labore
mollia contorto descendunt stamina fuso.
Vincunt Tithoni, vincunt et Nestoris annos.
Phoebus adest cantuque iuvat gaudetque futuris,
et laetus nunc plectra movet, nunc pensa
ministrat.
Detinet intentas cantus [1] fallitque laborem.
Dumque nimis citharam fraternaque carmina
laudant,
plus solito nevere manus, humanaque fata
laudatum transcendit opus. " Ne demite, Parcae "
Phoebus ait " vincat mortalis tempora vitae
ille, mihi similis vultu similisque decore
nec cantu nec voce minor. Felicia lassis
saecula praestabit legumque silentia rumpet.
Qualis discutiens fugientia Lucifer astra

---

[1] cantus *Gertz*: cantu. *Perhaps* carmen.

---

[1] In legend, Tithonus, son of Laomedon King of Troy
(see above) reached a great old age; Nestor, wise and eloquent
Greek hero in the Trojan war, lived for three generations.
[2] Nero (Emperor 54–68) was fond of playing music, and
singing in public.

444

As age by age the pretty thread runs down the golden
days.
World without end they spin away, the happy fleeces
pull;
What joy they take to fill their hands with that de-
lightful wool!
With speed the task performs itself: no toil the
spinners know:
Down drops the soft and silken thread as round the
spindles go;
Fewer than these are Tithon's years, not Nestor's
life [1] so long.
Phoebus is present: glad he is to sing a merry song;
Now helps the work, now full of joy upon the harp
doth play;
The Sisters listen to the song that charms their toil
away.
They praise their brother's harp and song, and still
the spindles run,
Till with good work beyond our span the busy hands
have spun.
Then Phoebus says, " O sister Fates! I pray take
none away,
But suffer this one life to be longer than mortal
day.
Like me in face and lovely grace, my peer in voice and
song,[2]
He'll bid the laws at length speak out that have been
dumb so long,
Will give unto the weary world years prosperous and
bright.
Like as the daystar from on high scatters the stars of
night,

aut qualis surgit redeuntibus Hesperus astris,
qualis cum primum tenebris Aurora solutis
induxit rubicunda diem, Sol aspicit orbem
lucidus, et primos a carcere concitat axes:
talis Caesar adest, talem iam Roma Neronem
aspiciet.   Flagrat nitidus fulgore remisso
vultus, et adfuso cervix formosa capillo."

Haec Apollo.   At Lachesis, quae et ipsa homini for-
mosissimo faveret, fecit illud [1] plena manu, et Neroni
multos annos de suo donat.   Claudium autem iubent
omnes

> χαίροντας, εὐφημοῦντας ἐκπέμπειν δόμων.

Et ille quidem animam ebulliit, et ex eo desiit vivere
videri.   Exspiravit autem dum comoedos audit, ut
scias me non sine causa illos timere.   Ultima vox eius
haec inter homines audita est, cum maiorem sonitum
emisisset illa parte, qua facilius loquebatur: " vae
me, puto, concacavi me."   Quod an fecerit, nescio:
omnia certe concacavit.

---

[1] illico *Gertz*: filum *Wehle*.

---

[1] The planet Venus as the evening star.
[2] A fragment from the lost *Cresphontes* of Euripides (Nauck,
452), which Seneca perverts from its meaning that one need
not grieve over the dead because they have left life's miseries.

As, when the stars return again, clear Hesper [1] brings
   his light,
Or as the ruddy dawn drives out the dark, and brings
   the day,
As the bright sun looks on the world, and speeds along
   its way
His rising car from morning's gates: so Caesar doth
   arise,
So Nero shows his face to Rome before the people's
   eyes;
His bright and shining countenance illumines all the
   air,
While down upon his graceful neck fall rippling waves
   of hair."

Thus Apollo. But Lachesis, quite as ready to cast a
favourable eye on a handsome man, spins away by
the handful, and bestows years and years upon Nero
out of her own pocket. As for Claudius, they tell
everybody

> to speed him from the house
> With cries of joy and solemn litany.[2]

At once he bubbled up the ghost, and there was an
end to that shadow of a life. He was listening to a
troupe of comedians when he died, so you see I have
reason to fear those gentry. The last words he was
heard to speak in this world were these. When he
had made a great noise with that end of him which
talked easiest, he cried out, " Oh dear, oh dear! I
think I have made a mess of myself." Whether he
did or no, I cannot say, but certain it is he always did
make a mess of everything.

5 Quae in terris postea sint acta, supervacuum est
referre. Scitis enim optime, nec periculum est ne
excidant memoriae quae gaudium publicum impres-
serit: nemo felicitatis suae obliviscitur. In caelo
quae acta sint, audite: fides penes auctorem erit.
Nuntiatur Iovi venisse quendam bonae staturae, bene
canum; nescio quid illum minari, assidue enim caput
movere; pedem dextrum trahere. Quaesisse se,
cuius nationis esset: respondisse nescio [1] quid per-
turbato sono et voce confusa; non intellegere se
linguam eius, nec Graecum esse nec Romanum nec
ullius gentis notae. Tum Iuppiter Herculem, qui
totum orbem terrarum pererraverat et nosse videbatur omnes nationes, iubet ire et [2] explorare, quorum hominum esset. Tum Hercules primo aspectu
sane perturbatus est, ut qui etiam non omnia [3]
monstra timuerit.[4] Ut vidit novi generis faciem,
insolitum incessum, vocem nullius terrestris animalis
sed qualis esse marinis beluis solet, raucam et impli-
catam, putavit sibi tertium decimum laborem venisse.
Diligentius intuenti visus est quasi homo. Accessit
itaque et quod facillimum fuit Graeculo, ait:

τίς πόθεν εἶς ἀνδρῶν, πόθι τοι πόλις ἠδὲ τοκῆες:

---

[1] se nescio *S*: illum nescio *inferior MSS.*: sibi nescio
Gertz.

[2] *V and L omit* et.

[3] non enormia *Gertz.*

448

What happened next on earth it is mere waste of time to tell, for you know it all well enough, and there is no fear of your ever forgetting the impression which that public rejoicing made on your memory. No one forgets his own happiness. What happened in heaven you shall hear: for proof please apply to my informant. Word comes to Jupiter that a stranger had arrived, a man well set up, pretty grey; he seemed to be threatening something, for he wagged his head ceaselessly; he dragged the right foot. They asked him what nation he was of; he answered something in a confused mumbling voice: his language they did not understand. He was no Greek and no Roman, nor of any known race. On this Jupiter bids Hercules go and find out what country he comes from; you see Hercules had travelled over the whole world, and might be expected to know all the nations in it. Then Hercules, the first glimpse he got, was really much taken aback, being aware that he hadn't yet even by then seen all the monsters in the world that he might be afraid of; when he saw this new kind of object, with its extraordinary gait, and the voice of no terrestrial beast, but such as you might hear in the leviathans of the deep, hoarse and inarticulate, he thought his thirteenth labour had come upon him. When he looked closer, the thing seemed to be a kind of man. Up he goes, then, and says what your Greek finds readiest to his tongue:

" Who art thou, and what thy people ? Who thy Od. i, 170 parents, where thy home ? "

---

⁴ *One inferior MS. has* domuerit.

Claudius gaudet esse illic philologos homines, sperat
futurum aliquem historiis suis locum.   Itaque et ipse
Homerico versu Caesarem se esse significans ait:

Ἰλιόθεν με φέρων ἄνεμος Κικόνεσσι πέλασσεν.

Erat autem sequens versus verior, aeque Homericus:

ἔνθα δ᾽ ἐγὼ πόλιν ἔπραθον, ὤλεσα δ᾽ αὐτούς.

6 Et imposuerat Herculi minime vafro,[1] nisi fuisset illic
Febris, quae fano suo relicto sola cum illo venerat:
ceteros omnes deos Romae reliquerat.   " Iste " inquit " mera mendacia narrat.   Ego tibi dico, quae
cum illo tot annis vixi: Luguduni natus est, Marci [2]
municipem vides.   Quod tibi narro, ad sextum decimum lapidem natus est a Vienna, Gallus germanus.
Itaque quod Gallum facere oportebat, Romam cepit.
Hunc ego tibi recipio Luguduni natum, ubi Licinus [3]
multis annis regnavit.   Tu autem, qui plura loca

---

[1] *For* Herculi *Iunius reads* homini.   *For* vafro (*so Iunius
again*) *MSS. have* fabro.
[2] Munatii *Rhenanus*: Planci *J. F. Gronov.*
[3] Licinus *inferior tradition*: Licinius *S, V, L.*

---

[1] Claudius had written a history of the Etruscans in 20 books,
in Greek; a history of the Carthaginians in 8 books, in Greek;
a history of the Roman state since 31 B.C. in 41 books; his own
biography, in 8 books; and a defence of Cicero.   He was fond
of speaking Greek and of quoting Homer : Suetonius, *Claudius*,
41, 42.
[2] Ilion: Troy.   The Cicones dwelt in Thrace near the river
Hebrus (Maritza).
[3] Febris had several shrines in Rome.
[4] *Marcus* would be Marcus Antonius under whose auspices

Claudius was delighted to find literary men up there, and began to hope there might be some corner for his own historical works.[1] So he caps him with another Homeric verse, explaining that he was Caesar:

" Breezes wafted me from Ilion unto the Ciconian land." [2] Od. ix, 39

But the next verse was more true, and no less Homeric:

" Thither come, I sacked a city, slew the people every one."

He would have taken in poor simple Hercules, but that Our Lady of Malaria was there, who left her temple [3] and came alone with him: all the other gods he had left at Rome. Quoth she, " The fellow's tale is nothing but lies. I have lived with him all these years, and I tell you, he was born at Lyon. You behold a fellow-burgess of Marcus.[4] As I say, he was born at the sixteenth milestone from Vienne,[5] a native Gaul. So of course he took Rome, as a good Gaul ought to do.[6] I pledge you my word that in Lyon he was born, where Licinus [7] was king so many years. But you that have trudged over more roads than any

Lugudunum became a Roman " colony " or city-settlement. If we read *Munatii* with Rhenanus, or *Planci* with Gronov, this is L. Munatius Plancus, founder in 43 B.C. of the colony.

[5] The old capital of the Allobroges and a Roman colony, in Gallia Narbonensis.

[6] Gauls irrupted into Italy and captured Rome in 390 or 387 B.C.

[7] A Gaul and a freedman made by Augustus procurator of Gallia Lugudunensis where he governed badly.

calcasti quam ullus mulio perpetuarius, Lugudu-
nenses scire debes, et [1] multa milia inter Xanthum et
Rhodanum interesse." Excandescit hoc loco Claudius et quanto potest murmure irascitur. Quid
diceret,[2] nemo intellegebat, ille autem Febrim duci
iubebat, illo gestu solutae manus et ad hoc unum
satis firmae, quo decollare homines solebat, iusserat
7 illi collum praecidi. Putares omnes illius esse libertos: adeo ilum nemo curabat.

Tum Hercules "audi me" inquit "tu desine
fatuari. Venisti huc, ubi mures ferrum rodunt.
Citius mihi verum, ne tibi alogias excutiam." Et quo
terribilior esset, tragicus fit et ait:

"exprome [3] propere, sede [4] qua genitus cluas,
hoc ne peremptus stipite ad terram accidas:
haec clava reges saepe mactavit feros.
Quid nunc profatu vocis incerto sonas?
Quae patria, quae gens mobile eduxit caput?
Edissere. Equidem regna tergemini petens [5]
longinqua regis, unde ab Hesperio mari

---

[1] *Buecheler omits* et *with some MSS. and would delete* lugu-
dunenses.
[2] quid dicebat *V*: quod dicebat *L*: quidquid dicebat *Rossbach.*
[3] exprime *S, V.*
[4] sede *Rhenanus*: sed.
[5] potens *S, V.*

---

[1] There were two rivers Xanthus in Asia Minor—one in the
Troad (the one mentioned here?) and one in Lycia.

muleteer that is always on hire, you must have come across the people of Lyon, and you must know that it is a far cry from the Xanthus [1] to the Rhône." At this point Claudius flared up, and expressed his wrath with as big a growl as he could manage. What he said nobody understood; as a matter of fact, he was ordering my lady of Fever to be taken away, and making that sign with his trembling hand (which was always steady enough for that, if for nothing else) by which he used to decapitate men. He had ordered her head to be chopped off. For all the notice the others took of him, they might have been his own freedmen.

Then Hercules said, " You just listen to me, and stop playing the fool. You have come to the place where the mice nibble iron.[2] Out with the truth, and look sharp, or I'll knock your quips and quiddities out of you." Then to make himself all the more awful, he strikes an attitude and proceeds in his most tragic vein:

" Declare with speed what spot you claim by birth,
　　Or with this club fall stricken to the earth!
　　This club hath ofttimes slaughtered haughty
　　　　kings!
　　Why mumble unintelligible things?
　　What land, what tribe produced that shaking
　　　　head?
　　Declare it! On my journey when I sped
　　Far to the Kingdom of the triple King,
　　And from the Main Hesperian did bring

___

[2] A proverb, apparently implying fairyland, the land of Nowhere. Cf. Herondas (Herodes), III, 76.

Inachiam ad urbem nobile advexi pecus,
vidi duobus imminens fluviis iugum,
quod Phoebus ortu semper obverso videt,
ubi Rhodanus ingens amne praerapido fluit,
Ararque dubitans, quo suos cursus agat,
tacitus quietis adluit ripas vadis.
Estne illa tellus spiritus altrix tui? "

Haec satis animose et fortiter, nihilo minus mentis
suae non est et timet μωροῦ πληγήν. Claudius ut
vidit virum valentem, oblitus nugarum intellexit
neminem Romae sibi parem fuisse, illic non habere se
idem gratiae: gallum in suo sterquilino plurimum
posse. Itaque quantum intellegi potuit, haec visus est
dicere: " Ego te, fortissime deorum Hercule, speravi
mihi adfuturum apud alios, et si qui a me notorem
petisset, te fui nominaturus, qui me optime nosti.
Nam si memoria repetis, ego eram qui tibi[1] ante
templum tuum ius dicebam totis diebus mense Iulio
et Augusto. Tu scis, quantum illic miseriarum tulerim,[2] cum causidicos audirem diem et noctem, in
quos[3] si incidisses, valde fortis licet tibi videaris,

---

[1] Tiburi *Buecheler* (*cf. Suetonius, Aug.,* 72.).
[2] tulerim *Haase*: tetulerim *Heraeus*: ⟨te⟩cum tulerim
Rossbach: ⟨e⟩go tulerim *Mariotti*: contulerim *S, V, L*: per-
tulerim *inferior tradition*.
[3] quod *S, V, L*.

---

[1] For his tenth Labour, Heracles brought back to Argos, of
which in legend Inachus was the first King, the oxen of three-
bodied Geryon in Spain by the Hesperian—the Western—
ocean, that is the Atlantic.
[2] Colline de Fourvière on which Lyon was built.

The goodly cattle to the Argive town,[1]
There I beheld a mountain [2] looking down
Upon two rivers: [3] this the Sun espies
Right opposite each day he doth arise.
Hence, mighty Rhône, thy rapid torrents flow,
And Arar, much in doubt which way to go,
Ripples along the banks with shallow roll.
Say, is this land the nurse that bred thy soul? ''

These lines he delivered with much spirit and a bold
front. All the same, he was not quite master of his
wits, and had some fear of a blow from the fool.[4]
Claudius, seeing a mighty man before him, saw things
looked serious and understood that here he had not
quite the same pre-eminence as at Rome, where no
one was his equal: the Gallic cock [5] was worth most
on his own dunghill. So this is what he was thought
to say, as far as could be made out: '' I did hope,
Hercules, bravest of all the gods, that you would take
my part with the rest, and if I should need a voucher,
I meant to name you who know me so well. Do but
call it to mind, how it was I used to sit [6] in judgment before your temple whole days together during
July and August. You know what miseries I endured there, in hearing the lawyers plead day and
night. If you had fallen among these, you may
think yourself very brave, but you would have found

---

[3] The Rhône and the Saône (Arar).
[4] A parody of the phrase, $\theta\epsilon o\hat{v}$ $\pi\lambda\eta\gamma\acute{\eta}$, god's blow, or as in
Apostolius viii, 89, c, $\theta\epsilon o\hat{v}$ $\delta\grave{\epsilon}$ $\pi\lambda\eta\gamma\grave{\eta}\nu$ $o\mathring{v}\chi$ $\mathring{v}\pi\epsilon\rho\pi\eta\delta\hat{q}$ $\beta\rho o\tau\acute{o}s$
(from Menander): no mortal can escape god's blow.
[5] *Gallus* means both Gaul and cock; the proverb plays on
his birthland.
[6] Claudius was fond of presiding over judicial cases.

maluisses cloacas Augeae purgare: multo plus ego
8 stercoris exhausi. Sed quoniam volo " . . . " Non
mirum quod in curiam impetum fecisti: nihil tibi
clausi est. Modo dic nobis, qualem deum istum fieri
velis. Ἐπικούρειος θεός non potest esse: οὔτε αὐτὸς
πρᾶγμα ἔχει τι οὔτε ἄλλοις παρέχει. Stoicus? Quomodo potest ' rotundus ' esse, ut ait Varro, ' sine
capite, sine praeputio '? Est aliquid in illo Stoici dei,
iam video: nec cor nec caput habet. Si mehercules
a Saturno petisset hoc beneficium, cuius mensem
toto anno celebravit, Saturnalicius [1] princeps, non
tulisset illud, nedum [2] ab Iove, quem [3] quantum quidem in illo fuit, damnavit incesti. Silanum enim
generum suum occidit propterea quod [4] sororem
suam, festivissimam omnium puellarum, quam omnes
Venerem vocarent, maluit Iunonem vocare.
' Quare ' inquis [5] ' quaero enim, sororem suam? '

---

[1] Saturnalitius *Iunius*: -cius *Buecheler*: saturnalia eius.
Lips deletes.
[2] illud, nedum *J. F. Gronov*: illum deum.
[3] ab Iove quem *J. F. Gronov*: ab iove qui *V, L*: ab iovem
qui *S*.
[4] propterea quod *or* propter quod *Buecheler*: propter quid
Lips (*rightly?*): *there are other suggestions*.
[5] inquis *Lips*: iniit *Rutgers*: inquit.

---

[1] Compare Diogenes Laertius x, 139: τὸ μακάριον καὶ
ἄφθαρτον οὔτε αὐτὸ πρᾶγμά τι ἔχει οὔτε ἄλλῳ παρέχει: " The
Blessed and Incorruptible neither itself has trouble nor causes
trouble to another."
[2] Author of *Saturae Menippeae* (now lost), which no doubt
burlesqued the Stoic " perfect man," *totus teres atque rotundus*.
In Stoic pantheism also this universe is round and identified
with god.

it worse than the sewers of Augeas: I drained out more filth than you did. But since I want . . .''

(Some pages have fallen out, in which Hercules must have been persuaded. The gods are now discussing what Hercules tells them and one of them is speaking to Hercules.)

" No wonder you have forced your way into the Senate House: no bars or bolts can hold against you. Only do say what species of god you want the fellow to be made. An Epicurean god he cannot be: for they have no troubles and cause none.[1] A Stoic, then? How can he be globular, as Varro[2] says, without a head or any foreskin? There *is* in him something of the Stoic god, as I can see now: he has neither heart nor head. Upon my word, if he had asked this boon from Saturn, he would not have got it, though he kept up Saturn's feast all the year round, a truly Saturnalian prince. A likely thing he will get it from Jove, whom he condemned for incest as far as in him lay:[3] for he killed his son-in-law Silanus, because Silanus had a sister, a most charming girl, called Venus by all the world, and he preferred to call her Juno. Why, you say, I want to know why, his own sister? Read your books, stupid: you may

---

[3] Because Juno was sister and consort of Jupiter (compare Petronius, 127, pp. 334–5). Claudius did *not* " kill " Lucius Iunius Silanus Torquatus, who was *not* Claudius's son-in-law but only betrothed to Claudius's daughter (by his notorious wife Valeria Messalina) Octavia. Silanus in A.D. 48 was accused (at the instigation of Agrippina who wanted Octavia to marry hers on Nero) of incest with his sister Iunia Calvina, and took his own life on the day in A.D. 49 when Claudius married Agrippina, daughter of Claudius's brother and therefore Claudius's niece. Cf. Chapter 10.

Stulte, stude: Athenis dimidium licet, Alexandriae
totum. ' Quia Romae' inquis[1] ' mures molas
lingunt.' Hic nobis curva corrigit? quid in cubiculo
suo faciat, nescio,[2] et iam ' caeli scrutatur plagas '?
Deus fieri vult: parum est quod templum in Britannia
habet, quod hunc barbari colunt et ut deum orant
μωροῦ εὐιλάτου τυχεῖν? "[3]

9   Tandem[4] Iovi venit in mentem, privatis intra
curiam morantibus ⟨senatoribus non licere⟩[5] sententiam dicere nec disputare. " Ego " inquit " p. c.
interrogare vobis permiseram, vos mera mapalia
fecistis. Volo ut servetis disciplinam curiae. Hic
qualiscunque est, quid de nobis existimabit? "[6]
Illo dimisso primus interrogatur sententiam Ianus
pater. Is designatus erat in kal. Iulias postmeri-

---

[1] inquis S, V: inquit inferior tradition.

[2] For corrigit Sonntag proposes corriget: for faciet Maehly
proposes fiat, Wachsmuth faciant. For nescio Buecheler and
others read nescit.

[3] So Lindemann and Schneidewin. But Waltz with some
reason reads τύχην: ΤΟΥΤΥΧΗΙΝ cod. S, for which ΤΟΥΧΗΙΝ
cod. V.

[4] tantum S, V.

[5] senatoribus non licere added by Buecheler.   nec sententiam
dicere licere Waltz.   There are other suggestions.

[6] existimabit inferior tradition: existimavit.

---

[1] Marriage with a half-sister was allowed in ancient Athens;
the ruling Greek Ptolemies of Egypt married their sisters.

[2] A proverb of unknown meaning. It may imply ironically
that people like choice things in Rome as everywhere else; or
that a mill where mice find only meal to lick is in good condition.

[3] Perhaps alluding to the mock marriage(to avert a prophecy)
of Gaius Silius to Claudius's wife Messalina (see p. 476 below)
or to the marriage of Claudius to Agrippina.

go halfway at Athens, the whole way at Alexandria.[1]
Because the mice lick meal [2] at Rome, you say. Does
this creature mend our crooked ways? What goes on
in his own closet I know not; [3] and now " he searches
the regions of the sky," [4] wants to be a god. Is it
not enough that he has a temple in Britain,[5] that
savages worship him and pray to him as a god, so that
they may find a fool [6] to have mercy upon them? "

At last it came into Jove's head, that while
strangers were staying around in the House it was not
lawful for senators to speak or debate. " My
lords," [7] said he, " I gave you leave to ask questions,
and you have made a regular farmyard [8] of the place.
Be so good as to keep the rules of the House. What
will this person think of us, whoever he is? " So
Claudius was led out, and the first to be asked his
opinion was Father Janus: he had been made consul
elect for the afternoon of the next first of July,[9] being

---

[4] This comes from the lost play *Iphigenia* of Ennius, the
full line as quoted being *Quod est ante pedes nemo spectat,
caeli scrutantur plagas.* " No-one looks at what is before his
feet—they all search the regions of the sky." (*Remains of Old
Latin*, I, pp. 310–311, L.C.L.)

[5] At Camulodunum, Colchester, after it had been made a
Roman colony (city-settlement) in A.D. 48–49.

[6] Again μωροῦ for θεοῦ as in Chapter 6.

[7] *p.c.* stands for *patres conscripti* " fathers " (that is senators)
" on the register."

[8] Cf. Petronius, Chapter 58 at the end.

[9] Probably there are two allusions here: (i) shortening of a
consul's term of office, so as to give more candidates a chance
of the honour; (ii) the normal Roman habit of doing public
work in the morning and relaxing in the afternoon, so that a
consul for an afternoon would be idle. In the Roman senate
the consuls designate gave their opinion first. So here among
the gods.

dianus consul, homo quantumvis vafer,[1] qui semper
videt ἅμα πρόσσω καὶ ὀπίσσω. Is multa diserte,
quod[2] in foro vivebat,[3] dixit, quae notarius persequi
non potuit, et ideo non refero, ne aliis verbis ponam,
quae ab illo dicta sunt. Multa dixit de magnitudine
deorum: non debere hunc vulgo dari honorem.
" Olim " inquit " magna res erat deum fieri: iam
Fabam[4] mimum fecistis.[5] Itaque ne videar in
personam, non in rem dicere sententiam, censeo ne
quis post hunc diem deus fiat ex his, qui ἀρούρης
καρπὸν ἔδουσιν, aut ex his, quos alit ζείδωρος ἄρουρα.
Qui contra hoc senatus consultum deus factus,[6]
dictus pictusve[7] erit, eum dedi Larvis et proximo
munere inter novos auctoratos ferulis vapulare
placet." Proximus interrogatur sententiam Diespiter[8] Vicae Potae filius, et ipse designatus consul,
nummulariolus: hoc quaestu se sustinebat, vendere
civitatulas solebat. Ad hunc belle accessit Hercules
et auriculam illi tetigit. Censet itaque in haec verba:

[1] quantumvis vafer *Rhenanus*: quantum visus fert *Ronconi*:
quantum via sua fert.
[2] quom *Haupt*: cum *Waltz*.
[3] vivebat *Buecheler*: vivat.
[4] fabam *Buecheler*: Φάσμα *W. S. Watt*: famam *or* fama.
[5] fecistis *Scheffer*: fecisti.
[6] fictus *Heinsius*.
[7] fictusve *Iunius, deleting* dictus.
[8] Dis pater *or* Dispiter *Schenkl*.

---

[1] Homer, *Iliad*, III, 109, where the expression is applied to
the long life of Priam, King of Troy; here the allusion is to
Janus's double face.
[2] Where there was a temple of Ianus containing a statue of
Ianus Bifrons, " Janus with two foreheads."
[3] *Fabam* is Buecheler's reading for *famam* (*cod. S*), or *fama*

as shrewd a man as you could find on a summer's day :
for he could see, as they say, before and behind.[1]   He
made an eloquent harangue, because his life was
passed in the forum,[2] but a harangue too fast for the
notary to take down.   That is why I give no full
report of it, for I don't want to change the words he
used.   He said a great deal of the majesty of the gods,
and how the honour ought not to be given away to
every Tom, Dick, or Harry.   " Once," said he, " it
was a great thing to become a god; now you have
made it a ' *Bean* ' farce.[3]   Therefore, that you may
not think I am speaking against one person instead of
the general custom, I propose that from this day forward the godhead be given to none of those who eat
the fruits of the earth, or whom mother earth doth
nourish.[4]   Whosoever is made, said, or portrayed to
be god, so as to contravene this decree of The Senate,
I vote he be delivered over to the bogies, and at the
next public show be flogged [5] with a rod among the
new gladiators."   The next to be asked was
Diespiter, son of Vica Pota,[6] he also being consul
elect, and a moneylender; by this trade he made a
living, used to sell rights of citizenship in a small way.
Hercules trips me up to him daintily, and tweaks
him by the ear.[7]   So he uttered his opinion in these

(*cod. V*), because in Cicero, *Letters to Atticus*, I, 16, 13, we have
fabam mimum as something absurd for ἀποθέωσιν. Cf. P. Eden,
in *Hermes* 92, 1964, 251 ff.; W. S. Watt in *Hermes* 83, 1955,
496 ff.

[4] Mankind is meant.   Homer, *Iliad*, VI, 142; VIII, 486;
Odyssey, VII, 332; Hesiod, *Works and Days*, 237.

[5] Part of the training.

[6] Diespiter, father of light, son of " Victress and Possessor."

[7] To signify that he was to be his witness.

" Cum divus Claudius et divum Augustum sanguine contingat nec minus divam Augustam aviam suam, quam ipse deam esse iussit, longeque omnes mortales sapientia antecellat, sitque e re publica esse aliquem qui cum Romulo possit ' ferventia rapa vorare,' censeo uti divus Claudius ex hac die deus sit, ita uti ante eum qui [1] optimo iure factus sit, eamque rem ad metamorphosis Ovidi adiciendam." Variae erant sententiae, et videbatur Claudius sententiam [2] vincere. Hercules enim, qui videret ferrum suum in igne esse, modo huc modo illuc cursabat et aiebat: " Noli mihi invidere, mea res agitur: deinde tu si quid volueris, in vicem faciam; manus manum lavat."

10 Tunc divus Augustus surrexit sententiae suae loco dicendae, et summa facundia disseruit: " Ego " inquit " p. c. vos testes habeo, ex quo deus factus sum, nullum me verbum fecisse: semper meum negotium ago. Sed [3] non possum amplius dissimulare, et dolorem, quem graviorem pudor facit, continere. In hoc terra marique pacem peperi? Ideo civilia bella compescui? Ideo legibus urbem fundavi,

[1] qui *Maehly*: quis.
[2] *von Leutsch would delete* sententiam.
[3] sed *inferior tradition*: et.

---

[1] Antonia, mother of Claudius, was niece of the Emperor Augustus; Drusus, father of Claudius, was son of Livia and step-son of Augustus; *diva Augusta* is Livia, wife of Augustus. Claudius secured divine honours for her.
[2] A quotation from an unknown poet. Claudius was fond of eating.
[3] Where occur the apotheosis of Romulus, the mythical founder of Rome (Ovid, *Metamorph.*, XIV, 815 ff.), and of

words: " Inasmuch as the blessed Claudius is akin to the blessed Augustus, and also to the blessed Augusta,[1] his grandmother, whom he ordered to be made a goddess, and whereas he far surpasses all mortal men in wisdom, and seeing that it is for the public good that there be some one able to join Romulus in devouring boiled turnips,[2] I propose that from this day forth blessed Claudius be a god, to enjoy that honour with all its appurtenances in as full a degree as any other before him, and that a note to that effect be added to Ovid's Metamorphoses." [3] The meeting was divided, and it looked as though Claudius was to win the day. For Hercules saw his iron was in the fire, trotted here and trotted there, saying, "Don't deny me; I make a point of the matter. I'll do as much for you again, when you like; you roll my log, and I'll roll yours: one hand washes another." [4]

Then arose the blessed Augustus, when his turn came, and spoke with much eloquence.[5] " I call you to witness, my lords and gentlemen," said he, " that since the day I was made a god I have never uttered one word. I always mind my own business. But now I can keep on the mask no longer, nor conceal the sorrow which shame makes all the greater. Is it for this I have made peace by land and sea? For this have I calmed intestine wars? For this, laid a firm foundation of law for Rome, adorned it with build-

Julius Caesar (XV, 745, cf. XV, 870—the coming apotheosis of Augustus). [4] Petronius, c. 45.

[5] The speech seems to contain a parody of the Emperor Augustus's style and sayings. Cf. *Res Gestae Divi Augusti*, L.C.L.

operibus ornavi, ut—quid dicam p. c. non invenio: omnia infra indignationem verba sunt. Confugiendum est itaque ad Messalae Corvini, disertissimi viri, illam sententiam ' pudet imperii.' Hic, p.c., qui vobis non posse videtur muscam excitare, tam facile homines occidebat, quam canis excidit.[1] Sed quid ego de tot ac talibus viris dicam? Non vacat deflere publicas clades intuenti domestica mala. Itaque illa omittam, haec referam; nam etiam si soror mea[2] Graece[3] nescit, ego scio: ἔγγιον γόνυ κνήμης. Iste quem videtis, per tot annos sub meo nomine latens, hanc mihi gratiam rettulit, ut duas Iulias proneptes meas occideret, alteram ferro, alteram fame; unum abnepotem L. Silanum, videris Iuppiter an in causa mala, certe in tua, si aequus futurus es. Dic mihi, dive Claudi, quare quemquam ex his, quos quasque occidisti, antequam de causa cognosceres, antequam audires, damnasti? Hoc ubi fieri solet? In caelo

[1] excidit *V*: adsidit *S* (*rightly?*): exsidit *L*.
[2] soror mea *Buecheler*: psora mea *Birt*: sura mea *suggests Russo*: sormea *or* formea. *P. Eden suggests* σφυρὸν *meum*.
[3] *Some inferior tradition omits* Graece *rightly?*

[1] M. Valerius Messala Corvinus, appointed praefectus urbi, resigned within a week.
[2] That is, a double " one ", the worst throw in dice-playing. If we read *adsidit* the meaning is quite different " as easily as a dog sits to " (to urinate). Augustus was a " plain " speaker.
[3] A proverb, like " Charity begins at home." The reading of the passage is uncertain; *soror mea* is only a conjecture, and it is hard to see why his sister should be mentioned.

ings, and all that—my lords, words fail me; there are
none can rise to the height of my indignation. So I
must borrow that saying of the eloquent Messala
Corvinus, I am ashamed of my authority.[1] This man,
my lords, who seems to you as if he could not hurt a
fly, used to chop off heads as readily as the dog's
throw comes tumbling out.[2] But why should I speak
of all those men, and such men? There is no time to
lament for public disasters, when one has so many
private sorrows to think of. I leave that, therefore,
and say only this; for even if my sister knows no
Greek, I do: The knee is nearer than the shin.[3] This
man you see, who for so many years has been mas-
querading under my name, has done me the favour of
murdering two Julias,[4] great-granddaughters of
mine, one by cold steel and one by starvation; and
one great-great-grandson, L. Silanus [5]—see, Jupiter,
whether he had a case against him (at least it is your
own if you will be fair). Come tell me, blessed
Claudius, why of all those you killed, both men and
women, without a hearing, why you did not hear their
side of the case first, before putting them to death?
Where do we find that custom? It is not done in

---

[4] Claudius's full title was Tiberius Claudius Caesar Augustus
Germanicus. The two great-grand-daughters of Augustus
here mentioned were Julia Livia, a daughter of Claudius's
brother the famous Germanicus (the other son of Nero Claudius
Drusus) and Julia, daughter of Drusus Caesar (not Emperor)
and Livia, sister of Germanicus. Drusus Caesar was a nephew
of Nero Claudius Drusus, father of Germanicus. Both Julias
were victims of Messalina's jealousy. The first mentioned was
exiled for alleged adultery with Seneca and allowed to starve;
the second was executed.

[5] See above, Chapter 8.

11 non fit. Ecce Iuppiter, qui tot annos regnat, uni
Volcano crus fregit, quem

$$\hat{\rho}\hat{\iota}\psi\epsilon\ \pi o\delta\grave{o}s\ \tau\epsilon\tau\alpha\gamma\grave{\omega}\nu\ \dot{a}\pi\grave{o}\ \beta\eta\lambda o\hat{v}\ \theta\epsilon\sigma\pi\epsilon\sigma\acute{\iota}o\iota o,$$

et iratus fuit uxori et suspendit illam: numquid
occidit? Tu Messalinam, cuius aeque avunculus
maior eram quam tuus, occidisti. ' Nescio ' inquis.
Di tibi male faciant: adeo istuc turpius est, quod
nescisti, quam quod occidisti. C. Caesarem non
desiit mortuum persequi. Occiderat ille socerum:
hic et generum. Gaius Crassi filium vetuit Magnum
vocari: hic nomen illi reddidit, caput tulit. Occidit
in una domo Crassum, Magnum, Scriboniam, † Tristionias, Assarionem, †[1] nobiles tamen, Crassum vero
tam fatuum, ut etiam regnare posset. Hunc nunc

---

[1] *Buecheler, following Birt, conjectures* tris homines assarios.

---

[1] Zeus (Jupiter) once strung up his own wife Hera (Juno);
and any gods whom he caught trying to free her he hurled from
heaven to earth (Homer, *Iliad*, XV, 17–24). He threw out his
son Hephaestus (Roman counterpart: Vulcanus) by the foot so
that, after plunging all day, he fell at sunset on Lemnos island
and was thus lamed for everlasting life (*Iliad*, I, 590–594).

[2] Messalina was in fact great-grand-daughter of Octavia,
sister of Emperor Augustus, whereas Claudius was grandson of
Octavia; so Augustus was *avunculus maior* (" greater uncle "),
that is, great-grand-mother's brother, to Messalina, but
avunculus magnus (" great uncle ") that is grandmother's
brother to Claudius. It is impossible to be confident about
the lurid details of Messalina's intrigues, shamelessness and
sudden fall. But it appears that she was in the end done to
death, without trial, by the agency of the powerful freedman
Narcissus who said he acted by Claudius's orders. See p. 476.

[3] Caius Caligula, emperor A.D. 37–41.

[4] Caius Caligula condemned to death Marcus Iunius Silanus

heaven. Look at Jupiter: all these years he has
been king, and never did more than once to break
Vulcan's leg,

> 'Whom seizing by the foot he cast from the Iliad I. 591
> threshold of the sky,'

and once he fell in a rage with his wife and strung
her up:[1] did he do any killing? *You* killed Messalina,[2] whose great-uncle I was no less than yours. ' I
don't know,' did you say? Curse you! that is just
it: not to know was worse than to kill. Caligula [3] he
went on persecuting even when he was dead. Caligula
murdered his father-in-law, Claudius his son-in-law to
boot.[4] Caligula would not have Crassus' son called
Great; Claudius gave him his name back, and took
away his head. In one family he destroyed Crassus,
Magnus, Scribonia, † the Tristionias, Assario,† noble
though they were; [5] Crassus indeed such a fool that
he might have been emperor. Is this he you want

(not the father of L. Silanus of Chapters 8 and 10), father of
Caius' first wife. Claudius caused the death of his " father-
in-law " Appius Silanus (cf. below, p. 468, n. 2) and of one of
his (Claudius's) sons-in-law (cf. Chapters 8 and 10). Appius
was the third husband of Domitia Lepida, mother of Messalina.
[5] Marcus Licinius Crassus Frugi was the father of Cnaeus
Pompeius Magnus, son-in-law of Claudius (to whom Crassus
was therefore joint father-in-law), whose daughter Antonia
Pompeius married. Scribonia was Pompeius's mother. We
do not know the reasons for their deaths. The reading
Tristionias cannot be right; nor does *Assario* occur as a name.
Many conjectures have been made. The whole corruption
may hide simply one name, *Aristionem*. The words *nobiles
tamen* might refer to the two preceding names only, in which
case Aristionem alone would not do; but apparently they
refer to all the names here given.

SENECA

deum facere vultis? Videte corpus eius dis iratis natum. Ad summam, tria verba cito dicat, et servum
me ducat. Hunc deum quis colet? Quis credet?
Dum tales deos facitis, nemo vos deos esse credet.
Summa rei, p. c., si honeste ⟨me⟩ ¹ inter vos gessi, si
nulli clarius ² respondi, vindicate iniurias meas. Ego
pro sententia mea hoc censeo:" atque ita ex tabella
recitavit: " quando quidem divus Claudius occidit
socerum suum Appium Silanum, generos duos
Magnum Pompeium et L. Silanum, socerum filiae
suae Crassum Frugi, hominem tam similem sibi quam
ovo ovum, Scriboniam socrum filiae suae, uxorem
suam Messalinam et ceteros quorum numerus iniri
non potuit, placet mihi in eum severe animadverti,
nec illi rerum iudicandarum vacationem dari, eumque
quam primum exportari, et caelo intra triginta dies
excedere, Olympo intra diem tertium."

Pedibus in hanc sententiam itum est. Nec mora,
Cyllenius illum colo obtorto trahit ad inferos, [a
caelo] ³

" ⟨illuc⟩ ⁴ unde negant redire quemquam."

12 Dum descendunt per viam sacram, interrogat Mercurius, quid sibi velit ille concursus hominum, num

¹ added by Haase.
² clarius S: darus V: durus L: durius Rhenanus.
³ a caelo is rightly deleted by Muret, though other suggestions
have been made.
⁴ added by Muret. It completes a hendecasyllabic line.

¹ Some such words as aio esse meum " I say he is mine."
² For all these see above. C. Appius Iunius Silanus was
not really father-in-law of Claudius; but Appius had married

468

now to make a god? Look at his body, born under
the wrath of heaven! In fine, let him say the three
words [1] quickly, and he may have me for a slave.
God! who will worship this god, who will believe in
him? While you make gods of such as he, no one
will believe you to be gods. To be brief, my lords:
if I have lived honourably among you, if I have never
replied too plainly to any, avenge my wrongs. This
is my motion ": then he read out his amendment,
which he had committed to writing: " Inasmuch as
the blessed Claudius murdered his father-in-law
Appius Silanus, his two sons-in-law, Pompeius
Magnus and L. Silanus, Crassus Frugi his daughter's
father-in-law, as like him as two eggs in a basket,
Scribonia his daughter's mother-in-law, his wife
Messalina,[2] and others too numerous to mention; I
propose that strong measures be taken against him,
that he be allowed no delay of process, that immedi-
ate sentence of banishment be passed on him, that
he be deported from heaven within thirty days, and
from Olympus within thirty hours."

The house divided and approved this motion.
Not a moment was lost: Mercury [3] screwed his neck
and haled him to the lower regions, " to that bourne
from which they say no traveller returns." [4]   As they
passed downwards along the Sacred Way, Mercury
asked what was that great concourse of men?   could

Domitia Lepida, mother of Messalina, wife of Claudius.   In
A.D. 42 when Appius rejected Messalina's lustful advances she
duped Claudius into executing him.
   [3] Called Cyllenius because he was supposed to have been
born on Mount Cyllene, in Arcadia in the Peloponnese.   His
Greek counterpart Hermes was escort to dead souls on their way.
   [4] The author of this saying is unknown.

Claudii funus esset. Et erat omnium formosissi-
mum et impensa cura, plane ut scires deum efferri:
tubicinum,[1] cornicinum, omnis generis aenatorum [2]
tanta turba, tantus concentus,[3] ut etiam Claudius
audire posset. Omnes laeti, hilares: populus
Romanus ambulabat tanquam liber. Agatho et
pauci causidici plorabant, sed plane ex animo. Iuris-
consulti e tenebris procedebant, pallidi, graciles, vix
animam habentes, tanquam qui tum maxime revi-
viscerent. Ex his unus cum vidisset capita confer-
entes et fortunas suas deplorantes causidicos, accedit
et ait: " dicebam vobis: non semper Saturnalia
erunt."

Claudius ut vidit funus suum, intellexit se mortuum esse. Ingenti enim μεγάλῳ χορικῷ nenia
cantabatur anapaestis: [4]

" Fundite fletus, edite planctus,
   resonet tristi clamore forum:
   cecidit pulchre cordatus homo,
   quo non alius fuit in toto
   fortior orbe.
   Ille citato vincere cursu
   poterat celeres, ille rebelles

---

[1] tibicinum *V, L* ("tootling of pipers ").
[2] aenatorum *Buecheler*: aeneatorum *Rhenanus*: senatorum
(sonatorum *inferior tradition*).
[3] *Lips suggested* conventus, *which may be right.*
[4] *Heraeus would delete* anapaestis. *The following arrangement in anapaestic tetrapodies follows the MSS. But the older*

it be Claudius' funeral? It was certainly the most gorgeous spectacle, got up regardless of expense, clear it was that a god was being borne to the grave: blaring of trumpeters, roaring of horn-players, an immense brass band of all sorts, so great a crowd, so great a concerted din that even Claudius could hear it. Joy and rejoicing on every side, the Roman people walking about like free men. Agatho [1] and a few pettifoggers were weeping for grief, and for once in a way they meant it. The Barristers were crawling out of their dark corners, pale and thin, with hardly a breath in their bodies, as though just coming to life again. One of them when he saw the pettifoggers putting their heads together, and lamenting their sad lot, up comes he and says: " Did not I tell you the Saturnalia could not last for ever? "

When Claudius saw his own funeral train, he understood that he was dead. For they were chanting his dirge in anapaests, with much mopping and mouthing:

" Pour forth your laments, your sorrow declare,
 Let the sounds of grief rise loud in the square:
 For he that is dead had a wit most keen,
 Was bravest of all that on earth have been.
 Racehorses are nothing to his swift feet:

---

[1] Unknown.

---

editors may have been right in treating the poem as a series of dipodies:

> Fundite fletus,
> edite planctus,

and so on.

fundere Parthos levibusque sequi
Persida telis, certaque manu
tendere nervum, qui praecipites
vulnere parvo figeret hostes,
pictaque Medi terga fugacis.
Ille Britannos ultra noti
litora ponti
et caeruleos scuta Brigantas
dare Romuleis colla catenis
iussit et ipsum nova Romanae
iura securis tremere Oceanum.
Deflete virum, quo non alius
potuit citius discere causas,
una tantum parte audita,
saepe et neutra.[1] Quis nunc iudex
toto lites audiet anno?
Tibi iam cedet sede relicta,
qui dat populo iura silenti,
Cretaea tenens oppida centum.
Caedite maestis pectora palmis,
o causidici, venale genus.
Vosque poetae lugete novi,

---

[1] saepe et neutra *ed. princ.*: saepe neutra.

---

[1] The Romans and the Parthians of Iran (Persians and
Medes are older names for them) recurrently quarrelled over
the control of Armenia. The allusion here would be to the
appeal of the Parthians in A.D. 49 to the Romans to have a
hand in deciding the Kingship of Parthia itself. Claudius
reminded the envoys of the supremacy of Rome. The
achievements of the Romans against the Parthians during the
reign of Claudius (who had no personal part in them) were none

APOCOLOCYNTOSIS

Rebellious Parthians [1] he did defeat;
Swift after the Persians his light shafts go:
For he well knew how to fit arrow to bow.
Swiftly the striped barbarians fled:
With one little wound he shot them dead.
And the Britons beyond the sea-shores which one
  sees,
Blue-shielded Brigantians too, all these
He chained by the neck as the Roman's slaves.
He spake, and the Ocean with trembling waves
Accepted the axe of the Roman law.[2]
O weep for the man! This world never saw
One quicker a troublesome suit to decide,
When only one part of the case had been tried
(He could do it indeed and not hear either side).
Who'll now sit in judgment the whole year round?
Now he [3] that is judge of the shades underground,
Once ruler of fivescore cities in Crete,
Must yield to his better and take a back seat.
Mourn, mourn, pettifoggers, ye venal crew,
And you, newer poets, woe, woe is to you!

too successful. The capable King Vologeses of Parthia
(A.D. 51–78) established his brother Tiridates as King of
Armenia in 54.

[2] After the invasion of Britain in A.D. 43 the Roman power
had, before the death of Claudius in 54, spread over southern
England and Wales; and the Brigantes between the Trent and
the Tyne were under Queen Cartimandua were becoming a
threat but were not yet even in clear conflict with Rome. But
the Romans had, through Cartimandua's treachery, at last
captured the great southern Briton Caractacus who was
displayed in Rome (and " pardoned ") by Claudius. The
" Ocean " is the Atlantic.

[3] Minos, in Greek tradition the powerful king of Crete, was
after his death made one of the three judges in the world below.

473

vosque in primis qui concusso
magna parastis lucra fritillo."

13 Delectabatur laudibus suis Claudius, et cupiebat
diutius spectare. Inicit illi manum Talthybius
deorum [nuntius] [1] et trahit capite obvoluto, ne quis
eum possit agnoscere, per campum Martium, et inter
Tiberim et viam tectam descendit ad inferos. Ante-
cesserat iam compendiaria Narcissus libertus ad
patronum excipiendum, et venienti nitidus, ut erat
a balineo, occurrit et ait: " Quid di ad homines ? "
" Celerius " inquit Mercurius " et venire nos nuntia."
Dicto citius Narcissus evolat. Omnia proclivia sunt,
facile descenditur. Itaque quamvis podagricus esset,
momento temporis pervenit ad ianuam Ditis, ubi
iacebat Cerberus vel ut ait Horatius " belua centi-
ceps." Pusillum perturbatur—subalbam canem in
deliciis habere adsueverat—ut illum vidit canem
nigrum, villosum, sane non quem velis tibi in tenebris
occurrere, et magna voce " Claudius " inquit
" veniet." Cum plausu procedunt cantantes: εὑρή-
καμεν, συγχαίρωμεν.[2] Hic erat C. Silius [3] consul

---

[1] *Deleted by Camden.*
[2] *Buecheler reads* συγχαίρομεν, *the actual word of the cry.*
[3] C. Silius *Muret*: consilius V, L: .c. consilius S.

---

[1] Claudius was fond of playing with dice.
[2] Agamemnon's herald in the Trojan war. Here Mercury
is meant.
[3] The " *Via Tecta* " " Covered Way " was at the northern
limit of the Campus Martius at Rome.
[4] The powerful freedman Narcissus, Claudius's secretary,
died shortly after Claudius.

> And you above all, who get rich quick
> By the rattle of dice and the three card trick." [1]

Claudius was charmed to hear his own praises sung, and would have stayed longer to see the show. But the Talthybius [2] of the gods laid a hand on him, and led him across the Campus Martius, first wrapping his head up close that no one might know him, until betwixt Tiber and the Subway [3] he went down to the lower regions. His freedman Narcissus [4] had gone down before him by a short cut, ready to welcome his master. Out he comes to meet him, smooth and shining (he had just left the bath), and says he: "What make the gods among mortals?" "Look alive," says Mecury, "go and tell them we are coming." Away he flew, quicker than tongue can tell. It is easy going by that road, all down hill. So although he had a touch of the gout, in a trice they were come to Dis's door. There lay Cerberus,[5] or, as Horace puts it, the hundred-headed monster. Claudius was a trifle perturbed (it was an off-white bitch he used to keep for a pet) when he spied this black shag-haired hound, not at all the kind of thing you could wish to meet you in the dark. In a loud voice he cried, " Claudius is coming! " All marched before him with clapping of hands and singing, " The lost is found, O let us rejoice together! " [6] Here were found C. Silius consul elect, Juncus the ex-

Odes ii, 13, 35

---

[5] On Dis, see above. Cerberus was the three-headed (or hundred-headed) monster which guarded the gates of Hades.

[6] With a slight change, this is a cry used in the worship of Isis and Osiris.

designatus, Iuncus [1] praetorius, Sex. Traulus,[2] M.
Helvius, Trogus, Cotta, Vettius [3] Valens, Fabius
equites R. quos Narcissus duci iusserat. Medius erat
in hac cantantium turba Mnester pentomimus, quem
Claudius decoris causa minorem fecerat. Ad Messalinam—cito rumor percrebuit Claudium venisse—
convolant: primi omnium liberti Polybius, Myron,
Arpocras, Amphaeus, Pheronactus,[4] quos Claudius
omnes, necubi imparatus esset, praemiserat. Deinde
praefecti duo Iustus Catonius et Rufrius Pollio.[5]
Deinde amici Saturninus Lusius et Pedo Pompeius et
Lupus et Celer Asinius consulares. Novissime fratris
filia, sororis filia, generi, soceri, socrus, omnes plane

---

[1] Iuncus *Sonntag:* iunius.   *Cp. Tac., Ann., xi, 35.*
[2] Traulus *Lips:* trallus.
[3] Vectius *Lips:* tettius *S:* tectus *V.*
[4] Arpocras *Buecheler:* Harpocras *ed. princ.:* arporas.
Pheronactus *Buecheler:* pheronattus *V:* pherona otus *S.*
[5] Rufrius Pollio *suggested by Reimar. There are other suggestions.* rufius pomfilius *S:* rufius pompei filius *V.*

---

[1] All these were lovers and accomplices of Messalina. C.
Silius, the most notorious of them, was consul designate in
A.D. 47. If the fantastic story is to be believed, Claudius
allowed a mock marriage of his wife Messalina with Silius, to
ward off some diviners' forecast of evil for " Messalina's
husband." Claudius's freedmen, especially Narcissus, took
action and brought about the fall and death of Silius and
Messalina in 48. Of the other persons mentioned by Seneca
here, Iuncus Vergilianus was a senator; Sextus Montanus
Traulus was a Roman knight and a lover of Messalina for a
few hours only. Marcus Helvius is otherwise unknown.

praetor, Sextus Traulus, M. Helvius, Trogus, Cotta,
Vettius Valens, Fabius, Roman Knights whom
Narcissus had ordered for execution.[1]   In the midst
of this chanting company was Mnester [2] the mime,
whom Claudius for good form's sake had made
shorter by a head.   The news was soon blown about
that Claudius had come: to Messalina they throng:
first his freedmen, Polybius, Myron, Arpocras, Amphaeus, Pheronactus,[3] all sent before him by Claudius
that he might not be unattended anywhere; next
two prefects,[4] Justus Catonius and Rufrius Pollio;
then his friends, Saturninus Lusius and Pedo
Pompeius and Lupus and Celer Asinius,[5] these of
consular rank; last came his brother's daughter, his
sister's daughter,[6] sons-in-law,[7] fathers- and mothers-

Trogus was Saufeius Trogus (we have no details); and Cotta
is otherwise unknown.   Vettius Valens was a medical doctor;
and Fabius is otherwise unknown.

[2] A dancer; one of Messalina's lovers and helpers.   He was
executed.

[3] Polybius helped Claudius in his studies and did other
secretarial work.   He was a lover of Messalina but was
accused by her and executed in A.D. 47.   Arpocras or Harpocras is known to have been honoured by Claudius.   But
Myron, Amphaeus, and Pheronactus (if these names are right)
are otherwise unknown.

[4] Of the imperial guard, Catonius in A.D. 43, Rufrius in
41.

[5] Pedo Pompeius is otherwise unknown.   Lusius Saturninus
and Cornelius Lupus were victims of the intrigues of P. Suillius;
Sextus Asinius Celer was consul in 38.   The cause of his death
is unknown.

[6] Julia, daughter of Germanicus and Julia, daughter of
Livia and Drusus.   Cf. Chapter 10.

[7] Lucius Silanus and Pompeius Magnus: see above,
Chapters 8, 10, 11.

consanguinei. Et agmine facto Claudio occurrunt.
Quos cum vidisset Claudius, exclamat: πάντα φίλων
πλήρη "quomodo huc venistis vos?" Tum Pedo
Pompeius: "Quid dicis, homo crudelissime?
Quaeris, quomodo? Quis enim nos alius huc misit
quam tu, omnium amicorum interfector? In ius
eamus, ego tibi hic sellas [1] ostendam."

14 Ducit illum ad tribunal Aeaci: is lege Cornelia
quae de sicariis lata est, quaerebat. Postulat,
nomen eius recipiat; edit subscriptionem: occisos
senatores XXXV, equites R. CCXXI, ceteros [2] ὅσα
ψάμαθός τε κόνις τε. [3]Advocatum non invenit. Tandem procedit P. Petronius, vetus convictor eius, homo
Claudiana lingua disertus, et postulat advocationem.
Non datur. Accusat Pedo Pompeius magnis clamori-
bus. Incipit patronus [4] velle respondere. Aeacus,
homo iustissimus, vetat, et illum altera tantum parte
audita condemnat et ait: αἴκε πάθοι τά τ' ἔρεξε δίκη
κ' ἰθεῖα γένοιτο. Ingens silentium factum est.

---

[1] stellas *S*, *V*, *L*: stelas *or* sitellas *Iunius*.

[2] XXXV (*Buecheler*) equites romanos CCXXI, ceteros
Rhenanus: XXX equites RU (romanos V *cod. L*) ceteros
CCXXI *S*, *V*, *L*.

[3] *Gertz adds* ille, *Wachsmuth* iste.

[4] P. Petronius *ed. princ.*: petronius *inferior tradition*.

---

[1] Appius Silanus; Crassus Frugi; Domitia Lepida;
Scribonia; See above, Chapter 11. Seneca here uses the
words *socer* "father-in-law" and *socrus* "mother-in-law" in
the sense of son-in-law's or daughter-in-law's parents. Crassus
was *consocer*, joint father-in-law, with Claudius.

[2] Mythical King of Aegina, after death made one of the three
judges in the world below.

[3] Passed by Sulla in 81 B.C. establishing a standing criminal
court to try cases of assassination and poisoning.

in-law,[1] the whole family in fact. In a body they came to meet Claudius; and when Claudius saw them, he exclaimed, " Friends everywhere, on my word! How came you all here? " To this Pedo Pompeius answered, " What, cruel man? You ask how came we here? Who but you sent us here, you, the murderer of all the friends that ever you had? To court with you! I'll show you where their lordships sit."

Pedo brings him before the judgment seat of Aeacus,[2] who was holding court under the Lex Cornelia[3] to try cases of murder and assassination. Pedo requests the judge to take the prisoner's name, and produces a summons with this charge: Senators killed, 35; Roman knights, 221; others as the sands and dust for multitude. Claudius finds no counsel. Il. ix, 385 At length out steps P. Petronius,[4] an old chum of his, a finished scholar in the Claudian tongue, and claims a remand. Not granted. Pedo Pompeius prosecutes amid loud applause. The speaker[5] for the defence tries to reply; but Aeacus, who is the soul of justice, will not have it. Aeacus hears the case against Claudius, refuses to hear the other side and passes sentence against him, quoting the line:

" As he did, so be he done by, this is justice undefiled."[6]

---

[4] This Petronius is known also from Tacitus, *Annals*, III, 49; VI, 45. He was *consul suffectus* in A.D. 19 and later proconsul. The point about Claudian tongue is obscure, but clearly this Petronius spoke like Claudius whose speech sounded thick.   [5] Petronius.

[6] A proverbial line. The MSS. are a muddle here, and I accept as Rouse did πάθοι τά τ᾽ἔρεξε of Curio and Schneidewin.

Stupebant omnes novitate rei attoniti, negabant hoc unquam factum. Claudio magis iniquum videbatur quam novum. De genere poenae diu disputatum est, quid illum pati oporteret. Erant qui dicerent, Sisyphum [1] ⟨satis⟩ diu [2] laturam fecisse,[3] Tantalum siti periturum nisi illi succurreretur, aliquando Ixionis miseri rotam sufflaminandam. Non placuit ulli ex veteribus [4] missionem dari, ne vel Claudius unquam simile speraret. Placuit novam poenam constitui debere, excogitandum illi laborem irritum et alicuius cupiditatis speciem [5] sine effectu.[6] Tum Aeacus iubet illum alea ludere pertuso fritillo. Et iam coeperat fugientes semper tesseras quaerere et nihil proficere.

15   Nam quotiens missurus erat resonante fritillo,
      utraque subducto fugiebat tessera fundo.
      Cumque recollectos auderet mittere talos,
      fusuro [7] similis semper semperque petenti,
      decepere fidem: refugit digitosque per ipsos

----

[1] Sisyphum *Buecheler*: sium *or the like*.

[2] ⟨satis⟩diu *Buecheler*: ⟨nimium⟩diu *Gertz*: ⟨iam⟩ diu *Waltz, Rossbach*: diu, *or the like, MSS*.: si nimium diu *Ball*.

[3] fecisse *Buecheler*: fecissent.

[4] veteribus *S*: veteris *V*: veternis *L*: veteranis *Rhenanus* (*rightly?*).

[5] speciem *Scheffer*: spes *S, V, L*: spem *or* species *inferior tradition*.

[6] sine fine et effectu *is the accepted reading here*: sine effectū *S*: sine fine effectus *V, L*: *This suggests that* fine *comes from* sine.

[7] fusuro *Buecheler*: lusuro.

----

[1] In Greek mythology, in the lower world Sisyphus a robber-prince was condemned to roll up a hill a stone which

A great silence fell. Not a soul but was stupefied at this new way of managing matters; they said there had never been anything like it before. It was no new thing to Claudius, yet he thought it unfair. There was a long discussion as to the punishment he ought to endure. Some said that Sisyphus had done his job of porterage long enough; Tantalus would be dying of thirst, if he were not relieved; the drag must be put at last on wretched Ixion's wheel.[1] But it was determined not to discharge any of the old stagers, lest Claudius also should dare to hope for any such relief. It was agreed that some new punishment must be devised: they must devise some new task, something with no effect, to suggest some craving without result. Then Aeacus decreed he should rattle dice for ever in a box with holes in the bottom. At once the poor wretch proceeded to his fruitless task of hunting for the dice, which for ever slipped away—

> " For when he rattled with the box, and thought he
>   now had got 'em.
> Both little cubes would vanish thro' the perfor-
>   ated bottom.
> Then he would pick 'em up again, and once more
>   set a-trying:
> The dice but served him the same trick: away
>   they went a-flying.

always rolled down again; Tantalus, a Phrygian, who be-trayed secrets of the gods, was condemned to stand chin-deep in water, unable to reach fruit to satisfy his hunger and thirst; Ixion, a King in Thessaly, attempted an indecent approach to Hera (Juno) and was in condemnation tied to an ever-turning wheel.

fallax adsiduo dilabitur alea furto.
Sic cum iam summi tanguntur culmina montis,
irrita Sisyphio volvuntur pondera collo.

Apparuit subito C. Caesar et petere illum in servitutem coepit;[1] producit[2] testes, qui illum[3] viderant ab illo flagris, ferulis, colaphis vapulantem. Adiudicatur C. Caesari; Caesar illum Aeaco donat. Is Menandro liberto suo tradidit, ut a cognitionibus esset.

[1] coepit *S*: caepit *V*: cepit *L*. *After* coepit *an inferior tradition adds* et.
[2] producit *V*, *L*: producere *S*.
[3] *Buecheler deletes* illum. *Maehly suggests* olim.

So still he tries, and still he fails; still searching
　　long he lingers;
And every time the tricksy things go slipping thro'
　　his fingers.
Just so when Sisyphus the hill-top touches with
　　his boulder,
He finds the labour all in vain—it rolls down off his
　　shoulder."

All on a sudden who should turn up but Caligula?[1]
He proceeds to claim the man for a slave: brings
witnesses, who said they had seen Claudius being
flogged, caned, fisticuffed by him. He is handed
over to Caligula, and Caligula makes him a present
to Aeacus. Aeacus delivers him to his freedman
Menander, to be his law-clerk.

---

[1] The emperor Gaius, Claudius's nephew and predecessor,
afflicted him with many insults but did also make him consul.
Seneca, in having Claudius condemned to useless attempts to
play dice, a punishment mild in comparison with others, may
be admitting that some of the *Apocolocyntosis* is unfair. In
spite of all his faults, Claudius did some good things for the
Roman Empire, and is not unfairly summed up by Dio Cassius
when he indicates that Claudius was not a bad man, but he
was in the power of women and of " slaves ", that is freedmen.

INDEX TO PETRONIUS

INDEX OF NAMES

The references are to chapters of the English translation as numbered in the Latin text. The Fragments and Poems are indicated by numbers with the letter F or P respectively prefixed.

487

PETRONIUS ARBITER

488

INDEX OF NAMES

INDEX OF NAMES

INDEX TO SENECA

INDEX OF NAMES

in Seneca's "Apocolocyntosis" and footnotes. The references are to the pages of this volume.

495

SENECA

INDEX OF NAMES

497

Printed in Great Britain by
Fletcher & Son Ltd
Norwich

THE LOEB CLASSICAL LIBRARY

VOLUMES ALREADY PUBLISHED

Latin Authors

AMMIANUS MARCELLINUS. Translated by J. C. Rolfe. 3 Vols.

APULEIUS: THE GOLDEN ASS (METAMORPHOSES). W. Adlington (1566). Revised by S. Gaselee.

ST. AUGUSTINE: CITY OF GOD. 7 Vols. Vol. I. G. E. McCracken. Vol. II. and VII. W. M. Green. Vol. III. D. Wiesen. Vol. IV. P. Levine. Vol. V. E. M. Sanford and W. M. Green. Vol. VI. W. C. Greene.

ST. AUGUSTINE, CONFESSIONS OF. W. Watts (1631). 2 Vols.

ST. AUGUSTINE, SELECT LETTERS. J. H. Baxter.

AUSONIUS. H. G. Evelyn White. 2 Vols.

BEDE. J. E. King. 2 Vols.

BOETHIUS: TRACTS and DE CONSOLATIONE PHILOSOPHIAE. REV. H. F. Stewart and E. K. Rand. Revised by S. J. Tester.

CAESAR: ALEXANDRIAN, AFRICAN and SPANISH WARS. A. G. Way.

CAESAR: CIVIL WARS. A. G. Peskett.

CAESAR: GALLIC WAR. H. J. Edwards.

CATO: DE RE RUSTICA; VARRO: DE RE RUSTICA. H. B. Ash and W. D. Hooper.

CATULLUS. F. W. Cornish; TIBULLUS. J. B. Postgate; PERVIGILIUM VENERIS. J. W. Mackail.

CELSUS: DE MEDICINA. W. G. Spencer. 3 Vols.

CICERO: BRUTUS, and ORATOR. G. L. Hendrickson and H. M. Hubbell.

[CICERO]: AD HERENNIUM. H. Caplan.

CICERO: DE ORATORE, etc. 2 Vols. Vol. I. DE ORATORE, Books I. and II. E. W. Sutton and H. Rackham. Vol. II. DE ORATORE, Book III. De Fato; Paradoxa Stoicorum; De Partitione Oratoria. H. Rackham.

CICERO: DE FINIBUS. H. Rackham.

CICERO: DE INVENTIONE, etc. H. M. Hubbell.

CICERO: DE NATURA DEORUM and ACADEMICA. H. Rackham.

CICERO: DE OFFICIIS. Walter Miller.

CICERO: DE REPUBLICA and DE LEGIBUS: SOMNIUM SCIPIONIS. Clinton W. Keyes.

1

OVID: HEROIDES and AMORES. Grant Showerman.
OVID: METAMORPHOSES. F. J. Miller. 2 Vols.
OVID: TRISTIA and EX PONTO. A. L. Wheeler.
PERSIUS. Cf. JUVENAL.
PETRONIUS. M. Heseltine; SENECA; APOCOLOCYNTOSIS. W. H. D. Rouse.
PHAEDRUS AND BABRIUS (Greek). B. E. Perry.
PLAUTUS. Paul Nixon. 5 Vols.
PLINY: LETTERS, PANEGYRICUS. Betty Radice. 2 Vols.
PLINY: NATURAL HISTORY. Vols. I.–V. and IX. H. Rackham. VI.–VIII. W. H. S. Jones. X. D. E. Eichholz. 10 Vols.
PROPERTIUS. H. E. Butler.
PRUDENTIUS. H. J. Thomson. 2 Vols.
QUINTILIAN. H. E. Butler. 4 Vols.
REMAINS OF OLD LATIN. E. H. Warmington. 4 Vols. Vol. I. (ENNIUS AND CAECILIUS.) Vol. II. (LIVIUS, NAEVIUS, PACUVIUS, ACCIUS.) Vol. III. (LUCILIUS and LAWS OF XII TABLES.) Vol. IV. (ARCHAIC INSCRIPTIONS.)
SALLUST. J. C. Rolfe.
SCRIPTORES HISTORIAE AUGUSTAE. D. Magie. 3 Vols.
SENECA, THE ELDER: CONTROVERSIAE, SUASORIAE. M. Winterbottom. 2 Vols.
SENECA: APOCOLOCYNTOSIS. Cf. PETRONIUS.
SENECA: EPISTULAE MORALES. R. M. Gummere. 3 Vols.
SENECA: MORAL ESSAYS. J. W. Basore. 3 Vols.
SENECA: TRAGEDIES. F. J. Miller. 2 Vols.
SENECA: NATURALES QUAESTIONES. T. H. Corcoran. 2 Vols.
SIDONIUS: POEMS and LETTERS. W. B. Anderson. 2 Vols.
SILIUS ITALICUS. J. D. Duff. 2 Vols.
STATIUS. J. H. Mozley. 2 Vols.
SUETONIUS. J. C. Rolfe. 2 Vols.
TACITUS: DIALOGUS. Sir Wm. Peterson. AGRICOLA and GERMANIA. Maurice Hutton. Revised by M. Winterbottom, R. M. Ogilvie, E. H. Warmington.
TACITUS: HISTORIES AND ANNALS. C. H. Moore and J. Jackson. 4 Vols.
TERENCE. John Sargeaunt. 2 Vols.
TERTULLIAN: APOLOGIA and DE SPECTACULIS. T. R. Glover. MINUCIUS FELIX. G. H. Rendall.
VALERIUS FLACCUS. J. H. Mozley.
VARRO: DE LINGUA LATINA. R. G. Kent. 2 Vols.
VELLEIUS PATERCULUS and RES GESTAE DIVI AUGUSTI. F. W. Shipley.
VIRGIL. H. R. Fairclough. 2 Vols.
VITRUVIUS: DE ARCHITECTURA. F. Granger. 2 Vols.

Greek Authors

4

ARISTOTLE: PHYSICS. Rev. P. Wicksteed and F. M. Cornford. 2 Vols.

ARISTOTLE: POETICS and LONGINUS. W. Hamilton Fyfe; DEMETRIUS ON STYLE. W. Rhys Roberts.

ARISTOTLE: POLITICS. H. Rackham.

ARISTOTLE: PROBLEMS. W. S. Hett. 2 Vols.

ARISTOTLE: RHETORICA AD ALEXANDRUM (with PROBLEMS. Vol. II). H. Rackham.

ARRIAN: HISTORY OF ALEXANDER and INDICA. Rev. E. Iliffe Robson. 2 Vols.

ATHENAEUS: DEIPNOSOPHISTAE. C. B. Gulick. 7 Vols.

BABRIUS AND PHAEDRUS (Latin). B. E. Perry.

ST. BASIL: LETTERS. R. J. Deferrari. 4 Vols.

CALLIMACHUS: FRAGMENTS. C. A. Trypanis. MUSAEUS: HERO AND LEANDER. T. Gelzer and C. Whitman.

CALLIMACHUS, Hymns and Epigrams, and LYCOPHRON. A. W. Mair; ARATUS. G. R. Mair.

CLEMENT OF ALEXANDRIA. Rev. G. W. Butterworth.

COLLUTHUS. Cf. OPPIAN.

DAPHNIS AND CHLOE. Thornley's Translation revised by J. M. Edmonds: and PARTHENIUS. S. Gaselee.

DEMOSTHENES I.: OLYNTHIACS, PHILIPPICS and MINOR ORATIONS. I.–XVII. AND XX. J. H. Vince.

DEMOSTHENES II.: DE CORONA and DE FALSA LEGATIONE. C. A. Vince and J. H. Vince.

DEMOSTHENES III.: MEIDIAS, ANDROTION, ARISTOCRATES, TIMOCRATES and ARISTOGEITON, I. AND II. J. H. Vince.

DEMOSTHENES IV.–VI.: PRIVATE ORATIONS and IN NEAERAM. A. T. Murray.

DEMOSTHENES VII.: FUNERAL SPEECH, EROTIC ESSAY, EXORDIA and LETTERS. N. W. and N. J. DeWitt.

DIO CASSIUS: ROMAN HISTORY. E. Cary. 9 Vols.

DIO CHRYSOSTOM. J. W. Cohoon and H. Lamar Crosby. 5 Vols.

DIODORUS SICULUS. 12 Vols. Vols. I.–VI. C. H. Oldfather. Vol. VII. C. L. Sherman. Vol. VIII. C. B. Welles. Vols. IX. and X. R. M. Geer. Vol. XI. F. Walton. Vol. XII. F. Walton. General Index. R. M. Geer.

DIOGENES LAERTIUS. R. D. Hicks. 2 Vols. New Introduction by H. S. Long.

DIONYSIUS OF HALICARNASSUS: ROMAN ANTIQUITIES Spelman's translation revised by E. Cary. 7 Vols.

DIONYSIUS OF HALICARNASSUS: CRITICAL ESSAYS. S. Usher. 2 Vols.

EPICTETUS. W. A. Oldfather. 2 Vols.

EURIPIDES. A. S. Way. 4 Vols. Verse trans.

EUSEBIUS: ECCLESIASTICAL HISTORY. Kirsopp Lake and J. E. L. Oulton. 2 Vols.

GALEN: ON THE NATURAL FACULTIES. A. J. Brock.

THE GREEK ANTHOLOGY. W. R. Paton. 5 Vols.

GREEK ELEGY AND IAMBUS with the ANACREONTEA. J. M. Edmonds. 2 Vols.

THE GREEK BUCOLIC POETS (THEOCRITUS, BION, MOSCHUS). J. M. Edmonds.

GREEK MATHEMATICAL WORKS. Ivor Thomas. 2 Vols.

HERODES. Cf. THEOPHRASTUS: CHARACTERS.

HERODIAN. C. R. Whittaker. 2 Vols.

HERODOTUS. A. D. Godley. 4 Vols.

HESIOD AND THE HOMERIC HYMNS. H. G. Evelyn White.

HIPPOCRATES and the FRAGMENTS OF HERACLEITUS. W. H. S. Jones and E. T. Withington. 4 Vols.

HOMER: ILIAD. A. T. Murray. 2 Vols.

HOMER: ODYSSEY. A. T. Murray. 2 Vols.

ISAEUS. E. W. Forster.

ISOCRATES. George Norlin and LaRue Van Hook. 3 Vols.

[ST. JOHN DAMASCENE]: BARLAAM AND IOASAPH. Rev. G. R. Woodward, Harold Mattingly and D. M. Lang.

JOSEPHUS. 9 Vols. Vols. I.–IV. H. Thackeray. Vol. V. H. Thackeray and R. Marcus. Vols. VI.–VII. R. Marcus. Vol. VIII. R. Marcus and Allen Wikgren. Vol. IX. L. H. Feldman.

JULIAN. Wilmer Cave Wright. 3 Vols.

LIBANIUS. A. F. Norman. Vol. I.

LUCIAN. 8 Vols. Vols. I.–V. A. M. Harmon. Vol. VI. K. Kilburn. Vols. VII.–VIII. M. D. Macleod.

LYCOPHRON. Cf. CALLIMACHUS.

LYRA GRAECA. J. M. Edmonds. 3 Vols.

LYSIAS. W. R. M. Lamb.

MANETHO. W. G. Waddell: PTOLEMY: TETRABIBLOS. F. E. Robbins.

MARCUS AURELIUS. C. R. Haines.

MENANDER. F. G. Allison.

MINOR ATTIC ORATORS (ANTIPHON, ANDOCIDES, LYCURGUS, DEMADES, DINARCHUS, HYPERIDES). K. J. Maidment and J. O. Burtt. 2 Vols.

MUSAEUS: HERO AND LEANDER. Cf. CALLIMACHUS.

NONNOS: DIONYSIACA. W. H. D. Rouse. 3 Vols.

OPPIAN, COLLUTHUS, TRYPHIODORUS. A. W. Mair.

PAPYRI. NON-LITERARY SELECTIONS. A. S. Hunt and C. C. Edgar. 2 Vols. LITERARY SELECTIONS (Poetry). D. L. Page.

PARTHENIUS. Cf. DAPHNIS and CHLOE.

PAUSANIAS: DESCRIPTION OF GREECE. W. H. S. Jones. 4 Vols. and Companion Vol. arranged by R. E. Wycherley.

PHILO. 10 Vols. Vols. I.–V. F. H. Colson and Rev. G. H. Whitaker. Vols. VI.–IX. F. H. Colson. Vol. X. F. H. Colson and the Rev. J. W. Earp.

PHILO: two supplementary Vols. (*Translation only.*) Ralph Marcus.

PHILOSTRATUS: THE LIFE OF APOLLONIUS OF TYANA. F. C. Conybeare. 2 Vols.

PHILOSTRATUS: IMAGINES; CALLISTRATUS: DESCRIPTIONS. A. Fairbanks.

PHILOSTRATUS and EUNAPIUS: LIVES OF THE SOPHISTS. Wilmer Cave Wright.

PINDAR. Sir J. E. Sandys.

PLATO: CHARMIDES, ALCIBIADES, HIPPARCHUS, THE LOVERS, THEAGES, MINOS and EPINOMIS. W. R. M. Lamb.

PLATO: CRATYLUS, PARMENIDES, GREATER HIPPIAS, LESSER HIPPIAS. H. N. Fowler.

PLATO: EUTHYPHRO, APOLOGY, CRITO, PHAEDO, PHAEDRUS. H. N. Fowler.

PLATO: LACHES, PROTAGORAS, MENO, EUTHYDEMUS. W. R. M. Lamb.

PLATO: LAWS. Rev. R. G. Bury. 2 Vols.

PLATO: LYSIS, SYMPOSIUM, GORGIAS. W. R. M. Lamb.

PLATO: REPUBLIC. Paul Shorey. 2 Vols.

PLATO: STATESMAN, PHILEBUS. H. N. Fowler; Ion. W. R. M. Lamb.

PLATO: THEAETETUS and SOPHIST. H. N. Fowler.

PLATO: TIMAEUS, CRITIAS, CLITOPHO, MENEXENUS, EPISTULAE. Rev. R. G. Bury.

PLOTINUS: A. H. Armstrong. Vols. I.–III.

PLUTARCH: MORALIA. 17 Vols. Vols. I.–V. F. C. Babbitt. Vol. VI. W. C. Helmbold. Vols. VII. and XIV. P. H. De Lacy and B. Einarson. Vol. VIII. P. A. Clement and H. B. Hoffleit. Vol. IX. E. L. Minar, Jr., F. H. Sandbach, W. C. Helmbold. Vol. X. H. N. Fowler. Vol. XI. L. Pearson and F. H. Sandbach. Vol. XII. H. Cherniss and W. C. Helmbold. Vol. XV. F. H. Sandbach.

PLUTARCH: THE PARALLEL LIVES. B. Perrin. 11 Vols.

POLYBIUS. W. R. Paton. 6 Vols.

PROCOPIUS: HISTORY OF THE WARS. H. B. Dewing. 7 Vols.

PTOLEMY: TETRABIBLOS. Cf. MANETHO.

QUINTUS SMYRNAEUS. A. S. Way. Verse trans.

SEXTUS EMPIRICUS. Rev. R. G. Bury. 4 Vols.

SOPHOCLES. F. Storr. 2 Vols. Verse trans.

STRABO: GEOGRAPHY. Horace L. Jones. 8 Vols.

THEOPHRASTUS: CHARACTERS. J. M. Edmonds. HERODES, etc. A. D. Knox

THEOPHRASTUS: ENQUIRY INTO PLANTS. Sir Arthur Hort, Bart. 2 Vols.
THUCYDIDES. C. F. Smith. 4 Vols.
TRYPHIODORUS. Cf. OPPIAN.
XENOPHON: CYROPAEDIA. Walter Miller. 2 Vols.
XENOPHON: HELLENICA. C. L. Brownson. 2 Vols.
XENOPHON: ANABASIS. C. L. Brownson.
XENOPHON: MEMORABILIA AND OECONOMICUS. E. C. Marchant. SYMPOSIUM AND APOLOGY. O. J. Todd.
XENOPHON: SCRIPTA MINORA. E. C. Marchant and G. W. Bowersock.

IN PREPARATION

Greek Authors

ARRIAN I. New version by P. Brunt.
PLUTARCH: MORALIA XIII 1–2. H. Cherniss.
THEOPHRASTUS: DE CAUSIS PLANTARUM. G. K. K. Link and B. Einarson.

Latin Authors

MANILIUS. G. P. Goold.

DESCRIPTIVE PROSPECTUS ON APPLICATION

CAMBRIDGE, MASS.   HARVARD UNIVERSITY PRESS
LONDON   WILLIAM HEINEMANN LTD